My Double Life

ALSO BY DON HARRON

Anne of Green Gables Vocal Score (2011)

Anne of Green Gables the Musical:
101 Things You Didn't Know (2008)

The Outhouse Revisited (1996)

Charlie's a Broad: Travails in Fern Parts (1994)

Charlie Farquharson's Histry of Canada: Reevized and More Expansive:
As Told to Valeda Drain Farquharson When It Was Too Wet to Plow (1992)

Keeping a Canadian Christmas (1991)

Charlie Farquharson's Unyverse (1990)

Cum Buy the Farm (1987)

Debunk's Illustrated Guide to the Canadian Establishment (1984)

Charlie Farquharson, Yer Last Decadent (1982)

Olde Charlie Farquharson's Testament:
From Jennysez to Jobe and After Words (1978)

Charlie Farquharson's K-O-R-N Filled Allmynack (1976)

Charlie Farquharson's Jogfree of Canada:
The Whirld and Other Places (1974)

Anne of Green Gables: A Musical (1972)

Charlie Farquharson's Histry of Canada (1972)

My Double Life

Sixty yeers of Farquharson around
with Don Harn

DUNDURN
TORONTO

Project Editor: Michael Carroll
Editor: Allister Thompson
Design: Jesse Hooper
Printer: Friesens

Library and Archives Canada Cataloguing in Publication

Harron, Don, 1924-
My double life : sexty yeers of Farquharson around with Don Harn / Don Harron.

Includes index.
Issued also in electronic formats.
ISBN 978-1-4597-0550-0

1. Harron, Don, 1924-. 2. Actors--Canada--Biography. 3. Humorists, Canadian--Biography. 4. Authors, Canadian (English)--20th century--Biography. I. Title.

PN2308.H37A3 2012   792.02'8092   C2012-903232-8

1   2   3   4   5   16   15   14   13   12

     Conseil des Arts   Canada Council
du Canada   for the Arts   Canada   ONTARIO ARTS COUNCIL
CONSEIL DES ARTS DE L'ONTARIO

We acknowledge the support of the **Canada Council for the Arts** and the **Ontario Arts Council** for our publishing program. We also acknowledge the financial support of the **Government of Canada** through the **Canada Book Fund** and **Livres Canada Books,** and the **Government of Ontario** through the **Ontario Book Publishing Tax Credit** and the **Ontario Media Development Corporation.**

Thanks to my old pal Christopher Plummer for the witty remark on the back jacket of this book.

Don Harron

Care has been taken to trace the ownership of copyright material used in this book. The author and the publisher welcome any information enabling them to rectify any references or credits in subsequent editions.

J. Kirk Howard, President

Printed and bound in Canada.

VISIT US AT
Dundurn.com | Definingcanada.ca | @dundurnpress | Facebook.com/dundurnpress

Dundurn	Gazelle Book Services Limited	Dundurn
3 Church Street, Suite 500	White Cross Mills	2250 Military Road
Toronto, Ontario, Canada	High Town, Lancaster, England	Tonawanda, NY
M5E 1M2	L41 4XS	U.S.A. 14150

In memory of my beloved parents,
who never hesitated to encourage me in my choice of profession

Contents

Introduction

After seventy-seven years as a professional performer in all aspects of the entertainment business, I have decided to hang it all up, sit on me arse, and read somebody else's book. After I finish *this* one. Have to get it all down and let it all hang out before I forget everything. In another two years I'll be four score and ten. That will make me a nonny-geranium.

Even now I suffer from short-term memory, which means I can recall events early in my existence, but I can't seem to remember where I hung up my pants last night. Years ago, when I turned seventy, I had lunch with the great Canadian novelist, journalist, playwright, and all-round wit Robertson Davies, who had just turned eighty.

I asked, "Rob, what's the difference between seventy and eighty?"

He gave me an avuncular smile and said, "Frequent urination and an inability to remember names."

I got much the same reaction later when I was in Nashville for a taping of *Hee Haw* and missed the eighty-fourth birthday of country music icon Roy Acuff by just one day. I said, "Wadjuh do on your birthday, Roy?"

He grimaced and replied, "Jest set on the tilet and tride to remimber names!"

I'll try. In my eighty-eighth year I have been through what Shakespeare might have called the Seven Stages of Man, plus a few more. Starting my professional career in 1935 on the banquet circuit as a boy cartoonist, I went on in 1936 to become a child radio actor even before the CBC got started. In 1942 I became a humble farm labourer in two Canadian provinces, and the next year joined an RCAF aircrew as a bombardier. I returned to civilian life without a medal but got my B.A. instead.

I became a radio actor again in 1945, and at the same time was a regular member of a theatrical stock company, the New Play Society, under Dora Mavor Moore. I have played ten years of Shakespeare in three different countries and done six shows on Broadway and four in London's West

End, eventually starring in both places. I appeared on several American TV series (but only in three Hollywood films!). In 1982 I received an ACTRA Award as Best Radio Host, and in 2002 a Gemini Award for Lifetime Achievement in Canadian television. In 1999 I was appointed one of Canada's representatives to the United Nations Year of Older Persons.

I have contributed to the writing of books and lyrics for six stage musicals, one of which, *Anne of Green Gables*, is approaching its fiftieth anniversary of annual performance in Charlottetown. In my time I have been host of a TV game show, *Anything You Can Do*; was at the helm of a CBC Radio public affairs show (*Morningside*) for five years, three hours a day; did a TV talk show from Vancouver (CTV's *Don Harron Show*); and was a forty-year stand-up comic, a five-year sit-down comic, not to mention a drag queen (I was Charlie Farquharson's rich-bitch city cousin, Valerie Rosedale!).

In 1980 I was made an Officer in the Order of Canada, and in 1996 I received the Order of Ontario (Hell, I'll take Orders from anybody!). I have had fifteen books published, two of them in English and the rest in broken Canadian, a language I would best describe as "Farquharsonese."

Looking back on my career, I realize that Charlie Farquharson is my only original creation. The rest have been adaptations based on somebody else's original work. (What about Valerie Rosedale? This book should be *My Double-Double Life*.)

But Charlie is based on my observations of real life. Furthermore, he has allowed me to express my views more completely than me. When I was host of *Morningside*, I used to get hate mail when I expressed political opinions similar to Charlie's. In sixty years, nobody ever did that to Farquharson! He is my second self, and in a way more truly myself than I am. Which is why I insist on sharing this memoir with him.

Perhaps I should give him some sort of formal introduction: Charlie is a Canadian institution. His wife thinks he should be *in* one. He was born inside a monologue in *Spring Thaw '52*. It was a four-minute delivery.

Considered the resident intellectual of *Hee Haw*, he spent eighteen years cultivating that particular branch of educational television, known to its participants as "Sesame Street for Grown-Ups." This was due to both shows requiring a similar twenty-second attention span.

Among his many awards is an Honorary Degree from Trent University, Doctor of Personal Experience (D.O.P.E.), and this year he got a special citation from the Royal Canadian Mounted Police. He doesn't want any more of these, because he only has one demerit point left.

He lives not far from Bobby Orr's birthplace in Parry Sound, Ontario, on Rural Route 2, one concession away from the old Orr house. When Bobby started out as a humble private for the Oshawa Generals, Charlie was busy thrashing about in the fields with his neighbours, or getting in the hay with his sister. Charlie did find time, between thrashings, for a game of work-up baseball in the fallow field beside his hardwood bush. The game was suddenly cancelled when Charlie slid into what he thought was third base.

But Charlie is basically a winter sport, and as an active athletic supporter he is more or less confined to assisting his wife and former sweetheart, Valeda, in the Parry Sound Mixed Curling League, where they have been sweeping together for many years.

He is also a man of many parts in the literary world, having written ten bestselling books (the others were duds), including *Charlie's a Broad*. It's a travel book, not a transsexual medical text.

With all his fame, Charlie has remained a son of toil covered in a ton of soil, a man outstanding in his field, because it's too far to go back to the house. So he is not afraid to go against the grain.

Ded Occasion by Charles Ewart Farquharson

Hear's yer four wurd: don't bleeve Don Harn!

He clames he cremated me during yer spring flaw of '52, in a four-minit delivry of a monotnus log. Wat a big fib!! I got born in yer normals way jist like everbuddy elts, except fer my breeches berth, witch meens I cum out feat first, and hav kep them feats parrlells to yer ground ever sints!

Wat Don Harn has writ about me is absoloot friction! But i did got born hard by Parry Sound, Rooriel Root 2, McKellar, not far frum the old Orr house wair Bobby's fokes still reeside.

But Harn don't menshun that now weer all part of metropopolitan Parry Sound, after we got amangelmated yeers ago by our Ontairyo premeer-that-wuz, Mike Harse and his uncommonly nonsensical resolutions.

First thing we lost wuz our pustoffiss. We mist it at first, but have becum a-custom by now to no stamps and mebby strikes. We jist hands our males to them Jeehovah Witlesses. Thair goin door-tuh-door ennywaze!

Speshul note to reeders: like yer fambly bibel, my words is best red owt lowd. So don't be afrayed to flap them rooby lips of yers wile die-gestin' my thots. Don't bee afrayed fer to git oral.

But I digest. Here's yer reel fore words to this book....

Don't bleeve Don Harn!

PART I

My Life B.C. (Before Charlie),
1935 to 1952

1: FIFTY PLUS

The Year of Our Lord 2002 was a golden one for me. I mean that quite literally. I celebrated the fiftieth anniversary of three Canadian institutions with which I had been connected from their beginnings: CBC Television, the fiftieth season of the Stratford Shakespeare Festival, and the birth of Charles Ewart Farquharson, appropriately enough on April Fool's Day.

Despite this rural connection, I am a city boy, born and earned my first bread in my hometown of Toronto. But I have lived and worked about a dozen years each in New York, Los Angeles, Nashville, and London, England. Still, I am drawn to the rural existence, especially in the non-wintertime. I have spent rapturous summers in Georgian Bay and Haliburton and had an alternate domicile for thirty-five years outside Barrie in rural Innisfil. As I write these words, I am in a cottage in the tiny community of Blooming Point on the north shore of lovely Prince Edward Island. My address is on Donnie's Lane (*not* named after me) on the eastern end of Tracadie Bay. Beyond the bay are the dunes leading to a glorious beach on the Gulf of St. Lawrence. On a June day, who would want to be anywhere else?

Mind you, country living requires an aptitude for home repairs. In the city you phone somebody. In the summer in Prince Edward Island, most fixer-uppers are too busy up until about Thanksgiving. I am absolutely useless when it comes to all of this. For proof I have an aptitude test taken in my teenage years, which states that I should deal with people rather than things, because I have a mechanical aptitude below that of the average dog.

Fortunately for me, I co-habit with Claudette, a gifted tinkerer with things mechanical. So here I am plunking out these words on a computer while my live-in love is outside our cottage preparing a mosquito trap she purchased at Home Depot. Do I feel worse than useless? 'Twas ever thus, during the course of four marriages. Which is why I acquired a reputation as a workaholic in other areas of endeavour. But on a farm I'm of less use than teats on a bull. How I managed to charge for my services as a hired man in two provinces beats me!

But constantly throughout this book I will rely on the hoary, musty companionship of my ol' pal Farquharson, acting as a Geek chorus to my many escapades. He has been with me since midway through my first marriage and has never once charged me alimony. On the contrary, he has been a constant source of revenue for sixty years. Last year I put him into a retirement home ... my place ... where he belongs on my bookshelf. But in print, in this book, he will be a constant commentator on all our foolish foibles. For instance:

2008 wuz yer biggest bust sints yer durty thurtys! All but a hanfull of Ewe-Ass yewconomicks experks bleeved that ther howzing boom of that yeer wuz a bubbil cud go on furever. So they give out lones to pore peeple hoo cudden possumbly payback. But then, them hy mucky muck finnanseers on Wallstreets, instedda stickin' around, jist soled them morgridges to uther banks!

This stoopid bleef in a dett-free fewcher cost ate millyun Norse Amerkens ther jobs. It cut yer saim swatch thru Yerp, speshly Grease, Porchgill, and IRA land. Has even coz rye-uts in mainline Chiner wen Yank Wallmart sails alluva suddin dry up! This brung on yer big bank bale-out, cuz Bracko Bananer in yer yer Widehouse bleeved they wuz all too big to fale, too ritch to jale!!

But at the same time, a hanfull of smarties on yer sock exchains, like yer goalmen-sacks, maid ther own fartunes outa uther peeples mizzery, by sellin shorts wirldwide. So now we has got arselfs at a majer crotch-rodes, between a depressed reesessyun and a reesessed deepressyun.

2: MY FIRST YEARS

Since this book really starts in 1952, I thought I should include a frank synopsis of the first twenty-seven years of my existence, which dealt with the beginnings of my seventy-seven-year career in this business. I was born in 1924, at home in Toronto, lying next to a naked woman, and I hope to leave this earth the same way.

My parents, bless them, were both enthusiastic amateur performers most of their lives. This was based on an affiliation with their church, Bathurst Street United, the centre of their social life. My father was in a Bible class, the Hustlers, while my mother's was the Joy Girls. (Please insert your own contemporary comment.)

At college Dad was the staff cartoonist on *The Varsity*, the university paper, and he kept on doing it in his spare time, performing his cartoon act at church banquets. He must have been good at it, because in 1929 he had an offer from King Features Syndicate to move to Chicago and be staff cartoonist. We didn't go because my mother didn't want to leave Toronto!

So my father stayed, working for his late father's establishment, Harron's Cleaning and Dyeing. But by 1935 it was a luxury trade. Everyone in those mid-1930s seemed quite resigned to walking around unpressed, if not unclean.

I like to think that my sense of humour comes from my mother. She loved to call my father inappropriate nicknames which had no basis in reality, like Fat and Big Bum ... and he would tease her about her newness to the kitchen, since she went straight from my uncle's insurance office to our first home. She would reply in baby talk: "Tant took, tut nanas!" (Translation: I can't cook but I can cut bananas!)

One of my father's nicknames offered me the opportunity for my first public performance at the tender age of fifteen months. By that time he had become superintendent of our Sunday school, and on its anniversary the tradition was that the sermon in church would be given by the super himself. So my mother proudly brought me along to view my dad in his glory. Unfortunately, I didn't get much of a view of him, because Bathurst Street Church is full of posts, and I was located directly behind one of them. I could hear my dad, but I couldn't see him, and in my infantile frustration I shouted out the only familiar name by which I knew him: "Ya big bum!" I was told I got the epithet out about five times, louder each time, before my mother and I reached the rear door of the church. Thanks for being there for my debut, Mum.

Most of my early rural contacts (on a more long-term basis) came from my mother's side of the family. Early on, I detected a difference in speech patterns between my own parents and my mother's cousins in Allandale, near Barrie. They were Owen and Mary Peters and their teenage son, George. I was fascinated by how they pronounced our surname as Harn, expressed between the teeth with a sphincter-like tension (which makes rural Canadians almost impossible to lip-read).

My mother, Delsia Ada Maud Hunter, was born near Barrie at Painswick, where her father Christopher Whiten Hunter ran the local post office. That was, until Wilfrid Laurier was elected in 1891. The job had been a sinecure provided by my grampa's allegiance to Sir John A. Macdonald. After Grampa Hunter lost his government job, no Hunter has voted for "them Grits" since.

Our present encumbrance Steevy Harpy claims to be a Tory, wun of them Regressiv Preservativs. But he had his ruts in yer Refarm Party under that Presstone Mannering. Petey Muhkay wuz at that time yer tit-you-lar hed of them Regressiv Preservativs, but he amangelmated with Harpy and they form a coaly-ishun (witch lader becum a durty wurd to enny Tory). But I think of Steevy Harpy as more of a suppose-a-tory.

My maternal grandfather retired at the age of forty-nine and was supported ever after by his son, my rich uncle Tom, a whiz in the insurance business. My chief task when I was in Dunbarton was swatting flies while my grandfather read Toronto's *Evening Telegram*. As my reward, his wife, my Nanna, spoiled me with homemade taffy and sandwiches which consisted mainly of white sugar!

Eventually the lack of electricity and plumbing in Dunbarton caused my uncle to move his aged parents into Toronto. To our place, not his. His wife wouldn't have put up with two elderly free lodgers. I moved out of my spacious bedroom into a smaller space. My grandfather's chief preoccupation was re-reading the Bible and strolling outside in the street with great dignity, shovel in hand, returning to my mother's peony bushes with a steaming load of "road apples."

Them wuz more innersent times I gess, yer thurtys and fartys.

I mind a call-gurl in them daze wuz sumbuddy worked fer yer Bell telly-fone. I don't mind any feemails hangin round Parrysound streetcorners with offrins of sax. In them daze all that kinda effurt wuz dun by voluntears.

And we never herd of a sexchange. We jist maid dew with wat we had. And nobuddy wuz on the pill. Our only methid of breth controll wuz wat we calls preematoor withdraw-all. That's like taken yer nite-trane frum Muntry-all and gittin off in Coburg!

So ther wernt no copulation explosion round about our parts. And our numbers allweeze staid the saim, cuz everytime a gurl got preggerunt, sum yung man left town.

I vividly remember my mother's antics one Hallowe'en when I was nine. I was dressed as a cowboy, and my job was to lead a heavy-draft plush horse up and down our street and stop at each door as I shouted "Shell out!" ("Trick or treat" is a later American intervention.) Inside that horse costume was Bryce Wylie's mother from down the street. She was the front of the horse, and guess who was the horse's ass? Delsia Ada Maud Harron.

I led my ungainly steed up to the door and shouted "Shell out!" As the amused householder handed out the goodies, my horse would slowly turn around, and I don't know how she managed it in that confined space ... but my mother scrunched up several brown paper bags and stuck them out the you-know-what-hole onto the householder's front steps as my horse retreated to another location!

3: GETTING PAID FOR IT

I started my professional showbiz life when I got involved with a Boy Scout minstrel show in 1935. I was a ten-year-old Wolf Cub and my scoutmaster wanted me to provide an interval in their show by doing the same cartoon act my father had been doing to earn a few bucks. His main work was running Harron's Cleaning and Dyeing, but in 1935 there was much more dying about it than cleaning. So for fifteen bucks a time, he travelled the banquet circuit drawing cartoons on big white sheets of paper with coloured chalks.

My dad was completely helpful, coaxing me through every phase of my ten-minute act. After the third night, a gentleman came backstage and approached me about doing the same act for his employees at their annual banquet. He was Basil Tippet of Tippet-Richardson, a cartage company that still exists today. If I would appear at the Round Room next to Eaton Auditorium above the College Street store, he would pay me fifteen bucks. My father's fee!

My dear dad, bless him, assisted me once again in my first professional job, and from then on I replaced him on the banquet circuit. A ten-year-old with coloured chalks is much more of a novelty than his father doing the same thing. A couple of months later, I was doing the chalk-talk act and a woman approached me about coming to her office and reading a script.

An advertisement for Don's father's Chalk Talk act, 1935.

"What's a script?" I asked.

She said never mind, just come along and read. I did, and when I finished she said, "Well, that takes it off the paper." I apologized, but she said I would now be doing a radio series three times a week at the princely sum of $2.50 a broadcast. It also involved rehearsing on the other three days of the week, at no extra charge. It seemed like a fortune.

Just before my radio series began, I started high school. When I entered the hallowed halls of Vaughan Road Collegiate, I was the only pupil wearing short pants. I feel an explanation is in order: I was only eleven and had skipped my last year of public school because I was in a double class. (Today it would be called grades seven and eight, but we called them Junior and Senior Fourth.) I spent far more time listening to the lessons of my upper classmen, so that when exam time for the grade above me came along, I decided it might be fun to try to bullshit my way through their curriculum.

When the results came out weeks later, I was taken down to the principal's office. I didn't know what to expect. By writing the exams a grade above my class I had managed to get an average mark of seventy-four! The principal suggested it might be better if I went right on to high school. He thought, and rightly so, that I might be bored to death listening to all the lessons I had spent the year overhearing.

In shorts, that's how I came to be the youngest Vaughan Road student. I was in awe of fifth formers like William Hutt, who had a moustache! That year he was a chorus boy in Vaughan Road's production of *Rio Rita*. Later we shared the first few seasons at Stratford, and Bill went on to be the festival's leading light.

I bought a CCM bicycle with my first month's radio pay, went careening down a steep hill to the studio, and ran into a taxi. It was all my fault, but he generously put my bike in his trunk and myself in the back of the taxi, and drove me to the station. When I came to my other assignment, reading a safety message to all kids listening, as was my regular assignment at the end of the show, the entire cast was choking with laughter as they clutched the velvet curtains of the studio.

Our series was cancelled when the Canadian Radio Broadcasting Commission suddenly became the CBC in 1936. It was because we had a sponsor, the Ontario Department of Highways.

That's why they calls it yer Canajun Broadcorping Castration! I never mind that guvmint commishun at all. In them daze i had a cristle set brung me in raddio pogroms frum as fur away as Pissburg. Lader we dun time with yer Seebeesea, but nowadaze Valeda and me is pritty well hung up on yer Rodgered K-bull.

4: BACK TO NORMAL (WHATEVER NORMAL IS)

My career zoomed in the opposite direction after that. A new block of talent was coming in from the West: John Drainie, Bernard Braden, Fletcher Markle, and Tommy Tweed under the direction of Andrew Allan. I was to become a junior member of that illustrious group, but not until after I returned from my Air Force service in 1945.

Among the displaced was a director I worked with occasionally, Sid Brown. He was bad-tempered but later when he became a lowly actor like me, his disposition changed. Relieved of directorial responsibility, I found him very affable and not at all without humour. In fact, he already had a wide underground reputation as the creator of a smutty but funny recording, *The Crepitation Contest*. For decades now fans have heard and roared at this farting duel between the champion Lord Windersmear and his Australian challenger, Paul Boomer, who was disqualified in the finals at the farting post for upping the tone of his performance by attaching blue ribbons to the seat of his britches.

But I was glad to resume a normal life. I was never really comfortable with my brief interlude of local celebrity. Especially when our Sunday school superintendent referred to me as "the boy genius," and I had to endure the downright hostility of my fellow Christians in Sunday school.

I was actually relieved to go back to high school full-time. I would be able to hang around after hours, blending in with the average population seeking teenage thrills by shaking up an Aspirin in a bottle of Coke. And playing my favourite sport, football. I got to play on the Junior B team, unlike years earlier in public school when I tried out for soccer. When the soccer team roster was posted, next to my name it said: Harron, Left Outside. I was shattered and went on home. I didn't realize it was actually a position on the team.

I played football for three years, and all that time without a helmet! Today's preoccupation with brain concussions in football and hockey makes me question my adolescent sanity.

The most exciting aspect of high school life was the proximity to girls, especially when they were wearing a kind of school uniform called a middy, with the skirt hoisted higher than regulation by about three inches. An invitation to meet and socialize with females in the auditorium after class was far more exciting than reading lines over a microphone. I put Orange Blossom brilliantine on my cowlick, hoping to make myself more acceptable.

Eventually I got a date and took Norma Helston to our annual formal dance. She was the butcher's daughter, and when I took her home to her apartment above the shop, instead of stealing a goodnight kiss, I asked for one! The air was fraught with tension as she counted the number of times we had been out together and finally consented when the total came to five. I should have grabbed that minx without so much as a by-your-leave!

To make up for my loss of radio income, I took a series of part-time jobs. I sold *Liberty* magazine door-to-door, without much success, and delivered pastries on my bicycle, trying to avoid potholes that would shake the meringue off a lemon pie. The closest I came to being rural was as a paid assistant to my Sunday schoolteacher on Saturdays selling vegetables at a so-called farmer's market in the heart of downtown Toronto.

I had heard the word *hybrid* mentioned in connection with corn, so I used the term as a selling point and passed on the information to my customers, much to the consternation of my employer. He told me to desist from dispensing such information, because hybrid corn was the kind that was fit only to put in a silo and fed to cattle.

I resigned and became a Saturday bag boy at a now-defunct super-market, Power Stores. I got the same salary as my former radio career, $2.50 a time. Through trial and error, I eventually learned to put the customer's eggs at the top of the bag and the canned goods at the bottom.

My most vivid memory of that time was in the employee lunchroom one Saturday upon hearing on the radio the news that France had fallen to Hitler's hordes. No one talked. Finally one man spoke up. "It'll take a miracle. A fuckin' miracle." Next week came the news of the successful evacuation of the British expeditionary force at Dunkirk.

Shore glad our boys got evaccinated crost yer chanel that day, and releefed they wuzn't dive-bummed by them Stookys and Messershits of Hitler's Lust-wafers. Mine jew, anuther mirrorkill wood soon be needed, cuz them krout Panzy Divishuns of yer Nazty party plan to evade yer hoamland of our Anglican Sacksons. Mysalf I wuz at the time a semmy-private in yer Royl Muskokey Dismounted Fut, station hard by Barry. I volumeteer but I never got over-seized. Jist spent the rasta Whirld Wore Eleven at Camp Boredom, standin on gard fer thee and me.

5: FELLED BY PHYSICS

I spent almost six years in high school, because of my failure in physics. The failure was really caused by my skipping class and shooting pool at a nearby establishment, the Mission. I noticed recently that it was at last living up to its name as an Evangelical Church. But I had to pick up physics if I wanted to go to college, so I stayed in high school an extra year. Coming up was my sixth consecutive year. It's supposed to take five, but the previous year I had written my physics exam and got twenty-two out of a hundred! The problem wasn't just my reluctance to embrace anything to do with the sciences, but it was also the teacher, J.C. Harston. For me the J.C. stood for Jesus Christ, because he was so convinced of his eternal rectitude. He was a severe disciplinarian to his own brood of children. I know this because he lived on the next street to us and every night I could hear the piercing tones of his whistle summoning his own kids home from the playground at a disturbingly early hour.

He was playful in his own way, with a constant air of mirthless jollity. Once he asked if any of us had a nickname. Foolish me, I was the only one who blurted out that I was sometimes called Bunt, a nickname my father gave me because at an early age I couldn't hit a baseball more than a few feet. So Bunt I now became constantly, accompanied by the snickers of the rest of the pupils. It got so I took to skipping J.C.'s class and taking refuge at the Mission. If I wanted a high school diploma, which would allow me to enroll in a university course, I would have to pass physics. Since it was the only course I was repeating in my sixth year, I decided to fill out my otherwise empty curriculum with a commercial course involving typing and shorthand. This meant I would be part of a class of thirty-five girls! The only other male enrolled in the course was my pal, Louie Libman. (Known to television audiences as Larry Mann, and now living in California.)

So we gathered, the thirty-five females and two males, for our first typing lesson with Mr. Smith. He told us all to place our hands just above the typewriter, ready to strike. He announced the first word: *IF*. We all duly typed the two letters. *IF IT*. Two more. *IF IT IS*. No problem so far. *IF IT IS IN!* I glanced across the room at Louie. One owlish glance from him and I was gone. We both let out a shriek of laughter.

End of the lesson for us. Mild-mannered Mr. Smith kicked us out of class. Next day we were let back in, and I am so grateful, because typing is the only technical skill I have ever had, and it has stood me in good stead. I got to be a whiz at shorthand but lost all of it as soon as I went on the farm. Which, as I explained, was the only way to avoid my writing that damn physics exam. It was either repeat that miserable experience or spend half a year on a farm from April to September, working twelve to fourteen hours a day, six days a week for $20 a month. I took the easy way out.

The Farm Service Force was a wartime organization putting urban high school students into agricultural work in an attempt to replace the professional labourers who had joined the armed forces. So the call went out to high school students to replace them. It was a way of "getting our year" if we left school in spring and went on the farm as hired help.

My mother knew of a second cousin by marriage who had a farm not far from where I had vacationed in my earlier days. Charles Hadden had an innate dignity, even a nobility, and as superintendent of the local Sunday school, he was extremely well spoken, despite being a man of few words. But his entire working wardrobe was something I was later to adopt: glasses, a weathered peak cap, and a roll-top cardigan sweater which I actually saw him buy one Saturday night in the town of Sunderland. I thought at the time, *You'll never catch me wearing anything like that!* Sixty years later, it's my only claim to fame.

It's wat yer hy-fashion mucky mucks calls a shawl-collard cardig-agin. I bot it frum yer old Eton cattlehog back in 19 ot 42, and has wore the blaim thing ever sints! And low and beeholden, you'll see it nowadaze fer sail to wimmen in yer fashnabull maggotzeens like Vague, or Harpy's Brazeer, or even up heer in Canda in yer Shatty-elaine.

The Haddens had a hundred-acre farm, predominantly dairy, near the little village of Wick, Ontario, between Greenbank and Blackwater. The big towns where you went on Saturday night for a haircut and an ice cream cone were Uxbridge, Port Perry, and maybe once a year, Lindsay. When I got off the bus in Wick, it seemed less like a village than a general store where the rubber boots stood next to the head cheese, and the local population on view at my arrival was a dog sleeping under a tree.

Grace Hadden, the farmer's wife, was waiting for me and drove me the half mile to the farm, too late for the midday meal. I was immediately put to work. My first day's job was harrowing. The task was to drag a device that broke up the lumps of freshly plowed soil into smaller lumps. Actually, horses did the actual dragging. I was merely put in charge of a team of them, or rather, the team was in charge of me. I went wherever they led me, and by choretime that afternoon I was starving. You might call it tea time, but there was no tea to be had in that barn. Just milk to be extracted from about thirty cows, and their milk was sold to someone else.

By this time, I was faint with exhaustion and a bit dizzy as I approached the barn to turn in my horses and help with the milking. I don't remember who turned in the horses. Probably Charles Hadden's ancient father, a tiny termagant who was supposed to be retired but managed to do all the things I was supposed to be doing.

The Hadden cows were milked twice a day. Fortunately for me, this was done by machine, and all I had to do was attach suction cups to the cows' teats. But the operation had to be finished by hand to get the few remaining drops. They were coaxed out of the cow by a manual process called stripping. I was never much of a success as a stripper doing hand jobs.

The thing that hit me when I staggered wearily into the cowbarn that day was the smell. Combined with my harrowing vertigo, the odour made me quite unsteady. Charles and Grace were most understanding of the rookie's condition. They told me to sit outside on the step of the separator room until I regained my composure. By now I was thinking seriously about catching the next bus back to Toronto and tackling that physics exam. The madness was momentary.

Because I was ravenously hungry, I asked senior Hadden what time the family had dinner. His cheery answer was "You've missed it!" Missed it? It was five o'clock in the afternoon, for God's sake! Only later did I realize that dinner in the country is lunch in the city. What I was anxious about was "supper." It turned out to be the best part of my day.

The Haddens were involved with a score of other farmers in a Beef Ring. Each member contributed one kill per month, in which the rest of them shared, and that night there was a glorious supply of meat on the table.

Mysalf I'm a mixed farmer, part grain part dairy part fruit with a chick or two on the side. Can't make a livin at any of them, and only beef i got is agin the guvmnt. Last spring our bull wandered off with another bull … takes all kinds don't it! So we bin tryna fix our cows up with wat they calls yer arty-fishul insinuation. But so far our cattle don't seem to want to take to the bottled stuff as long as they thinks they kin still git draft!

6: DOWNCAST ON THE FARM

My second day I was in deep shit. Literally. I was given the early morning pre-breakfast task of shovelling the cows' other contributions to the morning milking. That done, I was taken to the sheep pen, now empty of its residents, who were vacationing in a nearby meadow. I remained penned up with their leavings. I suspected the stuff hadn't been disturbed in years. What faced me was layer after layer of their ancient offal, stratified like geological formations. But fate had chosen only me to uncover these layers.

Little did I realize, up to my knees in the stuff, that not much more than a year later I would be sleeping in a sheep-pen. That was when, in 1943, as a newly recruited Acey Deucey, the lowliest member of the RCAF, I was billetted in the Coliseum of the Canadian National Exhibition. I spent a month where the sheep used to crap in my bed, but then I was promoted to the bull pen, where God knows what kind of carnal doings went on, and spent my third month upstairs in the room next to the Dog Show, commonly known as the Cathouse.

Back to 1942. My third day I was sent to clean out the chicken house, which was a fairly dry operation compared to what the cows offered. But believe me, a fine spray of chickenshit hanging in the air can do a lot more damage to your vocal cords, not to mention your morale and *joie de vivre*.

However, all that was bliss compared to the pigpen. I had read a lot of claptrap about how intelligent swine are and how clean they actually intend to be. But nothing in my rural experience ever compared with the olfactory anguish I suffered when I did time in the pen with their offal remains.

By the end of the first week I had settled into a kind of routine. In the grey hours of dawn I brought the cows in for milking. After morning chores, breakfast was the main event, lots of meat and not much milk, but I got used to tea with just a drop of the precious stuff. Every week I would help Charles load up the city milk truck with big cans. Freud would probably deduce that that's what stirred my interest in the upper part of the female anatomy. But I became more of a leg man shepherding those cows back and forth at both ends of the day.

I was never allowed near the tractor. I worked with horses. My favourite was a twenty-six year old Percheron named Pearl, a name I later chose to be Matthew Cuthbert's buggy companion in *Anne of Green Gables*.

On the manure spreader, Pearl was pretty well in charge as I took off my shirt, closed my eyes, and basked in the sunrays. At the end of a day on the spreader, my back would be flecked with brown. But not, alas, by the sun.

Charles Hadden had a four-year-old son, Donald, and because of our names, we spent time together. We later became good friends, but at age four his chief function in life seemed to be emptying either his sphincter or his bladder. I recollect two well-remembered phrases: "I do stream" and "I do pile." As a city slicker, I soon learned to follow his example of relieving oneself outdoors. Monkey see, monkey doo-doo.

I don't think I earned my $20 wage that first month, but I was handed my precious emolument anyway and immediately took off for a weekend in the city. I had retained my touch-typing skills by keeping in touch with three different girls. I managed to take out all three in the space of my two and a half days in the city (matinee and evening performances included), but I didn't manage to get in the hay till I got back to the farm.

I'll skip the details because none of it resulted in my losing my virginity, but the most vivid impression on my return to the Hadden farm was that the barn didn't seem to smell any more. This gave me some temporary comfort, until I realized with a shock that if the barn didn't smell, maybe to those three city girls I was the one that did!

7: GETTING READY FOR A GANG-THRASH

My monthly salary was raised to $25 during the month of August. That's when the local farmers got together to harvest their wheat, oats, and barley in a co-operative venture that involved travelling to each other's home turf. It was a joyous time. I became what you might call A Happy Stooker. To stook (rhymes with puke, not cook) is to stack together several sheaves of grain which have already been bound together by twine into a neat bundle by a machine called a binder. The stooker makes a pile of the upright sheaves ready for them to be pitched into the threshing machine. (But it's thrash, not thresh.)

This is all water under your bridgework now, because in an age of air-conditioned combines with FM radio and CD players, stooking isn't needed any more. That's why it's called a combine — the whole threshing operation done in one swell foop.

But that stooking operation was my first real introduction to the dialect of local farmers and their hired hands. That's where I heard constantly the kind of speech that I eventually gave to Charlie. I think it's a third or fourth generation dialect out of Lowland Scotland and Northern Ireland. Americans these days make fun of our Canadian pronunciation of the word *outhouse*. To them we're saying *oothoose*. To us, the Yanks are saying *aout hayouse*. But to me our version of *out* has the same timbre as a bloodhound baying to the moon.

By the time I was ready to go back to the city, I had a thorough grounding in the regional dialect that bespoke my original heritage. I was speaking "broken Ontarian" like a native. I used it first in a rural radio drama, *Summer Fallow*, and later onstage in Harry Boyle's play *The Macdonalds of Oak Valley*.

Never mind. I enjoyed my co-workers' thrash talk in the harvest fields. It wasn't about politics or even sports, and there was a distinct absence of dirty jokes. Instead it was mostly about family relationships.

Do yuh mind her, Big Bertha? She wuz a Leitch. Wun of yer old Flesherton Leitches. But Bertha wuz a Rumball on her father's side, wun of the old Port Perry Rumballs.

No, no, yer wrong there, them Rumballs is cuzzins to us, my Ant Willeena she wuz a Canningtin Rumball on her mother's side. Bertha her famly wuz in trucking, yer Hoare transports peeple, so bertha wuz wun of yer old Oshawa Hoares.

But my most cherished memory of those days, which can still warm the cockles of my stomach, was the threshing suppers with their bounteous array of food. We would all traipse in for "dinner" shortly after noon to steaming fresh cobs of corn, mounds of mashed potatoes, heaping helpings of yellow beans, platters of well-done roast beef, and jugs of hot gravy followed by seven different kinds of pie! I think I tried every one of them.

After a twenty-minute nap it was back to the fields, and about four o'clock the women would bring us out lemonade and homemade cookies. That would keep us going till about seven, and the feast would start all over again at supper. Threshin' time on and off the Hadden farm were my best days.

8: COLLEGE DAZE

From my six months on the farm in 1942, I had saved $120 out of my salary of $125. That sum was enough, in those days, for a half semester at college! So I joined Victoria, the United Church college at the University of Toronto, in an arts course, Social and Philosophical Studies, that when shortened for familiarity was called Sock and Fill. It was just the ticket for me — airy discussions about the arts where vagueness and bullshittery beckoned.

When I enrolled, my previous professional experience as an actor counted for nothing. I auditioned for the only broad comedy role in Shaw's *The Devil's Disciple* for director Earle Grey. Instead, he assigned me a non-speaking part, a Hessian officer who attends the treason trial at the end of the play. I hesitated at this comedown, but when I saw the costume, all white breeches, high black boots, and a bright scarlet tunic, I figured the whole outfit might be a "chick magnet."

On the dress rehearsal of *The Devil's Disciple* I did as I was told, just sat there during the trial. They gave me a wig that made me look like Apple Mary, and nobody bothered to apply any makeup. Also, after the dress, the director was furious at my lack of reaction during the trial. "This chap Dick Dudgeon is on trial for his life! Surely your character should be at least curious, old boy! Do you by chance speak any German?" I told Mr. Grey that I had one year of it in high school. "Then express yourself, laddie! Show your concern! And for heaven's sake, chappie, get someone to put some makeup on you!"

Next night was the opening performance of three. The new wig they gave me was all tight curls, instead of the drab tea cosy of the night before that made me look like Dame May Whitty. The co-ed in charge of me also slathered on the makeup in a generous fashion, including flaming rouge for my cheeks. After I put on the wig I looked a good deal like Harpo Marx.

When the trial scene finally arrived, I was a-flutter with nerves, anxious to prove myself among these amateurs. I took Earle Grey's notes seriously. From the very beginning of the scene my eyes flashed with unfulfilled curiosity as I used my limited high school German to express my confusion as to what was taking place. *Vas haben sie gesaght*? (What did he say?) *Ich weiss nicht vas soll es bedeuten*! (I don't know what's going on!).

Everyone seemed to be watching me throughout the trial scene. But not because of my performance. My exaggerated gestures had caused a slight rip at the knee of my skin-tight britches. I was completely unaware that the rent had started travelling toward my crotch, causing a tension in the audience that exceeded the one caused by Mr. Shaw's play.

No notes for me after the performance. I was summarily dismissed by Earle Grey himself and told *not* to come back for either of the following nights!

Ironic footnote: in 2008 I was given an Earle Grey Gemini Award for lifetime achievement in radio and television. That night I told the story of my rank failure in my college theatre debut. So in accepting the award I sang (off-key I'm sure) to the tune of "Getting to Know You" from *The King and I*: "Thank you, Earle Grey, despite the fact that you have never been 'PRECISELY MY CUP OF TEA!'"

But farming wasn't about to release its hold on me. Instead, the call came from the West to bring in the biggest bumper crop Saskatchewan had since the early 1930s. With most of its hired men already overseas, the Prairie province was urging anyone, even college students to help bring in The Big Haircut.

It was considered a patriotic duty to help out, but the big attraction for me was that I would be well paid for my efforts, not twenty bucks a month, but $6 a day! Over a period of five or six weeks I could earn enough to pay my fees for the second semester! At home I talked excitedly of nothing else. My mother dutifully prepared for me three days' worth of baloney sandwiches as she listened to my constant Regina monologue!

Them prayery provintses is call that becuz so menny times they bin brung to thair neez. If it wernt drout er rust, it wooda bin grassed hoppers, caterpillers, or even frate rates. Them provintses wuz compleatly at the mersey of yer ellamints, and offin without no crap insurience. This yeer it wuz so wet out west ther feelds cooden be worked till joon. Yer risk in bean on the sock markit is nuthin cumpair tuh sprayin' yer seed intuh the ground.

So it was shortly after my eighteenth birthday that this young Lochinvar set out for the West. We were to take a train full of colonist cars, the same mode of travel that brought immigrants out west at the turn of the century. There was no sleeping accommodation, but it was only a three-day journey with one stopover in Winnipeg. Overhead, above the seats, were panels which when lowered could serve as a kind of hard-shell bunk.

I began to eat my never-ending supply of baloney sandwiches. By the end of the first day I was dispensing them freely to my travelling companions. Every few hundred miles or so the train would stop for a quarter of an hour, and we would all pile out and fill up the seats of a little railside restaurant, not to mention the washroom.

9: ON TO WINNIPEG, LEADING TO THE REGINA MONOLOGUE

Manytober: meenin "yer place ware evrybuddy cums together fer to part-take of yer grate spearits." Them spearits needs to be lifted regler, on accounta the hole place is so blaim flat ... Floody flat. That's why Ottawar thinks sumtimes uv sendin water wings to all them dry farmers.

It was a relief to get away from the bone-aching sleeping arrangements on our train and have an overnight in a cheap but comfortable Winnipeg hotel. I cannot reveal the name of that hotel, not due to senility, but because I stole one of its towels. On to Saskatchewan. Next stop was Regina, described by one of their own local smartasses as being "entirely on the wrong side of the tracks."

Sasquatchyouwan: a old Cree wurd witch means "My gol that's a swift curnt!" A Yank tooryist wunce ask a lokel inhibitant jist wair he wuz in Canda, and wuz tole "Saskytoon Sassakatchyouwon!" he deeside fer tuh keep on drivin' till he cum to sum place wair they speeks Anglish.

Regina in 1942 seemed to have a lively nightlife. Before being assigned to our first farm, we had a night on the town. A bunch of us Eastern punks and bums (as Calgary premier Ralph Klein was later to refer to such as us) went to a dancehall, the Trianon, which advertised future name bands like Don Messer and Mart Kenney. But the current combo seemed quite adequate. They were sufficient to allow us to get in contact with some of the local girls.

Our departure to Moose Jaw, where we would be assigned to a farm, was delayed a day until the following morning. So Archie and I decided to while away the time at a bowling alley, and we accidentally ran into two so-called debutantes we had squired the night before. They were busy setting up our bowling pins. On to Moose Jaw, the only city in Canada named after Brian Mulroney.

I was assigned to a farm in Chaplin, forty miles away. I arrived to find the farmer at breakfast. The remarkable thing about him was his wardrobe. He had the same peak cap, glasses, and grey roll-top sweater worn by Charles Hadden in Ontario. I thought *My God, are they franchising them now?*

He was a miserable man to work for, and so were his meals. After six days the rain came down. My farmer made a fist and shouted at the sky, "Goddamn Patterson government!"

But the crop was the biggest in a generation, and the farm was vast by Ontario standards, about 1,500 acres growing nothing but wheat. With no livestock there were no chores to do. At $6 a day the job looked like a cinch. But at the end of a long day I felt that I had well and truly earned the money. Have you ever been so bone-tired that you couldn't sleep? That was my condition throughout that first week.

And hungry, too. No splendid harvest dinners, just more baloney and boiled spuds, with a vague promise of Hungarian partridge that never materialized. And gloom, constant gloom served up by farmer Bill, with constant complaints about the Liberal government in Regina.

My second week was a welcome change. I was shifted to the farm of Paul Hammer, a German immigrant with five daughters and no sons, but each of those girls was stronger than me. Since 1939 I had been conditioned to regard Germans as the enemy. Here I became a willing member of a truly happy family. The meals were much better, too, with lots of sauerkraut and Braunschweiger sausage.

But midway through that first week in October, there was a huge snowfall! It's not unusual in the West. I waded through ankle-deep drifts to get to their outdoor privy, carefully selecting pages from Eaton's catalogue, keeping the ladies' underwear portions until I was forced to use them. The snow brought the harvesting to a complete stop.

After years of drought, the bumper crop could not be brought in from the fields. From my own point of view, I wasn't going to make nearly enough money to pay my tuition fees. I said a warm farewell to my new German friends and went back to Moose Jaw to apply for any work available.

I got a job near the U.S. border in Estevan cutting wood with a bandsaw for a Russian farmer with a heavy-handed but basically jolly sense of humour. Both Russian and German employers were brief but pleasant interludes at the same moment when German and Russian armies were locked in deadly combat on the Eastern front. Saskatchewan was a world away, and for me, multiculturally ahead of its time.

The woodcutting ended sooner than I had hoped, and I returned to Toronto and my university education. In that brief time I had learned a bit about my country and its people, but when the occasion arose to use my newfound knowledge of a rural Ontario dialect, I shied away from the opportunity.

In January my university staged a big fund drive for European War Relief for those refugees upended by the conflict. There were reps from each arts college to arrange the entertainment. I became the Hick from Vic in red underwear and a set of buckteeth. But when I opened my mouth to speak, instead of the by-now familiar-to-me twang of Charlie Farquharson, out came a pale imitation of Edgar Bergen's other dummy, Charlie McCarthy's hick sidekick, Mortimer Snerd. So I missed the chance to celebrate Charlie's seventieth anniversary with me this year, instead of the sixtieth.

Thair's nuthin fer to sellabate. Don Harn's bin livin offa my a-veils fer long enuff!

I came home with not enough money for tuition, so before Christmas I signed on as a temporary janitor at a Toronto high school, where I was assigned to scrub out the swimming pool with what I considered to be a toothbrush. I did double time working the graveyard shift at the post office and made my tuition fees just in time.

10: ISN'T THAT WHEN YOU DECLARE BANKRUPTCY?

Despite my shameful stage debut, I was welcomed into the ranks of the Victoria College Drama Club, mostly because it was wartime and able-bodied males with theatrical experience were few and far between. After the big production at Hart House where I had made my drastic entry, the Drama Club was now involved in a one-act play competition with other arts colleges.

Vic's choice was *Riders to the Sea* by J.M. Synge. The play consisted of a bunch of Irish women keening (i.e. moping) over the corpse of a family member washed up on the beach. I had read the play in high school but didn't remember any male role in it. I had forgotten about Bartley, the corpse. So I was chosen to lie there in state with no lines of dialogue, unseen by the audience, moaned over by sobbing females. There was only one performance, so I amused myself by staring back at the keening women and making all kinds of goofy faces while they sobbed over me. The Vic drama co-eds were not amused, and I wasn't asked to participate in their next venture. Our college won the award.

But despair not, dear reader, because before the school year ended I emerged as a genuine drama award winner. A couple of fourth-year actors at Vic were anxious to try some of the meatier roles provided by William Shakespeare. Jack Coleman, just prior to enlisting in the navy, wanted to do a scene from *Macbeth*, while Ralph Hicklin, later to be drama critic of Toronto's *Evening Telegram*, longed to don the sober threads of *Hamlet*. They appeared in a brief, condensed version of soliloquies from both tragedies.

These were two acts of a theatrical evening, to be judged by Professor Robert Finch of University College and the Vic librarian, Miss Honey. What was needed to fill out the evening was some lighter material sandwiched in between the two tragic heroes. Somebody suggested *The Proposal* by Chekhov, a light but classic one-act farce. I was cast as a nervous hypochondriac who is trying to woo his landowner's daughter and can't help running off at the mouth in his hysterical nervousness. This time I would get to speak in English!

The tickets were not reserved, and neither was my performance. I remember swallowing great gobs of water, and some of it got sprayed on the front row of our audience. Sandwiched in between Shakespeare's tragic heroes, we Chekhovians became tragic relief and got a very positive audience response. At the end of the evening came the adjudication. Robert Finch was a distinguished professor of romance languages and a published poet in his own right, but he stood no chance against the iron will of Miss Honey. *Hamlet* and *Macbeth* were both shut out of the winner's circle, and the Best Actor Award went to my own shamefully hammy performance, water spray and all. Perhaps it was a portent of my life to come.

Professor Finch all but winced as he was forced to hand the trophy to me. It was like the ones handed out for excellence in athletics, a felt crest in our college colours, scarlet and gold, depicting our college and the name of the activity. Finch almost cracked a frosty smile as he handed me my limp felt crest with the two letters *VD*.

I treasure that trophy and keep it fondly to this day. So when people ask me what I got out of my college theatrics, what do you think I tell them?

11: NERVOUS IN THE SERVICE

After being unceremoniously ordered out of my Hessian chick-magnet grandeur, the next uniform I put on was that of a private in the University of Toronto COTC (Canadian Officers' Training Corps). I was given battle dress to wear once a week.

Battle dress was the lowly grunt's only uniform in His Majesty's Army, and the college version consisted, I suspect, of ill-fitted rejects from the regular army. But going to and fro on Toronto's streetcars, I was often taken for a member of our regular armed forces. The cheery smiles and the odd thumbs-up only deepened my eighteen-year-old guilt at remaining on the home front while others my age were preparing for the eventual assault on the beaches of Europe. Other, wiser heads on those streetcars took me for a "zombie," a conscripted soldier who refused to serve overseas.

Either way I was miserable. My father, a veteran of the First World War, with the Military Cross, had rejoined the army with the rank of major and was now stationed in an Army Trade School in Hamilton. As the only man left at home, I started to chafe at my civilian existence. Especially since the regular army officer in charge of our unit looked down his nose at our collection of saggy-baggy intellectual misfits. He was always clearing his throat, and I expected at any moment that he was going to spit on the lot of us.

The COTC went to camp that summer in Niagara for two weeks. It was during a route march that I got a dandy second-degree burn on my arms. That weekend I still had the bandages on when a bunch of us college-boy commandos crossed the border to visit the Buffalo USO. I got a great deal of sympathy from the canteen hostesses about my war wounds. I slunk back across the border burning with shame and determined to enlist in September 1943 instead of going back for a second year at college.

I never got overseized. I wuz still standin thair wen it cum yer evasion of Yerp on VD day. Oney danger I ever cum up agin wuz goin to breckfust every mornin ware they use to put sumthin' in our serial to make us never mind the girls. It wuz call yer salty peater. The wife thinks that that darn stuff is finely startin to work!

In the fall of '43 there was a big demand for aircrew. Night bombing raids ended with more and more RAF and RCAF airmen in German prison camps. With my high school pal, Bill Bremner, I went downtown one September morning just before my nineteenth birthday, to enlist in the RCAF.

Bill didn't get past the eye test. He was colour-blind. I passed with flying colours and was sworn in after undergoing the required electro-cardiogram.

Next day in my green tweed suit I reported to #1 Manning Depot, CNE grounds, and lined up with others to be issued a uniform. When it came my turn, the corporal in charge told me that I wasn't to be fitted with a uniform because there was something wrong with my electrocar-diogram. When I checked with the medical office, I was told I had an enlarged heart.

Immediately I felt a thumping in my chest, and I had great difficulty getting to sleep that night because that alarming thump never stopped. The next day I reported back for discharge from the Air Force and was told that there had been a mistake. Somebody else's electrocardiogram was mixed up with mine.

I got my new uniform and joined a platoon of raw recruits under a drill instructor. He must have been a religious man, because every so often he would raise his eyes to the sky and proclaim, "Father, forgive them, for they know not what they do." When he dismissed us, he told me to wait behind. I was starting to get a persecution complex, but this interruption was a pleasant surprise. He looked me straight in the eye and asked, "How do you tie your tie like that?" I told him it was a Windsor knot, with one extra layer of knot, invented by the abdicated King Edward VIII when he was Prince of Wales. I tied one on with my instructor and headed for my next assignment: the Harvard Step Test.

This was designed to test heart and lungs by stepping up and down a three-foot platform for four minutes. Suddenly my heart was in my mouth when I heard the shrill cry of *"Bunt!"* ring out. The officer in charge of the test was my old high school physics teacher, J.C. Harston. With him looking on and grinning like an obelisk, I don't know how I ever passed that test.

In that barracks I heard other familiar sounds: the familiar clenched-teeth twang of a rural background. I felt very much at home among these rural would-be aviators. But all of us in that sheep-pen were scheduled to be transported to a radically different part of our country, the Initial Training School in Victoriaville, Quebec.

12: DOWN TO EARTH IN QUEBEC

An Initial Training School is where you are taught the rudiments of flight and then appraised to determine into which part of an aircrew you would fit. My three-month stay in Quebec ended my dream of becoming a Spitfire pilot. Simply because I was left-handed, the powers-that-be pronounced me fit only to drop bombs on people from a great height.

Most of my time in La Belle Province was spent in a classroom. Day after day we studied far harder than I ever had before. Not only were we future bomb-aimers expected to drop the explosives, we also had to learn the art of celestial navigation and an ability to gauge wind currents, both direction and speed.

Sometimes we were summoned to a large room called the Theatre. There we would be addressed by our leader, Wing Commander Dawes, heir to a brewery of the same name in Montreal. He would usually lecture us about fire prevention, and occasionally, after partaking of too much of his family's product, would institute fire drills at three o'clock in the morning.

Victoriaville is in the Eastern townships, and despite its name the population is mostly French-speaking. On weekends I went to nearby Richmond, an English-speaking community, and I was billeted with a local family. I ended up the sole guest of a Mrs. Kelley who had recently lost her son, an RCAF officer who had the misfortune, on returning from a mission overseas, to walk into the propeller of his plane. Mrs. Kelley seemed to regard me as the reincarnation of her son. It was a fairly onerous duty, and I was glad to return to barracks.

I had very little contact with the people of Victoriaville, but I did manage to connect with one of the local girls. Her name I never did find out, but she told me to call her Fluff. I decided to invite her to the final dance before we returned to Ontario. That evening I called for her at her home. I was received by a middle-aged male I presumed was her father, but all I got in greeting was a grunt, and was then ushered into the parlour to await my date.

While I sat there in the parlour, I could hear the French chatter of two or three people in the kitchen. None of them came to speak to me, and I felt rather like a German officer in occupied France. Conscription was a sore issue in Quebec, and I presumed most of those remarks in the kitchen were directed at me. When Fluff arrived in a low-cut dress and reeking of perfume, she had nothing to say either as we waited for a taxi.

At the dance, Fluff was very chatty and seemed to be familiar with most of the males. I learned from one of my bunkmates that I had dated the town "bicycle," so called because she had been ridden by everybody. When I took her home, I was reluctant to get a goodnight kiss, but Fluff did the job for me, tongue well down my throat. As I turned to go, she was wide-eyed with surprise. "You doan wann to phoque?"

I don't know if I replied. All I know is that I turned down tail and ran. Back in the barracks I spent quite a bit of time gargling with Listerine. I am ashamed to confess that I went through the Second World War without losing my virginity.

Mysalf, I don't clame to be by-lingamal, but I hav tride fer to git a bit uv a handel on yer garlick langridge as spoke in Cuebec.

Mesdams et messoors: my ladies and my sisters

Jimmy sweeze appel charolais Far-queue-harson: my name's Charlie Farquharson and I squeeze my own apples …

Et je serais heureux de sez affaires … i'd be happy to have sixteen affairs.

13: DAYLIGHT SWEEPS OVER LONDON, PARIS, AND BRANTFORD

Transferring to the Bombing and Gunnery school in Fingal, Ontario, changed my preoccupation with sex to a concentration on the delicacy of my stomach. My third day was the occasion of my first flight, a weathercheck in a Harvard trainer. I shouldn't have mentioned that I had never flown before, because the pilot did some aerobatics to impress me. My stomach was full of two helpings of bacon-and-melted-cheese sandwiches, and if I had had any cookies I would have whooped them, too. As we looped the loops, the only receptacle handy was my wedge cap. By the time my cap finally dried out, it looked like a veteran of several tours of bombing missions.

This aerial baptism of barf haunted the rest of my flying career. I now realized I had a delicate stomach, but I didn't want my superiors to find out.

When we started bombing runs in Avro Anson Mark Twos, more than once I would have to stay behind and clean out the bomb bay that I had decorated. This would make me late returning to the hangar. Once I was so preoccupied with my upset stomach that I failed to notice a plane taking off on the same runway. I guess the pilot didn't notice, either, because as he passed me the wing of his plane clipped the top of my head. It drew some blood. Not a lot, but I did have to have the crown of my head shaved by a nurse, so for weeks I resembled a Franciscan friar.

When I walked out of the MO's office that day, there was my commanding officer on the other side of the door, at twenty-five years old already a veteran of two tours of overseas operations. He suggested I come to his office and have a chat. He told me that I had been noticed cleaning up a mess I had made on more than one occasion and wanted to know why I hadn't mentioned it to anyone.

I told him it was because I hoped that by avoiding the issue, it wouldn't interfere with my getting my wing as a bomb-aimer. He said my getting bilious wouldn't necessarily interfere with my graduation, but it was important for him to know that I had gotten sick in training, because if the authorities weren't aware of my tendency to hurl my lunch until I got overseas, I would be judged LMF.

I didn't know what that meant. It sounded like a current commercial, Lucky Strike Means Fine Tobacco. But it meant Lack of Moral Fibre. He smiled and said, "Now that we know what to expect, you will be able to proceed overseas."

I have chosen to downplay the two years, 1943–45, of undistinguished service spent in the RCAF. I did not get overseas as a bomb-aimer. I ended up with the rank of pilot officer, despite the fact that I got frequently airsick and was caught cleaning out my bomb-bay.

14: A BUM AIMER

The night we bomb-aimers graduated from Fingal, we were treated to a Hollywood movie. It was *The Purple Heart* and was the story of an American bomber crew shot down over Japan. The Purple Heart was awarded to the bombardier, played by Farley Granger, and the reason he was awarded that medal when he got back to the States was because the Japanese had cut off both his hands in reprisal, since those fingers were the ones that had dropped the bombs on them. We graduates left that film to go back to our barracks, where most of us threw up.

Next posting for me was at Crumlin, part of London, Ontario, at a navigation school. Here I wasn't expected to drop bombs, thank god, but I was expected to know where I was when we were up in the air, and the exact location of where we were going. I'm afraid I was often all up in the air when I was up in the air. I don't know how I got through this course.

I considered the fact that I never got the chance to become a pilot because I was left-handed to be rank discrimination. In my test-bombing flights at Crumlin, I would frequently gauge the amount of wind correctly, but I would be dead wrong about its direction. This resulted in my dropping a bomb on a farmer's manure pile some miles from my target. It was an eleven-and-a-half-pound practice bomb, and it couldn't have killed anyone, but it sure made a mess. He was working on his pile at the time, and without scraping anything off, horse, wagon or himself, he drove seventeen miles to complain about being violated. But I was in shit, too. I was hauled up in front of my wing commander and forced to stand there while the farmer related the whole incident. All I could think was *With people like that, we cannot possibly lose this war!*

Ten years later, when I did a monologue entitled "Th'Ex" (about the Canadian National Exhibition) in *Spring Thaw 1952*, I tried to re-create my memory of that stalwart farmer. My rural character had no name at all. But he kept referring to his friend Charlie Farquharson, who was the assistant convener in charge of the CNE semi-finals for the horseshoe pitching. Sample line: "Ya never heard of Charlie Farquharson? My gol ... isn't that a coincidence!"

Ignore this guff with yer undivide detention! To begin at my big innings, us Farquharsons is in no ways frictional. Our incesters immy-grunted to Canda frum IRA land in them hungry farties. (not yer 19 but yer 18 farties.) They got kick out of Ballyhilly in yer county's Antrim by the same overlards of Anglican-Saxafones as had boot our saim peeple outa Scotland yer senchry afore that.

They kick us offa our hy-lands cuz our Anglow-Sexist landlards wanted to raze sheep on ther akers instedda Scotchmen (on accounta yiz kin skin a sheep morn wunce!) So sum of us Farquharsons immygrunted over to Ire-land. It were hard by yer county Dunny-gall in yer north parts, witch is call Ulcer.

All they groo wuz taters, witch wuz all wat wuz ever on yer men-you evry blessed day. Until wun yeer ther taters tern black. (wirst virey-uss sints yer bloobonnits plaig!)

That's wen Ire-land becum part of yer Thurd Wirld, like Affagahanstand or Bangyerdesk! So our Anglish oversneers jist round up my lot fer shippin' overseize. That's when our bunch of Farquharsons lit out fer Uppity Canda. We wuz yer boatpeeple of them daze jist like them Veet Napammers sayin by-gons to Sy-gon.

Some of them stayed. When I was in Belfast a few years ago researching *Charlie's a Broad,* I looked up Farquharson in the city's phone book. I found to my dismay that there were only three of them, but when I looked up my own name, I found eighty-two Harrons. I phoned a couple and found that they were very vague about their origins. One woman, a Harron by marriage only, claimed her own ancestors were Huguenot lacemakers from France driven out after the massacre of Saint Bartholomew in the seventeenth century. She insisted on pronouncing her family's origin as Huge Noses.

Farquharson is a Gaylick word frum yer Utter He-brides. It meens "vurry deer wun" and probly defurs to yer Scotch cost of keepin up livin' in them daze. We is deesent frum yer Thaina Fife, Mickduff, hoo wuz told to "lay on" by eether Mac or Beth in that old Jakesbeer play by yer Beerd of Ayvon. But that wuz afore our family got clobberd at Clodden by them Anglish mercymarys, wen our Boney Prints Charly hadda drag his way outa our country dress up like his gurlfrend, Flory Mickdonald, before taken refuse in Fran's.

That's wen we wuz took over by them Sassynackers (Anglican-Sacksons). Not wanted, us Farquharsons lit out fer sumwares elts in wun big ewe-turn. It were over tuh IRA land, naimly Bellyfast. Not reelizin' how trew that naim wuz to becum, wen blite hit ther taters, witch wuz all they ever had t'eat. Canda sounded morn more like yer last retort.

Sum of our immygrunts landid up in Cuebeck, hard by Gross Eels. (but summa them kick yer buckit thair durin their qwornteens peeriods.) Wun branch of our Farquharson fambly landed on yer Cape Bretons, hard by Aunty-go-nish (and they bin Anty-gonishtick ever sints!)

Our bunch lit out frum them Noo Brunsicker Loylists fer Uppity Canda, got all the way up yer Parrysound, then went lumbring off inta yer Mustkokey bush, ware we bin groundid ever sints.

Suddenly we were invaded by a bunch of tailors from Toronto measuring us all for officer uniforms. This was a total surprise, because none of us knew whether we would get a single wing, much less an officer commission. Some of our bomb-aimers were former army officers who, after the invasion of Europe, June 6, 1944, volunteered for aircrew in an act of pure unselfish patriotism. When our final results came out, one of the army volunteers, a former major, had his rank reduced to flight sergeant. I, the knight of the weak stomach with the poor sense of direction, became a pilot officer! Evidently my marks on the ground in the classroom counted more than my time in the air.

It was totally unfair, but nineteen-year-old Pilot Officer Harron, covered in guilt, still donned the flat cap, the white scarf, and the greatcoat without a qualm. Until I stepped outside the tailor shop on the base and received my first salute from a non-commissioned officer. He was a warrant officer first class, a grizzled veteran bedecked with the ribbons of the First World War. As soon as he saw me, he snapped his arm straight from the shoulder. I returned the salute limply and slunk back to my barracks, red with shame.

Major Harron and Pilot Officer Harron, 1944.

15: AN OFFICER AND A GENTILE MAN

Now that I was winged and commissioned, the next move for me was a commando course in Maitland, Nova Scotia. Presumably this was a toughening-up process before being sent overseas. But before that, I was granted another seven days' leave.

I headed to New York. As an officer, nothing was free as it had been on an earlier trip when I was a humble Acey Deucey. But my daily pay had gone up from $1.30 to $6.25, so I didn't mind the change at all.

Through a dating service for servicemen, I ended up at a tea dance in a synagogue, and a date with a socialite to go to a Broadway play.

My date was a budding actress who lived in the Barbizon Hotel for Women. I arrived resplendent in my RCAF uniform with my *Dawn Patrol*–like white scarf, and my officer's flat hat with the wire removed to give the impression that I was a veteran of several tours of "ops." I gave the receptionist the name of my date. She plugged in the switchboard and contacted the young lady by saying "Miss Allardyce, there's a West Point cadet here to see you."

This budding actress took me to see a play: *I Remember Mama*. It was a wholesome family drama, and I would much rather have watched briefly attired chorus girls. My date reacted over-enthusiastically to the performance of a young actor. I thought the way he slouched and stammered his lines was pretty untalented but neglected to say so. His name was Marlon Brando.

Sooner than I expected, it was time to leave the Big Apple and head for the Maritimes. Maitland was nothing but a mess hall, a dormitory, a gymnasium, and an assault course to test the stamina of any would-be commando. Our days consisted of strenuous efforts attempting that assault course, plus thirty-mile route marches. The amazing thing is that after all this physical effort, we spent our evenings playing floor hockey!

Weekends we were free to do what we liked. The nearest town was Amherst, and we flocked there to attend a Saturday night dance. I met a nice girl who invited me to Sunday dinner, at which her mother cooked venison. It was after church, so I became a weekend Catholic for several weeks entirely because of that delicious deer meat.

My next posting was Lachine, Quebec, and from there our flight would be sent overseas. But before that, we were granted embarkation leave in Toronto. I remember saying a fond farewell to three different girls in one weekend.

The third date was a late-night one with a wealthy blonde whose parents were away at a Muskoka cottage. It turned into a four-hour necking session to the voice of Frank Sinatra. From the sounds coming from my date that night, I could have lost my virginity, but I didn't have any preventive preparations.

My stay in Lachine was just as brief and anti-climactic. Demand for aircrew in Europe was winding down rapidly. The flight before mine was ordered to England, but they never saw any action, except for pleasure yachting in Bournemouth that summer of 1944. The rumour was that my flight was to be held back as a secret weapon against Japan. They put us on indefinite leave and sent us home.

I arrived back home in Toronto with orders to report to Manning Depot on December 12, 1944, the day before my mother's birthday, still remembered by many a Toronto oldster as the Day of the Great Snowstorm.

Daylight sweeps over London, Paris, and Brantford.

16: CIVVY STREET

I think the most dangerous mission in my entire wartime service was getting from my home at 162 Pinewood Avenue in the borough of South York down to Manning Depot on the grounds of the Canadian National Exhibition on December 12.

The snow was so deep and the wind so strong that there were no buses running. I had to fight my way down to St. Clair hoping that there would be a streetcar. It was eight o'clock in the morning, but the sky was totally black and the snow was well past my knees. My assignment was to report in person, and I was determined to obey orders.

After I fought my way against the elements to St. Clair, a miracle appeared eventually in the shape of a streetcar. I arrived for my appointment only a half-hour late, but the whole vast place was absolutely deserted. Nobody else seemed to have made the effort. My next assignment was to find my way back home. Before that, I finally ran into another human. He was a WAG (Wireless Air Gunner) with two tours of ops over the skies of Europe to his credit. Dunc Chisholm had a lot of funny stories about his overseas experiences. He confessed it was his desire to get into show business.

I told Dunc about my early career in radio and added it might be easier than us getting back home that day. Dunc figured the teen market would be the one to go for, and together we roughed out a series of half-hour radio shows with the title *It's High Time*. As we were regaling each other with ideas, an RCAF underling appeared to tell us to go on home and try getting out of uniform some other time.

The next day I got a phone call from Dunc to say that we had an appointment to pitch our teen show idea. His father knew Jack Brockie, the PR headman at Eaton's Department Store and the man in charge of the Santa Claus parades.

I mind the last time I wuz down to Trawntuh fer yer Sandy Claws prade. I had brung sum aigs fer our ritch bitch cussin Valerie Rosedale. She persists in payin me holesail not retale, so I jist don't bother cleanin' them off. On my way to Santy's prade I run into a cupple of them Yorickville hippos with beerds down to ther bellybottom drores hoo arst me fer to step intuh thair pad. I tole them steppin into a pad is the kinda thing us Farquharsons tries to ignore in our barnyard.

Terns out all they wanted wuz fer me to sine ther partition fer to leegal-ize that Maxycan laffin teerbacker, yer maruhjewahyena. I tole tem ide sine her, but only if that dopey stuff wuz giv away free to peeples over yer age of sexty-five!!

Four days later, Dunc and I appeared in Brockie's office both wearing our Air Force Reserve pins attached to the lapels of our new grey flannel civilian suits. When Brockie asked what the pins were, Dunc told him that it was the insignia of the secret weapon our government was holding in reserve for the war against Japan.

It didn't take long for Brockie to turn down our project for a high school radio series, but his assistant, my old pal, suggested a job for me. Bill Bremner remembered my cartoons in our high school magazine, and also my imitations of the characters in *Looney Tunes*. His suggestion was that I wear my grey suit at Easter, plus a set of buckteeth, a bunch of fresh carrots, and a headdress with rabbit ears provided by Eaton's PR staff. Then I could draw cartoons of Bugs at a series of Easter parties on the toy floor, not to mention a bunny hop for disabled children at Casa Loma.

I agreed to the deal. It felt good to be in the spotlight again, however brief. But this was the middle of December, and Easter was months away. I had to get other employment. Dunc and I parted, promising to keep in touch. Much later I got him a non-paying job playing Shakespeare for Dora Mavor Moore, something Dunc had never tried before. He wasn't very good, but neither was I, as his sidekick Andrew Aguecheek, which I over-acted shamelessly.

My mother made the next suggestion about civilian employment. Her older brother Tom was a junior partner in an insurance firm, and she was sure he could offer me some kind of a job. Fully aware that I would jump ship at Easter to get my Bugs in, I signed on as a file clerk in his insurance office.

By the end of the third day, I was stupefied with boredom. Announcing my abrupt resignation, I explained to my uncle that I had secured other employment. I hadn't, but I had a good idea where I could find some: Jack Brockie got me a job selling shoes in the Eaton's annex.

The annex was the poor relation of the main store, and its shoe department sold cheap footwear with soles made out of stout paper.

Our temporary staff in the shoe department could boast, much later in life, of some distinguished salesmen. One of them was Allan Lawrence, who later became attorney general of Ontario under Premier Bill Davis. The other celebrity-to-be was Elwy Yost, who became the genial host of a long-running Saturday night film series on TVOntario.

But I had more important things on my mind than selling paper-soled shoes. There was that two-day job promised me by Jack Brockie for which I would be remunerated $15 — the same fee Basil Tippet had paid me nine years earlier for cartooning at his firm's banquet. Still, it was good to be back in some form of show business. All the while, I had atop my new grey flannel suit a headpiece with huge floppy ears. Never mind. I was to spend most of the rest of my life in a far more outlandish costume as Charlie Farquharson.

I hooked up again with my old college chum, Ralph Hicklin (the one-act Hamlet). He was now was involved with a theatre group, the Village Players, who created drama in a barn.

The Village Players was an amateur theatre group under the direction of Dora Mavor Moore, a retired actress who had been prominent in the British professional theatre. Although her company was amateur, many of the actors were the cream of Toronto professional radio who worked for her for nothing to keep their talents fresh.

In the spring of 1945 I was taken by Ralph Hicklin to see an evening of one-act plays. I remember Noël Coward's hilarious *Fumed Oak* as one of them, plus a dramatic scene from *Green Grow the Lilacs* (which had been turned into the musical *Oklahoma!*). After the presentation, Ralph introduced me to Dora Mavor Moore, who seemed to have a gleam in her eye when we met. It wasn't sexual; to her I was a rarity, a young male not in uniform and available for her theatrical purposes. She told me she was planning a tour of army hospitals, entertaining wounded troops and trying to make them laugh with the famous English farce-comedy *Charley's Aunt*.

This made me feel that I could do something to contribute to the war effort. I accepted Dora's offer. The only theatre experience I had was a public school presentation of *Uncle Tom's Cabin* at Humewood Public School. I was eight years old and played one of the little black boys that hung around Tom's cabin. All I remember was the trouble I gave my mother when my blacking came off on the sheets every night.

Oh, yes, I also played Peter Cratchit in our grade eight production of *A Christmas Carol*. I had one or two lines of dialogue.

We gathered for the first rehearsal of *Charley's Aunt*. Barbara Kelly and Jane Mallett would alternate in the part of the real Charley's aunt. The name Jane Mallett I remembered. When I was on leave in Toronto and went to the Active Service Canteen on Adelaide Street, the entertainment was provided by the Arts & Letters Club, with excerpts from their spring revue *Town Tonics*. It consisted of two people performing skits and monologues. One was Freddy Manning, a campy, dumpy middle-aged man who served as a perfect foil for a tiny lady with a big smile and the dirtiest laugh. This was Jane Mallett, making fun of all the high-society people in Toronto in a way that would have made those same people laugh at themselves, as well. I had such a good time but didn't have the nerve to wait around and tell her how she had made me snicker. It was years later, when we performed in *Spring Thaw*, that that same woman advised me to take on the persona of a much older person if I wanted to succeed with political humour.

17: BACK TO THE BOARDS

April 1945, and the first rehearsal of the Village Players hospital tour. Things went well with this professional cast, except for me. I felt completely out of place.

The rehearsal over, I was the only one asked by Dora to stay behind. Ralph Hicklin had told me she represented a great tradition of culture. As a child she had sat on the knee of various friends of her academic father, Dr. James Mavor. His pals included Bernard Shaw, William Butler Yeats, and some bearded man named Tolstoy.

That night in her living room, instead of dismissing me because of my clumpish efforts, she patiently showed me how to cross a stage without bumping into the furniture.

I don't remember getting one laugh during our tour, but at least I didn't disgrace myself. A year later, when the Village Players decided to become a professional theatre, the New Play Society, I was asked to join at a salary of $7.50 per performance.

But that was a year later. In the meantime I had to make a living, and my father came to my rescue. Both parents had always been understanding and even encouraging about my early forays into theatre, even though my mother hoped that someday I might settle down and get a desk job at the CBC.

After D-Day, my dad resigned his commission and went back to the civil service. He knew I planned on going back to university, so he managed to wangle me a summer job with the Ontario Department of Education.

My main duty was to take exam papers from every school in Ontario to various rooms in Queen's Park, where examiners would assess and mark them. It was the only time in my life that I remember being a clock watcher. The job was absolutely mind-numbing. No wonder that after hours I fled to Dora's barn. Summer was a busy time for the Village Players, and I was thrust into the middle of it. We put on what my air force buddies would have considered pretty artsy-fartsy stuff.

First thing we did that summer was a play by Lorca, *The Shoemaker's Prodigious Wife*. Unlike his other more serious Andalusian plays, this one was a farce. I played the part of a nine-year-old boy. This essential information was never put into the program, and when the play was reviewed by *Evening Telegram* drama critic Rose Macdonald, she gave me a rave review: "Donald Harron is superb as the idiot."

Next I was given the leading part in a two-character, one-act play by William Saroyan entitled *Hello Out There!* The role was that of a young man in a Texas jail who is accused of rape and is befriended by a teenage girl who is hired to keep the jail clean.

What I remember vividly is the sessions the two of us had with our director, Herb Gott. He was an actor, an attractive young man with a full beard, and Dora had given him his first assignment as a director. He turned out to be first-rate. The only thing lacking in him were both arms. He had lost them in a horrific accident riding the rails during the Depression.

When Herb performed in radio, as he did quite often, someone had to stand beside him and turn the pages of the script. As a stage director, he seemed to have memorized the entire script.

In the audience one night was CBC's wonderboy Fletcher Markle, who was writing, directing, and producing a summer series of his own, *Sometime Every Summertime*. He hired me for one of the items of that series, but even before that he told Andrew Allan about me with such enthusiasm that I found myself on the last show of the season of the now-classic series of radio dramas begun in 1944 and lasting into the first years of the television era.

The Stage series was really our first National Theatre, with original Canadian radio dramas to display the talents of leading actors. The plays were a mixture of classic adaptations along with original scripts.

Stage 45's final offering was a drama by agriculture expert Harry Boyle celebrating the arrival of V-E Day. I got a chance to use my rural accent. The rest of the cast wondered what I was doing, but not Harry. He was a farm boy from Wingham, Ontario, and he still talked that way himself. He must have told another producer about me, because I ended up an occasional performer on the farm radio drama series *Summer Fallow*. Charlie Farquharson was struggling to be born, but for the moment his rustic dialect was being used by me in straight drama.

I never took off nobody's part but my own. I jist sat thair in my seet givin a big clap to udders like the wife bein a harpy and our boy Orville with his rotten roll band, yer Running Sores. Altho' I wood jist as soon hav lissen to Don Messy.

On VJ day we celebrated victory over Japan. It also marked the dropping of the first (let's pray they are the last) atomic bombs on Hiroshima and Nagasaki. For Don Harron, that day was simply a matter of an audition for a part in a radio sitcom, *Penny's Diary*, written by the clever young woman who played Penny herself, Patricia Joudry, and aired over station CFRB.

CFRB stands fur Charlie Farquharson, retard bankrupt. Bein' retard is even wurse than gittin tired all the time.

The role I tried out for was that of Penny's boyfriend. My only competition for the role was John Aylesworth, later in life the one to hire me for *Hee Haw*. I gather that by then he must have forgiven me for the shameful ploy I pulled that day. I appeared at that audition in my air force uniform while everyone was celebrating the victory over Japan. I got the job.

So by the time I was to start university again in September, I was beginning to make a modest living as a radio actor, coupled with the fact that I was living at home rent-free, and as a veteran (no medals, no overseas duty, no shame whatsoever) the government was prepared to pay my tuition, as well as an allowance of $75 a month for any expenses incurred in my pursuit of higher learning.

18: BACK TO CLASS

Starting college again in late September 1945, I also had a new professional career in radio. In addition to the CFRB sitcom, I was included in the list of actors regularly hired for Andrew Allan's Sunday night series, *Stage 46*. Also, there were school broadcasts at times in the morning when I should have been in class. I skipped the class, not the broadcast, although such a procedure was extremely rare in that era with the students that returned from the war. After fighting the enemy in Anzio and Caen, they were thirsty for higher learning. Attendance was overflowing at lectures, and some students sat on the floor because there was no more room. It was an exhilarating atmosphere, so different from the 1960s, when skipping classes to occupy the dean's office as a form of protest became a badge of honour.

I registered in a course called Philosophy and English, although I preferred poetry to Plato. The English part of my curriculum would include lectures with Northrop Frye, who had impressed me in 1942 with a public lecture on satire. Speaking of satire, in addition to the double workload of radio and lectures, I was asked to help create Vic's annual satirical show, *The Bob*, a nineteenth-century tradition that had persisted. It consisted of merciless lampoons of authority figures on staff.

I was assigned to write the first half of the show, and the second half would be written by two Vaughan Road Collegiate colleagues of mine, Ben Bramble and Bruce Quarrington. I decided that the theme of my part would be the return to college of the veterans. It would contain original songs, my first attempt at this formidable field of endeavour. I hummed the tunes to a fellow undergraduate, Lorne Watson, a piano whiz, who turned my off-key humming into recognizable forms.

But before that I had to deal with a domestic tragedy. I arrived home on a bright September day to find my beloved grandmother in a panic. She seemed unable to speak but pointed toward the stairs to our cellar. At the bottom lay my ninety-six-year-old grandfather. No one else was home, so I suddenly became the head of the household.

My grandad was dimly conscious, and my grandma had placed a pillow under his head. I phoned for an ambulance and sat by his side. I was devoted to my Nanna, who spoiled me regularly by making me plates of taffy and brown sugar sandwiches, but I had always had mixed feelings about Bampa.

I couldn't understand an able-bodied man retiring at the age of forty-nine because he lost his post-office job when Wilfrid Laurier replaced John A. Macdonald. For the next fifty years he seemed to do nothing but read his Bible, smoke his pipe, and listen to Sunday sermons on the radio.

The ambulance arrived at last. Two attendants picked up my grandfather, a tall man over six feet, and hinted that his hip was broken. I hated to leave my grandmother alone, but I knew I had to provide the necessary information at the hospital. During subsequent visits, lying there with a pin in his hip, he didn't seem to recognize anyone. After a week I barely recognized him. I was shocked at his appearance; he already looked like an emaciated corpse. My grandad passed away on September eleventh, 1945, and my darling grandma five weeks later. There's something inevitable about that particular period of time that affects long-married couples. My own dear parents both passed away in the 1970s, first my mother, then my father, and it happened in that same period of time, five weeks to the day from each other.

Mum and Dad ready for Halloween.

My favourite memory of my grandma is from not long before the tragic accident. My grandfather boasted of having read the entire Bible many times, and though he couldn't go to church, he was often visited by a retired minister, who would pray with him by the hour. I mean that literally. Once I peeked into our living room and there was the long-bearded minister seated between my grampa and my gramma. He was praying. He must have been at it for quite some time, because when Nanna saw me peeking at the three of them she mimed the action of winding Reverend Mr. Garnham up like a gramophone.

19: THE HICK FROM VIC

After the twin funerals, I took refuge in a heavy work schedule. In addition to radio jobs and lectures, Dora Mavor Moore cast me in the first Vic Drama Club production of the '45–'46 season, Thornton Wilder's *The Skin Of Our Teeth*. It's a cartoonish version of the story of mankind, represented by Mr. and Mrs. Antrobus, their son Henry, and the sexy housemaid Sabrina.

But first I had to write one half of *The Bob*. The Bob of the title was a real-life college janitor when Victoria College was located in Cobourg back in the mid-nineteenth century. He used to entertain undergraduates with solos on his violin, tell jokes and stories, and comfort them with apples. By the time I got there it was a full evening in Hart House Theatre with under-graduates giving caricaturish impressions of the president of our college, Walter T. Brown, and the dean of the entire university, Canon Cody.

Instead I referred to the president in a song entitled "Let's Do It Up Brown." It was sung by a jug-eared freshman, Jack Pearse, who became a lifelong friend, and I have sent two of my daughters to Tawingo, his summer camp near Huntsville. There he conducts daily sing-songs and nobody does it better.

I hummed this tune to Lorne Watson at the piano and he put it down on paper in the form of musical notes. I have been rescued by composers all my life, and Lorne was the first of them. The plot I stole, too, although I knew I was doing it. It was loosely based on the Gene Kelly/Frank Sinatra film *Anchors Aweigh*, about two sailors on shore leave. In my case they were two sailors returning to college, and they were played with great energy and enthusiasm by Alan MacNeill and Jack Pearse. Al McNeill was the actor who won the comedy part of Christy from me in 1942, in *The Devil's Disciple*, my ill-fated venture with Earle Grey.

A columnist on our daily newspaper, *The Varsity*, E. Ross Maclean (known to his campus readers as Eros) wrote that red underwear and a rube accent was becoming a trademark of mine, since I had already appeared in the same garb and with the Mortimer Snerd bit on several college charity engagements for war relief. Consequently he referred to me ever after as "the campus cutup." I forgave him years later when he hired me to do Charlie Farquharson on *This Hour Has Seven Days*.

20: LET'S GET SERIOUS HERE

Almost immediately I was plunged into rehearsals for *The Skin of Our Teeth*. Dora Mavor Moore had a rather stately approach to the broad comedy of the first half, but she seemed very much at home in the serious aspects of the second. The play has a sharp shift from farce into near-tragedy. My character Henry Antrobus, the son of the family, is the "mean little kid" Red Skelton used to talk about. He doesn't appear in the second act, but in the third he wears the mark of Cain on his forehead and seems to predate but relate to the rise of Fascism.

We opened to the standard three-performance run. On opening night I got lots of laughs, but alarmingly for me, those laughs continued in the third act in an atmosphere of nihilistic destruction, where they aren't supposed to. The family of Man is trying to start civilized life again, but the figure of Henry Antrobus with the mark of Cain stands in their way. Many in the audience had seen me in the long underwear spouting Danny Kaye at the *Bob*, and they rewarded my tragic figure with howls of laughter.

Friends and family congratulated me on my success, but I knew I had failed. My next acting assignment was to play a scene from *Hamlet* on a school broadcast. It made me more than a bit nervous to realize I was asked to play the great tragic figure of all time. So much so that when I did the show and came to the suicidal line, "I do not set my life at a pin's fee," I ended up shouting "I do not set my life at a Finn's pee!"

Perhaps the hick from Vic was doomed to be the campus cut-up. That certainly seemed to be the case in the following months as I continued my string of light-hearted college engagements, including master of ceremonies at a campus beauty contest. Canada's most admired literary critic, Northrop Frye, was appointed head judge. He made the clever wisecrack that as head judge it was a shame he wasn't allowed to examine other parts of the body.

When I later wrote an essay for Frye, he gave me a B-minus, and in his remarks he said, "This is mostly BS, but you do have a knack for making complex ideas simple."

One of the contestants in that beauty contest was the entry from Vic, a young co-ed dressed in a green Shetland sweater that matched her mid-calf length skirt of the same colour. It nicely set off her hair, which was a glorious shade of red that accompanied her freckles.

But she was the only contestant who kept her eyes firmly on the floor. She was obviously petrified. Due to her monumental shyness, my heart went out to her. When the results of the contest were revealed, the only person who voted for her was Northrop Frye. She seemed relieved not to win. The information on the contestant sheet said that her name was Gloria Fisher from Gravenhurst, a graduate of Toronto's Branksome Hall and a winner of several scholarships in French and German.

I later saw her attending Frye's course in Religious Knowledge, an event that was always packed with students from other faculties, including Medicine, Dentistry, and Science. Frye's approach to Christianity was absolutely riveting. He linked the belief in the Resurrection to the pagan rites of tribes like the ancient Incas.

Although I didn't drink coffee, I invited Gloria to Murray's Restaurant to discuss Frye's ideas. She was so impressed with him that she was seriously thinking of giving up her scholarships and enrolling in the same Philosophy and English course as me. I was impressed by the fact that she seemed to understand the ideas in that lecture better than I.

I had spent my first year back at university so busy that I didn't have time to find a girlfriend. I would MC a campus event and then watch couples evaporate into the night while I went home alone. When Gloria suggested we meet up again, it was to discuss the other courses I was taking. I had snared a true intellectual, and this was her idea of a hot date ... talking Frye and Plato.

Besides acquiring a girlfriend, I was still leading the busy double life of university student and radio actor. There was the theatre. At one point, and close to exam time, too, I was involved in two productions at the same time. Dora wanted me in her production of *The Taming of the Shrew*, and Andrew Allan cast me as the lead in Eugene O'Neill's *Ah! Wilderness*, which would open two days after the Shakespeare play closed. Radio jobs started to proliferate at the same time. The pace was dizzying.

Budd Knapp gives Don the facts of life in Ah! Wilderness, *1946.*

I don't remember much about *The Taming of the Shrew* because I opened the play. I played the young Lord in the Induction at the beginning of the evening, but left immediately for rehearsals of *Ah! Wilderness*. It is O'Neill's least serious play, a warm nostalgia for the America of the first decade of the 1900s. Andrew Allan had assembled (some might say bullied) some top-flight radio actors to work for nothing: Budd Knapp, Tommy Tweed, Claire Drainie, Lloyd Bochner, Andrew Allan's current girlfriend Sandra Scott, and the actress who had played my mother in that 1936 radio series, Arden Keay.

Ah! Wilderness was the most popular production the Village Players had ever attempted and was decisive in convincing Dora that her company of amateurs should go professional. This was strengthened by the arrival from overseas of her talented son, Mavor. He was a most important influence in my life, because Mavor Moore soon became the founding father of Canadian musical comedy.

21: I GO PRO AGAIN

I wrote my exams in the midst of a flurry of other activity, so consequently I did my best to entertain the examiner with bullshit. This was easier with literature and history than philosophy. I came to the conclusion that I had chosen the wrong course. Philosophy deals primarily with ideas rather than facts, and teaches one to generalize rather than particularize. As an actor I should have been studying psychology.

The exam results came out when I was visiting Gloria's home in Gravenhurst. Her father was a country doctor with a pronounced Huron County accent that I later appropriated for Charlie Farquharson. He was a dedicated man who went out on calls at all hours of the day or night.

Parry Sound is nowares neer yer Urine County! This Harn idjet has mix up yer norse Ontario with yer souse.

While I was enjoying Gloria's mother's superb meals at the dinner table, the *Globe and Mail* published her daughter's (and my own) exam results. Gloria came first in her Modern Languages course, and surprise, surprise, I tied for first place with a girl from Trinity College in Philosophy and English. I gathered new respect for the power of bullshit.

But after her usual triumph Gloria was determined to change her course to mine, not because of me, but due to the brilliance of Northrop Frye. She would lose the grant money from all her scholarships, and her parents later received a large bill for her tuition and residence fees. I felt guilty that I had been a part of all this.

I kissed the scholarship rebel a temporary goodbye and headed back to Toronto. Toward the end of August I got a call from Dora Mavor Moore to an important meeting of the Village Players. Her living room was crammed with amateur actors. Her son Mavor was back from the army but working now at the United Nations in New York. He was present at that meeting and promised to stay active in the theatre group. Next on the agenda was a vote on whether the Village Players should become professional.

The result was close. Many in the group considered acting a part-time hobby and had other full-time jobs. I must confess I voted for the outfit to stay amateur. My third year in university was coming up and radio work was increasing. I had been suddenly cast in a weepy soap opera entitled *Soldier's Wife*, and to my surprise, was also chosen to represent two separate sponsors on two different radio series: one a kids' program about the RCMP, *Men in Scarlet* for Orange Crush, and in the other I was to be a newsboy on the Canadian cut-ins for the soap sponsor of the American network show *Big Town*. My job was to shout: "Wuxtry! Wuxtry! Get your Lifebuoy here!"

In addition to all this, I had agreed to write the entire show of the 1946 edition of the Vic *Bob*. What was I thinking! I was thinking that Dora would lose her shirt if her players went pro, and I had enough on my plate without adding to that concern. The vote wasn't a secret ballot, but an open show of hands. The amateurs among us lost. As soon as the vote was announced, Dora said the Village Players would now be called the New Play Society.

The plays would be performed in a lecture hall of the Royal Ontario Museum, just across from Victoria College. The 1946 season featured plays that would be considered classics rather than contemporary products of Broadway and the West End. The first would be the turn-of-the-century Irish folk comedy, Synge's *The Playboy of the Western World*. I figured I would read it sometime between university lectures.

To my complete surprise, I was cast in the title role. Common sense told me to turn it down, but common sense has never been part of my makeup. The fee was $7.50 per performance, which would take place on two consecutive weekends, making it a run of four performances and a salary per production of $30. I was getting more than that to shout "Wuxtry" on my Lifebuoy commercial cut-ins. But speed-reading the play, I realized it had the flavour of authentic folk comedy. My character was called a playboy because the local girls think that he is a kind of hero, since he has been adventurous enough to kill his father. That dad appears later in the play and spanks me for my tall tales.

The lecture hall at the museum was hardly a theatre. The stage was tiny, as were the dressing rooms, and worst of all, there were no toilet facilities. If you needed to relieve yourself, it was across the hall from the entrance itself.

Sometimes the rehearsals would conflict with my commercial radio duties, and that was where I came into conflict with Dame Dora. She didn't understand the demands of Mammon, so pure was her love of the arts. So I took to inventing tall tales about how I got delayed. Eventually I told her that if she would allow me a little liberty to fulfill my commercial commitments, I would work for her for free. Her eyes gleamed, and I lost a mere thirty bucks every few months.

My conflict with commercialism was relieved somewhat a few weeks later when I was fired from that soap opera. It seems I had been making fun of the inane dialogue in the scripts, never on the show, of course, but rehearsals seemed to be a time when everyone in the cast relaxed and "kibitzed a bit." One day the producer, an absentee landlord most of the time, happened to be in the studio when these antics were going on. He assumed that I was the leader of the revels and wanted me off the show. The next day I was released. Looking back, I realize that I was really relieved.

I also had trouble with my other commercial assignments. I was told that I pronounced the name of the company's product incorrectly. I called the drink Orange Crush, with two syllables on the first word, instead of the way ordinary Joe Blow orders it ... as one word: "Gimme a Ornjcrush." However, I didn't lose that job and kept it by slurring my diction. But how I held on to my Lifebuoy commercial, I cannot fathom, because I was working on the other side of the microphone with a madman named Allan Macfee.

Allan has been a legend at the CBC as someone who is absolutely fearless about committing pranks. Later, as staff announcer associated with the comic antics of Max Ferguson, he was given scope for his wicked sense of humour. But when he did the farm market reports, he would often insert the names of members of the Royal Family among the agricultural products.

As the announcer across the mike from me on the Lifebuoy commercials, he would try to make me laugh. And he succeeded. More than once I would say "Get your Lifebuoy here!" and end with a helpless giggle. Why I was never fired from that job I will never understand.

22: THE PEEBOY OF THE WESTERN WORLD

I finally got a chance to play a farm lad in *The Playboy of the Western World*, but with a southern Irish accent. My ancestors came from Northern Ireland, where the dialect is much harsher. I still remember a poetic speech I got to deliver in that play. I still remember every syllable of this beautiful declaration of love: "And we'll be making mighty kisses with our wetted mouths, til I'd feel a kind of pity for the Lord God Himself sittin' lonesome in his golden chair."

Being Irish, the *Playboy* play involves a lot of drinking, since it takes place in a pub. This proved to be a problem for me, who was, as they say, at the back of the room when the kidneys were given out. Once I entered that snug (pub) I was never offstage, and as called for by the script, had to toss back many a toast. By the time the curtain came down on the first act on opening night, I was in dire need of a pee. The only dressing room was shared by actors of both sexes, so the sink was no option. There was no chance to go during intermission, because the only washroom was out front and used by paying customers. But there was a break at the beginning of the second act where I wasn't onstage. I made my way through a secret passage to the back of the theatre.

Peeking through a doorway, I crossed my legs and waited for the customers to go back to their seats. Eight minutes, that was my deadline. Bladder almost bursting, I dashed into the nearest washroom as soon. I flew into my temporary refuge and looked frantically about for a urinal. There weren't any. I was in the ladies washroom. My bladder was close to overflowing.

The only cubicle was occupied. In desperation I invoked the actor's time-hallowed privilege when *in extremis* ... I peed in the washbasin. Midway through my evacuation the toilet in the cubicle flushed and an elderly woman emerged, staring at me with horror. I stood frozen with embarrassment, unable to say a word. As she left she gave me a look that would wither winter wheat. I don't know if she returned to our theatre, but I had no choice.

For some reason I wasn't asked to be part of the New Play Society's next production, *Oedipus Rex*. Too bad, because I had a nifty idea for a musical version, including the hit song "I Got a Girl Just Like the Girl That Married Dear Old Dad."

23: BOBBLING THE BOB

I turned my attention, not to lectures or essays, heaven forfend, but to *The Bob*. This time I was responsible for the whole show, which gave me more than a slight sense of panic, because I had been busy being a playboy. Hart House was unavailable, but when we applied for Massey Hall, the hallowed institution said okay! It would be the first time our annual revue was performed off-campus since 1887.

I was too busy to attend rehearsals, so I did not cast myself as a performer. But the script was mine, written during the previous summer, and I was ready again to hum songs to my friend Lorne at the piano. Jack Pearse offered to conduct rehearsals for me. He was my lead performer, along with a short, funny little guy named Allan Beckett.

When I finally got to rehearsals, Al Beckett was still short and funny, but he couldn't remember his lines. This continued into the actual performance at Massey Hall. I will always be grateful to Jack Pearse, but I started to feel about Beckett the way King Henry II felt about his Becket: "Will no one rid me of this troublesome @#% ... priest?"

Although I wasn't supposed to appear, I got applause after the many prompts I had to prompt Beckett, at one time having to appear from the wings to deliver him his lines. The only positive part of the show that night was an opera parody, "La Traviesti," which incorporated substitute lyrics for such classics as "O Solo Mio" and the quartet from *Rigoletto*.

This resulted in a standing ovation, and I rewrote it for the 1950 edition of *Spring Thaw* as a comment on the possible amalgamation of Toronto and its suburbs. (Which didn't happen until years later under Mike Harris's Common Sense Revolution.)

24: DANCING FOOL

The New Play Society's name was still confusing audiences. They did a play by Ronald Duncan with music by Benjamin Britten entitled *This Way to the Tomb*. During the day, the space outside our auditorium had a sign advertising the production, and it was full of confused museum visitors wandering around looking for the resting place of some ancient dead person. Also, the public wasn't sure whether it was a society for putting on new plays, or a new society for putting on old plays.

So Mavor talked his mother into putting on one new play a year. Think of it, a world premiere! In Toronto! He chose well. Lister Sinclair was a brilliant young lecturer in mathematics. His *A Play on Words* really started the tradition on that series of seeking out Canadian writers. Although young, he seemed to cultivate senility by growing a scraggly beard which other actors named "The Armpit." Also he had difficulty walking, always carried a cane, and lagged behind the others in their way out to lunch. I lagged along with him, because Lister read a complete book every day and was always anxious to share his comments. For me he was a walking encyclopedia.

His play *The Man in the Blue Moon*, starring the world's greatest radio actor, John Drainie, was well received by local critics with one exception. Nathan Cohen wrote for the *Canadian Jewish News* and often expressed considerable vitriol in print. His evaluation of Lister's play was no exception, and he laid it on with a trowel. Lister got his revenge the following year when he was asked by the CBC to review Cohen's first play put on by the New Play Society, *Blue Is for Mourning*, part of a planned trilogy about Cape Breton miners.

Lister's dissection of Cohen as a playwright was witty but just as vicious as the victim's accustomed style. Lister ended his review with a fervent plea that the would-be playwright would be deterred from such a misbegotten quest as extending this disaster into a trilogy. Such was the critical climate Toronto was accumulating in its postwar attempt to be another New York.

Just before my essays mounted up and exams loomed after that, I was cast in William Saroyan's *The Time of Your Life*. This was to be an all-star production directed by Fletcher Markle, who had cast himself in the leading role. The supporting cast included Lorne Greene, Mavor Moore, and CBC head producer Frank Willis. The cherry on the parfait for me was the appearance of Jane Mallett and her husband Freddy, an instructor at Upper Canada College, playing the bit parts of a high-society couple slumming in this sleazy bar. Just to hear that dirty laugh of hers once again was reward enough.

I was cast in the part Gene Kelly played in the original Broadway production: Harry the dancer. I think I was chosen, certainly not because of my dancing, but because my character wants desperately to be the funniest comedian in the world, and when his routines flop, he reverts to dancing.

In desperation I took Gloria to the Palace Pier to see Lionel Hampton and his orchestra. There I saw a black couple dancing in a way that was unfamiliar to me. They were boogying! Some of their moves reminded me of strippers I had seen at the Casino Theatre. I watched that couple all night, taking notes in my mind. Most of what they did was too athletic for me, but I felt I could always fall back on their general choreography.

The Time of Your Life had a black character, Wesley, played by a jazz pianist, Wray Downes. He coached and coaxed me along, playing riffs to help me in my combination boogy-bump-and-grind, as I looked as if I were trying to screw myself into the floor. I got away with it, and the production itself, with its local broadcast celebrities, was a huge hit.

Dora had closed her first season with an invitation to a local Chinese theatre to repeat their production *Lady Precious Stream* on the Museum Theatre stage, complete with an interpreter providing a narrative in English. To complete her second season, she added something that the Stratford Festival was to copy ten years later.

Les Compagnons de Saint-Laurent, under the direction of a Catholic priest, Père Legault, was Montreal's premier French-language theatre. I barely understood a word that they said, but they performed Molière's *Les*

Precieuse ridicules with such skill, such style, such daring, and such obvious enjoyment that the language barrier didn't matter.

25: MOVIE CRAZY

That was the title of a wonderful Harold Lloyd film in the 1930s in which he played a young man crazy to get into the movies. I myself had fantasies, not about starring in films but in writing scripts for them. I was so busy between my studies, my radio work, and my occasional theatre appearance, that I rarely had time to think about my secret ambition.

But the summer of 1947 constituted a lull. I was once again up in Gravenhurst with Gloria and her family when our results appeared in the paper. She hadn't done as well in changing her course to mine, but it didn't seem to bother her, although it certainly flummoxed her parents. To console her I thought of proposing, but I didn't have the money for a ring. Radio jobs seemed few and far between, so I decided to wait for her birthday next February.

Fletcher Markle had retained his enthusiasm for my work, and after the Saroyan play he was off to New York to produce a radio series for CBS. He told me he wanted to include *Ah! Wilderness* in that series, with me reprising the role. This was in the days before green cards and employment restrictions across borders, and I eagerly awaited the call from New York. It finally came late in August when I was flat broke, but I borrowed the fare from my understanding parents and took the train. I was to be put up in the Algonquin Hotel, the Broadway actor's home away from home. I protested to Fletcher that I couldn't afford such surroundings, but he assured me it would be taken care of.

I met the cast in the CBS studio. I didn't know their faces but recognized many of the voices that I had listened to for years. The role of my father would now be played by an actor I had seen and admired in *Citizen Kane*, Everett Sloane.

My girlfriend would be played by a young Broadway actress, Anne Burr, and I was invited to dinner with Fletcher and her at the legendary Toots Shor's, where I had my first taste of vichyssoise, and the sight at the next table of an actor I have always envied, Montgomery Clift.

Fletcher told me that in addition to this radio series, he was expected to deliver a film script to a Hollywood studio, but he was without an idea. All he had was a title: *There Was a Young Man*. Sounded to me like the first line of a dirty limerick.

When I was returned to the Algonquin Hotel, Anne and Fletcher came along with me. The penny finally dropped. It seems that at dinner I was playing the role of a "beard" — a man who comes along with a couple having an affair and gives the mistaken impression that he is the woman's date. I found this out when I realized that my room at the Algonquin Hotel was part of a suite occupied by Fletcher and Anne.

I was assigned to a much smaller room, and Fletcher warned me to beware of the hotel manager, who had a distinct predilection for young men. I shoved a heavy piece of furniture against the door as a precaution. I decided to tell Fletcher the next day about a film idea I had which existed at this time only in my mind, but would fit his title.

I didn't get much sleep that night. Over breakfast (Anne Burr didn't do breakfasts) I told Fletcher my idea. My central character was a baby-faced teenage seventeen-year-old who lies about his age and eventually becomes an RCAF fighter pilot. During the Battle of Britain he distinguishes himself in the air, and on the ground, too, when he is seduced by his wing commander's wife.

He returns to Canada and enters university but finds he can't make it with co-eds because he's hooked on cougars (older women). After a string of lusty affairs he finally falls for a girl his own age. This time it's true romantic love, and he worships the girl's purity. The irony is that she turns out to be a nymphomaniac, has her way with him, and tosses him aside for the next conquest. In despair, the young man drives his sports car off the end of a dock to a watery grave.

Fletcher's eyes gleamed with relief, and he told me that we'd work on it over the weekend. I spent the weekend at the Markles' house in Scarsdale, where his wife Blanche held the fort. Fletcher liked my plot idea of the multi-affairs, but he said the Hays Office would intervene. In those days their rules dominated the film business, and in their view nobody slept in a double bed or kissed with their tongues, and adultery was a crime punishable by death. So all those nice older women in my little story would have to end up murdered.

I protested that my hero was not a psychopath, just a mixed-up kid with a DFC and Bar. "It's the Hays Office! You can't commit a sin without being punished for it. That takes care of the kid driving off the dock."

What about the nympho who drives him to suicide? "We won't have her go all the way. Make her a cock teaser." I worked all weekend so that by the time I got to the radio show I was really tired, but the result was that I was so relaxed that I seemed to give a good performance. At least, Everett Sloane told me so, and that was enough for me.

There Was a Young Man never got made into a movie. Fletcher said he would "polish" my idea after he finished the next radio show with Mercedes McCambridge, the queen of New York soap operas. I saw Fletcher a couple of years later at his home in California, and by that time he had divorced Blanche and married Mercedes.

I got back to Toronto with fifty bucks in my pocket, no desire to make the rounds of New York casting agents, and disillusioned about writing for films.

26: THE HOSPITAL

I spent most of the hot, humid summer of 1947 in a hospital room, and very nearly left it feet first. When I arrived home from New York, it was a nice surprise to be hired for the Wayne and Shuster radio show. They were doing a summer series for NBC in direct opposition to Martin and Lewis, appearing on CBS at the same time. After rehearsal we sat and listened to their rivals. Johnny Wayne pronounced the fate of Dean Martin and Jerry Lewis. "We're gonna do better with Americans than those guys. They aren't gonna last! You know why? 'Cause we're corny and they're not!" Maybe Ed Sullivan agreed, because our Canadian team became the most popular comedy act on his show, while Martin and Lewis went their separate ways.

I never worked again for the Canadian duo ... well, not for the next twenty years, when I appeared as Charlie Farquharson in the late 1970s on a show in which they did a musical spoof, "Sam of Green Gables." I only got the job back in 1947 due to my friendship with their radio producer, Jackie Rae. I got to know him on the roof of the Central YMCA, where we tanned together, both us being admitted sun-sluts to the core.

His family was off in England that summer, and he seemed to be at loose ends. My parents and my sister were away up north, so Jack and I planned to join them in a few days. It was a good thing I invited Jack to bunk in for the night, because he probably saved my life. After a late-night meal that was not healthy for either of us, we retired late, but I was up early with violent stomach pains. I decided I had food poisoning, so I took a laxative. Jackie started looking through the Yellow Pages for a doctor and stopped at the first name he came across: Abbott.

Dr. Abbott turned up, tall and tanned. He prodded my abdomen and I hit the ceiling. I gasped. "Is it food poisoning?"

He ignored me and said to Jackie, "Get an ambulance before his appendix bursts!" I don't remember much after that except the siren blaring on the way to the hospital.

As soon as we arrived at Western Hospital, they shot my rump and rushed me to the operating room. It was a local anaesthetic, so I could watch the whole operation in the reflector of the lamp above me. Next morning, Doctor Abbott dropped in wearing his golf togs and told me I would be home in three days.

I was, but I didn't feel at all good. I phoned Gloria and told her what happened. She caught the next bus. When she arrived I was in agony and couldn't even remember the name of the doctor who had performed my operation.

Gloria phoned her father, who located Dr. Abbott through the medical directory. He appeared after his golf game and told me to get up, walk around the garden, and keep walking till the pain went away. He told me I had pleurisy, gave me a shot of sulfa, and left. (I found out later that if I'm allergic to anything, it's sulfa.) The more I walked, the more it hurt. The pain got worse, and so did my temper. I remember telling my would-be fiancée to get the hell out of my house. She marched as far as the phone and called her father. She described my symptoms and her father said, "It can't be pleurisy. Hold on. I'll get Kinsey at the Western."

Dr. Kinsey, a chest specialist, arrived in a matter of minutes to declare I had a pulmonary infarct. I weakly asked him what that meant. "Blood clots in the lungs." Exercise of any kind was the worst thing for it. And in my case, so was the sulfa, which provoked a violent reaction. Dr. Golfcart Abbott had neglected to give me any penicillin. To counter this I was doomed to receive an injection in one buttock or the other every three hours for weeks on end.

This was June, and as I said before, I ended up spending the rest of that summer in that hospital. Between the ever-present buttock injections, I was visited first by my parents and sister Mary, then Gloria, and even her father, who could ill-spare the time from his heavy duties back in Gravenhurst. Also on the hospital staff were several interns I had known in high school, and they used my room as a regular meeting place where they could sneak a smoke and talk shop, a language completely foreign to me. So I sat and read Toynbee's *A Study of History* as they gossiped and puffed away. One of them had nicknamed me "Baldy" after I got my first brush-cut. He was already losing his hair while mine stayed put.

I was visited by my university's director of theatre at Hart House, Robert Gill. I had met him socially but had never worked with him, and was surprised when he appeared at the end of my bed. He was there to offer me the leading role of Oedipus Rex in the first production of his season, Cocteau's *The Infernal Machine*. Despite my condition, I was sorely tempted.

Dr. Kinsey said no. "Nothing strenuous for at least three months." His word prevailed. But before Gill left the room he offered me the lead in his second drama of the season, Maxwell Anderson's *Winterset*, about the Sacco-Vanzetti terrorist trials of the 1920s. It was the part of Mio, who seeks justice and revenge for his father's unjust execution. The character is a kind of contemporary Hamlet, and Burgess Meredith had made him memorable on Broadway. It was another chance to play a tragic hero.

27: BACK TO WORK

In mid-September I was released from Western Hospital. Unlike spring, the fall had always seemed to me the time when things begin. I would be in time for the first lectures of my third year of classes. The New Play Society was getting ready to start its third season with a nice mix of the West End and Broadway. The last play of their season was an adaptation of Hugh MacLennan's Canadian classic, *Two Solitudes*. Exam-time notwithstanding, I was determined to be in on that.

I received an invitation to see the newest edition of *The Bob*, and I was more than keen to attend, because I understood it involved the Vic undergraduate who wrote the nasty letter to *The Varsity* about my own 1946 version. His name was Norman Jewison, and I was more than a little curious to see what he was up to! What he was up to was an old-fashioned minstrel show, something my mother and father had been involved in when I was a kid. But in postwar Canada, I considered such a project nothing but racist. I did think some of the lyrics were clever. I had the satisfaction of concluding that Jewison would never make it in show business.

My attention turned from watching college buffoons to rehearsing *Winterset*, a higher form of theatre. The first act ends on a dramatic high as Mio, my character, makes the decision to confront the judge who wrongly condemned his father to death. The moment of decision is illustrated by Mio lighting a cigarette, taking only one drag, then throwing it to the ground, stomping on it, and heading for the judge's house as the curtain falls.

The only problem with this climactic scene was that I didn't smoke. Not since I was nine years old, and the material I used then was only cedar bark. I delayed the dramatic decision in rehearsal by forgetting to bring matches, so I mimed the process with an unlit cigarette.

On opening night matches were provided by stage management, and I did the act of lighting up, inhaling deeply, and throwing the cigarette on the ground. My only problem was that I was so unused to smoking that I couldn't gauge distances. I held the match a good six inches away. The smoke remained unlit, which lessened the dramatic effect of that final gesture.

Next night I was determined not to repeat the mistake. This time I held the match so close that I practically singed my eyelashes. The play was only on for three performances, and I think I got it more or less right on the final night. But one thing puzzled me at the curtain call. Mio befriends a little girl, Miriamne, and they both die at the end of the play as the curtain comes down.

It came down to thunderous applause, but there were also snickers from some members of the audience. Nobody laughed when I couldn't light my cigarette or almost burned my eyelashes, so why would they mock me in death? That closing night they gave the cast pictures taken during the first of the three nights of the production, and there was my answer. Robert Gill had staged our death scene so that Mio and Miriamne fell in exactly the same position. We lay side by side like two colts who had died jumping the same fence.

28: NO TIME FOR TRAGEDY

I decided to stick to comedy. The *Varsity* announced the creation of an *All-Varsity Revue*, to be directed by ... Norman Jewison. I had suggested Jackie Rae, but he wasn't a student. Suddenly I got an invitation to participate, and it came from that same Jewison. Our first meeting started off rather awkwardly, but by the time the Revue was actually put onstage, Norm and I had become friends, a relationship which has endured ever since.

I did only one number in that revue, a Spike Jones–type assassination of the lovely ballad "Laura." I asked a favour of Murray Davis (the actor who had played Oedipus due to my convalescence). He was requested to stand there and sing the song absolutely straight, while I roamed about the stage with various props making a mockery of the lyrics.

My newfound friend, Norman Jewison, next wanted me to help him with a pep rally in Varsity Stadium the night before a football game between our Varsity Blues team and the Queen's University's Golden Gaels. We devised a sketch in which Norman played the coach of the Queen's team, and he got lots of laughs. The guy was a natural performer, I was forced to admit. When he introduced the members of his team, I was in the middle of two other guys and wearing a football sweater worn backward with a huge letter Q in front. The other two had sweaters with the numbers *4* and *2*, and when we stood together with me in the middle, our message to Queen's University was "4 Q 2"!

All this time I was attending lectures, writing essays, and doing the odd radio show. But I couldn't resist when Dora cast me as a villain in *The Little Foxes*. I played Leo, a nasty piece of work, and I enjoyed every minute of it. I also got a black friend of mine from Trinity College, Art Bell, cast as one of two coloured servants. The other was a professional actress, Kay Livingstone. Both Kay and Art were actually black, so my favourite moment of the whole run was reading Augustus Bridle's review in the *Toronto Star*.

He wrote: "The negroes ... Kathleen Livingston and Arthur Bell ... are both so excellent you'd think them actual negroes." More than once I had seen quotes from Gussie Bridle's reviews in *The New Yorker's* department of Rich Warm Soft Beautiful prose, but this time he outdid himself. He made no mention of who did the effectively accurate makeup.

29: SPRING THAW

The stage adaptation of Hugh MacLennan's *Two Solitudes*, about tensions between Anglos and Francos in Quebec, was being written by another Hugh: Kemp. It never arrived, because Hugh had a day job in a Montreal advertising agency and all of a sudden there was an assignment for him to do a campaign blitz on toilet paper. Ten days before we were to start rehearsal, the actors of the New Play Society had nothing to end their season.

Dora was in shock, but Mavor was on hand to remedy the situation. He was still spending summers with the United Nations in New York, but he managed to be around at this crucial time. He knew exactly what to do in this emergency, and the one resource he had in mind was the lady of the dirty laugh, Jane Mallett.

Jane Mallett is now a theatre next door to the Canadian Stage (both projects initiated by Mavor Moore), but back then she was merely Toronto's queen of revue comedy, an able successor to another Toronto girl who had gone abroad in the 1920s, Beatrice Lillie.

Jane's annual revue at the Arts & Letters Club, *Town Tonics*, was uppity Toronto's comedy event of each season, so Jane was Mavor's prime reason for daring to put on a topical revue on such short notice.

He knew he needed some kind of a script to start with. The great radio series *Stage 48* had just concluded its third season with Tommy Tweed's highly topical look at the unionization of a department store. The target was Eaton's, and it never happened in real life, but Tommy's script was well received, with a brilliant pun in the title, *It'll Never Get Well If You Picket*.

Casting had to be done in a hurry. One of the New Play Society regulars was Peter Mews, who had been in the army show with Wayne and Shuster. In that show he was paired with Connie Vernon. Since being demobbed, both she and Peter had been working in department stores designing window displays, Connie for Simpson's, Peter for Eaton's. How they managed to rehearse with us without quitting their day jobs was a wonder.

Connie was an excellent foil for Jane Mallett when they did a sketch about sketching in Muskoka. The script also called for a romantic entanglement; Mavor went outside the box and hired lovely Frosia Gregory, the singer with her husband Bob Shuttleworth's orchestra at the Granite Club. As the constant juvenile, I was chosen as the other half of the romantic pair; a straight man in a broad comedy.

Mavor didn't use Tommy's wonderful "picket" pun as the title of our show. It became a song in the show. Instead, he took a suggestion from the producer of the *Stage 48* radio series, Andrew Allan, who suggested he call the show *Spring Thaw*. In his mind it meant a time when people in this frigid country were ready to come outside their dwellings and bask in the sunshine. But the disappearing snow uncovered a motley assortment of items, all kinds of crap, including animal. It revealed in a way what had been going on all winter. This theme gave us carte blanche to do a self-spoofing review of the Canadian scene during the previous winter. That's why *Spring Thaw* was eventually called a Review instead of a Revue.

In the program was a timely note to explain the title: "When the spring thaw comes, all sorts of things appear: the birds, the flowers, the shovel you lost under the snow, holes in the road and so on. But most particularly, mankind becomes tetched with a strange lightness of the heart and the head, and therefore without another word of excuse, we begin our review."

There were also some Mavor Moore songs, written in haste I'm sure. "You're Always in Love in the Springtime" came from his pen, as well as one entitled "Spring Thaw." The finale of the show was headed by Jane with the entire cast doing a takeoff on a high school historical pageant. I was Laura Secord's cow.

Dora sat out front all through rehearsals with a glum look. Her dream of a classical company of actors doing Synge, Shaw, Shakespeare, and Sophocles was being shattered by the foolishness going on in front of her eyes. To think that it was being committed by her pride and joy, her own son!

We opened, appropriately, on April Fool's Day. It was a full house. Box office sales had been brisk for the three-night run. Dora wondered why the audience was laughing so hard at this foolishness. By the third night she was having to turn customers away from the sellout show.

It was held over for an extra sold-out weekend. Six consecutive performances in Canadian theatre in those days constituted a long run. Dora finally realized that the receipts at the box office would allow her to plan another season of Shakespeare and Shaw, not to mention another *Spring Thaw*. Mavor felt that the instant success of this "review" boded well for the future of Canadian plays. That summer, back at the United Nations, he started writing one. It opened the 1949 season of the New Play Society.

30: SCHOOL AGAIN! SCHOOL AGAIN!

The day after *Spring Thaw* closed in 1948, I had to write my final exams, leading to an Honours Arts degree. In addition to my honours subjects in English Literature and Philosophy, I had been taking a pass-course in European history. It involves far less serious study than the honours equivalent. When I came to write the exam the day after being onstage at the Museum Theatre, I found the history questions much more challenging than expected.

Instead of panicking, I went into my mode of the professional entertainer. In other words, I attempted to charm the ass off the examiner, whoever he or she would be. It was only after I had finished that I was informed that I had written the Honours history exam by mistake, not the Pass option. The results didn't come out for another month, but I ended up with a mark of 74. A remark of Lister Sinclair's came to mind: "You can slide a lot farther on bullshit than sandpaper."

When the results came out, it was my graduating year. I headed my course again, and as a result I was awarded the Sanford Gold Medal in Philosophy! Almost immediately I received an offer from Trinity College to join their staff, not as a professor, or a lecturer, but what they called a "reader." The salary was ... get this ... $600. Not a month — a year! Earlier that semester, I had already turned down the chance to apply for a Rhodes scholarship. It was tempting, but I knew my limitations and preferred to stay onstage instead of wandering where I didn't belong, in the groves of academe. I also thanked the Provost of Trinity for the opportunity to wear a gown over a guaranteed future of naked poverty

When I turned down that job offer, I happened to be playing the small part of the tailor in a Trinity College outdoor production of *The Taming of the Shrew*, directed by my old nemesis, Earle Grey. But this time he was in dire need of an actor who could play comedy to replace a drunken actor who had disgraced himself at the opening night performance. Somebody at Hart House recommended me as a quick study. (The part consisted of eight lines of dialogue!)

It was Earle himself who called me at home. He didn't seem to remember heaving me from the Victoria College cast and welcomed me warmly as someone who was helping him out of a tight spot. In rehearsals I decided to give the tailor a slight stammer, which ended up in performance as a nervous tic, building to a pronounced stutter, and lapsing into absolute gibberish. This tended to remind anyone who saw it of Danny Kaye. The fact that I got big laughs from undergrads in the audience saved me from another dismissal.

As soon as I finished my tailoring, I hightailed it to Gravenhurst to propose marriage to Gloria. There was no chance of marriage until she graduated, but I wanted to lock up the deal with an engagement. I bought a reasonably priced ring and managed to hide it in her breakfast napkin. The gag fizzled when the ring flew out of the napkin and onto the floor. Nobody noticed but me, and I had to go under the table to find it. But all the Fisher family seemed glad about the oncoming nuptial a year hence, when Gloria would be an honours B.A. like her fiancé, eh!

Lotsa yung sitty peeples seams to git ther eddication by degrees. Sum after gittin' ther B.A. or B.S., goze on to git ther M.A. or M.S. and sum goze all the way and ends up with yer PHD. We all nose wat B.S. stands fer, M.S. is more of the saim, and PHD is the saim blaim thing, jist piled hire and deeper.

31: OH! CANADA?

Flush with a bit of money from her *Spring Thaw* hit, Dora decided to set up a permanent company of six actors, with a whopping salary of $30 a week. I was one of them, along with Lloyd Bochner, Glen Burns, Bill Needles, Pegi Brown, and Robert Christie. Thirty dollars a week was more than Dora ever paid herself.

British born, she didn't have the same interest in a Canadian play as her son did. So the 1949 season the NPS had the same mix of classic and slightly modern standards that you would find in an English repertory theatre. But due to the commercial success of *Thaw*, interest by Canadian writers in penning their own projects for the theatre started rising again.

Morley Callaghan, the drinking pal in Paris of Ernest Hemingway, was well established in Canada as a successful novelist, with several to his credit. Encouraged by Nathan Cohen, Callaghan submitted to the New Play Society a play he was still working on.

Dora didn't quite to know what to do with it, but her son did. The play was *To Tell the Truth*, and it had some of the innocent whimsy that Saroyan had put into *The Time of Your Life*. Mavor urged his mother to option it for production in the present season. Dora cautiously agreed, remembering how the cash flowed in from their all-Canadian review. It would be staged just after New Year's, when ticket returns were at their lowest.

First up in the fall season was Shaw's *You Never Can Tell*. The reason for the title was that Shaw was well-known for heavy themes: *Saint Joan*, *Heartbreak House* — but this time he wrote what was for him a bit of fluff, a commercial piece that involved feminism but was basically a light-hearted tribute to a waiter who dispensed the wisdom of the ages in a down-to-earth, almost folksy way.

I was cast as Toby Robins's twin brother, one of a playful pair, full of teasing and good spirits. Toby was still a teenager who had impressed as a very young Miranda in Dora's production of Shakespeare's *The Tempest* when she was still in high school. Now she was a full-fledged professional and the best-dressed young lady I have ever seen. To play her twin I had to match her head of coal-black hair. I did it, not with dye but with lamp black, which looked effective onstage, but was even more effective in darkening my dear mother's sheets. She shrugged it off as her contribution to the arts. I didn't get in trouble with Dora by being late for rehearsals, because my involvement with the CBC this time was as a writer, not a performer. I was thrilled to change categories and worked on the scripts at home whenever I had spare time.

I was commissioned to write a series of scripts for the CBC Schools Department on Roman family life. I submitted a sample script entitled *Roman Manners* and was summoned to CBC headquarters on Jarvis Street, the best-known house in the red-light district of Toronto. The legend was that the CBC was the only non-profit business on that street.

The head of the Schools Department was rumoured to be a former distributor of porno films, and his assistant, my producer, was a raven-haired femme fatale who looked as if she belonged to the Charles Addams family. I was told by these two that my script simply would not do. When I asked why, I was informed that the dialogue sounded too "Lister Sinclairy." I considered that a great compliment, since I ranked the wit of my friend Sinclair just below that of Shaw. They wanted changes in my script. When they told me what they were, I pressed them to be more specific. They faffed a lot in true civil service mode and when pressed even further, the former porno-dealer finally stood up as he prepared to leave and said "Look, just take it back and make it duller."

I threw the script in the nearest ashcan. Who was I kidding? I was an actor, not a writer. The first Canadian offering of the season was right up my alley to bowl the audience over. It was Harry Boyle's *The Inheritance*, adapted from his radio play *The Macdonalds of Oak Valley*, an Ontario farm family dominated by a tyrannical Scottish father. Frank Peddie played the role to the hilt.

I played his younger son. His older son was played by John Drainie. An accident early in life had left John with a permanent limp which limited his appearances in a visual medium, but his talent under any circumstance was never limp, but glowing. I was excited by the chance to be his kid brother and try out my acquired Ontario rural dialect (harrrrd by the barrrrrn).

It didn't make much of an impression on the rest of the cast, or on the audience or the critics, either. Jack Karr, the *Toronto Star* critic, reported that "As the chief protagonist, Don Harrison as the rebellious son plays his part in a workmanlike manner, but seldom alleviates his surliness with any feeling of warmth." I decide to put my quaint turn of speech in mothballs, so when *Spring Thaw '49* came along, I never thought about using my rural accent.

But before that it was back to the classics. We went with Ibsen's *Ghosts*, a play about the hypocrisy of piety and the ravages of inherited syphilis. I played the young man who suffers from his father's indiscretions, and by curtain fall as a result is going blind. We opened out of town (just like

Broadway shows!) in Orangeville. The audience seemed not to react to much of anything until the final curtain, when I kept repeating, as I went blind, "Give me the sun! Give me the sun!" I heard a juvenile voice from out front whisper loud enough for me to hear, "Lookit that, Oswald! He's goin' nuts!" When Essa Ljungh did a radio production of the play later that season, he cast Drainie in that role, not me.

I agreed. Besides, I was too busy with the next show, Morley Callaghan's *To Tell the Truth*. The action takes place in a bar staffed by a young flute-playing poet. That was me, a non-flute player who had to learn to synchronize to a record with mixed results.

Nathan Cohen attended rehearsals. He seemed to have formed some sort of bond with Morley. When I made a comment that I thought Callaghan's script was about as profound as a comic strip with the cartoon character Krazy Kat, Nate bristled and said, "You better look again. Krazy Kat is profound satire!"

I must have been wrong, because the play opened to very respectful reviews, and miracle of miracles, it was almost immediately optioned by the Royal Alexandra's boss, Ernie Rawley. Two weeks after we closed at the 400-seat Museum Theatre, we were rehearsing in the 2,000-seat Royal Alex, the first Canadian play to be presented there in its forty-two-year history.

Almost immediately the rumours started in the Toronto press about a move to Broadway. No fewer than three producers were coming up to look it over. There were further reports during our two-week run that no lesser lights than James Stewart and Margaret Sullavan were being sought for the leading roles.

This dismayed the entire Canadian cast except me. I got to loathe playing Callaghan's wishy-washy little "friend of all the world." The most satisfying moment I had onstage was during the last matinee at the Alex. Lloyd Bochner was usually careful in ripping Dianne Foster's blouse to express his jealousy of little me. This matinee he accidentally ripped her bra as well as her blouse, and there for all to see were her naked breasts.

I immediately covered them with my own body, and she sighed with relief. For some reason I suddenly remembered an old joke and whispered to her as we moved offstage, "Lady, if yer gonna drown them two little piglets, woodya save me the one with the blue nose?"

She didn't laugh. Nor did our play move to Broadway.

32: WAITING FOR THE THAW

Back at the museum, Dora was busy with a production of Somerset Maugham's comedy about middle-aged lust, *The Circle*. Heading the cast was Jane Mallett, so the laughter would be guaranteed. I was cast to join her in the second edition of *Thaw* in April, but in the meantime, even though I was a post-graduate, I got myself involved in another edition of *The All-Varsity Revue*.

It was a chance to do something I've always been nuts about: silent screen comedy. When I was an eight-year-old taking swimming classes at Central YMCA, after the swim they gave us cocoa, and with it old silent movies featuring Charlie Chaplin, Buster Keaton, Harry Langdon, Chester Conklin, and the Keystone Kops.

Lorne Watson was still around doing graduate work and was willing to improvise a silent film–type score that would accompany my attempts at pantomime. I performed this skit one afternoon at Convocation Hall, imitating various old film stars as I ambled back and forth across the stage in various guises, and doing quick changes in the wings. My memory of it is a bit hazy as to how I managed going through the changes.

This was a one-night or rather one-afternoon stand, and almost immediately after that Mavor Moore called me for a meeting about the writing of *Spring Thaw '49*. There was to be no plot this time, just a series of topical sketches that would amuse Torontonians. Jane Mallett was returning, and so were Connie Vernon and Peter Mews.

Mavor added a performer with lots of comedy experience, Eric Christmas. He was a recent English immigrant who had made a career in Canada appearing in Christmas pantomimes. For *Thaw '49* he added some old music hall routines that won great audience response.

I contributed two sketches, and I can barely remember one of them. It was a satire on our tabloid newspapers of the day, *Hush* and *Flash*. I called then, naturally, *Hash* and *Flush*. It was sung by the 1837 newspaper editor, William Lyon Mackenzie, and called "We Get All the Dirt from Muddy York."

I don't really know how well my tribute to silent films went, because I was too busy changing costumes to notice. The only rehearsal I got was without Charlie Tisdall's help at the piano. He couldn't play the rehearsal for me because the audience was already in the theatre filling up the seats for opening night. The atmosphere was pretty frantic as we opened our second *Thaw*.

We ran for two weeks with packed houses.

The success of another *Spring Thaw* and the vague Broadway rumours that still persisted about *To Tell the Truth* brought a rash of Canadian plays to Dora's desk. She didn't know what to do with them, but Mavor did. He planned the next season of the New Play Society to be all-Canadian.

At last, he declared, the New Play Society would live up to its name. The budding playwrights he wanted for the new season were well established in other fields, like Harry J. Boyle, Andrew Allan, and John Coulter, who was preparing a drama about Prairie rebel Louis Riel.

Dora was taken somewhat aback by the idea. She agreed to renew *Spring Thaw*, but she had planned her season to include maybe another Greek tragedy, and certainly a Shakespeare. Mavor showed her the playscript he had been working on while summering at the United Nations. It was entitled *Who's Who?* It was not a naturalistic work, but rather an Expressionist story of a mega-tycoon of the Toronto business community. It traced his life from age eight to eighty, interrupted occasionally by an aged heckler sitting in the audience.

When Dora was told that Lorne Greene (CBC National News Voice of Doom) wanted to play the title role in *Who's Who?* she shrewdly agreed to have her son's play open the 1949–1950 season.

33: WEDDING BILLS

During rehearsals of *Spring Thaw*, Eric Christmas approached me about co-writing a radio sitcom. Since I would become a married man soon after the last performance of *Thaw*, I welcomed the chance for some extra income. Eric must have been a busy little beaver in the halls of the CBC, because by the time we opened our little stage show, we had a deal for a summer series with the head of programming, Budd Walker.

Budd insisted that we needed an extra writer of experience to fill out the writing team. He suggested Lister Sinclair, and to my surprise Lister accepted. I couldn't wait to work with him. Script discussions among the three of us began as soon as *Thaw* had its opening night. The final script had more Lister than Eric or myself, and in retrospect, it resembled a kind of "*Goon Show* for Ph.D.s." But not with the zany results of that popular whacko show created by Milligan, Sellers, and Secombe for the BBC almost ten years later.

Toronto reviewers would have none of our show. They dismissed it as obscurantist piffle and arrant snobbery. The role of the nerd in entertainment would have to await *The Big Bang Theory* some sixty years later. Budd Walker insisted on a meeting next day, and before he could say anything, Lister offered to resign from the enterprise.

I was startled, but Eric Christmas grinned, and Budd accepted. Lister left immediately, and Eric was quick to suggest that the original title *Keep in Touch* should be kept and used to illustrate a recent Cockney immigrant's adventures in Canada, played by him, and relate in letters to family back in England. I sat there silent but relieved that the original concept of a sitcom had been retained, and also the fact that I had another chance to make some pre-marital money. Despite the fact that I had never been to England, Eric felt that the two of us should work separately on alternate scripts.

Since my fiancée was up to her ears in exams, I attempted the second script, but I eagerly awaited Eric's first, and his approval of my efforts. Gloria and I planned to marry in 1949, the week after her exams finished.

Before that I had to turn out a *Keep in Touch* script on my own. Without waiting for Eric's version, I plunged ahead and in a white heat of creation turned out thirty pages in a couple of days. Unfortunately, I was so brain-dead from fatigue that I left my script on the streetcar on the way to the CBC, and despite frantic efforts at recovery, I was unable to retrieve it.

I never had a stag party the night before my wedding. I spent the time at home staring at my typewriter trying to recall the original thirty pages. On my way to the chapel that wedding morning, I had my dad drive me to the CBC building first to drop off a hastily re-created version, from memory, of my original script.

Gloria and I were married in the tiny Hart House chapel by a minister who was a friend of her family. After the ceremony we had the wedding reception at the Old Mill, where a few friends waited.

Gloria was a virgin, and so, I swear to God, was I. We honeymooned on Manitoulin Island. Then we spent a rewarding time at her home in Gravenhurst. Her father was a dedicated country doctor and at the same time secretary of the Ontario Medical Association, whose head was another doctor, a dedicated surgeon named Charles E. Farquharson. There is a school in Toronto named after him, Charles E. Farquharson Junior High.

When I first heard that name uttered in Doc Fisher's own Huron County twang, I fell in love with it and was determined to use it someday. This was 1949, and it would be three years, after a two-year sojourn in England, before I had the opportunity.

34: BACK TO THE SALT MINES

I wasn't at all sorry I had married. Gloria was a loving wife, and she made me so content in our domestic life. She was always a receptive audience for my more inane remarks. She turned out to be a highly compatible companion.

As a newly married man I had to get back to work and pay some bills, including that new car I bought for my parents. By the way, it didn't last long. My father hadn't driven since 1932, and on their vacation at Camp Billie Bear, the car ended up in a ditch and became a total write-off. Fortunately, my folks were spared, give or take a few scratches and bruises.

We newlyweds needed a place to stay in Toronto. Mavor and his bride Dilly were decamping their digs for the summer while Mavor made his annual pilgrimage to the United Nations in New York. So we subletted their Toronto apartment on very reasonable terms.

Keep in Touch, the sitcom I co-wrote with Eric Christmas, sort of lumbered on thanks to his Cockney authenticity. I think it appealed to Brits who were homesick for over 'ome, but I don't think it registered much with the Canadian public. It came to a sudden end in early summer.

Fortunately for me, other radio work was immediately offered by my fellow sun-slut, Jackie Rae. On that YMCA roof I had often given my impressions of the hired men I had worked with on "yer thrashin' gang." Jackie, ever the performer since childhood, did a pretty fair imitation of my rustic accent, and he thought I would fit in with a summer assignment he'd been given.

This time I would be performing as well as writing. It was a hoedown show headed by Bobby Gimby, on summer hiatus from CBC Radio's most popular show, *The Happy Gang*. I had never been fond of that kind of music. When my late grandfather would tune in to Don Messer and His Islanders, I would walk out of the house. But I was hired to present the various country music numbers on the show, and money was money.

I needed a name for my rural announcer, so I harkened back to my days on the Hadden farm. No, I didn't call him Charlie this time. Across the road from Haddens was the farm of Orville Short, so I ended up with the name Harry Shorthorn. I was paired with an American impressionist, Dick Nelson, who seemed to be stranded in Toronto. He chose the name Luther Duckett for his by-cracky character.

Together we were to provide verbal continuity between musical numbers. It was written by me, and Dick was a pleasure to work with. As he said as Luther Duckett: "By cracky, that there Rudy Hansom sings with lotsa jinicker, purtier'n a pink pig at market time!"

Then Harry Shorthorn would chime in with: "You ain't jist whisslin' Dixie. He's a regler ring-tail snorter of a wham-snapper of a rang-dang-doo!"

By hinkus that'd be Bobby Gumbo and his mewsickle aggravation goin' like a three-horse team over a wood bridge at a smart trot! I bleeve you cud have danced to the drum on that toon! And that fiddle! You'd wonder how she cud sound so blaim sweet jist by sumbuddy draggin the tail of a horse acrost the guts of a cat!

This sort of exchange of rural dialogue went on until Mavor came back from New York. We started rehearsing his own play, *Who's Who?*, as the initial presentation of the fourth season of the New Play Society. That meant that Gloria and I had to find other lodgings. While I was doing the by-cracky bit on radio, she had scoured the rental columns and managed to find a furnished flat next to a dentist's office in the far West End. We had to share a bathroom with the dentist and his nurse during office hours.

We soon found out that they were using the bathroom for their extra-marital sexual appetites. Their antics amused us at first, but later I think my bride became envious of their furtive situation.

35: ALL-CANADIAN!

Rehearsals began for *Who's Who?*, the life story of a Toronto mega-tycoon of business. Mavor's style was Expressionistic. Lorne Greene would sit and watch while another actor played him at an earlier stage in life. Namely me. Also, the action was interrupted occasionally by a heckler who questioned the validity of the evidence presented. This was played by a long-time veteran CBC Radio actor, Alex McKee, a down-to-earth, no-nonsense performer who breathed reality. Some members of the audience really believed he was one of them.

I was cast as the younger version of the leading role, from age eight up to late middle age. When I asked seventy-five-year-old McKee how to play age, he said, "Just relax. That's all aging is. By that time you've stopped worrying."

The author never got to see the second half of his own play at its world premiere performance. Mavor was stricken with acute appendicitis at intermission and was rushed to the hospital for emergency surgery.

There was a new critic in town, Herbert Whittaker. He was taking over the drama desk at the *Globe and Mail*, and he gave the play a rave review. But I don't think anybody saw his review, because it was hidden away in the back of the paper with the want ads. All Toronto newspapers had only one thing to write about that next day: the burning in Toronto harbour of the *Noronic* with heavy loss of life. Reality had intruded with a vengeance and wiped our efforts at drama out of the picture.

Andrew Allan's *Narrow Passage* was next, and I was delighted to work with the man who had made the rehearsals of *Ah! Wilderness* so enjoyable.

The play itself was a bit like Noël Coward in Muskoka, but with fewer laughs. I again played opposite the lovely Toby Robins. Herb Whittaker described it best in his review: "As the sensitive, hag-ridden musician, Donald Harron played with what we have come to recognize as this young actor's flair for presenting the highly-strung and desperate." I was starting to get typecast as tragic relief.

The next production was Mavor's concession to mother Dora, Shaw's *Heartbreak House*. It is a searingly bitter portrait of England on the brink of the First World War, but it contains great moments of savage humour. I was hoping to be part of it when Mavor threw a curveball at me. He wanted me to direct the next show.

Directing a play for me was not exactly typecasting. I was flattered but terrified. John Coulter's *Riel* was about Canada's most famous rebel, who caused two full-scale uprisings in the nineteenth century. I had met Coulter before at Toronto's Arts & Letters Club. I was fascinated by his thick northern Irish accent, pure Belfast.

I reluctantly accepted Mavor's offer, provided he would play the title role. He was still heavily involved with the United Nations but promised he would travel back and forth to fulfill both commitments. The part of Sir John A. Macdonald I felt could be filled by a member of our permanent company, Robert Christie. He was so successful in the role that he spent a good part of his subsequent career acting as our first prime minister.

Forget farming — as a director I had never worked so hard in my life. My bride was magnificent, bringing me hot meals on the spot because I was unable to leave the rehearsal hall (washroom duties excepted!). I had my problems with desertions in the cast. My Bishop Taché was a shy guy, Les Rubie, who had hung around for several shows playing walk-ons. He turned out to be a wonderful archbishop.

I then had difficulties with Coulter. I wanted to reverse the order of scenes in Act One to de-emphasize the role of Riel's mother, who I considered to be an ultra-religious bore. But he said simply that he preferred to see the play as he had written it. He won. I would face the same battles later in my career, when I was the writer of musical comedies.

My biggest problem was getting the title role to appear for rehearsal. The United Nations must have been in crisis, because Mavor was spending more and more time in New York. When he did appear, he had a very shaky mastery of his many, many lines. I started to panic and it showed in rehearsal. Bob Christie, who had been wonderfully prime ministerial in rehearsals, now assumed the same duties offstage. He literally took command of the production. He told me to stop fussing over the technical details and just allow the cast to get on with the job.

When Mavor didn't show up for our dress rehearsal, I had an absolute tantrum. He had no understudy, so I ended up playing his role, script in hand, while I doubled in my own role, Thomas Scott. I was in the ludicrous position of condemning myself to execution. It's a miracle that Mavor arrived back in Canada for opening night, because the day dawned in Toronto after a three-foot snowfall. The inclement weather did not prevent several veterans of the 1885 Rebellion from attending the opening.

Mavor looked resplendent in his dark wig and bristling moustache, but he still had a shaky mastery of most of his lines. After my character was shot, I spent the rest of the evening hiding under the floorboards of the upstage raised platform. In my hands I clutched a copy of the script as Mavor orated above me, and more than once I had to come through with a prompt prompt.

I breathed a sigh of relief when we finally got to hang Riel in full view of the audience. As musical background, the "Te Deum" was sung a cappella by a quartet of boys from St. Michael's Cathedral. I was backstage by that time, and as the final curtain came down and the audience burst into applause, the four lads then swung into their own arrangement of the blues classic "Tell Me How Long the Train's Been Gone!" It was unheard except by me backstage, and I realized what a gift the monsignor of St. Mike's had bestowed on us. Later they became a professional quartet: The Four Lads.

Mavor was receiving an ovation. In spite of everything, his performance was magnificent. The *Evening Telegram*'s Rose Macdonald wrote that Mavor's Riel was "one of the best-rounded and most convincing performances of his career, retaining the centre of the stage without elbowing out the other characters."

I never directed a play again, even though that opening night provided our playwright with a new career: the Riel business. The courtroom trial in the play's second act was based on actual historical transcripts and continues to be performed every summer in Regina. Mavor later wrote an opera, *Riel*, with music composed by Harry Somers. But for the moment he was content to rest on the opening night laurels and to contemplate his next venture, the title role in *King Lear*.

36: IT'S A BASTARD!

In the 1920s and 1930s, *Hamlet* was considered the apex of Shakespeare's achievement. Possibly this was due to the popularity of psychoanalysis fostered by both Freud and Jung. Even in the 1950s, among New York actors, every one of them seemed to be visiting a shrink on a regular basis.

King Lear seemed to picture a bleaker landscape savage in its ferocity, a different kind of horror from the personal psychosis in *Hamlet*. But after the excesses of the Second World War, concentration camps and atomic bombs, the heath that Lear stalked in his madness seemed not quite so unfamiliar territory. His rants spoke a bleak message directly to the postwar mind. Hamlet was an heir to the throne but deprived of his job; Lear was a retiree by his own choice and led himself to his own undoing.

I don't know why Mavor decided he should play the title role. He was just past the age of thirty but had never been cast in the juvenile roles I inhabited for so long. He maintained, at a young age, what the Earl of Kent attributed to his master Lear, and that was "authority." Perhaps his precocious maturity would work for Shakespeare's most difficult tragic role.

Our production was done under the most difficult circumstances. First, the rehearsal period for this epic tragedy was ten days. You heard me. Second, Mavor came to the first rehearsal and blew his throat out shouting on that blasted heath. He had to go straight to his bed. For the next eight days! This made the trials of Riel seem like a walk in the park. He finally appeared for the dress rehearsal.

Dora was the director of this operation, in her Battle of Britain Churchillian mode. We actors all appeared dutifully every day without our sovereign. I was the bastard son Edmund who watched the deliberate blinding of his poor father with no emotion.

I think it's the best part in this play, because the bastard is not only a villain, but he's a sexy one, keeping both of Lear's older daughters on an adulterous string, the two-timing bastard. Oh, he gets his comeuppance at the end of the play, slain by his hard-done-by brother Edgar, but until then he has a raunchy good time and even gets to say the word "Fut!" (Whatever that means!) It's a part I loved so much that I have managed to play it twice more since.

Our dear Dora, soldiering on, had created a blasted heath out of our tiny stage. She had always maintained all that was required to do Shakespeare were "two boards and a passion!" The NPS didn't have a board, and the passion was still in bed with laryngitis.

Finally, Mavor appeared for the dress rehearsal and proceeded to whisper his way through the entire play. But the man seemed to be at his best when everything was going wrong. In full voice opening night, he strode our fourteen-foot heath with true madness and majesty. He knew his lines perfectly and could even invent some blank verse if the situation called for it. And it did. When Lear enters a hovel to get out of the storm on the heath, he is supposed to find a footstool, which in his madness he mistakes for his second daughter Regan.

It wasn't there. The stage manager was sitting on it in the wings, script in hand, ready to jog Mavor's memory with a prompt. Without missing a beat, Mavor asked, "Where is the stool, Fool?"

Poor Jack Medhurst shrugged as if to say, "What the hell do I know?"

Then Mavor pointed offstage to where the stage manager's rump was and ad libbed, in perfect iambic pentameter, the following completely improvised speech: "Arise, Fool, and bring me yonder joint-stool, and you and I shall jointly sit upon't!" All this made up on the spot, with elision as the final touch: "upon't."

37: WAITING FOR THE NEXT THAW

King Lear closed to good reviews and good business, and Mavor started getting ready for the third annual *Spring Thaw*. Before that we had another Callaghan play to do, following last year's success, which had ended up by transferring to the Royal Alex.

But *Going Home* saddled the two leads, Toby Robins and Gerry Sarracini, with the most lugubrious dialogue this side of soap operas. I was lucky. I played a thoroughly unpleasant person who got to be drowned at the end of the first act. I never took a curtain call but hurried home on the Bloor streetcar to a home-cooked meal, sometimes by my mother-in-law visiting from Gravenhurst. When she noticed me writing sketches for *Spring Thaw*, she told me she thought I should be paid for them, a royalty for each sketch besides my $30 actor's salary.

In subsequent negotiations with a stone-faced Dora, I managed to eke out from her coffers $2 for a sketch and 50 cents for a blackout — per performance! I was still in trouble with her for sneaking in my radio jobs.

I found my mother-in-law, Martha Fisher, just as formidable as Dora. After supper one evening in our dentist-shared flat, she said something that startled me. We were alone because her daughter had just burned the roast and stormed off to bed. Gloria was always understanding when I goofed, but if she made a mistake, it was door-slamming time.

My mother-in-law put the charred remains of the roast in the garbage and heated up some Campbell's soup. As we sipped, she asked, "Why don't you and Gloria go to London?"

"What for?"

"To see some first-rate shows, for goodness' sake! Isn't that part of your job, to see the best theatre in the world?"

The next day I booked passage to London. Gloria was thrilled. We were due to sail two days after the run of *Spring Thaw* was complete.

The week before rehearsals started, Jane Mallett hired me as her second banana for a couple of concert dates in Montreal. I was basically her straight man, but she allowed me to do a couple of political monologues, as well. It was fun being her foil in some of her *Town Tonics* material, but my own political stuff went over like a lead balloon.

On the way home Jane explained the difficulty to me. "Although you're at the ripe old age of what — twenty-five, you still look like a teenager onstage. So when you criticize the government, older people in the audience think you're just being a smartass." She told me I should do what the ancient Greeks did: hide their identity behind a mask. She didn't mean a *papier-mâché* creation. That mask should be simply the creation of a much older person who had acquired the wisdom associated with maturity.

I thanked her for her advice and promptly forgot about it, until two years later in *Spring Thaw '52*, when I finally had enough sense to hide my own political opinions under the peak cap of Charlie. Ignoring this good advice for the moment, I decided to do some *Spring Thaw '50* casting on my own. One night after a *Lear* performance, I was sitting at the counter of a restaurant next to a "real character" who sounded like one of the old Borscht Belt comics who appeared occasionally with Milton Berle in the early days of television.

I summoned up my courage and broke the ice with "So whadda yuh do for a living?" His answer was brief: "Ennuh-tainmint." When I pressed him for further details, I found he was a stand-up comic who worked stags and smokers, and every summer at the Jewish hotels in the Muskoka area. I asked him if that included Gravenhurst, and he laughed as he told me he worked one summer hotel near that town that used to be a Nazi prisoner of war camp. I pumped him further about his background and found that in the 1930s he had belonged to a Toronto drama group, Theatre of Action, doing plays by Clifford Odets. He added, "We wuz probly a buncha Commies, but what the hell did I know from pollticks."

The short and long of it was that Mavor was glad to get a Yiddish flavour into *Spring Thaw*, because our theatre seasons had been sustained by Jewish theatregoers. I saw Lou Jacobi as someone who could play the lead in the mock opera I had written for the Victoria College *Bob* three years before. Completely rewritten, of course, but still a spoof of grand opera.

A situation had arisen in Toronto politics that called for such operatics: the amalgamation of the suburbs to form Metropolitan Toronto. It was the subject of endless discussion in the spring of 1950.

I titled my mock Italian opera *La Traviesti* and created a part for Lou as a Sicilian-type bandit, Taranna. He spent his time rounding up reluctant suburban villagers with names like Zcarr-boro, Yetobico, Swansi, and Mimi-co, and forcing his attentions on a weeping female in transit named Teetisi. (Her first name was Carmen, known to her intimate friends as Streetcarmen.)

Lou was a big hit in this, and so was Pegi Brown. Mavor re-hired Lou on the spot for *Spring Thaw '51*. Pegi also triumphed in her takeoff of Barbara Ann Scott.

Spring Thaw '50 was an even bigger hit than its two predecessors. The original run of three weeks was extended for another two. Everybody signed up for the extension, except me. There was no discussion about whether this shmoe would go on. I had a ship to catch. I really wanted to stay, but I had already paid for the tickets. Five weeks in Europe, including two in England.

38: INNOCENTS ABROAD

The Harrons had one night in New York before we embarked for England. Next morning, awfully early, we boarded our ship from a pier on Manhattan's west side. It was the *Georgic*, sister ship to the *Britannic*, which had served as a troopship during the war. Our ship had spent five years of the Second World War lying at the bottom of the Red Sea! It had only recently been exhumed from the depths and was making the return trip of its second-coming maiden voyage going back to Liverpool.

It still looked and felt like a troopship. The ship did not yet have separate staterooms for two. We were separated by sexes and booked in separate cabins with three or four other strangers. Gloria immediately took to her bunk and spent the rest of the voyage seasick.

I preferred being up on deck in the fresh breezes with the entire Atlantic Ocean as my vomitorium. The ship served five meals a day if you included elevenses and fourses, with hot beef bouillion served on deck at all hours. I kept bringing care packages of food to Gloria, but it was steadily refused.

We docked at Liverpool on the Whitsuntide holiday. The would-be Beatles were probably still in grammar school at the time. We managed to get our luggage to London, where we put up at the Charing Cross Hotel. It was a railway hotel, and I'll swear that the trains ran right through our room. First thing Gloria did was buy a newspaper and look up the theatre listings. Our hotel was on the Strand, and so was the Aldwych Theatre, which advertised *A Streetcar Named Desire*.

I had read back in Toronto that Bernie Braden had recently joined the cast, which included Vivien Leigh and its director, Laurence Olivier. We strolled along the Strand.

Our experience at the Aldwych that evening was a definite let-down. The main problem was the accent chosen by Vivien Leigh. It seemed to be Irish, nothing to do with New Orleans. Bonar Colleano, the Stanley, talked like somebody from Brooklyn. Braden, as Stanley's buddy Mitch, sounded all right to me with a Southern Comfort drawl, but he was about a foot short to fulfill the physical demands of the role. My friend was no hulking giant, as Mitch is supposed to be.

We decided to go backstage and make "nice noises." It was crowded back there, evidence of audience approval. Bernie soon appeared with a large American in tow, Daniel Mann, who had been hired to re-direct Olivier's production, since Vivien was leaving for Hollywood to do the film version of *Streetcar*. Danny Mann, I found out later, had been part of that same Theatre of Action company in 1930s Toronto in which Lou Jacobi had been involved. He took one look at me and asked, "You American?"

I said, "No, Canadian."

His reply surprised me. "What the fuck's the difference?"

Bernie explained that Mann was looking for a minor replacement in the cast, the part of the young man who collects the subscription money for the local newspaper, and has a nice flirtation with the leading lady. The actor who played him was leaving for a British film, and the part would be cast the following morning. Bernie suggested I appear at that audition.

He also took Gloria and me for an after-theatre supper, along with the leading man, Bonar Colleano, who wore a worried frown throughout the meal. It turns out Bonar was starting a BBC Radio comedy series the following week, and there was no script. To make a long story short, by the end of that evening, Gloria was taken home by cab to the Charing Cross hotel, while I was driven to the luxurious Grosvenor House hotel off Park Lane, to rewrite a radio script for Mr. Colleano. It was now shortly before midnight. *The Bonar Colleano Show* was a BBC Radio sitcom starring the namesake of the show as a dashing young playboy in contemporary London. His sidekick was to be played by a Canadian actor, Paul Carpenter.

With a Canadian and an American to write for, I didn't feel too insecure about the language. As I completely rewrote Doug Haskins's script, I threw into it every old gag I knew, including some from previous *Spring Thaws*. I wrote all night, and I was still there the following morning, having finished my version of the script by 10:30 a.m.

Bernie phoned to remind me of the audition for that small part in *Streetcar*, and I took a cab to the Aldwych Theatre. The area outside the stage door was crowded with about seventy actors. The stage manager appeared and asked if any of them were American. Three of us put our hands up and all the rest were told to go home.

The three of us were taken onstage. The first to read was a son of English actor Clive Brook. I didn't know the other auditionee, but he didn't seem to know how to act. So Danny Mann gave me the job, and I was to start at tomorrow evening's performance. When I got back to the Charing Cross Hotel, Gloria told me that Bernie had phoned to say they wanted me to co-write Colleano's radio series with some English writer.

I had two job offers, one in radio and the other in the theatre. The theatre job paid twelve pounds a week, and the radio-writing fee was more than three times that. That totalled an income of about 50 pounds a week in a country where the average workman's wage was closer to 10 quid. We hadn't been in London twenty-four hours.

39: LONDON LIFE

Gloria and I cancelled our plans for a three-week tour of Europe and prepared ourselves to settle down in London for an indefinite period. She dutifully went through the rental ads in one of the London papers and found us a flat with ev.mod.con. (every modern convenience) and a shared k.and b. (kitchen and bathroom) in the suburb of St. John's Wood. This was immediately cancelled by Bernie, who told us that St. John's Wood was "not a good address."

Instead, he suggested that we move into his old digs near Sloane Square, just off the King's Road next to the trendy borough of Chelsea. Gloria kissed goodbye the twenty pounds she had already paid for painting and decorating. We moved to 34 Lower Sloane Street, a tall, red-brick, three-storey Victorian house. Instead of two furnished rooms we had only one (it's called a bedsit), and we still had to share kitchen and bathroom. The landlady was red-haired, slightly buck-toothed and fiftyish, and welcomed us as if we were close relatives of Bernie.

I had to get to British Actors' Equity and become a member so that I could legitimately appear on the West End stage that night. This would not be an easy task today, but back in 1950 it was automatic that I could join their union as a member of the British Commonwealth.

When I arrived at the theatre for a rehearsal with director Danny Mann, I was told that I would certainly be going on that night, and it would be the last performance for Vivien Leigh before she left for America. Meanwhile, the new cast had already been rehearsing for at least a fortnight.

After the rehearsal, in which I was word-perfect, Danny Mann asked me to stay behind after the others had "taken five" to go to a pub. "I just want to time your scene to find out how long it runs. So don't give me any acting, just repeat the lines." I did as I was told, but I thought it an odd request. When I got through the scene, Danny leaned in and said in almost a whisper, "That's exactly how I want you to play the part."

I knew his background included the theories and practice of Constantin Stanislavski, which became all the rage in America as "method acting." But whatever this advice was, it remains a simple lesson that I will never forget.

Before the curtain went up, I was taken by the stage manager to meet "Miss Leigh." She was very jolly, with a firm handshake, and she sounded very much what I later understood was "county English," spoken by landed gentry in tweeds and pearls as they roamed their rural estates.

Onstage she reverted to that strange Irish-like dialect. I hoped that film director Elia Kazan would correct her. (He did. Her accent was strictly from the American South, just as she had exhibited years before in *Gone with the Wind*.) The scene we played together lasts for only two minutes, but it's one of the finest "brief encounters" ever written. We went through the scene in her dressing room, and her only comment was "Jolly dee! Bang on!"

My role was that of the paperboy who comes collecting for the subscription to the *Evening Star*. Blanche DuBois was really a genteel nymphomaniac, and the scene amounts to a seduction of me by her that never comes to fruition. She addresses me with "You look like a young prince out of the Arabian nights." The audience laughed. English audiences are probably more familiar than Americans with the original story, which ends with sex every night after the tale is told. Vivien bristled at the audience response and muttered something under her breath. It sounded to me like "Kents, Kents."

I wondered if she wanted me to go for cigarettes after I got offstage, until I realized what she was expressing. The scene over, I went to the cubbyhole that was my "dressing room" and tried to relax. When we took curtain calls, I was hoping to meet her husband, but all I saw of Sir Laurence Olivier was a shadowy figure in the back seat of a limousine waiting for his leading lady.

40: SCRIBBLE, SCRIBBLE!

It seems to me in retrospect that I went directly from the stage door of the Aldwych Theatre to the Paris Cinema in Lower Regent Street, where the first script of *The Bonar Colleano Show* was being rehearsed. Actually it was the next day, Sunday, when all this happened. The young writer was a very affable kind of bloke, full of funny stories that had nothing to do with the script. He was considered by the BBC as a "young hopeful." He was silent at the rehearsal when I found myself throwing in script additions all by myself. Even after the broadcast started.

It was an audience show, and they reacted very well. Evidently Colleano and Paul Carpenter had developed a following as rakes about town. They were charmers with a knack for currying favour not only with audiences, but the all-powerful daily newspaper columnists. Consequently the initial reviews were quite favourable. All that crossed my mind was that I had twelve more of these scripts to write ... more than likely all by myself.

I took to writing in my cubbyhole in the Aldwych as well as at our flat. But the typing seemed to bother our landlady and the other denizens.

Bonar wanted me to bring my portable typewriter along on his after-theatre forays into London's night-life. I hesitated. Still, it was my chance to observe a real playboy in action, which was the theme of our series. One of Bonar's pals bore an astonishing resemblance to film star John Mills, and Bonar sometimes used this to lure young dishy girls to Paul Carpenter's luxurious flat. I was holed up in the john, pecking away until someone needed to use the facilities.

Eventually I became so desperate for typing time after my performance that I ended up at BBC headquarters at the Aeolian Hall in New Bond Street. The kindly concierge would let me in before midnight and come round to let me out four or five hours later.

41: CENTRAL HEAT

Back at our one-room flat, landlady Ginger Ewen was becoming a problem. It seems her constant chatter drove Gloria up the pipe. My wife would get out of the house to roam art galleries and museums to avoid contact. When she finally got back to our lodgings and Ginger would knock on our door for a chat, Gloria would pretend not to be home. On the other hand, I welcomed the fact that Ginger was having an affair with the local butcher. Meat rationing was a real problem, but not at 34 Lower Sloane Street.

We had been in London for almost six months, and our circumstances were changing rapidly. For one thing, Gloria started having morning sickness. My bad. The London fogs were moving in, and the prospect of putting coin after coin into a gas meter that warmed only one side of us at a time did not thrill us as a prospect. The Romans had brought central heating to Britain almost 2,000 years ago, but it seems that when they left, it left with them.

Close to Marble Arch was an ugly modern block of flats called Park West. It was across the street from some lovely old terraced houses, and it lacked the chic address of Chelsea, but by God, it was centrally heated. We could stare at the lovely ancient houses from the windows of our warm, unfashionably ugly apartment. I signed a six-month lease.

All of a sudden, unemployment loomed. *A Streetcar Named Desire* was going on tour in October, and I was determined not to go with it. Then *The Bonar Colleano Show* came to an abrupt and tragic end. In true playboy style, Bonar was killed in a car crash. Opinions vary as to whether it was carelessness or suicide. I hoped it was the former. He always seemed so sunny and sure of himself.

With supporting a family of three looming in the future, I was really worried. Life had been so spectacularly easy since we arrived in London, and now I had to face reality. My constant friend-in-residence Bernie Braden offered to introduce me to his agent, Olive Harding. She was a warm, motherly woman who look me to lunch at an expensive restaurant and told me the first thing to do was to write brief, chatty letters to all the theatrical management in London, asking for an appointment.

There were thirty-two of them, and I got back thirty-one replies, with cordial invitations to pop by and have a chat. This often involved a cup of tea and a biscuit. It was all so civilized, unlike New York, where they were usually blunt and sometimes ill-mannered. Mind you, nothing came of all this civilized British treatment. The next person to hire me for a London play was the one man, Henry Sherek, who had never answered my request for an interview.

Olive also sent me on an interview for a film. *Streetcar* was still in town, but many actors managed film jobs in the day while appearing onstage at night. The interview was with Shepperton Films, outside London at Walton-on-Thames, an hour's journey on a train.

When I got to the casting office, I was greeted by another motherly lady. She asked me about my film career, and I was forced to tell her it was non-existent. She shook her head and tried to swallow a snicker. Suddenly her phone rang, and after a while she looked at me with new intensity and asked if I could dance. I asked her if she meant socially, because I thought I could manage a slow foxtrot.

"What I really mean is … can you move your head and arms to music?"

"Sure. I guess so." I was glad this didn't involve feet.

"Then would you go on the set now? They're waiting for you."

Dazed, nay, stunned, I was whisked away. I was practically hurled into a dressing room and emerged wearing a Raggedy Ann wig and a ruffled clown shirt. Before I could stand up I was invaded by a makeup artist who gave me beestung lips and purple patches on my cheeks.

I was on the set of *The Tales of Hoffman*, the dance film that followed on the success of *The Red Shoes* and with the same star, Moira Shearer.

I was to be an extra in a number entitled "The Trish Trash Polka." As I stood there with the pale young man who had slapped the costume on me, another, even paler young man pulled up beside us, quite out of breath. I still remember their exchange of dialogue to this day:

"Derek, I'm so terribly …"

Derek interrupted immediately. "You're late, you're late, you silly thing! Too many drinkypoos I'll wager!"

"I'm late? Maybe ten piddly-fucking minutes!"

Derek pointed at me. "Never mind, we have another dancer to take your place. So back to Lunders with you, tardy pants!"

I had stolen a job from a member of the Sadler's Wells Ballet. I was about to intervene on his behalf when Derek goosed me up a ladder. There were six holes at the top, five of them filled with bums. I was shoved into the sixth and told from below to "Just do what the others do."

I did. My hands moved in concert with the owners of those five other bottoms whenever the music started. After two hours of this, we broke for lunch. I sought out Derek and tried to tell him how important it was for me to be back in London at the Aldwych Theatre by at least 6:00 p.m. Derek said they were supposed to knock off at five but warned me to be back bright and early the next morning. And no drinkypoos.

Much later, when I got to see the film, I tried to figure out which set of waving hands were actually mine. I couldn't. At least I was seven pounds richer for my first film experience, and I could always put on my theatre credits that I had been a member of the Sadler's Wells Ballet.

42: JOBBING AROUND

My first film experience was soon followed by my first television experience. It was a ninety-minute television drama about the United Nations. I took an audition and found myself cast as an American undersecretary of state. It was a smallish part and I got away with it all right.

Back home, television didn't exist for Canadian actors. We used to watch Milton Berle on the *Texaco Star Theater* on the Buffalo station, but the screen was so full of "snow" that it hardly seemed worth the eye strain. It seemed that British TV had been going on a lot longer. It was still live, like radio, which made it more like theatre to me. Except that if you blew your lines, there was no way you could be rescued.

The cast of the U.N. drama was comprised mostly of theatre actors. One prominent member of the cast was in his late seventies, and in rehearsal he kept having trouble remembering his lines. He assured the director he would be "all right on the night."

On air, the old fellow was fine until his big confrontation scene with the Russian ambassador. As they say in the theatre, he "dried" completely. But the old actor's lips never stopped moving as he pretended to engage the Russian with passionate eloquence in an earnest plea for understanding. The rest of us were equally mute and open-mouthed. This silence went on for what seemed like several minutes ... actually, it was probably about forty-five seconds ... before the Russian, played by BBC veteran Arthur Young, realized what he must do. He ad libbed a paraphrase of what the old actor had probably said to him, and got the scene back on track, because the old bugger who had muffed his lines suddenly remembered the rest of them and was able to complete the scene as rehearsed.

We all breathed a sigh of relief as the drama continued the way we rehearsed it. However, the BBC switchboard erupted in pandemonium as irate viewers called in to protest that they had been short-changed by an inefficient government management, because in England you have to pay a hefty licence fee to watch television. And hear it, of course. But back in the studio we all gathered round to congratulate the old actor for his feat of daring.

After that experience, the next month I spent doing the rounds of all the theatrical producers I had wooed by post. They were, without exception, very hospitable and usually offered me tea with a biscuit, or a "chocky bikky." What none of them offered me was a job.

It was time to look outside London. One hour away by train was Brighton, where a repertory company was doing a season at the Dolphin Theatre, including American plays, a different one every week. The Dolphin was next door to the more prestigious Theatre Royal, which was a frequent pre-London stopover for plays on their way to the big time. But the box office did well because its prices were much cheaper, six shillings for the best seats and only one and six to sit in the upper circle.

I auditioned in London for director Stella Linden. I got the sense that she was more interested in my company offstage than as an actor onstage, but a job is a job. The play we were to do was an old American farce, *Separate Rooms*. My role was the leading one, but in reality I was more or less a straight man to the second banana, the actor playing my sardonic older brother, who got the funny lines while I got the girl.

Next week's play was Terrence Rattigan's West End hit *While the Sun Shines*, a comedy about love and life among wartime airmen. The lead was Ronald Howard, son of the immortal Leslie, and a thoroughly decent bloke.

At one point in the play, my assignment was to leap across the stage clad only in a towel. I decided I should douse my bone-white body in top-to-toe tan-like makeup. Opening night as I dashed past Ronnie in my new hue, I heard him singing a tune that was popular at the moment, "Orange Coloured Sky." Except that he had changed the lyric to "Orange Coloured Guy."

43: GRACIE AND ORSON

Bernie Braden came to my rescue again and got me a job that would allow me to stay in London and out of carnal trouble. He had been signed as scriptwriter for a radio series with Gracie Fields. This was for Radio Luxembourg and was produced by Harry Allan Towers. His firm, Towers of London, was not associated with BBC but produced several series of sponsored strictly commercial radio shows broadcast from a pirate station somewhere off the coast. The actual shows were done in a London studio.

Gracie Fields lived on the Isle of Capri but was persuaded to come to London and record a twenty-six-week radio series that would be done in a month. This was how Towers worked. The pay for his stars must have been good, because he also hired Orson Welles to narrate a series of classics like *Dr. Jekyll and Mr. Hyde*, both played by Laurence Olivier.

Bernie introduced me to Gracie, the Lancashire lass who had been adored by millions. She was one of the sweetest but also one of the saddest celebrities I have ever met. I got the feeling she would far rather be back home on Capri with her new husband, an ex-garage mechanic, than being what Harry Towers described her: "An idol in the hearts of millions."

My first assignment was writing a Seventeenth of March Irish show. Orson Welles had showed his displeasure at some of the narrations he had to deliver. Harry hired me to rewrite them. I used to bring Orson my efforts while he was lunching in true Rabelaisian style at a Piccadilly restaurant. Between bites he never asked for rewrites, but I'm sure the genius ad libbed my changes later to his own satisfaction. As a conversation icebreaker, I told him about the time I had met him backstage at his *Lear*, and he roared with glee at the memory of that production. He was eating an enormous meal but he never invited me to partake of any of it.

Suddenly an acting job in London appeared for me, this time from my Canadian connection. Andrew Allan, dean of our country's radio directors, had come to London to be with his fiancée, Dianne Foster, who was due to appear in an Agatha Christie whodunnit at the Fortune Theatre. But my job wasn't a theatre one. The BBC considered Andrew one of the top directors of radio drama, and they asked him to do a drama series while he was in town.

I was hired for one of the episodes, starring Ralph Richardson. What a thrill! He was the other linchpin to Laurence Olivier's tenure at the Old Vic, with unforgettable performances as Falstaff and Peer Gynt, which I had unfortunately never seen. I was thrilled to be in the same room with him, much less share a microphone.

Sir Rafe, as everybody called him, seemed incredibly ill at ease when we started rehearsals. He fumbled and fluffed almost every line on the first read-through, and we weren't even on mike as yet. I was astonished at this seeming attack of nerves and assumed it would disappear when he got in front of a microphone.

It didn't — if anything it got worse. I was used to live radio, not the pre-recorded technique we were using, but thank heaven this enterprise wasn't live. The rest of the cast waited patiently while Sir Rafe's long speeches were taped over and over again. The only emotion both in the studio and the control room was overwhelming sympathy for a great actor in an unfamiliar situation. A couple of weeks later I took Gloria to the theatre to see Ralph in J.B. Priestley's *An Inspector Calls*. He was utterly magnificent in rendering a flawless performance.

Gracie Fields went back to Capri and Orson Welles went God-knows-where. I was temporarily "at leisure," but again I was rescued from rank poverty by Bernie.

His new radio series, *Bedtime with Braden*, was even more successful than the previous one, *Breakfast with Braden*. That one used the talents of the most successful team of comedy writers at the BBC, Frank Muir and Denis Norden. That's probably why Bernie took advantage of the presence in England of the man I considered the best Canadian humorist since Stephen Leacock: Eric Nicol.

Bernie proposed that I join this distinguished pantheon of comic masters as a junior writer. I couldn't believe my luck. My job was to contribute five minutes each week of a half-hour radio show, and the money was better than acting in repertory in Brighton.

I was invited to an introductory script session with the other writers. But after that I would be on my own, sending my five-minute contribution in each week. I had never met the writing team of Norden and Muir, and the first surprise I got was watching them arrive for the conference. They both drove up in tiny sports cars and proceeded to unwind their six-foot-four frames from within the confines of that limited space. I don't remember either of them using that situation as material for their comedy.

44: TAKING THE VEIL

My agent, Olive Harding, sent me to audition for a play entitled *The Seventh Veil*. I had known it as a film, and a highly successful one. The most memorable moment was when James Mason, as the guardian of a schoolgirl with ambitions of becoming a concert pianist, played by Ann Todd, suddenly and viciously beats the girl across her hands and arms with his walking stick while shouting "If you won't play for me, you shan't play for anyone else!"

Now it was to be seen onstage. Todd was repeating her screen role but without Mason as her tormenter. He had decamped for Hollywood, and a couple of years after that, he joined Canadian actors onstage for the second season of the Stratford Festival. An important role was Todd's psychiatrist, played by Czech actor Herbert Lom, and he agreed to repeat his performance onstage.

Ann is taught to dance the waltz by a young American who functions as a kind of first love. That's the part for which I auditioned. It was at the Prince's Theatre, a huge venue which the management felt could be easily filled by the lustre of a beautiful film star.

I stood onstage with the prompter and read a love scene. I heard some vague whispering out there in the darkened theatre and then a crisp "Thankyew" from director Michael MacOwan. I was back on the street wondering where my next job was coming from. By the time I got back to our warm little apartment, Gloria was jumping up and down. I had won the part and rehearsals started the following week.

Ann Todd was delivered to the stage door in a Rolls-Royce driven by her husband David Lean. For some reason, I expected our star to be rather cool and distant, but she turned out to be warm and sunny, and incidentally, the most beautiful woman I had ever seen.

My character in this play was a trumpet player. Fortunately, I never had to play the damn thing, but I was supposed to teach her how to waltz. She already knew such a thing, but I didn't. My dancing credits were limited to a slow foxtrot while placing my lips on the forehead of my dance partner. Three mornings a week, director MacOwan arranged for me to be led around a studio floor in three-quarter time by a hearty, no-nonsense lady who trotted me about like a Lipizzaner stallion on a short rein.

Other than that, rehearsals were fun and went well. Everyone seemed to get along, and MacOwan made us all feel like a happy family. Out-of-town opening was in Brighton next door to the Dolphin at the Theatre Royal. The management put us all up in a hotel.

Don with Ann Todd in The Seventh Veil, *1951.*

David Lean turned up for our out-of-town opening, along with an actor who had played the small part of Herbert Pocket in Lean's brilliant adaptation of *Great Expectations*. I was able to congratulate the actor on his success in that role, and he seemed genuinely surprised that I had noticed his performance. His name was Alec Guinness.

Our next stop was the cavernous Manchester Opera House. No microphones in those days, so we upped the volume of our dialogue. The audience received us warmly, but nothing like the mob scene at the stage door after the performance.

I was so tired, I went to bed hungry and found my way to my digs. It was late at night, and no food was available, so I went straight to bed and got up early to assuage my gut. In the boarding-house dining room, the table was set for eight, with nary a soul in sight. A little man, and I do mean little — he was not much more than three feet — came and sat down beside me. I asked him when breakfast was going to be served. He pointed to a sideboard behind me loaded with food, all of it I found out later was luke-cold.

While I helped myself to room-temperature scrambled eggs and cold toast, the room began to fill up with other guests, three or four more, all of them male and none of them higher than the first entrant. For someone who cannot claim to be five foot ten, I was suddenly a giant among men. It didn't give me any great satisfaction. I just remained puzzled by this whole occurrence until I made my way back to the theatre on a tram and passed a billboard which explained everything. It said in big letters: NOW PLAYING AT THE HIPPODROME: SNOW WHITE AND THE SEVEN DWARFS!

45: ANOTHER OPENING NIGHT

Back in London, our premiere at the Prince's Theatre was a glittering affair, with an entire audience shouting "Welcome back!" when Ann Todd made her entrance. The critical response was more tepid, especially regarding Leo Genn in his ability to replace the sadistic intensity of James Mason.

So the play closed a bit sooner than expected, but perhaps it was all for the best, because I was able to get a cab to take Gloria to the hospital after her water-bag burst. Instead of the skittish female she could be, at this point she had the calm grandeur of Mother Earth.

We had a dinner guest that evening, Andrew Allan. Gloria had prepared a cheese soufflé, and before I got us both into that cab, she gave Andrew explicit instructions on when to take it out of the oven. As I saw her disappear into the obstetrics wing at Paddington St. Mary's Hospital, her last thoughts were again about the damn soufflé. But Andrew had taken direction well. By the time I got back, he was eating it.

I went back to the hospital next day to await the event but found that I already had a baby girl! I was allowed in to see her before I took flowers to her mother. The baby had a thatch of black hair and a brown complexion, all of which seemed to disappear in a week or so, and I had a blonde baby with pink cheeks.

Gloria said we must call her Martha, after her mother, and I said what about a second name? Gloria said she couldn't decide right away. But wonderful Ann Todd had agreed to be godmother and showered our baby with gifts, so Ann became little Martha's second name. We got a personal visit from Ann to see the baby named after her. Along with her came David Lean, but it wasn't just to see our baby. He had liked my performance in *The Seventh Veil*.

He asked if I would appears in his next film, *Breaking Through the Sound Barrier*. Ann's father would be played by Sir Ralph Richardson.

I hesitated, thought it over, and made a decision that shocked Gloria to the core. "Thanks for the offer, Mr. Lean, but I don't think I can sustain an English accent with any authenticity." He smiled, Ann looked a bit rueful, and they left. Gloria was absolutely in shock.

"Do you know what you've done, you idiot! You just turned down a major role with the best film director in the world! Are you out of your mind? You've always been good with accents!"

Another overseas visitor was drama critic Herbert Whittaker, who gave me a report on *Spring Thaw '51*. Great success, but not as good as last year, was the consensus. Herb told me he was off to Stratford-upon-Avon to see some Shakespeare. The theatre at Shakespeare's birthplace had chosen to do *Henry IV, Part 1* and *Part 2*, with Richard Burton as Prince Hal, Michael Redgrave as Hotspur, and Anthony Quayle as Falstaff. The stage had been re-designed for these productions by Tanya Moiseiwitsch. It looked like the Globe Theatre of Shakespeare's day and was a harbinger for what Tanya would do for Stratford, Ontario, ten years later.

Quayle did the standard Falstaff, but Redgrave did a Northumberland accent which was historically correct but resulted in him spraying the stage with his spittle. The performance that stayed in my mind was the quiet authority of Burton's Prince Hal.

There was a Montreal actor in the company, Leo Ciceri, so Herbert took me backstage to meet him. He played Pistol, one of Prince Hal's low-life companions, and understudied Burton.

All the way back to London on the train I thought about the fun I had had playing that Bastard in *King Lear*. I determined to get back to Shakespeare somehow, standing with one leg placed in front of the other and speaking in iambic pentameter. I knew that it probably wouldn't happen in England. I had already turned down the role of an Englishman in a film.

46: LEAN TIMES

I got a call from Lean's production office offering me the part of an air transport command pilot in one scene of *Breaking Through the Sound Barrier*. The scene was about four minutes long, and the pilot was either Canadian or American, so I felt up to it.

I was given a dressing room at Shepperton Studios next to the great man himself, Ralph Richardson. There was a Harley-Davidson parked outside his dressing room and from within the room came the most godawful screeching sounds. It seems he had decided to increase the range of his considerable accomplishments with two things he had never before tried: motorbike riding and violin playing. I hoped his motorcycle would make less noise than his damn violin.

I was told in the makeup room that Sir Rafe swooped in every morning on his charger dressed like a Hells Angel. He was playing Sir Geoffrey de Havilland, pioneer inventor of jet flight, so I supposed he felt this was a close approximation for the demands of the role.

When I was ushered into the studio itself, there was Nigel Patrick, who played Ann's husband in the film, and a cameraman, a lighting man, plus the great director himself.

"Hello, Donald, old boy. Know your lines yet?"

"Yes, Mr. Lean."

"It's David, dear heart. Feeling a bit chilly?"

"No." Actually, I was trembling like a leaf. Nerves.

"A bit nervy perhaps. Just to relax ourselves, let's just say the lines once or twice. Old Nige here has just remembered today is matinee day, and he has to bugger off to London in about an hour. So first let's just go over the dear old lines the same way you must have done them this morning in your bedroom."

Nigel grinned at me. "And if you forget the bloody words, just make 'em up. I always do."

I felt more relaxed now, so we ran through the entire scene, and I felt surprisingly relaxed as I waited eagerly for the first take.

"Now that was just splendid, Donald. As I knew it would be," Lean then said. "In fact, I had my camera running all the time you were talking, and I'm sure it's going to look just right in the dailies. So, dear boy, there's no reason why you can't go on home right now to that wonderful baby. I'm sure old Nige will give you a lift."

Once again I had a lesson in acting from a master of the craft.

Less is more.

47: BACK TO THE BOARDS

The Arts Theatre just off Leicester Square was London's equivalent of off-Broadway. When George Bernard Shaw died in 1950, the Arts put on a display of every one-act play he ever wrote. I attended several of them, including some I never knew existed. It saddens me to hear that the festival in his name in Canada is cutting down on the Shavian experience. Perhaps instead of Shaw's longer socialist sermons, they should revive his perky one-acters.

It was also the theatre that introduced a young Cockney actor named Maurice Micklewhite in an experimental comedy entitled *Next Time I'll Sing to You*. I saw his authentic Cockney performance. Next time he appeared onstage, he had changed his name to Michael Caine.

The Arts put on a new play contest. The judges were to be Alec Clunes, Peter Ustinov, and Christopher Fry. Fry was the current London sensation, and his poetic verse style was considered to be the modern successor to the mantle of Shakespeare. He had a play earlier at the Arts, *The Lady's Not for Burning*, which soon transferred to a major West End theatre and ended up on Broadway.

I was in one of the winning new plays, *Poor Judas* by Enid Bagnold, better known to her aristocratic neighbours in Brighton as Lady Jones. I auditioned for the director, Roy Rich, and won the part of a young officer in the Royal Canadian Engineers. I was not happy about any of my dialogue, which sounded to me much more upper-crust English.

Lady Jones came to rehearsal and took me to lunch. I found her a delightful combination of two Ediths: Evans and Sitwell. She asked me why I was upset about her dialogue. I told her that my character in the play never sounded like any Canadian I had met.

"But I knew the young man quite well. He was billetted with me during the war, one of the most fascinating, articulate creatures I had ever met. Died after D-Day, unfortunately."

"What was his name, Lady Jones?"

"His name was Sanderson, Captain Graham Sanderson."

I almost choked on my turbot. "I knew him, Lady Jones! He was my commanding officer in the COTC."

"The CO what?"

"It doesn't matter, Lady Jones, but you're absolutely right, Captain Sanderson was everything you say he was."

I tried to change my dialogue to the way I thought Captain Graham would have said it.

The lead actor was Robert Harris, known among actors as the poor man's John Gielgud. He had the same mellifluous voice but none of Gielgud's commercial success. But the performance that stole the show was a brief one (one scene) by the legendary Irish actress Maire O'Neill, one of the founders and mainstays of Dublin's Abbey Theatre. She was the actress who had created at the turn of this century the role of Pegeen Mike, the heroine of *The Playboy of the Western World*.

Almost eighty now, she shuffled onstage, and without even trying, wiped out the rest of us standing there. A less charitable person might have said that she knocked us all out with the gin on her breath, but it had nothing to do with her superb artistry. I told her about my own involvement with that play, and she described the rehearsal period which ended up with herself and Synge falling in love. I was sure some of my favourite lines came directly from that relationship.

During the run we got the terrible news that there was a disastrous fire at the Abbey Theatre. To Maire O'Neill it was like the loss of her own child. After the show that night, Maire and I went to a nearby pub to drink the night away ... me, ginger beer and her, something stronger. She did all the talking, and she told me how she had learned the lines of *The Playboy* directly from the author.

I asked her if she still remembered those lines. "Ach! Wun er two mebby." I recalled my favourite lines that Christy says to Pegeen Mike: "And we'll be astray in Erris, gamin' in a gap of sunshine, with yourself stretched back unto your necklace in the flowers of the earth, and makin' mighty kisses with our wetted mouths til I'd feel a kind of pity for the Lord God is sittin' lonesome in his golden chair!"

Maire looked at me with a twinkle and quoted the next line. "I'd be nice so, is it?" Then we might not have been word-perfect, but the rest of the scene seemed to flow effortlessly between us. We laughed and cried some more and drank a final toast to the dear old Abbey and another one to the memory of John Millington Synge.

48: A FIRE AND A FRY

There was another fire, this time in the Arts Theatre where I had just played *Poor Judas*. It happened the night after we closed the play, and lots of actors volunteered to come in and help salvage what was left. It felt as if London's wartime spirit hadn't left as we all chipped, sanded, and scrubbed away at the charred remains. It made me wonder if Canadian actors would have gathered round in the same manner.

One day, coming home from this task, Gloria told me I had a phone call from Christopher Fry. I wondered what he wanted with me. I soon found out.

"Hello, Mr. Harron, this is Kit Fry. Have you by any chance seen my play *A Sleep of Prisoners*?" I confessed I hadn't. "There'll be a ticket for you tonight. Do come along and have a peek, and tell me if you're interested in the part of Peter Able."

I went. It was playing in a bombed-out church off Piccadilly Circus on Lower Regent Street. The play itself was a kind of dramatic string quartet for four actors playing soldiers who are captured by the enemy in some war of the future. Locked up in a ruined church for the night, each one dreams a fitful dream drawn from Old Testament stories.

I saw the author after the play, plus the director, who turned out to be Michael MacOwan, who had been so pleasant to work with on *The Seventh Veil*. They had both seen me in *Poor Judas* and told me the part of Peter Able was mine for the asking. No audition necessary. I told them to count me in.

I was still puzzled about why I was chosen when Denholm Elliott had been so dazzling in the role. Turns out that Denholm was set to play Ann Todd's brother in the film role that I had turned down. But I knew that London actors regularly mixed film and theatre jobs. Denholm had to leave the cast because the play was going to New York!

When I eventually saw the *Sound Barrier* film, I was touched by Elliott's performance as he crashed to his death, desperately trying to please his father by becoming a pilot, even though he always got airsick. I thought, *I was certainly qualified in* that *department*! Both Fry and MacOwan had seen me in relatively undemanding roles, a fraction of what would be required of me as Peter Able. I had a big job to do.

While I was leaving for New York, Gloria and the baby and the good doctor, her father, would be heading for Gravenhurst. Before we left, there was time for an orgy of theatre-going, and we wanted Doc Fisher along. It turns out I found a good babysitter in Norman Jewison. He had come over to London to try his luck and had found a nice job writing comedy for a BBC-TV series, *Starlight Hour*. My old Vic-Bobber came to babysit whenever we asked and never wanted a shilling in compensation!

Lena Horne was in town, so I went to the legendary Palladium to see her. To open her act she hired Bernard Miles, who I remembered as a wonderful film actor specializing in characterizations of the lower classes.

Miles came onstage at the Palladium wearing a kind of billowing smock and a floppy hat, a typical English farmer. He was pushing a wagon wheel that looked as if it was covered with pigeon droppings, and in a Wessex accent he said, "Oim gunna take ee 'ome and mike a ladder outen it." The audience fell apart.

The constant laughter reminded me of the sage advice Jane Mallett had once given me. I had been a year and a half in London, and it made me more aware of being Canadian than had the past quarter century in Canada. It wasn't just the fact that I was surrounded by the English speaking in a rash of funny dialects. It was the Canadian visitors and even long-time Canuck residents in London I met who made me realize that my own countrymen spoke in a way that was just as amusing.

I used to go often to Canada House in Trafalgar Square to read copies of the *Globe and Mail,* and there I would meet all kinds of Canadians. A lot of them were like the kind of person I had worked with in my farm days, and when they spoke it was often with a mouth held tighter than a sphincter. "Superfine Binder Twine Number Nine!" These, I kept reminding myself, were *my* people.

That English performer at the Palladium opened my mind to the comic possibilities of a rural Canadian accent. Someday I hoped to win that same amount of laughter.

On our last night in London the three of us, Doc, Mom, and Pop, left the baby again with Saint Norman and went off to the opening of the Old Vic's '51–'52 season. The play was *Tamburlaine* by Christopher Marlowe, very rarely done in the past 400 years, and it brought back to the Vic one of its most dynamic former wartime tenants, Tyrone Guthrie.

The play is a Grand Guignol of conquest and violence. We watched three hours of butchery and mayhem, culminating in Tamburlaine the Conqueror's "ride in triumph through Persepolis" as his opponent-king, played by Leo McKern, dashed his brains out against the bars of his cage. Thumbing his nose at the theatrical establishment, Guthrie had chosen to play the title role the most unfashionable, old-fashionable "ham" actor in all of England, Donald Wolfit, wearing a ghostly, almost Kabuki-like white painted face.

Guthrie was the real star of the evening as far as I was concerned. At one point actor Lee Montague was shackled and strung up high in the flies onstage left. Onstage right, a group of actors drew their longbows and took aim. There was a whoosh of sound and instantly their high-flying victim was full of arrows. There were no arrows from the longbows. I don't know who or what made that whooshing sound, but those arrows suddenly appeared because they were hidden in the folds of his costume!

Although Broadway-bound, I wanted some day to come back to England and work for Tyrone Guthrie.

49: GOING TO CHURCH

Our New York venue for *A Sleep of Prisoners* was St. James Episcopal Church at Madison Avenue and 71st Street, a ritzy part of town. It looked for all the world like a Gothic cathedral. I said to our director, "My God, Michael, you would never put prisoners of war in a place like this!" St. Thomas's in London was a small Romanesque building, a little parish church that had suffered bomb damage during the Blitz. The only thing the two edifices had in common was that they were both churches.

Michael was too busy checking the acoustics under the high-vaulting nave. From just below the pulpit he started reciting lines from the play. I was halfway back and couldn't make out a thing he was saying. The pulpit had a microphone, but none of our action took place there. Michael said we couldn't use microphones because the wires would truss us up like turkeys, tripping us over power cords when we needed to be loose for the fight scenes.

Lucille Lortel and Luther Greene appeared. She is gone now, but her name remains on one of the most successful off-Broadway theatres in Greenwich Village. These were the producers who had booked us into this grand venue, and from the ecstatic looks on their faces, they were convinced we had brought them a sure-fire hit. Christopher Fry was box-office gold after the New York success of *The Lady's Not for Burning*.

Both producers were more concerned about our play as a social event than about the sound. When Michael suggested we needed to move the venue because of the acoustics, both protested that we would never get the carriage trade if we moved downtown. We were stuck with this inaudible ausable chasm.

My first task was to learn the many fight sequences. The British cast seemed to light into this with enthusiasm, since mine was the character who usually got beaten up. First Leonard White as Cain slugged me as Abel, then I got slaughtered as Isaac, and Stanley Baker made a hari-kari mess out of me as Absalom. After that it was actually a relief to simply walk through a fiery furnace.

Our lighting expert and the sound man were working feverishly to turn this mock-cathedral into a workable theatre. In the meantime we actors shouted our way through rehearsals. The play was full of animal cries expressing Old Testament passions, especially when we were dancing in the fiery furnace. Those cries sounded great as they bounced off the walls. When it came to the dialogue, the magic of Kit Fry's verse was lost in the Gothic rafters.

One thing our dilettantish producers were good at was getting publicity. One day the celebrated *Life* magazine photographer Eugene Smith showed up at a rehearsal. His photo session went on for eight hours, but he was so enthused that we didn't mind taking the time. The proofs were so good, Smith thought it was possible we could end up on the cover of America's most famous picture magazine. That would seal the success of a national tour, whatever the reviews.

Our opening was on a Monday, and on Sunday in the drama section of the *New York Times* was a wonderful cartoon of the four of us by the elegant caricaturist Harry Hirschfeld. The two previews went amazingly well, possibly because we were playing to a small number of people, all of them sitting down front. Most of Broadway's British contingent was part of that audience, and they all seemed to appear backstage to wish us well.

I wish I could remember the opening night performance, but it remains a blur. Even though technically the opening was off-Broadway, thirty blocks from the theatre section, our cast did the traditional pilgrimage down to Sardi's restaurant on 44th Street to await the newspaper reviews. They weren't good. I think the critics were looking for the frothy wordplay and sexual byplay of *The Lady's Not for Burning* instead of this grim, muscular retelling of tales from the Old Testament.

All of them, however, praised the actors to the skies. *The New Yorker* critic Wolcott Gibbs described the cries of anguish we all made as comparable to the sounds that came from the throat of Laurence Olivier as Oedipus Rex when he discovers he is married to his own mother.

Eugene's wonderful photograph of me as Absalom did not make the cover of *Life* magazine. Instead that particular issue displayed a full colour image of Ginger Rogers, who had arrived in town with a new play that lasted only a few days. There was, however, within the same issue, a glorious four-page display of our production. Thanks to Eugene Smith and *Life*, our producers received offers to present our play in churches all over the United States.

Which was just as well, because we only ran for five weeks in New York. So we set off to tour the country. First stop was the Rockefeller Chapel at the University of Chicago. Unfortunately, it gave us much the same problem as our New York venue ... vaulted ceilings and vague acoustics. Next was a synagogue in the same city, Temple Sholom. The acoustics were better, the reception was much more sympathetic, and I was invited to give an address in the temple on the sabbath, Saturday.

I realized I was in a play about the Old Testament that had to be explained to most of the audience afterwards. Mind you, the farther we got from Broadway the more understanding we got from audiences. We performed in non-conformist chapels, flat-roofed wooden structures that provided us with the proper acoustics.

Always the local minister would approach us before we went on and took a moment to bless our endeavours. The English actors got a little fed up with this and took to spending their after-show hours on a project new to all of them: burlesque strippers. The habit started in Chicago when they went to Minsky's and saw a toothsome number named Ricky Ginger Jones. After that it was a compulsory late-night tour of other city venues starring Cupcakes Cassidy, Princess Domai, and even legendary ecdysiasts like Ann Corio. I remember being dragged by my Brits to an amateur strip show in Ohio featuring well-past-middle-age ladies, who my fellow actors felt bumped and ground with the best of them.

The tour lasted four months, and at one point, in Washington, Gloria joined and brought our Muffin with her. Somehow the little one got a case of measles and the pair had to be shipped home pronto. Before they left, Gloria let me know that being the wife of an itinerant actor was not a life she would choose, and she hoped that I would consider becoming a writer rather than an actor.

I did not take kindly to that thought, but she had a point. The fights I had to go through every night were usually on stone floors, which played hell with one of my knees as it was slammed down hard every performance. Eventually I developed a condition called "water on the knee" and had to get medical attention before it threatened to derail my career.

I had spent all my time onstage (and off, now that I think of it) being British. To keep my accent consistent, I applied it offstage, as well. The Brits and I ended the tour as good pals, and Leonard White became a life-long friend. I visited his south coast home near Brighton several times. But before that, as our American tour was ending, Gloria rejoined me in New York for a bout of theatre, and we stayed in a cheap hotel on 42nd Street off Times Square. Cheap! It cost eighty-five bucks for the whole week, and if you were smart you didn't let your bare feet touch that floor. Despite the lack of sanitation, I think that's where the next little Harron was created.

50: GOING HOME

I'd been away two years, and there were changes. The New Play Society was known mainly now for its annual *Spring Thaw*, the run of which seemed to get longer and longer every year. Eventually, it eclipsed the Society itself by becoming a year-round event with a national tour.

Sharing the museum venue with Mavor and Dame Dora was a new venture, Jupiter Theatre. When I arrived on the scene, they were staging *Socrates*, a play by Lister Sinclair. I had done the radio version three years before. On radio I had played the juicy, showy part of Alcibiades, the sophisticated and inebriated playboy of Athens, but now it was under-taken by a young actor from Montreal, Christopher Plummer. When I finally got in to see the play, I was dazzled by what this Plummer kid had done with my old part.

Soon after that we both met on the *Stage 52* radio series, where we were cast in an obscure Restoration comedy, *The Man of Mode*. Frank Perry was in it, too, and both of us played the usual juvenile roles. But the title role of the rake was played by the newcomer, Plummer, and though he was younger, the richness of his voice exuded an air of maturity. Clearly this actor was no threat to our juvenile careers, because he was a full-fledged leading man. And a charmer off-mike and on, because before I knew it he had borrowed twenty bucks from me with a cheery "till next time."

The insecurity I felt around this new major talent made me make one of the worst decisions I ever engineered. The New Play Society welcomed me back with open arms and offered me the role of Captain Bluntschli in their production of Shaw's *Arms and the Man*. It's a good part, full of down-to-earth common sense and warm humour, compared to the blustering and posturing antics of the other leading character, Sergius.

I decided to hell with common sense, I wanted to make a splash in a part Chris Plummer would have made his own. But he wasn't playing it, thank God, so I suggested to Dora that Bob Christie and I change parts. She looked extremely puzzled, but good-natured Bob, the one who had saved my directorial butt during *Riel*, shrugged, smiled, and agreed.

The whole thing should have been a comic romp. It wasn't. I gave one of the worst performances of my career, and the reviewers agreed. Chris Plummer would have been sensational.

Soon after that debacle, I was stunned to find that the rival Jupiter Theatre wanted to hire me to co-star with Lorne Greene and British guest star Honor Blackman in Sartre's *Les Mains Sales*, translated as *Crime of Passion*. I couldn't believe my luck. Honor Blackman was a Bond girl, correction: *the* Bond girl (Pussy Galore), who had married a Canadian and was spending time in Toronto. I was to spend my time onstage being cuckolded by her, and because of it, assassinating Lorne Greene. What bliss!

Rehearsals were a delight because of her, and the Voice of Canada, Lorne, approached this role as a student learning his stagecraft again after all those years in radio. I hated the thought of assassinating such a thoroughly nice guy. There were only the three of us, and it was a happy experience.

Spring Thaw '52 was approaching. Mavor Moore took me to lunch and told me he wanted to star me in that year's edition. He said, "You've been away in England, Herb Whittaker has kept tabs on you with fond mentions of your progress, and you've just come back from Broadway. That spells stardom in this town, and that's what you'll be to *Spring Thaw*'s box office."

"But, Mavor, I can't sing or dance !"

"Oh, God, don't I know it. But we need you to write sketches, and perhaps you can do a monologue of your own!"

"About what?"

"Anything. As long as it's Canadian."

51: BIRTH OF A NOTION

Spring Thaw '51 had been a solid success, despite the inevitable remark by Nathan Cohen: "It's not as good as last year." The 1952 edition looked promising with the original '48ers returning: Jane Mallett, Connie Vernon, Peter Mews, and Pegi Brown. I agreed to contribute five sketches and to think about a monologue.

A welcome addition to the cast was Norman Jewison, who had come back from England to prepare for the advent of television. He wanted to direct, but he was still making a living as an actor. Before I arrived back on the scene, he had a hit acting in Jupiter Theatre's production of a Dalton Trumbo play. Normie also volunteered to write material for our show and anticipated his future film *Rollerball* with a takeoff on game shows entitled "Boggolo!"

The longest sketch I wrote for that year's edition was "Hollywood! And Fine!" It featured Jane Mallett as an aging Gloria Swanson–like film star, Crystal Stutz, who was being replaced in a big-budget movie by an Italian actress named Edna, who turns out to be a big brown bear.

But the biggest hit of the show was a musical number written by Cliff Braggins, "The R.M.C." It was sung by a quartet that included Connie Vernon and Peter Mews. It was about the Royal Military College in Kingston, and it opened the second half with a bang, so much so that the audience demanded an encore as soon as it had finished. I have never seen this happen before or since.

My own monologue was tucked away in the middle of the first half of the show. I wore my father's old blue serge suit, which was too short in the leg for me, just like many of the actual farmers that I had seen visiting the Canadian National Exhibition. They seemed to have a deep sunburn on their neck and forearms (farmer's tan), but the forehead remained bleached white because of the cap they always wore to shield their eyes.

I remembered as a child seeing those shy men with sunburned necks and pale white foreheads wandering around the Horse Palace and the Coliseum. It seemed to me, even at an early age, that they were what the Exhibition was really about. It was at heart an agricultural fair. So I did my best to re-create that feeling.

My farmer came onstage wearing a Lowney Young Canada Indian headdress because he had made a purchase in the Pure Food Building. He pondered whether to spend the rest of his meagre money on the freak shows on the midway, or the grandstand spectacle that evening.

The audience didn't know what to expect when they first saw me come onstage, but when I opened my mouth to speak, there was what the critic Edmund Wilson called "the shock of recognition." Because everyone in that audience at some time or other must have met or overheard such a man.

I had no name for my rural character, and the only name used in the monologue, "Charlie Farquharson," did not belong to the farmer I was portraying. But his name, which I stole from the head of the Ontario Medical Association, seemed much more appropriate than Harry Shorthorn. After *Thaw* finished, I started to use the name whenever I appeared.

Perhaps I should let you in on the entire four-minute delivery of the birth of the character that shares this book.

I spose this here's yer fountain Charlie Farquharson told me about. It's the only water fountain I seen so far. The rest has all bin soady.

Say, pardon me there, Billy, wood yiz have the right time? Haff past two? Oh my gol, I've only got twenty-five after one! But I spose yers is on city time?

Beg pardon? No, I'm not frum Trawntuh. Jist cum down fer the day to see th'Ex.

Wisht I'd brung the hole famly fer to see that big show they have over to yer grand stand. It'd be awful eddicational. My oldest boy, he's fourteen and a half and he's never yet seen a live American.

Mysalf, I don't git down every year. Last time I wuz over to that Poor Fud bilding evrybuddy wuz shoutin' "six bars a hat and a bag all fer twenny fie sents!" This year it seems to be 75 sents and bring yer own bag!

She sure is a scorcher over to that poor fud place. Mind you, it ain't the heet that duz it, it's yer humanity. She's not neer so crowded over to yer hores palace. That's nex to that other aminal bilding they calls yer colossalinoleum.

Taint all that much fun in yer horse palace walkin' up and down all them rows of stalls. I'll be kinda glad to git back home and see the front end of a horse fer a change.

I wuz over to yer auty-o-motives bildin fer to look at sum of them liddle Yerpeen cars. They have yer steerin' doofus on the gee side stead of the haw, ya see. I bleeve they do that becuz yer Anglishman's wife duz all the drivin'.

Oh my gosh, talkin' bout drivers, hav yiz tride that fool of a ride down yer middle-way called yer auto-scooter wirl? They hav these here tiny cars about this high. They'd be Anglish I spose. Wellsir, you pays yer dime fer to git in them, and th'idee is fer to ram it into the tuther fella's car jist as hard as yiz kin go and evrybuddy hoots and hollers fer to beet the band. Don't understand why them Trontuh peeples lines up fer to pay ther dimes fer that. Accorn to the papers they do the same fool thing down town evry day of the week!

Don't tell nobuddy, but I heer ther havin' troubles with the financys of these here exhibitionists. I know one of them offishuls persnally, do yuh see. You probly herd of him ... Charlie Farquharson. He's the assistant conveener in charge of the semmy-fine-alls fer yer hores shoe pitchin'.

You never heard of him? Well, isn't that a coincidence! I know fer a fact that Charlie, he's honest. Don't know the meenin' of the word crooked. Minejew, ther's a lot of other words Charlie he don't know the meenin of eyether.

But say, you has to watch sum of them jaspers down that middleway! Oh, arnt they the fancy talkers them Jimmy Didoes! I take everything they say with a dose a salts.

One side show they had wuz what they called the dubble-headed boy frum Borneo. The hole thing it wuz a fake! Oh, he had the two heads all right, but I don't bleeve he wuz from Borneo atall. Looked more to me like a cuppla fellers I went to school with in Parry Sound.

They had a beerdy lady there too. Well, she had the beard all rite, but fer a woman she wuz gittin' pritty thin on top. My gol. I seen more hair on ten sents wirth a bacon.

The nerve of sum of them peeple down yer middleway! I went and bot sum of that pink stuff that sticks to yer teeth. Wat they calls the dental floss. Smart jacky dandy wat sold it to me tried to gimme my change in American money. I told him. I sed them Americans don't stand fer our nashnul antrum, I don't see why we should stand fer their money. They have a national antrum of ther own down there ... it's called "My Country, Wat's it to Thee?"

But lemme tell yuh, the best show of all on that middleway wuz give by the tattooed woman. Her name is Britannica, yer yuman encyclical-peedieerast. She's well worth yer wiles lemme tell yuh. Eddicational too. She has the grate Alberta train wreck of 1919 tattood rite there on her stummick, and fer 15 sents extry, she'll re-enact the hole incident by moving her abominable mussels.

Gess I better start movin' over to yer bandshell, fer I'm darn sure the bandshell she's not movin' over to me. (horselaff)

Like the old sayin' sez, Billy, if the mounting won't cum to Hamilton I gess Hamilton'll hav to go to yer mounting.

I was still never sure whether the audience laughed at what I said, or simply at the way I said it. But from their response, I had found the mask that Jane told me to adopt, and I was forever grateful to this great comic artist for that advice.

Spring Thaw '52 was the last New Play Society production to play in the Museum Theatre, because it had now become a union-operated venue. Our tenure there had been a strange mixture, live theatre among the mummies, dinosaur skeletons, and totem poles. Hereafter *Spring Thaw* would be homeless, wandering around seeking a temporary lodging to rest its laurels. Actually, its success and continued existence marked the end of the New Play Society as a producer of plays, except for that annual review every spring, and an occasional Christmas pantomime. CBC had been checking out Mavor as a possible head of their new television network.

That autumn of 1952 Dora opened the New Play Society School of the Drama in a small facility near Yonge and Bloor. She was doing what she had always done, encouraging the young to have a passion for the theatre. That was the definition of theatre she always cherished: "two planks and a passion." She never made a dime for herself out of all this. The Winston Churchill of Canadian theatre would survive into her nineties. An annual series of awards for excellence in theatre are still given out each year in her name.

52: TV DAZE

The summer of 1952 involved the acting community of Toronto in a mad scramble to get ready for the advent of television. Radio actors who had made a good living for years started to worry about their future. A recent stage company like Jupiter Theatre suddenly found actors, well-known nationally to radio audiences, lining up to audition for theatre roles. Before this they had ignored the "bare boards" with their undivided attention.

Mavor did get that offer from the CBC and was now in charge of television production. Fledgling directors appeared who had never previously had any connection with TV. Among them was Norman Jewison, who was working his way up rapidly from dolly pusher to variety producer. Also from Vancouver came another Norman, Campbell.

I was involved during the summer when the CBC decided to tape a truncated version of Jupiter's production of *Crime of Passion* with the same theatre cast. Lorne Greene and I were rank virgins, but Honor Blackman had been doing English television for years. I had fun learning to tone down my histrionics, but not so much joy adapting to the technical complexities of camera positions. One inch out and you were offstage.

My *Spring Thaw* farmer appearance also got me a chance to work with a DJ from a Hamilton radio station. I had heard about Gordie Tapp vaguely but had never met him. He was a jolly type and full of self-confidence. We did a dry-run version of his radio show, but it never appeared on subsequent television. That had to wait another seventeen years, when we hooked up on *Hee Haw*.

The biggest surprise in that pre-production period was getting an offer from TV producer Bob Allen to write every other script in a twenty-six week adaptation of Stephen Leacock's classic *Sunshine Sketches of a Little Town*. The lead character, Peter Pupkin, was to be played by an unknown theatre actor, Timothy Findley, who years later told me that my working on scripts turned him from an actor into a full-fledged writer.

The job of hosting the variety show, *The Big Revue* and performing the comedy sketches was divided up among three different groups, alternating every third week. The second week starred the gorgeous singer Phyllis Marshall. CBC was way ahead of the American networks in giving a black performer her own show.

The third team consisted of me as co-host along with Toby Robins. The two of us would also perform a sketch about newlyweds. In addition I was called upon to do a weekly monologue standing beside a rural mailbox in the guise of my new character, Charlie Farquharson.

But first we all had to appear on a preview of the whole season. The opening night of CBC Television started off on the wrong foot. The logo and its call letters came on upside down! The first face to appear on that black-and-white screen was that of a bank robber, Edwin Alonzo Boyd. He had escaped from prison and he and his gang had knocked off three banks that same day. This was followed by speeches from various Ottawa bureaucrats and songs from Royal Conservatory opera singers. I was introduced among a gaggle of other performers making their maiden voyage.

I was in my own suit, not my father's, and along with the others I was supposed to say something about the new season. Instead I decided to be topical. When called upon to speak, in the voice of Charlie Farquharson, I heard myself saying: *I hear tell about sum banks in Trontuh got rob today by outside parties.* (Pause.) *Makes a change!* This provoked such a weird reaction from the official party that MC Drew Crossan explained I was quoting from a character I had created who would appear on *The Big Revue*.

The next day I started rehearsing a ninety-minute drama for a television series entitled *General Motors Theatre*. The play was John Galsworthy's *Justice*, and I played the young man who is falsely accused of theft and jumps out of a window to his death rather than serve an unjust jail sentence. When Herbert Whittaker reviewed this he said that TV was my medium, implying that my face was perhaps too small for the stage! The CBC response was so positive that I ended up being in a *General Motors Theatre* drama about every third week of the season.

Next came my debut on *The Big Revue*, and I was concerned about what my Charlie should wear hanging around that rural mailbox. I knew what he *should* wear: the peak cap and grey rolltop sweater I had seen on my Ontario employer, Charles Hadden, and the identical outfit I saw on that Saskatchewan farmer. But I had none of these.

Next door to the studio where we rehearsed was a smaller one that did the weather report. This involved an authentic meteorologist, Percy Saltzman, who became well-known for finishing his report by tossing his piece of chalk in the air, without ever failing to catch it. He made that nightly report to a puppet called Uncle Chichimus who looked an awful lot like Mavor Moore. The puppeteer was John Conway of the New Play Society, and his ambition was to create another puppet, an animal called Mavor Moose. Didn't happen, more's the pity.

I went to that studio during rehearsals because I had seen Norm Jewison leaving the CBC café wearing a battered peak cap. I heard he was the floor manager of the puppet weather show, so I peeked in the little studio next door, and there it was on top of his head. It belonged originally to his father Percy, who used to wear it while "pulling his cukes" at the family cottage at Lefroy, Ontario. I asked Norm, as an old Vic man, if he would mind lending the cap to me until the next day. I was starting to explain why when I noticed the director of the show was wearing a thick grey cardigan with a shawl collar. It looked exactly like the one I had seen on Charles Hadden and my Saskatchewan grumpy farmer!

I asked Normie to introduce me to his director. Norman Campbell was recently from Vancouver, but the sweater was something he had worn during the war as a meteorologist on Nova Scotia's Sable Island. (*Got the wool offa the backs of them ponys, I figger.*)

He was surprisingly cordial for someone engaged in putting on a television show at any minute, and when I asked him if I could borrow that sweater overnight, he whipped it off in no time and proceeded to go on with his light cues. I thanked both Normans profusely and stole out of the studio with my plunder. Stole is the right word, because I never returned either garment. They will be an exhibit in the Canadian Theatre Museum.

I also stole the name of Charlie's wife and former sweetheart, Valeda, from dear Norm Jewison. He had a cousin in Warsaw, Ontario, named Valeda Drain. Many years later, I was sitting offstage, waiting to go on in a P.E.I. theatre to rehearse my act as Charlie Farquharson, when a strange woman came and sat down beside me. She was about my age, with tangerine hair, and she whispered, "I'm your wife and former sweetheart!" It was Valeda Drain.

Dear Norman Campbell has gone to his reward now (no one deserved a reward more), but I plan to make it up to Victoria University's own ex-chancellor, Norman Jewison, by letting him wear the hat and tattered sweater as he plays a Prince Edward Island farmer when we do the film version of our musical, *Anne of Green Gables*. Norm does the Charlie Farquharson accent just as well as me, and I look forward to him dressed like Charlie, saying, "Mail boat didn't make it across? Isn't that a caution ... Mainland's been cut off again!"

Changing the subject, I remember how busy all of us actors were that year, and the problems it could cause. There was so much television work that we began to be invaded by British actors who wanted to join our gold rush. This prompted my *Spring Thaw '49* alumnus Gerry Sarracini to moan "Oh, to be in England, now that England's here!"

In addition to all this employment, there was still radio, with its school broadcasts and soap operas and a new season of one-hour dramas on Andrew Allan's *Stage 52*. Canadian actors have never been as busy before or since. It was not unusual for an actor to be in a radio studio at 8:00 a.m. for rehearsal and do a live broadcast to schools for 10:00 a.m. The actor might then have to hightail it down to the brand-new rehearsal studios on Sumach Street to rehearse a one-hour TV drama. I remember spending all day at home adapting a chapter of *Sunshine Sketches of a Little Town* into a half-hour television script, handing it in to the production office on Jarvis Street, and arriving just in time at the Museum Theatre, a half hour before I would be onstage in *The Lady's Not for Burning*.

In addition to all that TV and radio activity, there remained an active theatre. The rehearsal schedule of *Lady's Not for Burning* began at eleven o'clock at night because there was no other time available due to television and radio commitments. This production starred Christopher Plummer and the Irish beauty Kate Blake.

I was in the cast because I couldn't resist Kit Fry's poetry, playing the clerk Richard, the same part Burton did with Gielgud in London. In one scene my job was to scrub the floor while Chris as Thomas Mendip and Kate as Jennet Jourdemayne had a love scene full of dazzling poetic images. For some inane reason the audience watched me instead, performing this humble task, to the detriment of all that lovely verse. It's the one and only time I was ever able to upstage Chris Plummer. That time I felt like the pet in the love triangle, and as you know, the animal always wins.

One Sunday morning, I forewent all this petty diversion and took a bus to Gravenhurst to see my new daughter, who was born in a Bracebridge hospital. Now the latest Harron was home with her mum and older sister Martha. It was Gloria's turn to name the baby, and she decided to call her by that grand old name, Mary. The combination of the two names sounded quite Biblical, Martha and Mary, the sisters of Bethany. A quick kiss all round and I was back on the bus to Toronto to the endless maelstrom that year.

Lady ran for three weeks at the lovely Hart House Theatre. Now that Patrick Macnee was here, Leonard White suggested we revive *A Sleep of Prisoners* for Easter week. He said he told me he wanted to raise Cain again with my Abel. The reception for us was warm. It was rewarding to bring that particular play to my hometown.

As 1952 ended, I took stock of myself and figured that I had spent most of its days working eighteen hours out of twenty-four. I had done more television shows than any other local actor, appeared onstage in four different plays, and written several scripts and sketches, as well. The result was I finished the year exhausted. I wasn't sure I could keep up such a pace for all of 1953.

As it turned out, I didn't have to.

PART II

Boarding the Bard,
1952 to 1955

53: STRATFORD-on-TARIO

In the summer of 1952, Tyrone Guthrie was at home in Ireland when he got a call from Tom Patterson. Patterson had called earlier that day but the postmistress had said "Nonsense!" to a call from that far away and went off to feed her hens. This almost cancelled the beginning of the world-famous Stratford Shakespearean Festival.

It was just before Christmas 1952 when Guthrie appeared at our Museum Theatre in Toronto to show Tanya Moiseiwitsch's design for a theatre in Stratford that followed closely the Globe Theatre of Shakespeare's day. I went there that evening, along with most of Toronto's arts community. Guthrie displayed a tabletop model of the stage that he and Tanya had planned. It looked familiar to me. I had seen some of it when I went to Stratford-upon-Avon, England, to see Burton as Prince Hal: an open stage, no curtain, and at the rear steps leading up to a balcony. Herb had introduced me to the designer of that set, Tanya Moiseiwitsch.

Here it was again with more of it jutting out into the audience. Guthrie explained: "This open stage is the one on which Shakespeare's plays were performed. But the design goes back much further than his day. The classic theatres of Rome and Greece had open stages like this."

About 1650, that sort of theatre went out of favour, and theatres with proscenium arches and front curtains came in, because of the vogue for opera which spread from Italy all over Europe. There was something new facing the front of the stage: the conductor. It was vital that all the singers see him to "get the beat." It follows that the audience should also be facing the stage, and a great gulf be arranged between them and the performers onstage.

This was partly because of footlights, which before electric lights were naked flames and a perpetual source of danger. There was another reason for this divide. It acted as a social chasm, separating a courtly and aristocratic audience from the socially inferior persons paid to entertain it.

But besides the artifice of opera, another tendency was at work: realism. For more than 300 years it has been the dominant aim of theatrical productions in Europe and America. But it can readily be seen that the living room onstage has no wall, and a thousand people are looking in and overhearing everything!

For about fifty years now the view has been gaining currency that Shakespeare's plays can best be produced in a theatre which at least approximates the kind for which his plays were written, for an auditorium arranged not in *front* of the stage but to a greater or less extent, wrapped *around* the stage. Whatever may be the drawbacks of this open stage, it has, I think, three *distinct* advantages over the proscenium.

The first advantage is artistic. By gathering the audience *around*, rather than spreading it *in front* of the actors, many more people can be close to the actors. Between 1,500 to 2,000 people can be seated around an open stage, none of them more than fifty feet away, and no seat farther than fifteen rows from the front. A proscenium house of equal intimacy could seat barely half that number.

I must admit that an open stage poses acoustic problems. All the actors, for part of the time, have their backs turned to one side or other of the house. When an actor's face cannot be seen, it is inevitably harder to hear what he is saying. The solution lies partly in the skill with which an actor can turn, so that without seeming to fidget, his face is never turned away more than momentarily from any one part of the audience, and partly in the skill with which the face of the listening actor reflects what his colleague is saying — but chiefly in the vocal technique of the speaker.

The open stage does make great demands on the actor's accomplishment, but no greater than is required for the actor to be heard in a large proscenium theatre without sounding noisy and false.

The second advantage of the open stage is economic. Arranging the audience *around* the actors is a better use of the cubic space of the auditorium — larger capacity means larger takings.

The third advantage is philosophic and may seem to some people to be no advantage, but a drawback. People sitting around an open stage cannot but be aware of other people doing likewise on the opposite side of the house. Behind and beyond the lighted stage you can descry, however dimly, other members of the audience. If you allow your attention to wander, you may even recognize them. But this is only if you let your attention wander. And even in a proscenium house, you'll get some pretty irrelevant and incongruous impressions. But, you may say, the mere fact of people in the background, spectators all around the castle of Elsinore or whatever it may be, is destructive of illusion.

Granted. But do we really go to the theatre in search of illusion, to be convinced that a palpable fiction is reality? I think not. After the mental age of about eight, we are no longer "taken in" by the theatre. Does this knowledge detract from our pleasure? Surely not; it enhances it. Surely, therefore, our pleasure in the theatre is occasioned by something other than illusion.

When great music conjures, as they say, your soul out of your body, is there any question of illusion? You probably lose for a little while all sense of time and space, but you do not suppose that things are taking place which in fact are not.

Likewise, in the theatre you may be rapt, rendered unaware of your immediate surroundings, but there is no illusion. You know perfectly well that you are at a play and you are just your same old self, who has been for a short time, like Bottom, translated.

A play is a ritual re-enactment of events arranged to form an intelligible and significant pattern. This pattern is re-created by the actors, for the audience, every time a performance is given. I can understand that there are those who believe that theatregoing is just fun, and that it is fun to be again a child, childishly thrilled by the make-believe, surrendering to the illusion.

For such people, the open stage will be less satisfactory than the proscenium. Those who take the theatre more seriously will, I believe, prefer open-stage presentation. Let me say again, I do not believe that the open stage should, or will, replace the proscenium. The latter is more suitable for many kinds of entertainment; but not for any and every kind. It is not, and will not, become a substitute for the proscenium. It is a valuable, and in some instances, indispensable alternative.

Thus endeth the lesson from a master magician of the theatre. I don't really know what Toronto's arts community thought of that presentation. All I know is that I had great difficulty going to sleep that night, partly because the next day I was to have my first meeting with the great man himself.

54: FACE TO FACE

The next day Tyrone Guthrie took his six-foot-five frame to Dora Mavor Moore's New Play Society Drama School office, on a second floor next to the Uptown Theatre. He was there to interview actors regarding a summer season of Shakespeare.

I had never met the man, but I was certainly aware of his work because I had seen a fair amount of it, so I was already an admirer before I finally met him.

I was told to prepare nothing in advance. Guthrie beckoned me into Dora's tiny office and had me sit in the only other chair. He seemed larger than the room itself. Before I could say my name he said, "Understand you've been doing a lot of work and having great success on the tiny box." I gathered he meant TV and nodded. "Not at all like real acting, is it?" Not knowing how to answer, I nodded again.

"Understand you've been Christopher Frying it." I nodded dumbly.

"What sort of thing do you want to do at Stratters?"

I looked absolutely blank. "At what?"

He sighed. "Stratford, Ontario."

I shrugged and said something like, "Oh, gosh, I dunno. Just want to be part of it. I'd be happy to sweep the stage."

I said this because I had heard about other interviews he had with some of our top radio actors. They had told him that they would be giving up lucrative careers for the summer and were not interested in being part of the theatre company unless they were offered roles of considerable size, commensurate with their established reputation. None of them appeared onstage at Stratford.

Guthrie made a brief scribble on his notepad and dismissed me with, "Jolly dee. V. grateful. Toodle-oo." Suddenly I was out the door and kicking myself for behaving like a blushing schoolboy. What a stupid thing to say about sweeping the stage now that I had four mouths to feed!

I think we were well into 1953 when the names of the acting company were listed, and the cast lists were announced. Luckily I was included in both plays. In *Richard III*, I was to play one of his minor henchmen, Lovel. I looked it up in my one-volume Shakespeare and found I had only three lines. It was better than sweeping the stage.

The other play, *All's Well That Ends Well*, was not included in my Shakespeare book, so I had to go the library to look it up. My character was named Bertram, and he seemed to be the young man that the main situation of the play was about, his rejection of marriage with Helena, the daughter of the court physician. I was stunned at being offered a leading role opposite the magnificent Irene Worth! Alec Guinness was listed in a secondary role, the King of France.

I was also amazed by the fact that we would be paid as much for rehearsal as we would for performing. I've never known this before or since, but it made my $400 weekly salary much more bearable after having made much more than that with all those performing and writing fees in radio and television.

A disappointment was the fact that the festival could not find me a place to live in Stratford itself. Instead, the Harron family was billeted on a farm three miles out, and since I didn't drive, I would have to travel by bicycle and pray for good weather. My situation was shared by fellow festival actor Bill Needles, who was booked with the same farm couple, Ed and Phyllis Cardwell. Phyllis was a big woman, and Ed was a small man, so small that as Charlie Farquharson might have said, *Ed, he looked like her caff!* Ed had the usual reservations about this culture stuff. I don't know that he had ever seen any Shakespeare, but he was convinced that "them actors talk like they got a buncha marbles in ther mouth."

Phyllis was a different cuppa tea. A big-boned blonde, she felt she had ties with show-business folks because years ago she had worked on the Buffalo night-boat with another busty blonde she claims was Mae West. Since this was probably about the time Mae was doing *Diamond Lil* on Broadway, the evidence really didn't add up.

Unlike her husband, Phyllis was very excited about the prospects of our festival. She glowed when she said she had already booked tickets for herself and Ed for that Alex Gwiness show. Ed snorted and headed for the barn to feed the horses. But his wife raved on. "I heard on the raddio that them festeral people got applications from as far away as Honey-loo-loo near the Hy-wayuh!"

Stratford is in the middle of rich southern Ontario farmland, and from the sounds the Cardwells made, it seemed to me like Charlie Farquharson country. Nearby communities such as Palmerston and Harriston were regularly pronounced as PAMMERSTON and HARSTON. Although my farmer character was not involved with the festival itself, he would have been very much at home with the elderly gents who sat on the benches in front of Stratford town hall, moving clockwise with the sun in winter, and counter-clockwise with the shade in summer.

Well sir the wife and former sweethart and me herd about this Shakespeer Festeral, and we looked her up on the map, and by gol, there she wuz ... Shakespeer Ontaryario, hard by yer Noo Hamburgs. So we druv down thair between hayin' and harvestin', but wen we got to this heer Shakespeer, my gol, ther wernt no festeral on atall, jist sum fella hoein' his turnups in a feeld. The wife ast him wair wuz yer festerall? He tole us the hole rang-dang-doo wuz ate mile down the rode in Stratford. So I sed wat in the sam hill is yer Shakesbeer Festeral doin' in Stratferd? Hoer feller sed he cooden figger it out neether. All he noo is ther wernt nobuddy in Shakesbeer plannin' on goin' yer ate mile to Stratfurd fer to see it.

55: LET'S GET STARTED

Before rehearsals started, the cast was invited to a reception to meet the local Stratford citizenry on the construction site, which was at the moment a bunch of concrete stanchions in a semi-circular bowl just above the town's baseball diamond. Guthrie, Alec Guinness, and Irene Worth were there. Before the locals gathered, Guthrie told us that we were up against several factions in the town who thought our enterprise was a foolish adventure that could only end in financial folly. Included among the opposition was the local newspaper, the *Stratford Beacon-Herald*. There had been quite recently a sneering editorial in reference to our grandiose attempt to build a national theatre in their little town.

Guthrie said, "Consequently, before we start rehearsals tomorrow, each of you will be assigned tonight to Sunday dinner with a Stratford family, who have agreed to take us in individually and feed us in an attempt to get to know us. Get to know them, as well. For they, not us, are the future of this venture."

He was introduced to the Stratfordians as Dr. Guthrie. He had been given this honorary degree by some British university, but his actors always called him Tony. In his speech to the locals Dr. Guthrie said that this Stratford project was not to build a national theatre. He thundered, "Theatres only succeed when they have deep roots in the community from which they arise. The theatre we are trying to build here belongs not to us, but the people of this town."

Gloria and I were assigned to have dinner with Gib and Elizabeth Jarrot. It was a wise choice. He was a doctor who had gone to medical school with Gloria's dad, the one whose phone calls to Toronto in my presence had given me the heaven-sent name of Charlie Farquharson.

The Jarrots were well aware of the local skeptics, but they themselves were two of the prominent citizens who were firm supporters of the committee that allowed Tom Patterson to bring Guthrie all the way from Ireland to discuss the possibility of a six-week summer festival. Gib told us that when Guthrie arrived for the first time, he shocked the committee with his first words of advice.

Evidently Tony told them that if they wanted to make money out of this venture, they had better forget about the Bard of Avon and hire a bunch of dancing girls from New York, the kind who could kick higher than their foreheads! Elizabeth Jarrot felt Guthrie was referring to the Rockettes, whose specialty was dancing on top of big red balls. Dr. Gib said with a snicker that Guthrie was really hinting that small town culture was a lot of balls.

On the other hand, Guthrie said if this committee was hell-bent on doing something significant for Canada, and adding to its growing postwar awareness of a country in search of a home-grown culture, then a short season of Shakespeare using Canadian actors might do the trick. As long as the committee was prepared, he added, to make up for a possible financial loss.

The rest, of course, is history. The current Stratford Festival is probably the most sustainable commercial theatre on this continent. But echoing Guthrie's dancing words of sixty years ago, the chief money-making centrepiece on the Festival Theatre stage is the revival of a successful Broadway musical, with the plays of Shakespeare in a supporting role.

The beginnings of the Stratford Festival in Connecticut, three years after we got started, tell a different story. It was started by a bunch of New Yorkers, the American Theater Guild, and they made little or no contact with the locals. On the shores of the Housatonic river they proceeded on their own to build a conventional proscenium arch theatre, like you'd find in any high school. But this theatre was carved out of expensive, imported Burmese teak wood. Not that many years later, this magnificent relic of an Asiatic forest was closed.

But back to Ontario and the first rehearsal of the first season. It was not on any part of the park that contained the festival site. It was across the river in a big tin shed that usually held the local agricultural exhibition during the Fall Fair. That June day the weather was a bit cold, made even colder by the metal chairs. It was pretty grim surroundings, especially if you have read Robertson Davies's witty account in his first festival book, *Renown at Stratford*. He tells how we rehearsed among a flock of fornicating sparrows, with the odd bird-turd, newly hatched egg, or even a fledgling corpse careening down amongst us as we rehearsed.

Alec Guinness, who was genuinely shy, held his script close to his chest as he mumbled the opening speech of the play. I sat less than ten feet away and even that close it was hard to hear anything he said. On the other hand, Irene Worth (pronounced *Eye-reeny*) as Richard III's scourge, Mad Queen Margaret, gave a full-throated cackle and launched into a tirade using her magnificent voice at full volume that thrilled us all.

When it came to the Canadian actors, first up was Lloyd Bochner as the doomed Duke of Clarence heading for the hoosegow with his jailer Brackenbury, played by William Hutt. Brackenbury had no lines in that scene, but Bochner uttered his long soliloquy in a faultless British accent. When Bill Hutt did get to speak his few lines, the accent was straight Canadian, much like he must have used when I saw him as a chorus boy in our 1936 high school production of the musical *Rio Rita*. He went on, of course, to become the Canadian mainstay of our festival.

It turns out Hutt was correct about keeping his Canadian speech patterns. When it came to the Duke of Clarence (Bochner) to be murdered by being drowned in a cask of wine, the two thugs who did it were played by actors I had seen onstage many times before, Bill Needles and Eric House. They must have rehearsed together the night before our first reading, because they both affected lower-class British accents which sounded vaguely to me like they came from Cornwall or Devon.

Guthrie stopped them before they got any further and said, gently but firmly, "This is a Canadian festival. We don't need any second-hand renderings of Loamshire or Mummerset. Please find a local equivalent."

Eric looked at Bill and vice versa. Then they both looked at me and Eric started to smile. He repeated the lines in a voice that sounded quite a lot like Charlie Farquharson. Guthrie pronounced himself delighted and the rehearsal continued. I was glad to have my creation onstage at the festival in any shape or form. Guinness seemed to loosen up after that, and by the end of the rehearsal he was matching Irene Worth decibel for decibel.

I don't know if Tony Guthrie had gone to dinner the night before with some local family, but I suspect he stayed home with his wife Judy and had her prompt him while he carefully memorized the names (and nicknames!) of every actor, apprentice, technical staff, and usher of our yet-to-be-born enterprise. He referred to every one of us by name, without any prompting, and proceeded to give every actor a description of the kind of part he was about to play. Even minor characters without a name were given brief but dazzling descriptions of what it meant to be a fourteenth-century peasant, servant, soldier, or clerk. Despite the chill, the entire company glowed with excitement in the thrall of a master magician.

After the rehearsal, Alec Guinness came up to me and recalled that we had met someplace before. I gave him the details of our meeting backstage in Brighton, involving David Lean and Ann Todd. He smiled at the memory of my praise of his performance as Herbert Pocket in *Great Expectations*. Then he asked me if I had any advice about how to deal with Canadian audiences.

Emboldened by his humility, I said there might be a communications gap with rural Ontarians who were not familiar with the Elizabethan mode of speech. Alec looked concerned. Perhaps, I suggested, he might acquire a Canadian equivalent, as Guthrie had suggested to our two would-be murderers, Needles and House. Guinness asked me to demonstrate. I repeated the first line of his opening monologue in my best Charlie Farquharson accent: *Now be yer winner of our disco tent....*

Alec blinked twice and believed me for about five seconds, but as soon as he noticed me holding in a suppressed snicker, he grinned all over as I said in Charlese: *By swinjer, Mister Ginny, walcom to our Canader Jakesbeer Festerall!*

After the read-through of the text, the rest of the first day of rehearsal was devoted to the Battle of Bosworth Field at the end of the play, under the martial gaze of a pacifist vegetarian. That's what Douglas Campbell was, and proud of it. Doug chose Bill Hutt and me to begin the battle, me facing the audience and Bill showing his backside to it. It was my decision as to when to begin hostilities by raising my sword with a blood-curdling cry, and the battle commenced up and down the stairs at the back of the stage. Bodies were hurled over the parapet and swords clashed frighteningly close to the patrons in the front row on all three sides of our platform stage.

My only other duty in the rest of the play was to catch the decapitated head of Lord Hastings when it was slung in a bloody bag (literally) by Richard III to his servant Catesby (Timothy Findley). The way Guthrie staged it, the rapid-fire exchange of a human head looked to me like the classic baseball triple play, Tinker to Evers to Chance. Naturally, the head of Hastings was a life-size replica of Dougie Campbell's head from our the props department. In rehearsal we used a soccer ball in a burlap bag.

One day after a rehearsal, Guthrie summoned me to his office. I had no idea why. I was soon to find out. Tony was displeased with the way Bob Christie was coming along as the Duke of Buckingham and suggested that I replace him. I was so shocked that he found my friend inadequate.

I knew that Bob and his wife had been part of the Old Vic company Guthrie had directed when Guinness played his first Hamlet. It was before the war at the castle in Denmark at Elsinore, where Shakespeare sets the locale of the play itself. I pleaded with Guthrie to give our mutual friend a chance, because it was so early in the rehearsal schedule. Tony gave me a fishy look but agreed to let the matter rest. This strange meeting initiated a bond between the two of us, which persisted through time. I felt that Guthrie, in seeking my advice, was treating me like the son he'd never had.

Later, closer to the actual opening night, we started rehearsing on site in the park itself. The tent had not yet arrived from Chicago, but the actors wanted to get used to the actual dimensions of the stage, so we were forced to rehearse in full daylight to the stares of curious onlookers. Guthrie thought this was an okay thing, part of his belief that the festival belongs to the locals.

This open-air venue made Guinness shyer than ever. He reverted to the low monotone he had given us in the opening read-through, but he kept Richard's pronounced limp. I sat on the brow of the hill beside two open-mouthed rural spectators. They had probably seen Alec in *The Lavender Hill Mob* or *The Man in the White Suit*.

"That'd be yer Alex Gwiness the movie man," said one.

The other replied, "Wat's he doin' right now?"

Number One said, "He's practisin' to be on that platform fer the consert they're gonna give."

Number Two: "I can't hear a blame thing what he's sayin.'"

The reply from Number One was: "He's not worrying about that right now. He's finished gittin' off all his words by heart, and right now he's workin' on his jesters."

Richard Crookback was moving about the stage now with that peculiar walk that Alec had adopted, a combination of muscular dystrophy and cerebral palsy which made him look like a man not in control of any of his limbs. As Alec clumped about, the self-appointed expert on things theatrical said to his less savvy companion, "He's doin' pritty good fer a feller with the arthuritis offal bad."

Charlie Farquharson was alive and well in Stratford.

56: SHOWDOWN TIME

Our fledgling festival was developing lots of problems. The summer of 1953 was beset by some of the most extreme climactic occurrences ever experienced in our part of the planet. Violent thunderstorms, frequent cloudbursts, even tornadoes, were regular visitors.

The other problem was financial, something about which we actors were never acutely concerned as long as they paid us every week. But rumours were flying that we might not make it to opening night. Evidently one phone call Guthrie made to Ottawa did the trick. Our benefactor was never revealed, but evidence points to our governor general, Vincent Massey. The first Canadian to occupy that post had published his own view about our cultural climate, the Massey Report. Evidently the Guv-Jen was prepared to put his money where his vice-regal mouth was.

At any rate, that outright gift was the winning combine that saved the bacon of the first season of our festival. It must have been a good fat check because the tent finally arrived from Chicago a scant seven days before opening night. A miracle worker came with the tent, fortunately for us. Skip Manley was an old circus roustabout and employed his skills immediately because right after the tent was up, the heavens opened and poured down another cloudburst.

Rehearsals went on amid the deluge. Guthrie strode about in the tent among the puddles, wearing ancient sandals and an even more ancient bathing suit, under an enormous yellow slicker. The string must have been older than the bathing trunks, because it gave way in the middle of rehearsal. Without any hesitation Guthrie merely stepped out of the trunks and continued stalking about in his slicker, giving stage directions, absolutely starkers under it.

When the cloudbursts finally stopped and the tent began to dry out, another big problem presented itself. Our stage was made of wood, which is acoustically good, but the auditorium itself was concrete. It made our voices ring hollow and our words largely undecipherable in most of the theatre. Opening night was now less than a week away.

Everyone started to panic, except Guthrie. He had a confab with our tentmaster while we stopped rehearsal. But Irene Worth was sitting beside a coil of hemp rope, and she said from where she sat she could hear the dialogue onstage perfectly. Immediately there was an order to a Chicago textiles company for 10,000 square yards of cocoa matting.

Believe it or rip, Notley, it arrived the day before we had our Sunday dedication service in the tent. Guthrie was insistent that our theatre venture be dedicated to the service of the Almighty, so he arranged to have our chaplain, the Anglican Archdeacon Lightbourne, be present, along with a local Presbyterian minister, a Catholic priest, and a rabbi.

There was no rain that Sabbath afternoon but a considerable wind billowed out the folds of the tent, so that it felt we were all of us on the good ship *Bluenose*, and well out to sea. Some members of the audience started reaching in their purses for Gravol. Despite this digestive diversion, the good ship SS *Festival* (Silently Subsidized) was about to be launched.

Lightbourne spoke first. We had all gotten to know him because he was a tower of support all through the days of early dissension from the town and its newspaper. He was also a source of comfort to the acting company in the rehearsal period.

Archdeacon Lightbourne dedicated our tent and all within it to the service of the Lord. This was echoed by the Catholic priest, who reminded us that theatre had its origins on the steps of the medieval church, where ritual was turned into drama for the people in the town square. Guthrie looked immensely pleased, because it echoed his deeply held beliefs about the profound place the theatre should take in the hearts and minds of a community. The rabbi was quite pleasant in his short remarks about what fun it was going to be to have an exciting new playhouse in our midst.

The local Presbyterian minister was the last cleric to speak, and he turned out to be the corpse at the feast. Picking up where the Catholic speaker left off, he agreed that theatre started on the steps of the church. But this disciple of John Calvin felt that the move outside its sacred portals was where the church went wrong, because the theatre became involved in temporal matters, while the church continued to devote itself to the spiritual and eternal.

He looked up at the roof of our tent, still swaying in the stiff wind, and said mournfully, "This temporary building is by no means eternal. The canvas of this tent may rot in four years or five. The very concrete of which these foundations are built, may crack in the next ten years. But the church is founded upon a rock, it is Eternal, and God's house will last forever. Theatre should learn its place in the divine scheme of things from its immortal predecessor, and deal only with matters of the Spirit."

I looked at Guthrie. He wore an impish grin. Then I caught sight of the local contractor who had built our theatre's concrete foundations, Oliver Gaffney. His face was absolutely purple with anger. Like Archdeacon Lightbourne, he was one of our festival heroes, because he had kept on working all through the financial crisis when it was not in the least certain that he would ever be paid.

By now our glorious ceremony had turned into a Presbyterian bummer. The good people of Stratford and outlying areas left our billowing tent as if deserting a sinking ship. As in Shakespeare's day, the Puritans had done their damnedest to condemn the birth of our theatre.

57: BIRTH PANGS

The last couple of days of rehearsal were panic-filled for our Canadian contingent. Opening night nerves arrived ahead of time. Guthrie had told us at that first rehearsal that some of the best acting ideas take place in one's bedroom. Without being facetious, he meant that if we would suddenly get a bright idea before retiring for the night, or even during a fitful, worrying sleep, it should be presented the next day at rehearsal, and it might "astonish the multitude."

I got an idea like that, not in the bedroom, but on my three-mile bike ride. I broached my idea to Guthrie during a break in rehearsal: my character Bertram's behaviour to Helena is inexcusable, refusing to marry her in full sight of the court. His only excuse, I felt, was in being embarrassingly immature. So I suggested to Guthrie that I play Bertram as even younger than my twenty-eight years. From his great height he looked down on me with a sharp eagle eye on my five-foot-ten frame below, and said, "Don't think so, old chap. It would be a case of mutton dressed as lamb."

I winced and nodded, suddenly aware of my own insensibility toward a great actress who was probably in her late thirties. I realized that in *All's Well* I was called upon to play the part of a spoiled brat. Bertram is the son of a countess, a young headstrong snob who arrogantly refuses the hand of Helena, the daughter of the doctor who, on her own, has cured the king of a fistula, whatever the hell that is. Because of this, the king allows Helena to select for marriage any young man of her choice. When my in-laws came to see the play, they were highly amused when they heard their son-in-law say with horror in his voice, "A humble physician's daughter my wife?"

One scene involved the whole company, plus a choir that was brought in for the occasion. The scene is a party to celebrate the curing of the king's illness. The choir was from the local United Church, and they were all thrilled to actually be onstage, instead of just singing in the wings.

Everyone in the regular cast was taking side-bets as to when the Great Director might unleash some of his profanity on these innocent church-goers. It didn't take long. During the first run-through of the party scene, it was interrupted by Guthrie thundering his way down from the back of the theatre, roaring out, "This is supposed to be a party! Why aren't you all deliriously happy for His Nobs here? The old boy is up and about again! Must you all be so *fucking ontaireeo*!"

Complete shocked silence followed this remark. Everyone was too polite to say anything, but there were agonized looks on several of the choristers. The exception to this was two women who still had social smiles on their faces. I realized that neither of these women had ever heard the F-word.

Rehearsal for Richard the Turd also involved a choir, as members of the coronation procession to crown the evil king as the conclusion of the first half of the performance. For this glittering occasion Tanya Moiseiwitsch had designed a dazzlingly red coronation robe with ermine trim that covered not only Guinness, but all of the platform stage.

Consequently, any procession that had to make its entrance was from the tunnels under the stage. These were dimly lit, so it was easy to get confused down there in the murk. The leaders of this procession were the youngest choirboys bearing huge candles at least half their size. Dress rehearsal night was the only chance these junior choir members were to get, and the tension below the stage was palpable.

The coronation scene dress rehearsal was stalled because the two little boys in the front of the procession just got lost in the gloom of those tunnels. Guthrie was under extreme pressure now and forewent his usual witty ripostes. In fact, he lost his temper, particularly at the two cringing kids at the head of the lost procession.

He told the two leading choirboys that they were behaving like five-year-olds. I looked at both quaking kids. They couldn't have been much more than five!

The next day was it: opening performance. We had a last rehearsal of the battle where Bill Hutt and I began the whole thing by raising our swords, and he waited for my warlike (I hoped) cry before we clanged them together. The battle had been rehearsed every day, and thanks to our pacifist choreographer, Doug Campbell, it was an intricate exercise in gymnastics orchestrated to thrill the crowd, especially those in the front rows who, like any 3-D film audience, would seem to be part of the fighting itself.

After the battle brush-up, Guthrie decided on a restful line rehearsal that took a lot of our tension and opening night nerves away. Then we were dismissed until half-hour. I was too tired and nervous to drive my bike all the way out to the Cardwell farm. What made me tired was that Battle of Bosworth Field, but what made me nervous was the fact that the night after that I would be playing a major role on that stage. The house of Alf and Dama Bell, both members of the original Festival Committee, had become a kind of rest home away from home for many actors. After I rested at the Bell ménage, I realized that I had left the script back at the tent. Thinking

I could fight off opening night nerves by concentrating on my lines for the next night, I hopped back on my bike and headed for the tent.

I grabbed the script out of my dressing room and was about to head back outside when I heard fluted, bird-like laughter coming from the stage. Out of curiosity I took a look onstage. There were the two gentle giants of our festival, Judy and Tony Guthrie, doing the very job that I had volunteered for in that long-forgotten interview a year before when I first met Guthrie in the confines of the New Play Society. They were wielding large mops and sweeping the stage.

58: MOMENT CRITIQUE

Late that afternoon the weather turned hot and dangerously humid. By curtain time, inside the tent was like steambath. The only consolation we actors had was that Tanya had had the good sense to design our Wars of the Roses armour in some kind of fibreglass, which weighed lightly on our spirits.

The play opened with Alec thrusting his leg over the upper parapet and delivering his soliloquy, "Now is the winter of our discontent." In addition to his cerebral palsy limp, he had added a piece of Scotch tape over one eye to add to his physical distortion. It worked. In the tiny part of Lord Lovel, one of Richard's henchmen, I had decided to go in the opposite direction. I made myself up to look rather like the wicked queen in *Snow White*.

The scene where Richard dares to woo a grieving Lady Anne over the corpse of her husband on the way to his funeral is traditionally a difficult one to make believable. It looks like pure perversion on the part of Lady Anne to accept the marriage proposal of a deformed monster while she is standing beside the corpse of her husband.

In rehearsal, Guthrie suggested that kinkiness might trigger this strange match, and he tried to persuade Amelia Hall as Anne to spit in Guinness's face. She was reluctant to do such a thing to our star guest, but by opening night she must have gotten up the courage to try it, because that opening night she hocked an oyster a longshoreman would have been proud of, and it lay glistening on Alec's cheek.

He grinned slyly and with his fingers transferred her glooey mess into his own mouth. The audience gasped, and Milly Hall seemed to faint on the spot. Maybe she did, because when Alec picked up her little body and slung it over his shoulder, she didn't move.

The air in the tent was a problem. There were more than a few faintings among the rows of seats. One moment that seemed to revive any would-be slumberers was when three of us threw the head of Lord Hastings around the stage in a blood-soaked bag. I don't know what was in it, but it was always damp at the bottom. Before he threw it to me, Alec used his fingers again, this time to taste the blood that oozed through the bottom of the bag.

Other actors have invented their own business for this grisly moment. Olivier's Richard peeked into the bag, looked puzzled at its contents until he turned it 180 degrees and then with a smile recognized the decapitated face of his enemy. Donald Wolfit ate grapes all the while and spat the seeds as he stared into the bag.

A blast from the CNR train heralded the beginning of the battle at the end of the play. As rehearsed daily, it was my job as Richard's evil henchman to decide when to begin the battle. My immediate opponent, Bill Hutt, represented the forces of Good, namely Bob Goodier as the Duke of Richmond, soon to become Henry IV (*Part 1*).

I stood centre stage facing the audience, and ready to raise my sword as Bill approached from the underground tunnel. The audience was deathly still, maybe still-born in all this humid heat. I hesitated in raising my sword because I was watching a member of the audience who had fainted and was being transported slowly along the aisle from hand to hand to the St. John's Ambulance man at the end of the aisle.

It looked as if they were passing a large hot dog at a football game. But what I noticed most is that the eyes of those people passing that limp body along were not on the poor soul with whom they were briefly involved. Those eyes were glued to what Hutt and I were about to do on this stage.

I relaxed completely. I knew the audience was on our side and that we would give them a good fight. Because of Tanya's stage design, nothing like this close combat, or combat this close, had ever been witnessed by a Canadian audience, and that night ours shrieked its approval. The standing ovation at the curtain call seemed to go on forever. Alec stepped forward and when the audience finally became silent, he said, "I want to pay tribute to the only man who could make this possible: William Shakespeare."

From my point of view, the festival was in like Flynn.

59: MORNING-AFTER BLUES

The Canadian critics agreed with me, but not our American cousins. The local critic, Ed Nigh of the *Stratford Beacon-Herald*, the paper that had been against the idea of a festival, wrote appreciatively of our efforts.

A strong booster from the beginning, the *Globe and Mail*'s Herbert Whittaker, gave us a rave, and said it was the most important night ever for Canadian theatre. "Up to Monday, the description of Stratford, Ont. in the Encyclopedia Britannica, as a 'city and port of entry of Ontario, Canada, and the capital of Perth County, situated 83 miles W.S.W. of Toronto by the Canadian National Railway, on the Avon River,' will still hold. After that date the important information and identification of the town of Stratford must include: 'Site of the annual Shakespearean Festival, opened by Tyrone Guthrie, Alec Guinness and the faith of the citizens of Stratford on July 13, 1953.'"

He added, among his praise for the performers, "A memorable production, and a memorable night in the theatre for Stratford and for Canada. The final word of praise must go to the people of this festival town, and to Tom Patterson's dream come violently and excitingly to life."

Tom is gone now, but playgoers assemble every season at the Tom Patterson Theatre, right by the bank of the River Avon. It is smaller than the Festival and the Avon Theatres, but it has the same open stage with the audience on three sides. And if you have a picnic lunch, the nicest place to munch it would be to cross the bridge over the Avon River to Tom Patterson Island not far away.

The wife and former sweethart and me et our sandwitches down by that river and fed yer wacks paper to them swans. You take yer averidge swan she's a ugly bird. Oh! Take a peck outen yer arm as quick as look at yuh! Reezin they keeps them thair in Stratford is cuz their river, yer Ayvon, ain't no river atall. She's jist yer artywhyfishul lake, and they hav to keep them swans about fer to eat up yer garbidge.

Mite jew they mite be pritty good eetin', mebby as good as yer Canader Goosed. We never et a swan fer Chrissmuss, but I betcha ther mite be a good lotta meat on that neck.

The news from New York was not so good. The *New York Times* review by Brooks Atkinson had been relayed to us through a telegraphic spy in the Stratford railway station. "Spectacular production, shallow performance. Miss Moiseiwitsch's costumes are bold and beautiful. When Guthrie sets opposing armies at each other's throats on the various stage levels, this is a Richard III that looks exciting.

"But Shakespeare's bloody drama of evil and consequence comes off at second best among such overpowering externals. As the scheming Duke of Gloucester, Mr. Guinness does settle down to work in the last act, when he plays a king hedged about with treachery and forced to fight for his life. These are the most coherent moments in the entire performance. Mr. Guinness is a brilliant comedian, and he plays the first two acts in a light, witty key of subtle persiflage. It is difficult to believe that any of the nobles could be won over by the frivolous Richard that Mr. Guinness describes in the first two acts."

In his autobiography written decades later, Alec wrote: "We knew the Festival had got off to a blazing start, in spite of my poor Richard." Nobody in our festival company would have agreed with that assessment.

Other American critics treated our efforts as a cow-town trying to be big-time. An exception was William Hawkins of New York's *World-Telegram*: "Canada's Shakespearean Festival opened last night with a history-making explosion by a production of *Richard III* that is nothing less than brilliant. Alec Guinness, playing the title role, and Tyrone Guthrie directing, offered a production of the bloody play with novel depths and excitement I rarely have had anywhere before. This Richard is far and away the best thing Mr. Guinness has been seen in on this side of the Atlantic."

60: SECOND WIND

We were about to appear next night in a play that, according to Guthrie, had not been performed professionally in over 200 years. He was solemn when he addressed us before the final dress rehearsal and didn't mince words when he said to the assembled cast, "We haven't made it, people. Not yet. But tonight we have another chance. So let's fucking well get on with it!"

We did. And we did it, too! Actually, *All's Well That Ends Well* turned out to be *exactly* what happened with all the critics. The morning after our premiere, the Canadian papers from Stratford and Toronto and London raved again, and the rest of them were almost uniformly ecstatic.

But this time the New York critics went along with them. Perhaps it was the unfamiliar play, or the novelty of the modern-dress approach, but mostly I think it was the radiant performance of our leading lady, Irene Worth, dazzling in her yellow Valentina gown. She was also the only member of our cast who understood all of Shakespeare's jokes.

The unanimous success of our second play meant that Tom Patterson's dream came true in more ways than one. His real hope was to save the faltering economy of his hometown after it lost the CN repair yards. Due to the instant success of this first festival, other businesses decided to locate in Stratford. Among them was a German industrial firm, Fisher Aktiens Gesellschaft. They put up a huge sign on their building with just the three initials of their company, F.A.G.

That old Messy-Ferguson of mine had bernt out her balls barings and I writ a deer John letter to yer John Deer peeple fer replacemints. They writ back that the best place fer to replace them wuz in the saim town as that Shakesbeer festeral so I druv down to Shakesbeer Ontario lookiin fer my parts. By gol, if ther wernt that same happy hoer doin his turnups as I seen last time. So I stop and ast him wair I cud find yer F.A.G.s.

He sed, thair all down in Stratford on the platform of thair big tense, takin' off Shakesbeer's parts. I tole him I needed my balls barings and I had look up yer inflammation in my Messy-Fergoosin letter, witch sed I wuz to be hedded fer yer Fishers Arbeiten Gazelle Shaft.

This termip hoer sed I never shafted a gazelle, but I'm hopin' this fall to git me a deer er moose up yer Algonkywin Park.

As fer yer fishin' is consern, that'd be me, and soons I finish turnippin I plans to git over to yer stone quarry hard by St. Marry's and git me sum chub.

After the opening night of *Richard III* there had been no party after to celebrate it. Tony Guthrie's assistant Cecil Clarke decided that because we had another opening the following night. Also he pronounced that "there will be nobody allowed backstage after the performance." He must have neglected to inform Alec Guinness, and when nobody visited his dressing room at the end of opening night, he was furious with the fact that not even the Festival Board had come backstage to say thank you for his efforts.

There was hell to pay over this, but Patterson's mother shelled out 700 of her precious dollars to throw us a nice do after the second night. It was a pretty great party. I hope Alec enjoyed the camaraderie as much as I did. It seemed to me that every important person I had ever met in Canada was there that night. The one person I wanted to be added to this glittering assembly was my wife. It had not been much of a social summer for her, looking after two little kids aged two years and six months. If it weren't for the consolation of reading Northrop Frye's books, it would have been bleak indeed.

Guthrie left us soon after the second opening night. He and Judy were travelling to Israel, where Tony would direct a production of *The Merchant of Venice*, a play that most people consider anti-Semitic. I suggested he get the Irish film actor Barry Fitzgerald to play Shylock. His grin lasted for a nanosecond, and then he said, "I'm surprised that you have gone as far as you have in theatre with such a paucity of gesture. I suggest a season at the Birmingham Rep or the Bristol Old Vic would do you good."

After our second opening night, the rest of the season seemed to be one continuous party. An Englishman, Dr. John Penistan, had a house on Ontario Street not far from the festival, and it became an open house for the actors. Each night it seems they gathered there, and the master of the revels was our Duke of Richmond, Bob Goodier. He had been a star comedian of *The Navy Show*, which I never saw, but he lived up to his reputation at the Peniston soirées. I only attended one of them, mostly because the booze flowed freely and I don't drink. Usually I biked my way back to my isolated little family.

But I will never forget to my shame the closing night shenanigans of that first Stratford season. In the spirit of *Spring Thaw*, I decided we should do a takeoff on both plays in our repertoire and call it *All's Well That Ends Richard*. I also thought the spotlight should be on the actors who had never had any lines to say during the season. As Richard III, I chose our assistant stage manager, Jack Merigold, a short, stout fellow who had performed quite hefty roles with the Royal Conservatory operettas, and who I knew had a good sense of humour.

The skits would take place well after the audience had left the theatre on closing night. Unknown to me, someone had left the doors open and curious members of the public flocked in, some of whom had never even been inside our theatre before. I had a moment of panic when the seats started filling up, because our takeoffs were a mixture of private jokes and pretty gamey ones.

To cut to the chase, the evening was a double-meaning nightmare and I was the principle cause of it. It ended that first season for me on a decidedly sour note. Alec Guinness refused to stay for the proceedings, and he was absolutely right. One person who did stay was my old friend, theatre critic Herb Whittaker, who looked at me very solemnly after this fiasco and said, "You have no sense of occasion."

The next day I caught Doug Campbell before he took off overseas and told him to get me a job at the Bristol Old Vic.

The call came sooner than expected. Evidently Doug had phoned Denis Carey, the Old Vic director, before he left Stratford, and for Carey my connection with Tyrone Guthrie was enough. I thought my wife would be pleased, because I wanted her to come with me, but she couldn't believe that I would give up all that future work in Toronto to chase the will o' the wisp of trying to correct my "paucity of gesture."

So it was with mixed feelings I took a train to New York before boarding a Dutch ship for England. Before I left I persuaded Gloria that she should accompany me later, along with older daughter Martha. Baby Mary would stay home with Gramma Fisher, who seemed delighted at the prospect.

I had kept in touch with Chris Plummer, telling him he should have been with us on the Stratford Adventure. (That's the title of a National Film Board movie they made during that first summer.) Chris invited me for lunch at the Algonquin Hotel, where he ordered snails for two. When I told him about our season he said, "Oh, God, I would have given anything to be there!" He pounded the table for emphasis and escargot shells went flying everywhere. He didn't suffer from a paucity of gesture.

I bent down under the table to pick them up. Plummer whispered fiercely, "For God's sake don't pick them up! What do you think waiters are for?"

I said, "Why the hell weren't you with us this summer?"

Plummer replied haughtily, "Some eunuch in Montreal who worked with Guthrie years ago on a radio series for the CNR said I was a hopeless drunk, and I guess Guthrie believed him." I found out later that Chris had been involved with the mistress of a CBC executive and the slander was delivered out of pure jealousy.

"I'll see Tony in London. I'll tell him it's a lie. Besides, Plummer drunk is better than all the rest of us sober."

He cheerfully dismissed my offer. "Don't bother, dear heart. I'm talking to the Theater Guild about their plans next summer for Stratford, Connecticut." Then he borrowed twenty-five bucks from me to pay for the lunch. "Till next time, old sod."

61: BRISTOL-FASHION, NOT TO MENTION PARIS

Early in September 1953 I flew to London, and before I travelled on by train to my new job at the Bristol Old Vic, I heard that the London Old Vic had done its own production of *All's Well*, which was still on the boards. I arrived a bit late and was shown to my seat in complete darkness.

One character that didn't fit into our modern-dress production was the court jester, Lavache, all cap and bells in the traditional fashion. At one point he said something witty, which completely escaped me, but the person in the seat next to me gave a full-throated laugh that sounded familiar. I turned to look at the source, because it came from the only person in the entire audience who understood such an obscure witticism.

Lo and behold, I found myself sitting next to my Ontario Helena, Irene Worth. We gave each other a quick, joyous hug and turned our attention back to the stage.

Over tea and crumpets she told me that the Guthries had come back from Israel and to look them up at their rooms in Lincoln's Inn Fields, not far from the Aldwych Theatre. The next day I made my way to that curious set of buildings called the Inns of Court.

The Guthries lived in tiny rooms with low ceilings, and the tall heads of both of them I can imagine sometimes brushed those ceilings. To me the place looked musty and Dickensian. I told Tony that I was following his advice and was on my way to join the company of the Bristol Old Vic. He looked pleased and added that he was glad I wasn't at the London Old Vic, because their contracts would have precluded me from being part of the second Stratford Festival.

Tony told me he was thinking of doing a wacky version of *The Taming of the Shrew* and wondered if I was interested in the part of Lucentio. Having worked for Earle Grey in the quad at Trinity, I was familiar with the play. Lucentio is a nice young man who is madly in love with the Shrew's younger sister Bianca.

Guthrie was surprised when I turned down the role. I told him my ambition was to become not a juvenile but a character actor, and the good doctor then suggested the part of Lucentio's servant Tranio, who gets up to all kinds of shenanigans to help his boss win the girl. I said that sounded more like it, and we adjourned when Judy brought the tea.

Judy told me that when Tony was directing at "Stratters-on-Avon," they had no lodgings but lived in a punt on the river, open to the skies. It was a fairly dry summer, thanks be, and when it came teatime, she just dunked the pot in the river.

Tony told me something I hadn't considered. The pay at Bristol was the same as the London Old Vic ... ten pounds a week to play and five pounds to rehearse. When I thought of all those TV and radio offers going a-begging in Toronto, I was starting to agree with my wife. I was embarking on a mission of madness. But to reinforce my original decision, I bought a book of Elizabethan hand gestures written by some English graduate student of theatre and took a train to Bristol.

When I got there, Doug Campbell introduced me to the director, Denis Carey, and his wife Yvonne Coulette, who was to be Doug's Cleopatra. I was hoping to get the role of Octavius Caesar, but instead I was assigned the part of the messenger Cleopatra has had whipped and beaten up for telling her that Mark Antony has married another woman. In my first letter to Gloria back in Gravenhurst, I was reluctant to tell her that news.

I shrugged, hoped for better parts in the rest of the season, and got myself a room at the Bristol YMCA. I vowed to keep the book of gestures by my bedside and memorize at least one of them every night. As soon as I could, I would start looking around for lodgings for my family. On our first rehearsal I got to meet the rest of the company. It seems I was in between the era of John Neville, who had just left for the other Old Vic in London, and Peter O'Toole, who was yet to arrive.

Gloria and our Muffin arrived before opening night of *A. and C.*, as it came to be called. I had found lodgings on the edge of town in full view of the famous suspension bridge. Next to the bridge was a row of eighteenth-century rooming houses called Prince's Buildings. The landlady showed me a ground floor flat overlooking the river. It was called the Avon. She didn't know about any connection to the one at Stratford in Warwickshire.

Then she showed me her pride and joy: one of the panes in the front window had scratched on it the letter *G*. She beamed and told me that the greatest eighteenth-century actor in all England, David Garrick, had lodged there, and left his initial on one pane of glass for future generations to swoon over. I signed a six-month lease on the spot.

The first thing Gloria wanted when she arrived was a hot bath for herself and child. The landlady told her she was only permitted one hot bath a week, and today was not her lucky day. Gloria looked at the bath. The ceiling was four storeys high, because the skylight went right up to the roof. That meant that any body heat was sucked up immediately, and the tepid water might be cold before it hit the tub. Gloria spent the rest of the time taking baths in the kitchen sink. I used the facilities in the theatre.

Looking back, I think a special medal for bravery should be struck for the wives of itinerant actors. Having stuck my wife without a car three miles outside Stratford, I had now succeeded in banishing her to an outer suburb of Bristol where the nearest cultural institution was the zoo. That suited baby Martha just fine, and on my day off every week I would take her there, where her favourite exhibit was the choc-ice booth.

The nightly whipping (twice on Wednesdays and Saturdays) I underwent in *Antony and Cleopatra* eventually passed, and I ended up in the next production, *A Comedy of Errors*, not as a comic but as a villainous conjurer, Doctor Pinch. Then came a real test of my English accent: a contemporary new play, *Old Bailey* by T.C. Worsley. Nothing to do with the London prison, it was about a person named Bailey who was old. But it was English and I was in for it. I began talking with that accent every moment of the day, even at home in Prince's Buildings. My wife said I sounded exactly like a screaming queen.

Then came an even bigger challenge ... a musical. Julian Slade and Dorothy Reynolds had great success with their first effort, *Salad Days*. Their new offering was a Christmas musical, *The Merry Gentleman*, i.e., Father Christmas. The title role was to be played by Doug Campbell.

There were three special additions to the cast. One was Jane Wenham, who was living at the time with Albert Finney. From the West of England Light Opera Company came Joan Plowright, later to become Lady Olivier, and Patricia Routledge, known to viewers of PBS television as Hyacinth Bouquet (Bucket) on *Keeping Up Appearances*.

To this talented group was added one Donald Harron as the love interest for soprano Jane Wenham. The fact that they raised my salary from ten pounds a week to fourteen precluded me from telling the management that I changed key every other note. Jane and I did a duet on "You're Always in Love in the Springtime." I never heard her complain once about my lack of musical talent. Maybe it served to underline her lovely soprano. I went through this whole business almost unaware of how musically untalented I was.

Since that time I have been asked on three different occasions to sing the part of Matthew in our own musical, *Anne of Green Gables*. The first time was by producer Bill Freedman in the London production. I didn't mention the fact that I change key. I just said I didn't want my own show ruined by Charlie Farquharson.

Gloria was not a singer, so she didn't notice my failings, but she did feel that this entire overseas operation had been a distinct waste of time. Leaving our other baby in Canada, what did I accomplish? I had no answer. I was determined to spend the rest of my savings from the year before taking her to the theatre in London, and maybe Paris, too.

But what about our two-year-old, Martha? Doug Campbell proved to be the answer to that problem. Back in London, he introduced us to his wife and her family, Dame Sybil Thorndike and Sir Lewis Casson. Granny Sybil (Shaw's original Saint Joan) loved to babysit Doug's children, and she was happy to add our Muffin to the mix.

Gloria had a cousin in Paris who had just taken a job with UNESCO. Paris in the spring sounded pretty good, and neither of us had ever been there. Her cousin, Mary Winston, got us a room in the heart of the city at the Hotel Moderne. The plumbing wasn't so: it consisted of no bathtub, just a tiny toilet and a large bidet.

Gloria, baby Martha, and me ended up doing all our bathing at Mary Winston's apartment, where the bathtub with a lid on it doubled as a kitchen sink. While she was busy with the United Nations, I walked the Boulevard Haussmann, and Gloria took Muffin to the Parc Monceau, where our two-year-old was astonished to find children her own age who could speak perfect French!

I managed to get tickets for *The Threepenny Opera*. The actress who played Madame Peachum dans le Faubourg de Chelsea was film star Françoise Rosay. Somehow the enterprise onstage, trying to make a Broadway musical out of Bertolt Brecht, just didn't work. But the next night Gloria got a real thrill when she saw in the flesh Jean-Louis Barrault. Now he and his wife Madeleine Reynaud were playing in Jean Giraudoux's *Pour Lucrece*.

We got back to England in time to catch the *Maasdam*, but the day before we were to sail, our daughter came down with chicken pox.

I had to go because rehearsals were starting in Stratford, but Gloria had to stay behind. The Cassons were kind to her, but the Campbell kids were on the ship with Doug and Ann and me, the only flesh-eater among a pack of vegetarians.

62: ONCE MORE INTO THE BLEACHERS

A delightful surprise awaited me when I got to Stratford for the start of the second season. The part of Petruchio, the tamer of that Shrew, was to be played by Mavor Moore. He had given up his plum job after two years as head honcho of CBC Television to become an actor again.

Another not-so-delightful surprise was the atmosphere of nervous-Nellyness in the mood of those who administrated the festival. It had changed from the feeling of triumph at the end of the first season to the "cautious Canadian" approach. Nevertheless, we actors hoped to do it again.

Guthrie hadn't changed; he had the same pioneer spirit as before. It was as if the first season had never happened and he was beginning the project anew. I was reminded of a quote I had read in Ken Tynan's first book, *He That Plays the King*. "Guthrie's weakness is that he has never learned from his failures. His strength is that he has never learned from his successes."

Guthrie arrived at our first rehearsal knowing everyone by name, and there were lots of new people. The part I had turned down was to be played by a good-looking young actor from the Ottawa Repertory Theatre, Bill Shatner. The role of the Shrew was to be played by another newcomer to the festival, Barbara Chilcott.

The part of the Duke in *Measure for Measure* would be played by Lloyd Bochner, who had acquitted himself so well last season in the spoken verse department. The Duke's replacement is really the leading role, and it would be taken by the festival's first guest star, James Mason. He was still a mighty big movie star, now resident in Hollywood, but back in the 1930s he was a member of the Old Vic Company under Guthrie, along with Charles Laughton. The news that he was coming to Stratford caused a real tizzy among the population.

Guthrie offered me the role of Isabella's noble brother, Claudio, and again I turned him down. Instead I asked for the part of Lucio, the ne'er-do-well fop who flitters about spreading gossip. Guthrie acceded to my wishes. He was getting used to my refusal to play dull, nice young men. The part of Isabella's brother would now be played by Douglas Rain, who understudied Guinness the year before. He was also my understudy in *All's Well*. I made sure to stay healthy and not let such a talented actor take my place.

Another surprise was the fact that Guthrie would not be directing but left it to his right-hand man in charge of production, Cecil Clarke. He had been invaluable in his job the first season, among other things finding an old European bootmaker to make fourteenth-century shoes for the cast. No one from England could recall Cecil directing anything, but he certainly had Guthrie's approval, and that was enough for us.

James Mason's arrival was slightly delayed, finishing up filming with Judy Garland in a remake of *A Star Is Born*. So we started rehearsals of *Shrew* first. We looked at Tanya's sets and costumes, and we knew that it really would be a Wild West show. Petruchio arrived in Stetson and chaps on a pantomime buckaroo. Guthrie was in his element, cocking a snook at tradition and upsetting all previous notions of this comedy classic. While we were onstage, he would wander among the rest of the cast seated in the theatre and ask the advice of the lowliest walk-on. I never saw him pick on any of these underlings, except to encourage them to exaggerate what they were doing.

Having seen Mavor play Lear and Riel and all kinds of roles in several *Spring Thaws*, I was glad that he had returned to acting. To my mind it was the thing he did best. I knew from experience that he was more than merely talented, but resourceful and imaginative under the most difficult circumstances.

Due to the slam-bang Wild West nature of Guthrie's concept, it was not totally surprising that at the first rehearsal Mavor broke two ribs. This would have sidelined another actor, but not Dora's boy. He carried on gamely. After two days of this agony, Guthrie summoned me to his office. He came right to the point. "I want you to take over the part of Petruchio."

I was stunned and offended. I made the remark that a couple of cracked ribs would only improve Mavor's performance. Guthrie was unamused and adamant. I asked why. Tony said that Mavor's traditional interpretation was totally at variance with his own concept of the role. As far as he was concerned, Moore was out and Harron was in.

I raised my voice a couple of decibels. "Well, what in God's name is your interpretation of the part? You sure as hell haven't told any of us!

During the second season of Stratford, 1954. Don as the villainous fop Lucio in Measure for Measure.

And that includes Mavor!" Guthrie accepted my little tirade and set about to patiently explain his concept of the role. It was completely opposite to the traditional notion. Instead of a ruffian full of braggadocio, Tony saw the role as a mild-mannered nice young man who was trying to bluff his way into a rich marriage.

I shook my head in disbelief. "Jesus Christ, Tony, you want Harold Lloyd!"

He replied, "Exactly!"

It was then that I exploded. I told Guthrie that it would have been nice if he had explained this before Mavor quit his well-paid job at CBC. He would now be unemployed with a wife and two children to provide for. I refused to take over the role.

"You don't want me, Tony. You've got Harold Lloyd standing in front of you every rehearsal, glasses and all!"

After my tirade all Guthrie could say was, "Who?"

"Bill Needles!"

"Done!" said Guthrie and we went back to a waiting cast after the lunch break. Mavor was dismissed without any apologies. He left the theatre as rehearsal resumed. I looked at Lloyd Bochner. His face said what I was thinking. As soon as rehearsal was over, we would rally round our friend.

Rehearsal resumed with Petruchio's entrance on that pantomime horse. Quiet, shy Needles took to the role like the proverbial duck to water. My hunch had been right, and Guthrie looked relaxed. His ruthless behaviour with Mavor didn't seem to bother him a bit.

Lloyd and I found Mavor having a cup of tea to relax his sore ribs. When I asked what his plans were, he smiled bravely and said, "To stay here, of course. I'm under contract to play Escalus in *Measure*." This was a doddery old man role, the kind Mavor had often played with great comic flair. He did the same the rest of the season at Stratford. But it was a middling role, and his two fellow New Play Society actors felt sorry for him and admired his guts.

Next rehearsal Tony decided that my character, the servant Tranio, needed a set of buck teeth. He sent me off to a Stratford dentist to be fitted. The message was clear: "If you don't want to play handsome young *jeune premières* then be prepared to uglify yourself." I went Guthrie one better. After trying on my new set of buckteeth, I went straight to the barbershop and got myself a Tony Guthrie haircut. This was similar to what new recruits get when they join the army. A real bean-shave. My dear wife raised her eyes to the heavens when she saw me, and my two little girls snickered a lot.

James Mason arrived for rehearsals and turned out to be the nicest guy. Famous for his glowering bulldog look in films, he immediately became one of us, joining the actors' cricket team and showing a talent for caricature. He spent some time drawing pictures of his fellow actors and handing them out as gifts.

It soon became apparent to the company that there were not strong hands at the helm. Cecil Clarke had been a colonel in the British army, but he lacked authority as a stage director. The actors wanted Guthrie to take over. Tony turned us down, because he was busy with the third production that would end the season, *Oedipus Rex*.

Clarke had been Guthrie's assistant for a long time. Tony considered him a valuable friend and refused to undercut him in this way. Eventually the concern of the cast became so great that Guthrie was forced to take over the long final scene of *Measure for Measure*, in which everything in the complicated plot gets resolved. The only bit of direction I got from Guthrie in the heat of dress rehearsal was "Why are you playing Ibsen?" In a flash I immediately saw the comedy aspects of the role and turned Lucio into a Renaissance fop.

Measure for Measure opened to bad press from the New York critics, especially for Mason. We all adored him by this time and took his plight personally. But the most violent reaction to his performance took place backstage at intermission on opening night. His wife Pamela Kellino stormed backstage and marched into his dressing room to tell him he was wasting his time here, and she had no intention of sticking around for the second half. I learned this from Mason's dresser, who was witness to this whole dreadful scene. His only comment was that "the witch should have been burned on the spot."

Next night, of course, was the first performance of our Wild West *Shrew*. The big boys from New York reversed gear and adored Guthrie's wacky conception, and so did the rest of the press. My teeth caused a spray and an audience laugh every time I spoke. Backstage I was confronted by the wife of a cast member, who had the same kind of teeth, but hers were permanently attached.

I felt so guilty that at the first opportunity, I asked Guthrie to let me try playing Tranio without the teeth. He agreed, and I got most of the laughs back anyway. One night Bill Shatner and I got enormous reaction from a scene that usually received only mild titters. We congratulated ourselves offstage on our success, until we were told that the excessive laughter was caused by a little squirrel that appeared through a hole in the flooring while we were onstage and stole the show.

For our second season the board felt secure enough to add a third production, *Oedipus Rex*. It fulfilled a long-held dream of Tony Guthrie to have it performed the way the Greeks did it 2,500 years ago, wearing masks and cothurnes (four-inch elevator shoes). This was to give the leading actors more god-like proportions. I was a member of the chorus led by Bill Hutt, and the title role, King Oedipus, was played by James Mason.

The opening performance was marred by coughing fits from the audience. It was not because they were bored. Guthrie had insisted on an authentic beginning by having his tall, tragic masked figures emerge from the primeval mists. The smoke machine worked just fine, but the body heat from the audience drew those mists in their direction, and the actors emerged on a smokeless bare stage.

For some reason my farm family from the year before, Ed and Phyllis Cardwell, came to the opening night of the play, which they had heard was about a sexy family. They were totally confused by the plot. Ed asked me a question after the performance. "Now tell me one thing. Was she his wife or his mother?"

Phyllis instead was fixated on Creon. She said, "I'm not too sure, but I know fer a fact that that there Crayon is her brother."

63: BACK TO BROADWAY

During that second summer of the festival, entertainment reporter Jock Carroll did a piece on me for *Maclean's* magazine entitled "He Doesn't Want to Be a Star." He described me as the actor who would rather learn than earn, someone who gave up $2,000 a week in television to work for an English repertory company for $28 a week. The first amount was exaggerated, but I was about to do the rep thing again. Douglas Campbell was busy all through the latter part of our season organizing a new group, the Canadian Players. He planned an initial offering of *Saint Joan* with his wife Ann Casson in the title role. The tour would go as far north in Ontario as James Bay.

Doug offered me the part of the Dauphin, the weakling French king who Joan always referred to as Charlie in Shaw's version. My long-suffering wife threw up her hands in horror. Once again she would be abandoned by her itinerant actor-husband.

She got part of her wish. Two offers from New York came my way just before I signed with the Canadian Players. One was to play the lead in a revival of Sean O'Casey's *Red Roses for Me*. The offer was made to me in person because the producer flew up from New York to Stratford in his private plane. I had always admired O'Casey. The New Play Society had done a good job of one of his masterpieces, *Juno and the Paycock*.

At the same time the Theater Guild contacted me to replace an actor in a play headed for Broadway. I had no idea how they had ever heard about me, but I realized later that the cast included Chris Plummer, and he was behind the offer. It was an Irish play, *Home Is the Hero*, about a man who comes out of jail after a long time in stir. The part offered me was that of the son, and it was a fantastic one. It was a definite offer at a good salary.

I read the O'Casey play and didn't like it, despite the fact that I've always been a fan. Also, I decided I would forego the Canadian Players offer in favour of the Broadway one. Doug Campbell was pretty miffed, and relations were frosty at the close of our season. My American producer was surprisingly generous and offered to fly me to New York to rehearse the other play. It's a good thing I took up his offer this time, because the next time he flew, his plane ended up at the bottom of Lake Erie and him with it.

Home Is the Hero was doing a pre-Broadway run in Westport, Connecticut. I had one night in New York before going there, and it happened to be the night of Hurricane Hazel. I was slammed against a wall in Shubert Alley by the wind and drenched with rain. When I reached Westport the next day, the town square was waist-deep in water. Since they hadn't broached the bad news yet to the actor I was replacing, Richard Lupino, I skipped the matinee performance and waded across the Westport town square in my shorts in knee-deep water to a movie theatre, where I had my first exposure to *Gone with the Wind*.

Don in New York, 1954, in Home Is the Hero, *with author and lead actor Walter Macken.*

Home Is the Hero is an Irish play about a man who comes home after five years in jail for killing a man in a brawl. The role was played by the author, Walter Macken, who had great success with it in his native Dublin.

I played his son, Willy, with a permanent limp since infancy, caused by my father tossing me in the air in a drunken fit. I decided to prepare for the part by putting a stone in my shoe to remind me of his affliction. I was surprised to find Chris Plummer playing a minor role in this production.

First thing Chris did was pay me back the twenty-five bucks he had borrowed from me when I was on my way to England. I was flattered he remembered, because I kept hearing stories about his unpaid tailor bills, and his other extravagances were common gossip in the company. A week later Chris borrowed back the $25, "till next time."

I had two days before I played it onstage, and ten days before we opened at the Booth Theatre on Broadway. The part of my sister was not a particularly good one, and Peggy Ann Garner left a Hollywood career to do it. Glenda Farrell, a prominent film actress of the 1930s, played her mother. Peg knuckled under to the Theater Guild management when they insisted she dye her naturally blond locks a funereal black. It made her look depressed.

We opened, and I remember getting good laughs in a scene with my girlfriend, played by a little cutie named Loretta Leversee. In the play she complimented me on the new suit I was wearing, and I replied in a mournful tone and a Dublin accent, "I'll probly be burried in it." The next day Walter Kerr called me one of the three best young actors in North America.

I would love to know who he thought the other two were, but I remembered what happened when Bernard Shaw told Cedric Hardwicke he was one of the finest five actors in the world. When Sir Cedric asked Shaw who the other four were, Shaw replied, "The Marx brothers."

It was the first time, and the last, that I got better reviews than Chris Plummer.

I had moved my little family to a ground-floor apartment in Greenwich Village, so I had to scare up other employment when the play closed after a month. My good reviews got me an offer of a film contract from MGM, and an appointment to meet their head of production, Dore Schary, in his New York office. At the same time MCA offered to represent me as my agent. Before I went to MGM, I met the MCA agent who wanted to represent me, Maynard Morris. He was not a very prepossessing figure, a jumpy, nervous, twitchy little man who seemed too anxious to please. But I was told by my fellow actors that he was the most important agent in New York, so I let him represent me in my talks with MGM. The "talks" took all of ten minutes, and they offered me a seven-year contract. Morris told me to turn it down. I didn't hesitate to agree, because I hoped to spend the next seven summers at Stratford, Ontario.

Meantime I got a definite offer to join Katharine Cornell and Tyrone Power in another Christopher Fry play, *The Dark Is Light Enough*. It wasn't full of flashy humour, but it did have Fry's lovely verse-play. The part was a secondary one, and so was the role offered Chris Plummer, but he got the chance to understudy Tyrone Power.

We both accepted the gig and made sure we could get out of it in case of a long Broadway run, because we were both headed next summer for separate Stratfords, mine in Ontario and his in Connecticut.

Power came to the first rehearsal directly from a film preview of the new British film *Romeo and Juliet*. Ty said the film didn't really get going until some old geek had finished telling you what was going to happen, but luckily "we got past him to where it was really happening." Chris had to tell him that the old geek was John Gielgud.

We were on tour for four months. First we played Buffalo, then our hometown, Toronto. I remember a CBC interview with Elaine Grand involving both myself and Plummer, in which she asked us about some of the more difficult passages in the play. Chris repeated some of the analysis of Fry's main theme that I had given in a similar interview in Buffalo. Just for fun, I interrupted him in mid-dissertation and said, "No, Chris, that's not what Fry meant at all." I proceeded to make up an alternate interpretation, completely at variance with what Chris had just said. Instead of being annoyed, he winked at me as I continued bluffing. Chris understood a bluff better than anyone.

On tour we shared a dressing room. Chris was always a half-hour late and slapped on a few quick dabs of makeup just in time to go onstage. He always never bothered to own a scrap of any of that stuff, preferring instead to delve into my makeup box. For Christmas I got him a present of an empty cigar box without any bottom to it. "What the hell's this for?" he asked. I offered to demonstrate how to use it. I merely put the bottomless cigar box over my own makeup lying on the table, and moved it over in front of his mirror. He accepted it with good grace.

We had a good time because we whooped it up after the show wherever we were in the United States. We sought out places where jazz was being played. I whooped it up without liquor and Chris made up for it in that department. But he never drank before or during a performance.

Opening night in New York was so-so. Katharine Cornell had been the leading lady of the American theatre, but the Fry verse did not flow trippingly off her tongue as it did with Dame Edith Evans. But I have nothing but pleasant memories of Katharine Cornell. Opening night she ordered champagne for everyone in the cast. I remember congratulating her on her generosity by mistakenly repeating the slogan of Canada Dry: "Gee, Miss Cornell, this must be the ginger ale of champagnes!"

64: BACK TO THE BARD

The Dark Is Light Enough closed just in time for Chris and me to head off to our separate Shakespeares. Plummer was going to Connecticut to open their copycat festival by playing Mark Antony to Raymond Massey's Caesar. I wondered if another Massey would come to the rescue of their festival the way his cousin Vincent had been the saviour of ours.

Unfortunately, Chris vanished soon after I found out that Tony Guthrie was in New York for a few days. Tony was on future theatre business before heading to Ontario for our third season. I met him for lunch at his hotel and told him what a good actor Chris Plummer was and how he should be with us at Stratford.

Guthrie sniffed. "I'm told on good authority that he's a hopeless drunk." I told him about our recent four-month tour in which Chris never touched a drop until the curtain came down. I had made my plea and hoped that it registered.

We got on to other topics, like Tony's choice of *The Merchant of Venice* for the coming season. I said, "Why are you doing this anti-Semitic play after six million Jews had been murdered in the Holocaust?" Tony told me to wait and see. His production of the play would be resolutely anti-Gentile. I told him I couldn't wait — I needed to know right now how he planned to do this.

Guthrie outlined a Venetian society in which the Gentiles were the country-club set, the type who lived off the stock market, while Shylock had to earn an honest living through usury, the only occupation allowed to a Jew. Antonio, the merchant of Venice of the title, has all kinds of deals going with shipping goods overseas. He is a rich homosexual who was having an affair with a young bisexual named Bassanio and keeping him in luxury. But Bassanio has his sights on a rich young heiress named Portia who has more bucks in the bank, and so Bassanio wants Antonio's blessing to fly the coop and go straight. It's Antonio's loan of the money for Bassanio to go a-wooing in Belmont that ends up with Antonio borrowing that money from Shylock. This financial arrangement ends up in the "pound of flesh" bond, which starts out as a joke from Shylock, but ends up in dead earnest when he loses his daughter Jessica to a Gentile.

That's Lorenzo, one of Bassanio's social set, who has fallen in love with Jessica, Shylock's only daughter. He has plans to abduct her and enter into a biracial marriage. Guthrie offered me the part of Lorenzo. I turned it down. I told him that after his description of the role, I wanted to play the bisexual goy-boy-toy Bassanio. Without any hesitation, Guthrie agreed.

Tony had hired a great actor, Frederic Valk, a Czech refugee from Hitler, to play Shylock. He had recently been acclaimed in London for his Othello. His nemesis in legal argument, Portia, was to be played by Frances Hyland.

During that luncheon, Tony and I went on to talk about the new director, Michael Langham. Guthrie said this third season was perhaps his own last year, and he would go on to other projects when Langham would take over the whole Stratford operation.

Don as Bassanio with Frances Hyland as Portia in The Merchant of Venice, *1955, during the Stratford Festival's third season.*

FRANCES HYLAND as PORTIA
DONALD HARRON as BASSANIO
The Merchant of Venice
SHAKESPEAREAN FESTIVAL 1955
Stratford, Canada

Oedipus Rex would be repeated this season, with Doug Campbell filling the platform shoes of James Mason. Again I risked Guthrie's displeasure by telling him I didn't want to be one of those "Seven Dwarfs" in that Greek chorus. I wanted a night off to stay home with my family. Without a murmur, my request was granted.

We rented the same house in Stratford, which certainly suited my kids, because they loved playing in the tar at the end of the street, much to the consternation of their mother. They were also getting old enough to ride with me on my bike, Muffin on the crossbar and little Mary in the basket at the front.

First rehearsals began with no read-through but plunging immediately into the play. Valk was not particularly tall, but his bulk gave him considerable presence onstage. Standing in the wings one day at rehearsal, he made the wry remark to me that if Shakespeare's plays were not written by him (a controversy still extant) then they must have been written by somebody else of the same name. He fitted in with the cast immediately.

Lloyd Bochner became his chief Jew-baiter. They were both played like Nazis in our production, which is ironic because Lloyd himself is Jewish. Bill Shatner, another Jew, was the bully boy Gratiano, boyfriend of Portia's maid Nerissa, and played by Michael Langham's wife, Helen Burns. She turned out to have a blissful comic gift.

The audience might not have known about the sexual goings-on between my bisexual Bassanio and Antonio, who was played by straight-as-a-die Bob Goodier. It was not spelled out. The only hint might have been a too-long embrace as I departed for Belmont to win Portia's hand. Smouldering looks, but no mincing ones.

There was an exciting new addition to the cast. The Prince of Morocco was given the booming voice of Lorne Greene. That's all the spokesperson of the national news needed to completely command the stage. He chose the gold casket, while I hung around in the background waiting to swing with the lead.

The true star of the production was Tanya Moiseiwitsch. Her costumes this time spectacularly invoked the spirit of Botticelli. As we did the first year, but not the second, the leading actors sat to have their portraits painted by Canadian artist, Grant Macdonald. I still own his portrait of me as Bassanio. With a black curly wig and Tanya's gorgeous Renaissance costumes, I must confess I looked like Elizabeth Taylor.

I gained a groupie that season. A bunch of Ottawa schoolgirls visited us one afternoon and among them was young Adrienne Poy, later Clarkson. She confessed to me just a couple of years ago that she was absolutely smitten with that gorgeously costumed hunk Bassanio. Quite a revelation from a governor general. Robertson Davies didn't quite agree. He wrote in his third Stratford book, "Donald Harron could charm the birds out of the trees, but he is a light comedian, not a romantic hero."

In the other play, Langham cast me as Octavius Caesar. It's a small part but worth it for the final moment at the end of the play when he and Mark Antony stare at each other and divide the world between them. Donald Davis was our Antony, compared with Chris Plummer's in the other Stratford. Robert Christie was our Caesar and Lloyd Bochner was the "lean and hungry" Cassius.

Bill Shatner played Brutus's servant and was there to assist at the death scene as Brutus commits suicide. One night there was a lot of laughter in that scene, the presence of which no one onstage could figure out. But Bill found out that it was that same damn squirrel from last year, climbing through that same damn hole in the stage and irreverently enlivening the solemn proceedings!

The night before we closed, I had a quiet supper with Michael Langham. He was basically a shy man, unlike the flamboyant Guthrie. He told me that next year he and Guthrie had agreed on him doing *Henry V* with actors from Quebec in the roles of the French. But best news of all to me was that the role of Hank the Sank, as we actors liked to call him, would be played by Christopher Plummer. So perhaps Guthrie had listened to me!

I was overjoyed, and more so when Langham said, "I'm directing. What part would you like to play?" Without any hesitation I told him I wanted to be the Chorus, the one who follows the troops and spouts exciting monologues as the campaign in France progresses. I suggested that I should start out in contemporary clothes and then maybe change into period costume as the war in France progresses. I would be coming back to Stratford for its (and my) fourth consecutive season.

What to do in the meantime? The man I turned into John A. Macdonald, Bob Christie, had a temporary solution. He had been hired to direct a summer stock production of *The Glass Menagerie* in a nearby summer theatre at Vineland. The Gentleman Caller was to be played by Bill Shatner.

What was not cast was the role of the son, Tom Wingfield, a character Tennessee based on himself. That was me. It's the best play Williams ever wrote, in my opinion, and a pleasure to be a part of, if only for a week. But in those seven days, Bob and I thought up another project to put on later in Toronto: an autumn version of *Spring Thaw*. I wanted to call it *Fall Freeze*, but Bob thought we might get in trouble with dear Dora and even Mavor, who was busy at the moment in negotiations to take over a new theatre at the foot of the city next door to the new O'Keefe Centre. It eventually became the Canadian Stage.

Looking up a Shakespeare dictionary, I came across a quotation, "the lover, the lunatick and the poet's eye in a fine frenzy rolling." So we settled on a title *Fine Frenzy* then set about getting a cast together. Our first and obvious thought was Jane Mallett.

Maybe the Moores weren't amused when we dragooned a pair of their recent stars, the utility man of all-time, Peter Mews, and a relative new-comer from the West Coast, Dave Broadfoot, to be part of our ensemble.

There were no reviews of *The Glass Menagerie* that I know of, but we all had a good time acting in that moving play. I thought that cut-up Bill Shatner did a lovely gentlemanly job of the Caller, probably paving the way for his Captain Kirk. I was okay, I think. Never sure without the reviews, which gives you some idea of my insecurity in non-character parts.

65: FRENZY TO OPEN

Bob Christie's and my thoughts were fixed on the short rehearsal period ahead before we opened our new revue at the Avenue Theatre just before Hallowe'en. It was a movie house gone bad due to network television, but it was just the right size for our stage efforts, about 400 seats.

We had to have some Shakespeare to justify the use of that title, so I wrote a sketch for Jane Mallett entitled "The Queen Elizabeth Way." The idea of the sketch was that the Bard was so successful with his plays that Good Queen Jane (sorry, Bess) got the idea that royalty should share in his royalties, because these new-fangled plays were catching on with the public. ("Nobody looks at a tapestry anymore.")

Jane was also featured in a film travelogue made from home movies provided by John Drainie. The idea was to take well-known local landmarks and pretend they were world-famous like the Arc de Triomphe and the Eiffel Tower, when actually we were looking at something in suburban Trawna. Jane made it work with her tony upper-class accent. She sounded exactly like a cousin of hers I had met who spoke in a manner where every vowel becomes a dipthong. I was to steal this kind of upper-class Canadian accent ten years later when I became a drag queen and created Valerie Rosedale.

I myself had the absolute gall, not divided into three parts, to play a disc jockey who drops all his records on the floor at the beginning of his program and has to resort to live imitations of musical classics like Jan Peerce singing "The Bluebeard of Happiness." Need I go on?

What about Charlie Farquharson in all this? Well, a fourteen-year-old girl named Marilyn Bell had just swum across Lake Ontario, so Charlie attempted the same feat, but down by Niagara-on-the-Lake, where the lake is only two miles across. I came out in Jewison's father's chewed-up cap and the by-now familiar roll-top cardigan of Norman Campbell, but underneath it was a set of long johns, and I had a pair of flippers on my feet.

I had a can of Crown Brand Corn Syrup, explaining that I would dowse my underwear in the stuff to keep warm. My opening line was: *I plan to start acrost as soon as she's cam.*

For the life of me I cannot remember a line of the rest of the monologue, because of what happened to me backstage after the opening performance. Norman Campbell and his wife Elaine were in the audience. I knew they were there, because Elaine has the heartiest, most infectious laugh that would gladden the heart of any comedian. After the show they came backstage, because, as Norman said, "I wanted to visit my sweater."

I had no intention of giving it back to him, but that's not the only reason he came backstage.

PART III

Little Orphan Anne with an E,
1956 to 1969

66: CARDIGAN REVISITED

Norman told me with a furrowed brow that the CBC had just granted him ninety minutes of television time to do with whatever he liked. (Can you imagine this happening today?) I asked why his brow was so furrowed. Why didn't he do another of those light-hearted musicals, like *We Take to the Woods* with Shirley Harmer and Bob Goulet?

Elaine thought a musical was a good idea, but neither could think of another one. So I told them that I had been reading a book to my kids that summer in Stratford: *Anne of Green Gables*. Usually when I read fairy tales I made fun of the text. ("Oh Daddy! Read it straight!") But this time I did read it straight, because I got as involved in the story as my kids did. Five-year-old Muffin was deeply into the orphan story, and three-year-old Mary was so used to being an orphan due to my peripatetic career that she went along with her older sister.

Norman had vague memories of seeing a film version back in the mid-1930s. I told him it was about a young orphan girl with an imagination so vivid that the only way you could render the way she expressed herself onstage would be to set it to music. Elaine said she would get the book out of the library and start reading it immediately. I think the thing that attracted Norman to the project was its 100 percent Canadian content. He told me he would check with the CBC management and let me know in a couple of days.

Two days later, Norman phoned me and said the CBC production of *Anne of Green Gables* was on. I would adapt the orphan novel into a libretto, Norman would write the music, and Elaine and I would share the lyrics with him.

As soon as *Fine Frenzy* finished, I was determined to get away from Toronto to the Muskoka Lakes, which had much more of a Prince Edward Island-like feeling. Finally, my dear long-suffering intellectual, Northrop Frye groupie Gloria would have a writer in the family. I had saved enough from the Stratford summer without having to grub around for bits of television in Toronto. That's all that seemed to be around. Norman Jewison had become CBC's number one director of TV variety, but when he asked their permission to do a half-hour drama, they refused his request. He packed up, went to the States, and ended up doing powerful dramatic films.

I was getting some offers from south of the border, too. Katharine Cornell had signed to do a *Producers' Showcase* version of her early stage success *The Barretts of Wimpole Street*, and she told my New York agent she wanted me to play the part of her youngest brother.

I realized that I had better do something about getting a green card. Americans were tightening up on Canadian actors, so I contacted my agent, who contacted an immigration lawyer. His solution? Bribery! He knew some American official in the Toronto embassy who was on the take for things like that. I came down from Muskoka and got my green card by paying this embassy crook the going under-the-table rate, U.S.$750. Today I understand that "Here comes the bribe!" would be more like $15,000.

I'm not worried about this information being in print, because I lost my green card years later. I did a benefit for Stratford in Chicago, and some official conned onto the fact that I lived in Toronto when I claimed to be a resident of Nashville. In the last twenty years so many Canadians have said to me, "I'm so glad you stayed here in this country." I didn't. I spent twenty years outside my own country. I'm glad I did, because it has given me a perspective on my native land that has served me (and Charlie) well as observers of things Canadian.

Writing in peaceful Muskoka with my wife and kids, I was able to finish up a rough draft of the script in three weeks. Tommy Tweed, a master of adaptations, was the one who taught me the first (and only) law of adaptation: "Be true to your writer." I had my baptism in adaptation when I wrote scripts based on *Sunshine Sketches of a Little Town*. I learned that both Stephen Leacock and Lucy Maud Montgomery had created such a following among European readers in the decade preceding the First World War that although their readers hadn't a very clear idea of where Canada was, they were faithful fans of both novelists.

Some theatregoers still think that the jokes in our musical are mine. I can assure you that 99 percent of them originated with Lucy Maud herself. An example is the moment when the schoolkids appear as the Fathers of Confederation in the school pageant, and Mrs. Pye asks Mrs. Lynde who they represent. Mrs. Lynde replies with firm authority, "That's the Last Supper."

I bought a book entitled *The Art of Dramatic Writing* by Lajos Egri. The one thing I remembered from that book was a simple statement: if you are going to write a play, you should be able to describe the essence of it in one sentence. My one-sentence capsule of *Anne of Green Gables* was: "The perpetual loser emerges as the winner."

Mark Twain described Anne Shirley as the dearest heroine in fiction since Alice in Wonderland. I went even further back to Cinderella. Orphaned by the death of her father, she faces life with a cruel stepmother and two indifferent stepsisters but is eventually aided by a fairy godmother. Marilla wasn't cruel, sometimes just indifferent, and Matthew Cuthbert was neither a godmother nor a fairy but turned out to be a sympathetic ally. But basically Anne was on her own in life's struggles, and the loser does emerge the winner.

The biggest problem I faced was that the original novel deals with a little girl aged about eleven who emerges at the end of the book as a young woman closing in on eighteen. This doesn't work onstage. You have to use the same actress throughout. The solution? Ignore all specific references to the passage of time and concentrate on the change of seasons. No mention on the passage of years. Anne arrives on the island in the spring, goes to school, then has a summer of ice cream and jumping off the roof with an umbrella, returns to school in the fall, gets a new teacher, resumes rivalries with Gilbert Blythe and Josie Pye, dyes hair green, gets Diana Barry drunk by accident. Spends the winter studying for a scholarship, and the cutting of that green hair turns a pig-tailed urchin into a bobbed-hair mature teenager. Spring brings a mixture of triumph (she wins the scholarship) and tragedy (Matthew's death). The play ends with Anne's reconciliation with both Marilla and Gilbert Blythe.

Next season will be the forty-ninth for the musical, and I am looking forward to our golden anniversary, but wishing that Norman and Elaine were here to celebrate with me.

So far the forty-five pages of adaptation represented only the bare bones of our musical. Next came the songs and lyrics. In the meantime, Norman had been too busy to read the book, but Elaine had finished it and we started work on the lyrics. This happened at their home in suburban Toronto, Norman at the piano in the living room, Elaine in the kitchen baking something to feed us in between bouts of creativity, and me on the sofa petting their chow dog, Puff.

Elaine kept writing lyrics for *Anne* even when she was in the delivery room. She sent the lyrics to Norman then gave birth. When he visited her immediately after the happy arrival, he congratulated her. First, on the lyrics she had written *in extremis* and secondly on the arrival of their son, Robin. Quoting from our new lyrics, Norm said, "We didn't clearly request a boy, but, boy, are we happy with the one we got!"

At the same time I left town with my spanking new green card, because I was able to accept a New York television job on the *U.S. Steel Hour*. I played Joanne Woodward's husband and Joan Blondell's son-in-law. There was a young fellow who was always around after rehearsals to squire Joanne to dinner before he went to his own theatre performance. His name was Paul Newman. He soon went into movies and out-Brando'd the local opposition in becoming the film hunk of all-time.

I cannot remember the name of the play we did, but I have vivid memories of its author, James Costigan, who was fascinated with my adaptation assignment and wanted to help. He did, too, giving me sound advice about the art. I found time to continue work on the lyrics for *Anne of Green Gables*.

I went to the New York Public Library to do research on the making of ice cream. I also added some lyrics to the ones Elaine wrote in a song, "Gee, I'm Glad I'm No One Else but Me." It's about Anne discovering to her dismay that the roads were the same colour as her hair. So I sent the new lyrics through the CBC office in New York, located in the U.N. building.

Two weeks later, Norman was still waiting for those lyrics. Time before rehearsals started was getting short. MCA was getting me TV offers for other shows in New York. I would be lucky to get back in time for the taping of the show. But more urgent was our lyric situation. It turned out the United Nations was being monitored by Senator Joseph McCarthy's Committee, checking for Communist influences in the United Nations. All those lyrics about red roads and red hair had seemed awfully suspicious to McCarthy's bloodhounds, and they intercepted our transmissions.

Casting for *Anne* went ahead without me. John Drainie was cast as Matthew. He had a good singing voice and a limp that prevented him from playing many parts in a visual medium, but it suited Matthew Cuthbert just fine. His sister Marilla was Margot Christie, wife to Bob, and Anne was somebody I had seen as Princess Winterfall Summerspring on *Howdy*

Doody, Toby Tarnow. So a nice Jewish girl from Saskatchewan was chosen for our Island orphan. She had already played the part in a radio adaptation for CBC.

I was marooned in New York with my successful U.S. television career. I got another *U.S. Steel Hour* entitled *Tragedy in a Temporary Town* by Rod Serling and starring Lloyd Bridges. It was about racism against Spanish-speaking citizens. I played a bully, the younger brother of a wonderful character actor, Jack Warden, who hits me when I hesitate to be a racist. He never touched me all through rehearsal, but on the actual show he hit me a wallop upside my head that had my lights spinning for several minutes. That's professionalism.

This show became quite notorious, because in the climactic scene Bridges forgot his lines because of the effort in taking a sledgehammer and smashing several bigots' headlights. In his frustration at his faulty memory, he shouted out instead "Goddamn it!" The next day this rated headlines on the front page of the *New York Times*.

I did get back to Toronto in time for the taping of our musical. One of the additions to the cast was *Spring Thaw* star Barbara Hamilton, who played Lucilla, the girl in Blair's store who waits on Matthew Cuthbert when he is too shy to tell her he wants to buy puffed sleeves. Barbara backed John Drainie up against the coffee-bean grinder, and John's flailing as he accidentally spun the wheels of it was one of the highlights of the show.

However, our show was in danger of becoming a complete bust, because the actress in the title role could not utter a sound. Toby Tarnow was suffering from some kind of food poisoning. To add to our troubles, Nonnie Griffin, playing Diana Barry, arrived on set with pneumonia. Her doctor forbade her to do the show, but like a trouper she disobeyed his orders.

I was panicking, but Norm Campbell was cucumberish cool. He told Toby to just mouth the words as she took up all the camera positions she had rehearsed. She had been given a pill to induce her to throw up, but it got stuck halfway down. Buckets were placed at strategic spots around the studio in the event the deluge happened.

The thing about live television is that opening night is closing night. There is no question of turning back. This is it. All I remember of the actual taping was that the little girl from Gravelbourg, Saskatchewan, managed somehow to give a full-fledged, full-voiced performance. Everyone else had their spirits rise to the occasion, and if you want, you can get the whole ninety-minute black-and-white miracle from CBC.

67: MY COUNTRY, WHAT'S IT TO THEE?

The TV debut of *Anne of Green Gables* was my farewell to Canada for the next ten years. I didn't know it at the time. I fully expected to be back for my fourth season at the Stratford Festival. But just before the taping of *Anne* I received a telegram from Michael Langham advising me that I was to play Fenton in *The Merry Wives of Windsor* and Bishop Scroop in *Henry V*.

Merry Wives is my least favourite Shakespeare play, and Fenton is the kind of vapid nice-young-man role a burgeoning character actor like me tends to avoid. As for the good Bishop, Lord Scroop was taken away to have his head chopped off almost as soon as he appeared. No mention of the plum role of Chorus that we had discussed last summer. I thought at the time that Langham had nodded his approval. I was wrong. So I fired off a telegram: "Scroop you, Langham!"

I called my New York agent the day before the *Anne* taping. John Houseman, the man who had produced the film of *Julius Caesar* with Marlon Brando as Antony, and had just completed the Van Gogh film with Kirk Douglas in the title role, was in New York and offering me a season at Stratford, Connecticut. I didn't even ask what roles. I told my agent to accept it.

Whenever I left my native country, I always took something of it with me. This time it was a wartime novel by the poet Earle Birney, *The Adventures of Private Turvey*. Nothing poetic about it. It's a Canadian version of the Sad Sack character so popular in the U.S. *Stars and Stripes* comic section during the war. The day after our taping, I read it on the train trip back to New York with great relish and determined that some-day I would please my wife by becoming an adapter again. She had been thrilled about my *Green Gables* assignment and hoped for more. Gloria told me the Toronto reviews of *Anne* were quite friendly, and Elaine told her there was talk of rerunning it the following season.

Before we took up residence in Stratford, Connecticut for the summer, I had a chance to return to Toronto and prepare to bring my brood Stateside with me. I also saw my parents and took time to do a television interview with my old high school pal Louie Libman, now called Larry Mann. He had me (or rather Charlie) guest on his late-night talk show for CBC-TV.

To prepare for it I was able to catch up on all the news, and the scandals. Politically there were plenty of them, including the Pipeline Scandal that eventually brought John Diefenbaker to power.

Round about this time them Merkens started comin' round our parts fer to stair at our assets. They thot Canda wuz a nacheral gas and wanted to take it all home with 'em.

Yer old Seedy Howe he wuz gonna let them, too. He had evrything rigged fer to sell us out without no time fer debait in yer Commonhouse.

Well sir, our primed minster Looie Sin Lorrent (ya mind him and his see-ways?) wuz figgerin' without yer leeder of yer oppsit posishun Long John Doofenbeeker, hoo wooden be shutup, and haznt sints, cuz he wuz allways fullabluster.

And that's jist wat he start up all by hisself. Long John start on yer windiest gabbin' match ever seen in Canda. Them Libreeals called it yer pipe-down debait. But John wernt noan as yer wind frum yer prayery fer nuthin' and he tocked hisself all the ways acrost yer floor frum yer oppsit-posishun to yer premeership. First thing he dun wen he wuz in like flin, wuz bring up yer billy rites.

But then there was *l'affaire* Gerda Munsinger, the German would-be Mata Hari supposedly involved with two Tory cabinet ministers.

The scandal, combined with a prison escape arranged for an ice-rink hoser, Lucien Rivard, brought the Liberals under Pearson back in again.

I'm sure I got the events all mixed up, but the interview with my old school pal went off without a hitch. I went back to New York to get ready for the Stratford, Connecticut, season.

68: STRATFORD-ON-THE-HOUSATONIC

The good news about the American Stratford was that by this time the Theater Guild snobs were out of the picture and the enterprise had been taken over by Lincoln Kerstein and John Houseman. I didn't know much about the former, except that he was the founder of the New York City

Ballet, but the latter impressed me with his credentials, starting with co-producing with Orson Welles and the Mercury Theater, and several good Hollywood film credits.

The bad news was that in two of the three productions I was cast in roles that I had turned down in the Ontario operation: in *Shrew*, Lucentio, and in *Measure for Measure*, the brother of Isabella, Claudio (another nice young man with no character parts). However, I had Scrooped my bridges in Ontario, so I decided to go with the flow.

Stratford, Connecticut, was almost as pretty as Stratford, Ontario. We rented a white-framed house on tree-lined Main Street.

The rehearsals started with *King John*, a play not familiar to me in any way. The title role was to be played by John Emery, who had just finished being John Barrymore in a film, *Too Much, Too Soon*, with Diana Barrymore, the famous idol's daughter. Considering the rest of her career onstage, the title was all too true. I saw her later in a play in Boston when she was almost too drunk to stand.

My role was the Dauphin, son of the King of France. Dad the king was played by Arnold Moss, a ham actor much given to spitting all over me when he emoted, which was most of the time. I was given something to wear almost as laughable, a crown with two unnaturally tall white projections that looked for all the world like a pair of rabbit ears. I also had to say a tongue twister of a line: "What lusty trumpet thus hath summoned us?" Try saying that three times fast without tripping over your tongue.

When it came to the rest of my costume, I missed Tanya Moiseiwitsch and her lightweight fibreglass armour. Our designer had been asked to give the characters epic proportions. He settled for gigantic rather than epic and studiously avoided porous materials. His materials were a kind of rubbery plastic.

Halfway through the first dress confrontation between the forces of England and France on a hot Connecticut afternoon, Houseman called a two-hour break, because twelve bodies littered the stage in various stages of dehydration. I was one of them. When I came to, Morris Carnovsky was still out cold beside me. We had to be cut free from our costumes, against the wishes of our designer.

During the break I read the reviews of *Henry V* in Ontario, and they were glowing, both for Chris Plummer and the French actors. No time for regrets about my decision. I had another cup of tea and put my faith in Houseman, who was acting like a true leader. We came back to rehearsal to find our costumes punctured, gouged, slashed, and gutted. The cotton padding that held in the heat was removed. We had a director who cared more about ourselves than our appearance. The designer cried sabotage; the cast cried "Hooray!" Houseman decided the cuts and slashes looked as if we were in a battle.

We opened a week later. Houseman had decided on back-to-back openings. *Measure for Measure* was practically modern dress. I was given a suit with a double-breasted vest. Houseman criticized the collar they gave me. "He looks like Tony Curtis!" I was flattered. My old part, Lucio, was played brilliantly by a blacklisted actor, Norman Lloyd. Morris Carnovsky had also been banned from both Broadway and television by the same bunch of bigots. This was the political climate of the Broadway theatre of the 1950s.

The audience took one look at our costumes and must have accepted the slashes in them as the marks of battle-hardened veterans. But the critics didn't accept our production.

The only vote of approval was from my three-year-old daughter Mary, and it wasn't for me, it was for John Emery. Little Mary thought King John was a lovely man because he wore a golden crown and proved he was a true king, because he was the only person onstage who got to sit down! (This critique from the now-heralded film director and scriptwriter of *I Shot Andy Warhol* and *American Psycho*.)

We faced the same disapproving bunch of New York critics the next night. Another mass pan, and this new-found festival would be out of business. But *Measure* got raves from the same critics, mostly, I suppose, because it was better than *King John*. The same critics had been kind to me personally. Brooks Atkinson of the *New York Times* complimented me on my rabbit-crowned Dauphin and "admired the perfection of Donald Harron's Claudio."

Houseman found that review before it appeared in print. Our press agent had helped all the critics make their telephone calls, and after they had gone, went to lock up the building. In a wastebasket he found a crumpled sheet of carbon paper. He brought it to Houseman, who held it up to the light. "Shakespeare's bitterest comedy has never seemed so delightful, and the acting on the Stratford stage has never seemed so accomplished. I urge you to ..." That was all there was, but it was enough to save the season. Houseman read it to us at the opening night party, which only became a party when that was made known.

We had a *King John* matinee the following day, but Houseman stayed up till dawn phoning friends in New York to get all the other critics' reactions to *Measure*. They were raves, too. This was probably *Measure*'s first exposure to a predominantly American audience, and they gave us prolonged, ecstatic applause. At the cast party we were exhilarated by the audience reception. The critics could have put us out of business, but we knew that word-of-mouth alone might save this festival from bankruptcy.

The *Taming of the Shrew* could now go ahead. It was to be directed by Norman Lloyd. The senile suitor of the younger daughter Bianca was played by Morris Carnovsky. He devised a great sight gag for his miserly character. When he opened his ledger to assess Bianca's dowry, moths flew out. The *Times*' Arthur Gelb called it "inspired madness."

In a way that describes the whole zany summer. *The Shrew* was another hit. The only distinguishing mark of my performance as Lucentio is that I prevented my understudy from ever appearing in the role when he was frothing at the mouth to do it. He already had the photo taken to be placed on the cover of the program for next season's festival. His name was Peter Bogdanovich.

Out of that first Connecticut season came an offer to audition for the New York production of the London hit *Separate Tables*. I practised my English accent on the train into New York by reading London magazines as if I were a BBC correspondent. I nailed the sucker. It probably meant my family and I could stay in New York all next season.

69: AT HOME ON BROADWAY

Separate Tables was a huge success in London, where it had run for two years. It consisted of two one-act plays by Terence Rattigan in which the leading actors have a chance to play totally different characters in each half, while the rest of the actors stay the same. Most of the original West End cast came across the pond.

The director was Peter Glenville. The role I was playing was that of a young medical student living in sin with his girlfriend in the first play, then married to her with a baby in the second one. I was paired with a gorgeous redhead, Ann Hillary.

Every performance, Ann and I ate dishes of Jell-O, which was pretending to be something else, I know not what. But after a long run of this on Broadway, my finger- and toenails had never been in better shape. The rest of the cast ate sliced apples which passed for chicken. By the time we left for Boston for a two-week pre-Broadway run, rehearsals for this cast were more or less a done deal. I was included in this leisure. I had brought along my copy of *The Adventures of Private Turvey*, the Charlie Brown/*Peanuts*–type loser in Canadian uniform during the last global conflict that Charlie Farquharson always referred to as World War Eleven.

While the British cast explored historical Boston and restaurants like Lockober's, Jake Wirth's, and Durgen Park, I holed up in my hotel room in the Avery and in two weeks knocked out a first draft of two out of three acts of a stage version of Birney's picaresque novel.

For some reason, Tony Curtis came along to our opening night. He confided to me that he could never stand on a stage anymore and repeat the same words night after night. I reminded him that he used to do that years before, when he was considered Broadway's cutest chorus boy in some now-forgotten musical. When he made his first film with Piper Laurie, *The Prince Who Was a Thief*, a standard joke among New York actors was that the billing should have used their real names, Bernie Schwartz and Rosie Jacobs in *The Prince Who Was a Gonef*.

I think David Niven was there that night, but he didn't show himself at the after-theatre party at Sardi's. But he must have attended our play more than once, because the film performance that eventually got him an Oscar was based note for note on Eric Portman's brilliant stage portrayal. The New York critics raved about *Separate Tables* as much as their London counterparts had done. It was so refreshing for me.

The week after we opened, my wife kept my bumptious kids away from me as I sat at my smoking typewriter finishing Act Three of my adaptation of *Turvey*. I immediately phoned Mavor Moore in Toronto. He was in the midst of a highly successful run of his musical version of *Candide* starring Bob Goulet in the title role.

It was a critical hit, but Mavor was prevented from taking it further because it conflicted with a planned Broadway production of the same Voltaire novel with Lillian Hellmann's adaptation and Leonard Bernstein's music. This was eventually directed by Tyrone Guthrie and got nine Broadway raves. Despite that, it closed after a very short run, due to its high intellectual content, I suspect.

At the Music Box Theater in New York, 1956, with Ann Hillary as Don's wife in **Separate Tables.**

Mavor had taken a lease on the same theatre where his musical opened. I guess he needed new product to fill the seats, because he told me to send him my script right away. Two weeks later he optioned it for performance! This was late October. By January, the worst month in the year for theatre, it was onstage in Toronto.

I wasn't there opening night, of course, because I had a job in another city, but the reviews were quite friendly, and I was bursting to see my work. But *Tables* producer Robert Whitehead was reluctant to let me go, even for a one-night stand. I had a very good understudy in Michael Lipton, who had become a good friend. On his advice I finally erupted and told Whitehead he was a lousy Canadian. I said this to the most successful producer on Broadway that season, with four long-run hits out of a possible six. He grinned amiably and finally let me take a quick flight to Toronto.

What a thrill I got! The play was directed by Bob Christie. My former Stratford understudy, Douglas Rain, played the nerdy title role. My old schoolmate Larry Mann was surprisingly good as the French-Canadian, Gounod, who defends Turvey from hospital bureaucracy when our hero becomes deathly ill.

The only serious flaws onstage that night were in my script. I realized that to reach its full potential, *The Adventures of Private Turvey* should have been a musical.

70: KISS ME, KATE!

Midway through the run of *Separate Tables*, I got physically very weak, so much so that all I could do was get out of bed, go to the theatre, do the play, and go straight back to bed. I barely made it through matinee days. My father-in-law told his daughter that it sounded like incipient mononucleosis. He arranged for me to have several shots of vitamin B12. It worked. I was soon right as the proverbial rain.

I had thought it might have been amnesia, because the night that Marilyn Monroe appeared in the fourth row at our theatre in a glittering white dress, I stopped my dialogue in mid-sentence and couldn't remember a line. Another memorable night with a legend was when I opened my tiny dressing room door one night after a performance and standing in front of me was Katharine Hepburn. Her face was blotched with freckles like a winter apple, but all the bones were firmly in their right place.

She spoke with that wonderfully clipped New England speech I remembered from *The Philadelphia Story*. "My name is ..."

I almost laughed in her face. "I know who you are, Miss Hepburn, and I'm honoured by your presence. But were you looking for Miss Leighton or Mr. Portman? They're downstairs three flights."

"I came to see you, Donald. I want you to be my boyfriend this summer."

I knew she meant business. Onstage business, not romantic dalliance. But she was offering me a part I had already played: Bassanio in *The Merchant of Venice*. Two days earlier I had received an offer from Michael Langham to play Laertes that summer to Chris Plummer's Hamlet. I presumed this casting was Chris's idea, and not just because he planned to use my box of makeup.

To say no to Katharine Hepburn would be like shaking your head from side to side when Winston Churchill offered you nothing but "blood, sweat, and tears." I turned Langham down and gulped an acceptance to the immortal Kate. The offer from Ontario came again the next week, and Gloria suggested I recommend Michael Kane, a Canadian actor she had just seen in an off-Broadway production of James Joyce's *Exiles*.

I knew Michael Kane, not to be confused with Caine. Our Canadian Kane was the prankster of all time. He once stopped construction of the Toronto subway one day by pretending to be the architect in charge of the whole project. He told the subterranean workers that they were fifteen feet off the mark in their drilling. Construction of this whole project stopped dead for several hours that day. In a more minor matter, he once hailed a Toronto streetcar, and when it stopped for him, he placed his shoe on the bottom step, tied the laces in a bow, and waved the driver to continue on his way.

One night at a drunken party in uppity Rosedale, he moved a by now comatose Chris Plummer into an empty bathtub, went out and bought several packages of lime Jell-O, added warm water to the mixture in the bathtub where Chris was sleeping it off, and encased him in Jell-O. Much later, Chris awoke from his drunken toot and found himself preserved up to the neck.

For this Kane was ordered out of the party by the host. Michael then went outside, climbed a tree, and hurled insults at the host through the open window. He did have a glorious speaking voice.

Langham wired back once more to say that he hoped I would reconsider Laertes, and he needed an immediate decision. Being shut out of Hank the Sank still rankled with me, so I recommended Kane for the part. Reluctantly, I must confess.

I wondered what mayhem Michael would get up to while replacing me that summer. I didn't have long to wait. Even before *Hamlet* opened in Ontario, Kane was fired for "a lack of discipline." He immediately sued the festival for "character assassination."

Meanwhile, my decision to go back to Disneyland-on-the-Housatonic created its own problems. It was arranged that I would rehearse on non-matinee days for a month in Connecticut and spend my evenings in the state of New York, sitting at one of those *Separate Tables*.

This sounded quite feasible, until the head of the New Haven and Hartford Railway committed suicide. The poor man's death caused his railway to experience the most delays and cancellations in its entire history. I remember more than once arriving late at Grand Central station and rushing across town at full tilt for the Music Box Theater. I often arrived bathed in sweat with only seconds to go before I was due onstage, calm, cool, and collected in tweeds. Once I passed a couple in Duffy Square and heard the woman saying, "We're gonna be late for the curtain!" They had tickets to my show.

71: BYE BYE BROADWAY

I finally got to stay in Connecticut, day and night, and my little family came with me as soon as the Bank Street School in Greenwich Village finished their season. Meanwhile, onstage at the festival, although Jack Landau was officially credited as the director of *The Merchant of Venice*, I soon found out that was not the case. The director seemed to be the star, Miss Kate.

She was pretty good, too, except that she should have told the leading lady not to cry so much. Guthrie always said that this was the audience's job, not the actor's. She mentioned the fact that her "beau" was sneaking in some weekend to see her. I knew who she meant, but nobody ever saw him sneak in and out. But after Spencer Tracy had been there, he must have given her some advice, because she never shed another tear after that.

Hepburn must have read my mind when we came to the scene where I choose the correct casket and win her for my bride. She said, "Donald, don't worry about the difference in our ages. When you choose the right casket and turn to kiss me, I shall be five years old."

We started to rehearse Houseman's own production of *Much Ado About Nothing*, which co-starred Kate with Alfred Drake. He was the leading man of American musical theatre, originator of the role of Curly in *Oklahoma!*

He made a stirring Benedick to Kate's Beatrice. I trembled in my boots when Houseman told me I was to understudy him and prayed for his good health every night. I had been given a real character part to play, the old man Verges, deputy to the constable Dogberry. I thought I might get a little Charlie Farquharson into my character, but as an old pony express rider he came off more like Gabby Hayes.

The idea of doing this Renaissance Italian play in a Lower California Spanish setting of the last century was a brilliant one. Houseman was credited with it, but he said the notion was really Kate's. It worked and looked brilliantly, and plans were made to tour the production all winter.

Soon after we opened, Kate invited me to dinner in her little cottage beside the Housatonic. She lived in monastic isolation in a meagre habitation and used to swim a mile every day in the river. Her appetite was just as stringent. Dinner with her was eating some nuts and berries and not much else.

I was starved by the time I went back to my place but full of the news that Kate had imparted to me. She felt it was about time that I went to Hollywood, because at the age of thirty-four I was "no spring chicken." To quote the Bard, and she did: "Youth's a stuff will not endure."

She wanted to alert her beau Spence about my coming, because he was about to make a picture at 20th Century Fox, *Love in the Afternoon*. It was about an older man getting involved with a younger woman, and that part would be played by the other Hepburn, Audrey. Kate thought I could be the young man she ditches to go with Spence. My New York agent told me he would "alert the coast" to this development.

But soon after that, I got an even bigger surprise. It was the last matinee of the season, a glorious day. After the performance I came out of the theatre into the sunshine. A British voice spoke my name, and I nearly jumped out of my skin. It was Michael Langham, waiting for me to come out instead of calling on me backstage. I wondered if he would have me sued for recommending the wrong Michael, namely Kane. But he had a thick manuscript with him.

I wasn't sure whether he had been to the play that afternoon. He never mentioned it. He told me that he had heard about my adaptation of *Turvey* and wondered if I would be interested in doing another stage adaptation, Heinrich von Kleist's one-act play *Zer zebrochne Krug* (*The Broken Jug*), in English.

Michael placed the script in my hands. It was a word-for-word translation by the University of Toronto's distinguished Goethe scholar, Barker Fairley. My adaptation was to accompany another Stratford production of *Two Gentlemen of Verona*. Both plays would tour briefly in Ontario and end up at the Phoenix Theater in New York.

He pointed to the manuscript in my hands and said "Read it over. Remember it's just a literal translation, and you can do anything you want with it, but I should like it to have a Canadian setting."

Without waiting for my reply, Langham turned and walked away. He made no sound, a habit no doubt acquired during his years as a prisoner of war. I didn't see him leave. I was too busy reading *The Broken Jug*.

72: CALIFORNIA, HERE I COME

The Stratford season over, I left it to Gloria to move out of our summer digs. She did and took our girls back to her parents' Gravenhurst home for that most wonderful of all Canadian months, September. Our future was up in the air, as usual.

I read the literal translation of *The Broken Jug* on the plane on the way to California. Gloria was over the moon at the thought that I would be back to play-writing again. I was not so sure. It was a heavy-handed one-act farce about a corrupt judge in a small German burg who gets his head cracked. That's when a young woman he tries to seduce takes her mother's precious heirloom as a weapon to defend herself against his advances. There was no other plot. It's about a jug that got broken. That's it.

I was met in L.A. by Edgar Small, son of my Hollywood agent-to-be, Lillian Small. He had been ousted from MGM at the same time that John Houseman had quit the company in disgust.

I have never been lied to as pleasantly as I have in Hollywood. In New York theatre people are downright rude, but they are direct in their approach. In London they are more polite, but just as direct. Never a cross word emerges from the lips of those in charge of the business of entertainment on the Gold Coast. It goes with the California climate, which Charlie Farquharson describes as *cam and bammy*.

Except for the spring floods and forest fires at all times of the year, of course. Then the atmosphere created by Mother Nature is most impolite.

Edgar Small drove me directly to my new temporary home, the Montecito, a Hollywood hotel on Franklin Avenue with a swimming pool for actors who couldn't afford the Chateau Marmont on Sunset Boulevard. The Montecito was in Hollywood, not Beverly Hills, and locals considered it to be in a rundown part of town, except for the restaurant down the street, Musso & Frank.

New York actors like Jack Klugman and Walter Matthau would lounge around the pool, waiting for a call back from their New York agent. Lesser lights would line up for their unemployment cheques a couple of blocks further down another street, just off Hollywood Boulevard.

There were distractions waiting for me. My earliest CBC mentor, Fletcher Markle, heard I was there and invited me to dinner with his newish wife Mercedes McCambridge, queen of the soap opera *Big Sister*. After dinner they took me to see the hottest new L.A. stand-up comedian, Mort Sahl. I envied his multi-layered political material and longed to do the same kind of thing, rather than trying my hand at film acting.

I started to think about the Canadian locale of the play Langham had handed me. The original German piece was about the early years of the nineteenth century. This corresponds roughly with our War of 1812. I owned Pierre Berton's two-volume history of that event and wished that I had brought it along with me.

One of the celebs who hung around the pool was Miss America, Lee Ann Meriwether, staying there and anticipating film offers. One night when

I was getting into the 1812 idea, I got a phone call from Lee, who said a bunch of the Montecito-ites were going to Grauman's Chinese Theater to see a movie preview and asked if I would like to come along. I told her I was trying to write a play. She thought that was much more exciting than merely seeing somebody else's story in a movie and hung up. I was the one who felt hung up. I thought, *I just turned down Miss America!*

Eventually, the reason I had flown all the way there surfaced. I was taken by my Hollywood agent to 20th Century Fox to meet the casting director for *Love in the Afternoon*. I was ushered into a big office, and there was a great bear of a man who embraced me like a long-lost son. I had never met Spencer Tracy, but I had been coached well by his lady love. I acted as if we had been friends for all time.

The casting staff were enormously impressed by this seemingly filial relationship, and my appearing in their picture looked like a cinch. A few days later I was told by Edgar Small that the deal was off, because Tracy had turned down the picture. It was given instead to some cowboy named Gary Cooper.

That meant I was at loose ends. Lillian Small invited me to dinner at a restaurant on Sunset Boulevard. I took a taxi, but it was driven by an unemployed actor from New York who didn't know his way around. He had to stop at a drug store to get his bearings. The phonebook revealed he was next door to the right place all along. I told him to buy a street map with the tip.

Lillian told me that she was getting some good response for a screen test with Columbia Pictures. Her son trundled me over there a couple of days later to discuss a possible test for a film version of Thomas Mann's biblical novel *Joseph and His Brethren*. (A film, incidentally, that never got made.) I was proclaimed as a big-time classical actor, and so I did the test. Nothing came of it.

I was next taken to meet Gene Roddenberry, the man who created *Star Trek*. He was a former Los Angeles cop with a flair for science fiction. Gene showed me the pilot film for the television series starring Jeffrey Hunter, who had previously played Jesus in the film *King of Kings*.

Gene told me they were dumping Jeffrey and wanted to replace him with an actor who could easily memorize all those numbers and scientific terms involved in the highly technical script. I made him laugh during the interview following the screening by telling him I was a word man, not a numbers freak. About a year later I was doing a *Mission Impossible* next door to the *Star Trek* set, and I said to my old pal Billy Shatner, "How do you remember all those numbers?"

After that no-go at Columbia, I was taken to Paramount to meet one of the nicest men ever, George Seaton. He had just finished directing *Teacher's Pet* with Clark Gable and Doris Day and invited me to the preview a few days hence. I knew that he had written and directed more than one of those Marx Brothers movies back in the 1930s, so I asked him what it was like working with that zany family of actors. Seaton said the main problem he had in directing them was that they all thought of themselves as writers rather than performers, so they spent most of the time revising the script. With good results, he admitted.

He agreed to test me for a Paramount contract. First I did a monologue, a courtroom speech by an impassioned Irish patriot, and then a scene from a Peter de Vries novel, *Comfort Me with Apples*, which Johnny Carson later did on Broadway. The results would be viewed by a panel of studio executives several weeks away. I fled back to Canada instead of hanging around that pool.

Back home I was interrupted in my playwriting in the nicest way, by lots of work as an actor. A teleplay, *The Prizewinner*, had been written by a young Canadian actor, Bernard Slade, to provide a nice role for himself. But the CBC decided that he shouldn't play the role. Instead they hired me. I found this pattern consistent. If you hang around the place, Canadian television ignores you with its undivided attention. If you "come from away," particularly a glamour capital like Hollywood, even if you have done nothing while you were there, back home you're a temporary celebrity.

In *The Prizewinner* I played a nerdy office worker constantly teased on the job by two office bullies. Eventually they cook up a scheme to convince him that he has won a big lottery. The bullies were played by Bruno Gerussi and Frank Peppiatt. I had known Bruno at Stratford, but Frank had been a copywriter at MacLaren Advertising until television arrived, and then he and John Aylesworth became variety performers. On a late-night show, *After Hours*, I remembered Frank as Clark Kent trying to change into his Superman costume within the narrow confines of a phone booth.

Frank turned out to be a natural actor, but he told Bruno and me that he was very nervous about "going legit." We spent a few pees in the CBC washroom telling Peppiatt about motivation and that kind of crap. He almost stole the show. But when my character, the prizewinner, found out that he had been conned, after having spent most of his imaginary gains, and putting his life in financial jeopardy, I'm sure there wasn't a dry eye in any Canadian home. It certainly affected my daughter Martha, who had hysterics until she was brought to our TV studio to prove her dad was okay.

The next week I did a Charlie monologue on a variety show, *The Big Revue*, and five-year-old Mary was told it was Daddy on the TV screen. She couldn't believe it because he didn't sound like Daddy, or look like him, wearing a cap and sweater that didn't belong to him. She cried even more when she was told that Daddy would be home soon in his own clothes, and a taxi was *not* being ordered to take her down to the studio.

Little Mary must have been even more puzzled by the fact that I referred to neither daughter as part of my family, but to some strange phenomenon called Orville.

We has jist the wun issyuh in our fambly, the only froot of our loins bein' our boy Orville who is in his sexth yeer in graid twelve. Or is it his twelfth yeer in grade sex? I dunno. But he don't seem to git the hang of bean in scool. He cant seam to add or distrack. And the only way he everr figgered out how to multyply wuz by watchin' our aminals out beehind our barn.

73: THE PLAY'S THE THING

While doing TV shows, I had been spending time at my folks' place in Toronto, always a pleasure because they're my greatest fans. But now that I had some free time, I went to Gravenhurst to work on my play about the War of 1812. My wife was supremely happy to be back with the father she adored and the mother she loved to fight with, and a husband who might someday turn out to be a writer.

The Broken Jug was a one-act farce, full of the usual chicanery and sexual dalliance. Beyond that, about what? As I said before, it's about a jug that gets broken. It was hard to get anybody interested in the War of 1812.

At least it was back in 1958. Now that the bicentennial of the event is here, the Harper government seems determined to celebrate it as an important moment in our history. It was part of their 2011 electoral platform.

I quote from the leading editorial in the *Toronto Star*, October 15, 2011:

> As part of a multi-year commemoration, the federal government has announced it is planning to spend about $28 million. Ottawa has announced several valuable steps, including up to a hundred re-enactments, upgrades to battle sites, such as Fort York, interactive tours, and a nationwide education campaign underlining the importance of the conflict. The federal government, however, should retreat from its ill-judged plan to locate a permanent 1812 memorial in the National Capital Region. By all means, build a monument, but not in the Ottawa area, which played no role in the war, and was home to only a few farmers and loggers two centuries ago.

Another quote from the *Toronto Star* letters to the editor column a week later:

> We must commend the federal government. In a time of fiscal restraint, it has found $28 million to celebrate our heritage for the war of 1812. It is ironic, however, that this is almost the exact amount the government will strip from the current political process in party funding. I guess we are getting a lesson in 19th century politics as well as the War of 1812. (Brian Dugdale, St. Catharines)

At that time, two centuries ago, our future national capital wasn't even called Bytown. It was more like bypass. My research back in 1957 taught me that farce was the right tone in which to describe this dumb war thought up by Americans while the British were busy fighting Napoleon in Europe. There was no such country as Canada. True, there were two Canadas, an Upper and a Lower, but in 1812 they had really little to do with each other for the next fifty-five years. We were less of a country at that time than the Iroquois Confederacy, which under their leader Tecumseh fought the hardest against this invasion. He really saved our country before it was a country, but the British never lived up to their promises to him and his people.

Why did this war happen? It was the Republicans fulfilling their "manifest destiny" and eager for war against Britain. They resented the British navy boarding American ships to search for British nationals who had deserted their ships. The main goal of the United States was to add the British North American colonies to their Stars and Stripes. Some Americans assumed that we wanted to be part of their expanding destiny. The main feeling I got from my research was that settlers on either side of the border did not want to fight settlers on the other side. They were farming people, and their prime concern was raising food. War to a rural population is a colossal nuisance, with those damn troops trampling your crops, slaughtering your livestock, conscripting your sons, and having hanky-panky with your daughters.

Mind you, serious military events happened in this war. Especially in Quebec, where the American invading forces were repelled at the Battle of Châteauguay near Montreal. Both sides believe they won the war. The Americans did defeat the British at the Battle of New Orleans, and Johnny Horton had a hit song to commemorate it.

On April 27, 1813, a fleet of fourteen American warships with 1,800 invading troops landed in Toronto (then called York) harbour. A force half that size tried to hold them back, and before abandoning their Fort York our troops detonated their own massive gunpowder magazine in an earth-shaking explosion, which killed the U.S. general leading the attack and 200 of his invaders. The Americans left on May 8, having looted the town of York and burned Upper Canada's legislative buildings. This inspired British troops to burn Washington, including the White House. Fort York was rebuilt and remains the largest collection of buildings as a living memorial to that war.

I decided to set my *Broken Jug* adaptation in a less active locale of that conflict, a tiny, if imaginary, pioneer clearing located in southwestern Ontario somewhere between the contemporary Stratford and Shaw Festivals. Niagara-on-the-Lake was on the front line of the struggle and suffered accordingly. Not far from it is Queenston Heights, where the monument to General Isaac Brock still dominates the landscape.

Ontarians regard the Battle of Queenston Heights as one of "our finest hours," and General Isaac Brock became a hero, even though he was shot dead almost immediately while leading an attack up the hill. Perhaps the real hero was a heroine, Laura Secord, who risked her life (and her cow) to get to the general to warn him about the American attack on Niagara. Maybe Harper can advertise her as our own Paul Revere: "The Yanks are coming! The Yanks are coming!" I hope the proposed memorial doesn't show her riding that cow.

What about the average Joe and his Joan living within range of the conflict? I found a British military man's appraisal of the attitude of our civilian population in Upper Canada during the year in which I set my play, 1813:

> My situation is most critical, not from anything the enemy can do, but from the disposition of the people. The population is essentially bad ... a full belief possesses them all that this province must inevitably succumb. This prepossession is fatal to every exertion; legislators, magistrates, militia officers all have imbibed the idea, and are so sluggish and indifferent in their respective offices that the artful and active scoundrel is allowed to parade the country without interruption, and commit all imaginable mischief.

The title character in my play was just such a rogue. In his small community he functioned as magistrate, parson, and real estate tycoon. (He has put the Crown lands in his neighbourhood under the name of his relatives, some of them still living, in Fifeshire.)

A British military officer, Major Clovell, is on his way to Detroit, and hopes to corral able-bodied young men in the community as recruits. The presence of the British military, and the possible appearance of the American freebooters in the same room, adds the proper tension to the situation.

I decided to concentrate on the rural population, with the inevitable bother to their existence caused by the military. I changed the title from *The Broken Jug* to *Adam's Fall*, not because of the Biblical implication necessarily, but it was about a corrupt local judge named Adam who got his head broken by a jug because he was trying to seduce the daughter of its owner. I added a stupid war and the history of that jug as told by a United Empire Loyalist en route from New Jersey to New Brunswick.

Michael Langham had said the most amazing thing to me when I accepted this assignment. He said that the set and costumes would be designed by the incomparable Tanya Moiseiwitsch. Then he told me a second amazing thing. Instead of him, the director, I as the playwright could cast the players. This meant using the actors who were involved in the other touring production, *The Two Gentlemen of Verona*, as well as other festival actors who would be available to me. I was amazed.

It was the same situation Shakespeare always had at the Globe. He wrote his plays based on the availability of the actors in that company. With that same freedom I was able to cast for my play superb Stratford actors like Douglas Rain, Bruno Gerussi, Anne Morrish, Tony van Bridge, Amelia Hall, and Powys Thomas. A dependable bunch of comic actors, and in the title role of Judge Adam, who presides at a criminal trial in which he himself was the culprit, there was no hesitation. I chose Douglas Campbell.

I was more concerned about the casting of Jessie, the owner of the jug. For that part I wanted Langham's wife Helen Burns, who had established herself as a first-rate comedian. But it was her serious moments that linger for me, describing to the British Major Clovell how she carried the jug from the Old World to the New, and then out of the new American republic.

Before I deal with the pre-Broadway tour of *Adam's Fall*, I think you might need Charlie Farquharson's assessment of this most "unreported" war in our history.

Why I bleeve in celibating yer bi-sextennial of that 1812 evasion frum yer Ewe-ass: this happen neer farty yeer after them Yanks' deeclairation of their deep-endents, seventeen seventy-sex.

Now that they wuz two sepratist countrys, Canader and yer Benited States started puttin up boarders, and makin' sure eech uther hadda go thru sum strange customs.

But ther wuz sum Yanks thot Canda by rites belong to them. They wuz a buncha Warshinton capitolists called yer Warhocks. They bleeved in sumthin' call yer "manyfisted dustiny," witch ment that if us Canuckers didden wanna becum anuther star in the firmamint of ther flag then them Yanks wood roll up ther fistic cuffs, dust off ther nuckles, and giv us a few stripes of our own.

And they ment it. I fergit how yer hole offal thing start up. But sum Yanky gum-boat had a shot-put acrost yer stern of wun of our friggits. At that time the rest of yer Roiled Navels was all tied up on yer playin feelds of Eatons, heddin fer Yerp to fite that new upstarter, Napolleum Bonusparts. Yer Birdishtars finely beet yer Frenched navvies hard by Trafalgar Square, wen they all went down on yer Water Loo.

But that wern't no help to us over heer, with 3,000 mile of fensless boarders. Mind you, them Yank hire-ups didden hav yer smarts wen it cum to woretime stragedy. It mite a bin eezier to git ther sneekers crost yer forty nine parrlells of lassitude, but insted they march bold as brass acrost yer Piecebridge and rite up to yer neerest Lorey Seecord.

Now Lorey she wernt of a mind to set around like wun of them fanny farmers. As soon as them Yanks set down to eat her outta house and home, she snuck out to the barn, determin' to pull something.

Yer lokel dairy queen tuck her prize Holesteen and rode it twenty mile barebones over to I. Sick Brock and tole him fer to hide in yer ambushes, cuz the Yanks wuz comin' over here!

Well sir, Brock he jist waded hard by Queensum Hites, then let them Yank evaders hav it in thair reer-gards. He pert neer beet the retreet offa them.

But sad to say he got hisself nicked in the frackass, wen a Yank bullitt bounced offa Rick O'shay, and giv our belubbered genrul yer rigger's morse.

Our grateful Steevy Harpy guvmint remembers both yer brave Brock and that fine upstand-in Holsteen farm gurl, and considers them to be both immoral.

And thair both still in bizness in Nagger Falls to this day, fer she's a boxa choclits and he's a hoe-tell.

Thair's sum yanks today as won't admits it, but wen you counts up allthe fites in that war, I think it end up on yer winside fer us Canajuns. Score 18–12.

But that shood giv yer Ewe Ass sum stratus-faction, on accounta now they don't hav to say that yer first time they ever lost a war was in Soused Veet Napam.

So lets jist let sygons be bygons.

74: SURPRISE, SURPRISE!

Having finished the second draft of *Adam's Fall*, I missed all the rehearsals of the play in Stratford and the opening at London's Grand Theatre, plus the subsequent run in Montreal. Why? I received the news that Paramount had picked up my option and offered me a seven-year film contract at the princely sum (I thought) of $750 a week.

My first assignment would be to appear at the premiere of George Seaton's film *Teacher's Pet*. I had to get back post-haste while Gloria had the job of getting herself and our two daughters out to California as soon as she could. Langham hoped I would get back for the engagement at the Royal Alexandra in Toronto, where we could do the final rewrites before New York.

Los Angeles was not an easy place for me to get around, because I had never learned to drive. So I stayed in a motel close to the studio and walked, because bus service was erratic. I met the Paramount publicity department, a really nice bunch of unpretentious people. I was shown the first fruit of their efforts, a mention in Hedda Hopper's column: "Paramount has succeeded in signing legit actor Donald Harron. They say he is a combination of Leslie Howard and Montgomery Clift. Wow!"

There were about twenty-five actors under contract to the studio, and one of our responsibilities was to appear in screen-tests with movie hopefuls. My first test was with a handsome young Texan named Ty Hungerford. He looked like a rodeo rider, but the scene he had chosen for his test was from *The Philadelphia Story*. I played Jimmy Stewart and Ty played Cary Grant. After we finished he slapped me on the back and said, "Ah thought yew played it more comical while I just done it more swave!"

There was a Jerry Lewis film in preparation, and I got an interview, but not a test, with director Norman Krasna. It didn't last long. He told me that I couldn't do comedy because I had a serious face. I considered this a case of facial discrimination and replied, "Tragic face. What about Buster Keaton?"

This was at a time when Paramount had practically stopped making movies. Those of us under seven-year contracts were loaned out regularly to television studios for their shows. The studio pocketed the money. I never found out how much I would have been paid, but the studio's weekly stipend was always there, and that was more than enough to live on. Gloria and the daughters arrived. She immediately rented a station wagon, and almost as immediately, with the help of my agent, found us a home. It was in the hills behind the Beverly Hills Hotel on Summitridge Drive. I have always loved Artie Shaw's recording of the same name, and we were told by my agent that we had a "good address."

This meant that we lived in close proximity to celebrities. Down the road was Pickfair, still inhabited by Canada's sweetheart, Mary Pickford, although she was a recluse. Above us maybe a quarter of a mile was Gregory Peck, and down the drive, just behind the Beverly Hills Hotel, lived Janet Leigh and Tony Curtis.

My wife was thrilled at my lack of acting prospects, because she felt it would give me more time for writing. I hardly had time to play with my children in the little wilderness behind my new house before I got the call from Michael Langham reminding me about the Toronto opening of our play.

75: ANOTHER OPENING, SAME SHOW

According to Langham, the reception of *Adam's Fall* in London's Grand Theatre was "so-so," which was disappointing, because the story itself took place not far away from London. The Montreal run was "very successful." Evidently Quebeckers had more interest in the events of our mutual history than our home-grown WASPs.

In Toronto, at the Royal Alex, I enjoyed watching my Stratford chums make my little play look professional. In the lobby I was asked by a reporter my opinion of Hollywood. "It's just Scarborough with millionaires, but there isn't any snow to shovel," was my reply. I added I was pleased to see a full house, and even more pleased with the acting.

Doug Campbell was properly outrageous and uproarious as the libidinous magistrate and Doug Rain was superbly servile as his sly clerk, Huish. Bruno Gerussi had real passion as the New World, proletarian groom-to-be, and his Old World elegant father played by Powys Thomas conveyed the sense of immigrant aristocracy trying to adjust to the wilderness.

I made up his surname of "de Moulinville" because it translated into Miltown, a popular pill of the 1950s that supposedly brought tranquility, and that's what Thomas brought to this turbulent farce. Ann Morrish as the bride-to-be and smasher of the jug over the would-be rapist's head was sublimely tearful. Millie Hall as the aboriginal housemaid Bridget Turkeyfoot brought an endearing looniness to the proceedings. Best of all, as I had hoped, was Helen Burns, as the owner of the jug. Two of the three critics agreed.

The exception, of course, was Nathan Cohen. His review was given next morning on CBC Radio from a studio next door to the one in which I was sitting waiting to be interviewed by commentator June Dennis. He said, "Donald Harron's little play has two weaknesses. It has no plot and no characters. " As Nate finished his broadcast with what he considered more important theatrical items, June and I were the next voices on air.

She said, "Let's just ignore what Mr. Cohen said." I insisted that the first thing she should do was ask me about Nathan's review. My mind was whirling with possible retorts, things I might say, and more importantly, things I should *not* say.

As agreed, June said, "Well, Don, what do you think of what Mr. Cohen said about you just now?"

I don't know where it came from, but here is what came out of my mouth: "June, I don't care what anybody else thinks. I admire Nathan Cohen. I admire him because he has what I haven't got ... plot and character. You have to admit the guy is a character, and what about the plot he hatched this morning ... to assassinate me! But I don't think of Nathan Cohen as a critic. I think of him as more of a performer, and I think he should be with us in Stratford this summer, in the title role of *Much Ado About Nothing*."

On to New York and the Phoenix Theatre, the leading off-Broadway house. It was located way downtown in lower Greenwich Village. I had been to that theatre more than once and was glad that it had been chosen for the end of the Stratford tour. But this time I was too nervous to sit in one of its seats. Along with Langham, I prowled nervously at the back of the theatre.

Gloria was ecstatic about what she saw. I thought the rewrites worked well, but I was intimidated by being back in New York on the wrong side of the curtain. The theatre was by no means full, and the next day only two papers had bothered to review us. They happened to be the most important, the *Times* and the *Herald Tribune*. Walter Kerr said more or less what I had said when I read the original play. "It's about a jug that gets broken. That's about it." I thought by adding the War of 1812 I had increased the dramatic and comedic level.

I got the feeling that Americans in general felt that particular war was confined to New Orleans, thanks to Johnny Horton's song. Brooks Atkinson was absent from the *Times*, but we did get a review written by Harold Clurman. He was a well-known director, not a critic, but his temporary taking over the reins for regular critic Atkinson ended up giving me my only rave. Clurman preferred my play to Shakespeare's "Two Gents of Verona"!

Don with Rosemary Harris in Christopher Fry's A Phoenix Too Frequent *for CBC-TV, 1958.*

The response at the box office was fairly underwhelming, and we didn't, to paraphrase a play title by Christopher Fry, stay at the Phoenix too frequent. During Stratford's fiftieth anniversary celebrations, no mention was made of my little effort. But back in 1958, I did get a New York response to me as a would-be playwright.

A Broadway producer, Joe Hyman, had written to see if I would be interested in adapting Robertson Davies's novel *Leaven of Malice* for a forthcoming New York production. As a raving Davies fan, I had already read the novel. In fact, a couple of years before, I had done a version of the first book of the Salterton Trilogy, *Tempest-Tost*, for CBC Television, which languished on some executive's desk, but nothing came of it. This new theatre project was to be directed by Tyrone Guthrie, and I wondered if my Stratford father-figure had anything to do with me getting the offer.

I personally felt that Davies's novels, all of which I had eagerly devoured, would be seen best as films rather than plays, in the vein of those delightful Ealing comedies that the British put out with such ease. However, egged on by a supremely delighted wife, I undertook the theatre assignment. At least it would let me be at home in Hollywood and able to watch my daughters grow up.

76: NOT A LOT ON THE LOT

There was no sign of a film role in the offing for me at Paramount. However, I assisted in another screen test, the prospect of which totally delighted me. It was for Canada's TV sweetheart, the girl from Horner's Corners, Shirley Harmer. She was up for a co-starring role in a Western for director Jean Negulesco, and we did a scene from *Comfort Me with Apples*. She got the part!

I was hired in one of those loan-out deals Paramount made with NBC's popular daytime show, *Matinee Theater*. I was borrowed for an old English stage farce, *On Approval*. Next, they sent me over to Desilu studios for a television remake of a 1930s film I had enjoyed hugely, *The Prisoner of Shark Island*, about Samuel Mudd. He was the doctor who repaired the broken leg of actor John Wilkes Booth after he assassinated Abraham Lincoln, leapt down to the stage, injuring himself in the process, hobbled backstage, then fled on horseback. Mudd knew nothing of all this, but despite his innocence, he was sent to a Devil's Island kind of prison under the supervision of a sadist.

Lucille Ball and Desi Arnaz weren't there when I was ushered into a boardroom to be questioned and assessed by several anonymous gentlemen. Some of them came up and looked me right in the eye at extremely close range. One of them told me that he had been in Toronto a couple of years before and had seen my father on television. I didn't think Lionel Harron had ever been on the small screen. I asked for details and concluded that what this man had seen was me doing a Charlie Farquharson monologue. I told him it was not my dad, but me, his only son. I don't think he really believed me.

Nevertheless, I got the job. Evidently, the group took a vote, and the ayes had it ... because of my eyes. Add a dash of moustache and I was all set to kill a Republican. I loved doing the part, because it felt as if I was being a Bastard again, as in King Lear.

Otherwise, I think I spent most of my time in Hollywood playing with my kids. For that I am eternally grateful, besides trying to write the second act curtain of that Davies novel into a play. These days a second act curtain brings to an end the whole show, but *Adam's Fall* had three acts and so did *Leaven of Malice*.

Gloria told me it was time to get back to work on that stage play. I didn't tell her that I had been agonizing over this project for some time. I simply could not get a decent second act curtain. While she drove the kids to school in Beverly Hills, I made a furtive phone call to the man who had optioned me, Joe Hyman, and told him my problem. He sounded almost sunny in his reply and told me that the original author, Davies, was very keen on doing the stage version of his own novel. I breathed a big sigh of relief. Before I knew it, I was agreeing with him wholeheartedly, and the *Leaven of Malice* project was off.

My year with Paramount was almost up, and there seemed to be absolutely no chance of getting a part in a film. I did get another interesting assignment from Desilu to do a television play with Ernie Kovacs. To me he was the original TV stand-up comic, even though he sat down to do it. Through television's earliest hours, he had always been there as a sublime entertainer.

In this teleplay he had the role of an amiable layabout who liked to wander the halls of a hospital pretending he was a doctor. He did it just to make people feel better. His co-star was Jean Hagen, who was unforgettable in the film *Singin' in the Rain* as the silent film star with the awful voice. My favourite scene was when the microphone concealed in her chest dutifully recorded all her thumping heartbeats.

Before I started rehearsals, I got the momentous news that Paramount had dropped me. Me and every one of its seven-year contractees, just in time for Christmas. Almost immediately I got a call from my agent in New York, Marty Baum, with an offer to go on the road with a play.

It was *Look Back in Anger* and the part was Jimmy Porter. The part was longer than Hamlet and was to have been played by John Barrymore Jr., who had been signed by Broadway by producer David Merrick to do a national tour of the most successful British play in years. The day after the first read-through, Barrymore Jr. phoned to say that the part was too much for him, and he would not be at rehearsal. Ever. The phone call came from his hotel room ... in Rome.

Merrick, known in the trade as the Abominable Showman, was at his wit's end. The first week in Washington would be played by the actor who had played the role in New York, Donald Madden. But he would not be available to open in Cleveland because he was due to start rehearsals in New York as Hamlet. I had seen this play in England with the actor who had created the role of the angry young man, Kenneth Haigh. I thought it the best part written in years and years for a young actor, longer than *Hamlet* and just as complicated.

Merrick was so desperate, he would accept me without an audition and was aware of my current television commitment, but would hire me for the entire tour as long as I could be in Washington by Christmas Eve. The salary was twice what I was earning on my Paramount contract. The airline ticket would be waiting at the airport. I would have that weekend to rehearse and open on Boxing Day in Cleveland.

I bought a copy of the play and took it with me to the television rehearsal. The cast included two young actors, Ann Carroll and Michael Landon. They offered to help me learn the lines. Because of their helpful attitude I didn't feel the panic that would have been perfectly normal. (Landon was one of the wittiest people I ever met.)

The entire atmosphere on that set was very amiable. Kovacs was very friendly, smoking eighteen foot-long cigars every day. (That's eighteen cigars, each measuring twelve inches, in case I have confused you.) Jean Hagen was helpful with my lines, too, and when we finished the taping Kovacs sent me home with no cigars, but a case of champagne.

So Christmas Eve on Summitridge Drive was quite Dickensian, except that this particular Bob Cratchit was walking out on his little brood without so much as a goose to give them. As Tiny Tim might have said, "God help us, every one!"

Don with "stage wife" Pippa Scott during the Look Back in Anger *tour, 1958.*

77: FORCED TO TOUR IN A TOUR DE FORCE

My Christmas dinner in Washington consisted of a cold corned beef sandwich, an even colder cup of tea, and lots of grapefruit juice to keep me awake. The next night I was in Cleveland for my opening performance. I was so scared, really scared, that this perennial agnostic got down on his knees and prayed to God to get him through this night of trial and turmoil. He hadn't heard from me in a long time.

Don with Elizabeth Hubbard, the "other woman," during the Look Back in Anger *tour.*

But He came through for me! The Cleveland reviews were ecstatic. I got a phone call from David Merrick thanking me for saving his ass and extending the tour another three months. One of the reviews turned out to be prophetic: "If Mr. Harron hasn't spent his life to here flouting the moralities, railing against the social order, and sleeping in any bed with any partner, then in the persuasiveness of his performance we must conclude that he is an actor ... a gifted actor. "

Next stop, Her Majesty's Theatre in Montreal. My most vivid first impression was being snuck past a line of pickets outside the CBC studios (among the picketers, I understand, was Réne Lévesque) to talk about the rave reviews. With one exception: Nathan Cohen came all the way from Toronto just to blast me, among other things, for a Lancashire accent that sounded to him like a bad parody of Stanley Holloway reciting "Albert and the Lion." His was the one review I stuck in my wallet to keep me from being conceited. It worked onstage, but not offstage.

The prophetic part of that first rave review I got in Cleveland is that sometimes a part takes over the actor. In Chicago, next stop, I sassed a talk show host. It was reported in the *Tribune* that "Don Harron, the *Look Back in Anger* star, looked back in anger at WBKB's Marty Faye the other night. Harron was devastating."

The ancient Greeks used to say that some god or demon takes over your body and rules your performance. But that's supposed to be only onstage. The madness took me over offstage, as well. I became Jimmy Porter twenty-four hours a day. That made for great fodder on TV talk shows.

But the Horny Young Man in the play who serviced both his wife and the female lodger in their tiny apartment certainly caused a personality change. Young women congregated at the stage door for autographs. To have women seek after me was a new experience.

Except for the "town bicycle" in Victoriaville, ridden by everyone, no woman had ever made a move on me that I remember. Until this American tour. After I took my curtain calls, I started to realize that some of the autograph seekers wanted more than my signature. In fact, the demand at the stage door was so constant, I was tempted to "knock off" (but not up!) a chick in every town we played. This became rather complicated when the tour turned into a raging success and Merrick booked us on a series of one-night stands. (Just like the ones I was having!)

I made sure not to dally with either of the two females in the cast. But my conquests on tour weren't all happy memories.

The nicest moment I had was a chaste one in Chicago. I got a phone call from Lee Meriwether, who I had turned down in 1957. Not this time. Lee came to see the play and we had dinner after. Then we went to her room and … wait for it! Danced all night. She was engaged to another actor, but that danceable evening remains one of my favourite memories.

Back on tour and now facing a new schedule of one-night bookings, I finally ended up too exhausted to play Denver, and my understudy had to go on. My in-laws had flown from Canada to see my performance. I was covered with genuine shame and remorse as I limply and wanly accompanied them to Los Angeles for the end of our tour. They showed genuine concern for my state of exhaustion. Man, did I feel like a heel!

Because I skipped the Denver engagement, there was a few days' rest before we opened at the Biltmore in Los Angeles. The tour had taken its toll on Gloria, too. She showed the strains that so many single parents share, being mother and father to two vigorous daughters. No brown-bagging it for my kids; they were served a hot lunch at home every schoolday.

She told me she wished she had worked in a bookshop instead of the life I had given her. I'm afraid I responded just like Jimmy Porter, treating my long-suffering wife with the same contempt that I had grown accustomed to doling out to my onstage wife every night.

The opening at the Biltmore turned out better than my home life. Rave reviews as usual. Even Hedda Hopper, who loathed the play, prophesied it wouldn't be long before I got myself a motion picture deal. Based on that, my Hollywood agent hired a press agent, who threw a big post-victory party to introduce me to the press. But on the very day of the do, my fellow actor Al Muscari broke his leg in a motorcycle accident, and I had to leave the press party before it even began to rehearse with Muscari's understudy for that night's performance.

Nevertheless, my press agent stayed on the scene, and she came away from the party (all serious business in Hollywood happens at parties) with an offer for me to appear in a big budget film with Joan Crawford, *The Best of Everything*. Irony of ironies, it's a story about what heels men are, and I was cast as the only nice guy among a bunch of testosteronic rogues. Robert Evans was the biggest heel who drove the pregnant girl he had an affair with straight to the abortionist without telling her why. I had to wait to find which heel I was chosen to play. It never happened.

But the *Anger* tour wasn't over. We still had San Francisco and the Curran Theater for a three-week stand. No *Best of Everything* screenplay available, so I bought a copy of the novel and took it along with me.

Since it was early summer, I also took along my family to Frisco for the first weekend so that my two daughters could watch me behave badly onstage. Somebody asked my older one, Martha, age seven, what she thought of her father's behaviour in this play. She replied, "Oh, he's worse than that at home."

78: END OF ANGER, BEGINNING OF EVERYTHING

I had been sending rave review after rave review to my New York agents. It's a good thing I didn't include the ones from San Francisco. In one paper I remember my performance being described by the critic of the *Examiner* as "pure Smithfield." I had to ask what the reference was, and I soon found out that Smithfield was a ham. That review never reached New York.

My agent, Abe Newborn, had been sending reviews regularly to Paddy Chayefsky, who had never heard of me. But he heard about me as soon as he decided to hire Tyrone Guthrie for the direction of his new play, an up-to-date version of the classic Jewish horror story, *The Dybbuk*.

Chayefsky insisted on seeing me in person, so I caught a midnight plane that would dump me in Dallas for twenty minutes, then on to New York on another airline, to arrive in Idlewild on a foggy Sunday morning. But not as foggy and groggy as I was.

Abe drove me to an office on Fifth Avenue, where Chayefsky and Guthrie were waiting. I don't remember anything about the interview, and I had never read a line of Paddy's play. All I know is that within five minutes I got the job.

They sent me on my way with a copy to read on the plane back home. But that wasn't until the next day. Abe had got in touch with another client of his, Sidney Lumet, who remembered directing me in that television show where Lloyd Bridges made the front page of the *New York Times* by saying "Goddamn it." I was invited by him to dinner with his glamorous wife Gloria Vanderbilt, and their guests Mr. and Mrs. Sandy Meisner. I had been a member of Sandy's acting class, along with Farley Granger and Peter Falk, so they made me feel I was not among strangers.

I was back at the airport next morning, driven by my other agent, Marty Baum. Instead of sleeping, I had devoured this script of Chayefsky's and loved it. A Dybbuk is a malevolent spirit that inhabits the body of an innocent person and transforms them into a loony. The exorcism ceremony to get rid of the Dybbuk is to be performed in a little Long Island synagogue, with a minion (ten men) and a rabbi. In the play they can only scare up nine, but when a young hungover lawyer (me) wanders in, they suddenly have their Tenth Man. The exorcism ceremony is performed on a young girl who seems schizophrenic, but when the evil spirit comes out during the ritual, it comes out of me, not the girl. I couldn't wait to start rehearsals.

I told Marty this on the way to the airport, but he said we should hold off signing, because a better offer had just come in. It seemed that Chris Plummer and Laurence Harvey had both auditioned for the role of Lancelot in a new musical, *Camelot*, and both had been turned down. Marty said, "So now they're interested in you!"

I reminded Marty that I couldn't sing. "If you want a real singer, phone the CBC in Toronto and get Bob Goulet!"

I found out later that Marty did what I suggested, couldn't find Goulet in Toronto, but then tracked him down in Bermuda, where he was playing stock with a bunch of other Canadians. You know the rest. It's showbiz history. Marty had to split the commission with Goulet's agent, who hadn't even bothered to submit him for the part.

On the plane I also did a quick scan of that novel, *The Best of Everything*. It seemed a typical feminist weepie, in which women were treated without respect by men who were mostly despicable. When I landed in San Francisco, I immediately phoned Gloria.

I told her that I got the part and we would be moving back to New York in September, but there would be time for a couple of weeks stopover in Canada first. She whooped with joy then told me her news: 20th Century Fox had decided to cast me in the role of Sidney in *The Best of Everything*.

"Sidney, who the hell is he? I skimmed the book but I don't remember any Sidney."

Gloria had read every word of the novel and said, "He's the only one in that office who has an affair, and then has the decency to marry the girl."

My answer was one big raspberry that sprayed the phone booth with my spittle. After all of my looking back with anger for five months, Hollywood had cast me as a dorky mealy-mouth. To get back to playing nasty Jimmy Porter for another two weeks was a bit of temporary relief.

But ticket sales were not going particularly well. The theatre management arranged for me to be on a morning television show operating out of the Top of the Mark, the roof garden of the Mark Hopkins Hotel. The other guest on the show was Jonathan Winters, who was doing a stand-up stint at a trendy nightclub called The Hungry I.

While waiting to go on, Winters was scratching away with a pen on some paper. It was a cartoon, and a pretty good one. I told him I'd started out as a cartoonist, so we whiled away the time doing caricatures of each other. We got along so well that we decided to spend the rest of the day together. We were both performing at the same time in the evening, so neither of us could see the other's show. So what we did, I guess, was put on an ad lib show for each other for the rest of that day. I ended up exhausted.

I got the impression that Winters had a manic mask he never removed in public but bubbled away all day indefatigably. I languished more and more throughout that day as he continually pumped out his tireless, and eventually tiresome, energy. We parted late in the day, he to whatever and me to take a belated and much-needed nap.

The next morning I opened the *San Francisco Examiner* to find Winters on the front page. He had left me and gone straight to the harbour, where he boarded a sailing ship, climbed its mast, and announced to the world that the Martians were coming. The result of that escapade landed him in a for-real "funny farm" for the next six months. I wondered if, as a one-man audience for that one day, I had helped to drive the man to the heights of desperation.

Years later he became for one whole season a regular guest on *Hee Haw*, where we actually got to perform together. I never brought up our encounter of ten years before, but I still noticed that off-camera he had never bothered to take off that mask. Nevertheless, he still remains one of the most brilliant improvisers and funniest human beings on this planet.

79: VAMPING TILL READY.

There was four weeks until I had to appear in front of the cameras for Fox. Instead of spending time with my wife and kids, this cad opted to go down to Laguna Beach and appear in a play. Mind you, I took the kids and they had a great time collecting abalone shells. Gloria felt we were wasting a perfectly good $1,000-a-month Beverly Hills home before we took off for Canada.

The play was a shortened version of Shaw's epic *Man and Superman*. I was given the title role, and my father-in-law was played by Patrick Macnee. It was a thrill to trill the rich language provided by Shaw. The passion in Shaw was intellectual, yet his big speeches are constructed like operatic arias.

Quite a change to return to Hollywood and the relentless girly prose of *The Best of Everything*. My first day on the lot I was sent for by Joan Crawford, who wanted to meet this classical actor, because she admired such performers as me and Laurence Olivier. I was ushered into her dressing room, and the first thing she did was offer me a Pepsi. First thing I noticed was that her shoes didn't match. One was leather, the other was plastic, and they were in widely different colours. I also noticed those wonderful eyes and that beautiful speaking voice that had turned her from a dancer into a world-famous dramatic star.

I had no scenes with Crawford in the picture, so the next time we crossed paths was at a screening of some daily rushes that had been taken a few days before. She was accompanied by two of her daughters, one of whom later wrote the tell-all book, *Mommy Dearest*. I happened to be accompanied by my two girls, Martha, eight and Mary, six, both dressed up in their best, and identically, much to the older one's annoyance.

The showing of dailies often involves the repeating of the same scene over and over but shot from different angles. It must have been very boring for the four young ladies. Joan's daughters were very silent, but they must have gotten a bit restless, because their mother kept up a constant barrage of hectoring. "Why can't you two sit up straight like Mr. Harron's daughters?" It seemed to go on and on until I made an excuse and fled the scene with my grateful progeny in tow.

I found out something alarming about myself watching other dailies of that film. I'm not very sexy on camera. In fact, when it comes to kissing, I'm really quite inhibited. This opinion was shared by the actress I was required to smooch. She said so in print. "He's not a great kisser, poor dear." No wonder they left the emotional stuff to Louis Jourdan, driving the high-fashion model Suzy Parker to suicide.

The Best of Everything moved locations to New York City, and there I met the author, Rona Jaffe. The first setup was in the garden behind the Museum of Art, and as we shook hands I asked Miss Jaffe why my character, Sidney, was such a wimp. Her eyes blazed and she said that he was the true hero of her novel. Sidney was "Mister Right"! She also told me that she had personally chosen me for the role because of the sensitivity in my face when they screened for her my Paramount Pictures test that won me that seven-year contract.

What could I say? I took her to a Broadway musical and ended up in her hotel bed. Jimmy Porter was still alive and kicking. I didn't meet her again for ... oh ... eighteen years. She came into the CBC studio as my guest interview on *Morningside* to discuss her new novel, *Mr. Right Is Dead*.

It was quite a strained, albeit restrained, exchange between the author of that book and her interviewer, Mr. Wrong.

80: A JEW IS BORN

The Harron family took the Superchief back to Chicago, and another train took us to Toronto. I had a joyful reunion with my mum and dad. I must be the neurotic actor's exception to the rule: I have never wavered in my constant adoration of both parents, even though my mum's idea of a successful career for me still involved a desk job at the CBC.

I spent the time in Gravenhurst teaching my brood how to swim and ride a bicycle. September in Muskoka was the most glorious clime of the year. But soon I had to make the trek down to smoggy, dirty Manhattan. Maybe that was why my wife's parents decided the two girls would be better off at school in Gravenhurst. After Gloria's experience with American primary education, she agreed that the girls should stay with their grandparents. I said nothing.

When we started rehearsals for *The Tenth Man*, Tony Guthrie and I found ourselves as two of three goys in a Jewish minstrel show. The only other exception was a charming Czech comedian, George Voskovec.

Guthrie's opening remarks to the cast, backstage crew, and producers echoed this situation. "Now, I'm hopelessly goy and would be very grateful for any Orthodox assistance."

Rehearsals began in an abandoned theatre on 42nd Street. There was no read-through. My character, Arthur Landau, is a neurotic lawyer who wanders into a synagogue well hungover after a bender. This occurs much later in the action, so I was able to sit back and enjoy watching the masterful Guthrie at work.

The cast was composed of mostly elderly Jewish actors. I was delighted to see my old pal Lou Jacobi among them. Two of the leading parts were played by actors from the Habima Theatre in Israel, including a seventyish munchkin, David Vardi. He soon acquired a reputation as a scene-stealer.

The role of the girl who is reputed to have a Dybbuk inside her was played by a pretty eighteen-year-old named Risa Schwartz. She was the adopted daughter of the great Yiddish actor, Maurice Schwartz. The story was that he found her in a European orphanage after her family had perished in the Holocaust.

I found the scene with her in the rabbi's office very difficult. I asked Guthrie for help. His advice was to keep pacing round and round the desk. I suddenly remembered a remark that Elia Kazan had made about Tyrone Guthrie. "For emotion, he substitutes locomotion." Nobody could bring a performer on or offstage like Tony, but in between those two events, the actor is on his own.

Don in The Tenth Man, *1959.*

I did seek Guthrie's help on another matter. Paddy Chayefsky was so enraptured with the subject matter that he tended to over-write his dialogue. It sounded too literary, with three adjectives for every noun. It probably looked okay on the printed page, but delivered out loud it sounded phony. I got Tony aside and asked him if he could cure Paddy's "adjectivitis." Our author was so enamoured of his director that Guthrie was able to slash epithets until the floor was littered with vowels and consonants.

We had Sundays off, and from my Greenwich Village apartment I took a walk to go over my lines. In one of the squares I recognized an actor I had met during my *Separate Tables* days, Jack Gilford.

He looked pretty melancholy, despite having one of the sunniest dispositions I had ever encountered. I asked if he was working. He said, "I'm still blacklisted." My casting genes were alerted. I knew blacklisting wouldn't deter Guthrie, so I took Jack's phone number and called Guthrie. By Monday afternoon Gilford was rehearsing the scene with Jacobi that turned out to be the comedy hit of the show. It was about the frustrations of getting somewhere, anywhere, on the New York subway system.

The entire cast was so marvellous that I didn't mind playing straight man to all of them. We didn't open in Philadelphia on Yom Kippur. Instead we all, including Tony Guthrie, went to the synagogue to pray. It was Guthrie's idea. I'm afraid it didn't mean much when the reviews came out. The local critics were frankly puzzled by everything we did. It looked as if we would be non-starters on Broadway. That included the review in the Bible of showbiz, *Variety*. Philadelphia was our only out-of-town stop. It seemed as if all our efforts had been in vain.

Our New York home (temporarily, we figured) was the Booth Theater, where I had garnered such good reviews in *Home Is the Hero*. We had two previews, the first sparsely attended, and the second was packed to the rafters at fifty bucks a crack. It didn't help. They either sat on their hands or laughed in all the wrong places, especially in the exorcism that ends the play.

The opening performance remains a blur. After the show we walked across Shubert Alley to Sardi's, where a party had been arranged on the upper floor. The lower floor is where the celebrities dine. Guthrie and Chayefsky came in and remained very quiet. It was like a funeral.

Eventually Tony talked to me about his plans to establish a repertory company smack dab in the very centre of America, which turned out to be Minneapolis. I had played that town on the *Anger* tour and reassured Tony that there was a genuine thirst for good theatre there. He then asked me if I was interested in joining him in that venture. I looked at Gloria, who looked back, very noncommittal, and I quoted from the Book of Ruth: "Whither thou goest, I will go."

Our press agent walked in with a piece of paper. It was the *New York Times* review by Brooks Atkinson. It began: "Being a genuine writer, Paddy Chayefsky can make the impossible happen. He has written an enchanting play." Before we could digest the rest of the review, a copy of the *Herald Tribune* appeared, with Walter Kerr's assessment: "It is a work of the creative imagination. Let me try to explain what a rare thing a work of the creative imagination is on Broadway...."

The funeral wake woke up and became a rave. Gloria stayed for the party but took a plane back to Toronto the next day.

We were involved in a monster hit. Being in a Broadway hit means a long run, and it also means all kinds of offers pour in that you can't possibly accept because your long-run contract won't allow it. My favourite offer was the leading role in a television series in which I would play a king who reverts to private life and goes to an Ivy League college.

All of our audiences were not as entranced as the critics. Often some would leave wearing puzzled looks. We found out why. Across the street from us was Gore Vidal's play *The Best Man*. It was a hit, too, a political comedy about Washington starring Frank Lovejoy in an obvious imitation of Richard Nixon. It was rumoured that more than one person in our audience after watching our senior citizens onstage in their little Long Island synagogue would ask the person sitting next to them, "Which one is supposed to be Nixon?"

81: A LONG, LONG WAY TO RUN

After the excitement of opening night died down, my Protestant upbringing didn't allow me to enjoy being in a hit. Therefore, I got sick with some kind of flu. It didn't prevent me from appearing each night onstage, but it did curtail my daytime activities. I spent most of the time in bed.

On the first day of this enforced convalescence I got a call from Virginia Leith, who had accompanied my friend Peter Baldwin to our opening night. She called to congratulate me on my reviews. When I told her about my illness, she offered to bring me some hot soup. I accepted.

Virginia was surprised to find that I was living alone in my apartment. She was doing the same thing, having given up California and hoping to make a go of it in New York. Her film career had started when Stanley Kubrick cast her as the only female in his first film, *Fear and Desire*, and she had gone on to make *A Kiss Before Dying* with Robert Wagner. Recently, she had made a quickie film, *The Brain That Wouldn't Die*, which she described as a piece of "shlock." It was made in a couple of weeks. Her disembodied head spent most of that time in a saucer of fake blood. Virginia wasn't looking forward to the premiere, which would take place in some small movie house in Manhattan.

Since I was "batching it," she offered to come again the next day and cook me something. I was hardly in a state to refuse. We shared a taxi to the theatre, and then she went on to have a dinner date with Mike Nichols.

Backstage at the Booth there was a minor riot in progress. Or rather a riot about something exceedingly minor. Comedy is no laughing matter to its participants, and tensions among the aged participants in our play led to backstage screaming matches, mostly one accusing the other of upstaging him. The chief culprit seemed to be the Israeli import, David Vardi, whom everybody called a *gonef* (thief) because he kept inventing bits of comic business during other actor's speeches.

Don with Virginia Leith, the next Mrs. Harron, in New York, 1960.

For some reason, I kept being designated as the arbiter of these dust-ups. Maybe the folks at CBS heard about these incidents and chose me to be the spokesperson to explain the meaning of Chanukah on television to other goys like myself. The problem is that I had to appear clean-shaven, while since I portrayed someone on a three-night bender, I had to appear eight times a week with three days' growth of beard.

I only shaved after the second show on Saturday, rather like the farm-hands that I had worked with, who only spruced up for Sunday services. During the day I walked around like a Bowery bum.

This didn't seem to faze Virginia Leith, who kept feeding me in my apartment, and her way of avoiding facial contact with me, I discovered one afternoon, was by reverting to oral sex. This happened almost before I knew it.

Virginia was quite free in discussing her sex life in Hollywood, where she had had affairs with Bob Hope, Frank Sinatra, and Richard Burton. I wondered if I was falling victim to the same thing I went through on the tour of *Anger*, identifying with the character I played. Not compulsive womanizing this time, but experiencing psychoanalytic angst, since my character was in the throes of analysis. During rehearsals our producer Arthur Cantor had arranged for me to meet several psychiatrists in their off-duty hours.

I met several of them all at once, and they more or less ignored me while they told silly jokes and acted like children after school. Looking back, I can understand why they behaved as they did. They wanted to release the pressure of listening to the troubles of others in fifty-minute doses several times a day.

It seemed to me that everybody in New York was in analysis. Woody Allen, it is said, has been going to his guru daily for nearly forty years. Virginia had been through all that and more. In California her analyst had her submit to sessions involving LSD. She said the experience was earth-shaking. She reverted to a stage when she was six years old, in search of a father who had deserted his wife and child.

I must confess she opened a whole new world of self-examination for me. She was a minor Hollywood actress, but she could quote Rilke and Kierkegaard. She gave me a book about self-analysis, which became my consent companion backstage. It was only much later that I came to realize Virginia gave great personal advice to everybody except herself.

Despite my unshaven state, CBS kept offering me that job hosting a Sunday series about the meaning of Chanukah. It didn't seem to matter that I wasn't Jewish. As a preamble I was asked to briefly promo the subject at a B'nai Brith luncheon and talk about the trials and tribulations of bringing *The Tenth Man* to Broadway.

I asked Lou Jacobi to give me something in Hebrew to round off the speech. He wrote it down phonetically and I memorized it faithfully without asking what it meant. I got a standing ovation! When I got back to the theatre for the matinee, Lou told me it was the cry of hope that Jews had expressed since their Babylonian exile: "Next year in Jerusalem!"

Oy veh ist mir! Maybe I was being a bit premature in 1959 about that 1967 war.

82: FAMILY MATTERS

Christmas was a-coming, and my extra-marital situation would come to a head, because my wife and kids and her parents were all coming to New York for the holidays. I hadn't seen Gloria since opening night, and my daughters since mid-September. This decision was made without consulting me, but I was partly complicit, because I had so enjoyed teaching them to ride bicycles and swim, knowing they would continue to be in such a safe environment. They came, saw the play, and we had a turkey with all the trimmings.

Doc Fisher left the day after Christmas to get back home to his many patients. My mother-in-law stayed behind. I was confused about the future of the girls. I wasn't sure whether they were coming back to Perry Street to go to the Bank Street school again, or retreat back to the sweet innocence of Muskoka.

I decided it was time to "fess up" to my wife about my behaviour on tour with *Look Back in Anger*. I did this when we were alone and at one point gave her an estimate of how many one-night stands I had clocked in a five-month tour. She sat very silent. Before I went to my theatre, we all went out to a cozy, elegant French restaurant for an early dinner. Momma-in-law didn't care for foreign food and stayed in the apartment to dine on leftover turkey. The kids were all excited about eating out in New York.

The whole holiday spirit seemed to prevail until Gloria suddenly hit me in the face with her fist using all her force. Both girls grabbed their mother, and also their father. She screamed at me until I fled uptown to my theatre. I guess she paid the bill. I didn't dare look my daughters in their faces as I left. I fled to the theatre but didn't go back to the apartment that night. Instead I phoned Virginia and asked if I could stay the night with her.

Arriving at the apartment next morning I was informed that my family was not staying but was taking a train to Toronto. This was followed by a grim-faced mother-in-law dressed in black, saying to everyone in the room, "I will *not* have a divorce in this family!"

I insisted on having some time with my two daughters. I took them for a walk and we passed a record store with the sounds of "Moon River" wafting out onto the street. We stopped to listen, and I quoted the lyric, "There's such a lot of world to see." I told them how much I missed them, but that whatever happened I would make sure that they would see lots of that world, because I would always be around, in some way, to make sure of it. They were both expressionless and dazed.

When we got back everything was packed and ready. I insisted on taking them to their train in Grand Central station, and inside the taxi it was a cavern of silence. As they boarded the train, the only one in my group who spoke to me was Martha Senior, my mother-in-law. "I hope you're pleased with yourself!" In a moment they were all headed back to Canada, and I was left speechless.

I didn't take a taxi back to my apartment. I walked the fifty-some blocks because I needed to think about my own life in this huge city. The one thing I didn't want to do was repeat what I had done on my country-wide tour. I wanted to be with just one person. I had so far, however briefly, had a highly successful love life with Virginia, but I didn't want to share her with anybody else.

We resumed our separate existences, she in her apartment and I in mine, but we recognized a mutual need. Virginia was a child of early divorce and still felt more or less like an orphan. She had a mother who lived in Los Angeles, but even when Virginia lived and worked in the same city there was very little contact with her mother. For the first time in my life, I felt like an orphan, too.

On New Year's Eve I welcomed 1960 by taking Virginia to the most sought-after party for any New York actor, Lee and Paula Strasberg's. Their lovely daughter Susan had just been cast for the title role in a stage production of *The Diary of Anne Frank*. We were losing Lou Jacobi for a major role in that production.

"All that glittered" was present to ring in the new year. Chris Plummer was there, and so was a very drunk Peter O'Toole. I made the mistake of warmly welcoming O'Toole to America, and he flared up and said, "Oh, fuck off, you idiot!" Virginia and I retreated in embarrassment. Evidently, Chris told Peter a bit later that he had snarled at Broadway's Tenth Man. Plummer led him to me, where O'Toole flung his arms around me and said, "Forgive a drunken old fool! I saw you in that play this afternoon and you were fucking mahvellous!" What could I do? I forgave.

Life went on in the new year, and so did the fights backstage at the Booth Theater. It was always the same problem, about who stepped on whose line with a bit of physical distraction.

Tony Guthrie dropped in on his way back from Minneapolis, where the repertory theatre to be named after him was going ahead. No squabbling among the cast that night. I managed to get a few moments alone with him in my dressing room and told him about my marital trouble. For a brief time we resumed our father-son kind of relationship, but this time I was the one seeking for his opinion. His reply surprised me. He didn't do any moralizing about commitment to family or the sacred nature of the marriage contract. All he said was "Accept yourself."

Okay, Tony! So I resumed my monogamous relationship outside my marriage. Virginia felt that the test of my feelings for her would be to witness the schlocky movie she had made. We went to a press screening, of her ninth, and last film, *The Brain That Wouldn't Die*. It was as bad as she had predicted.

In retrospect, fifty years later, I don't really know if I was being true to myself when I made her feel better by proposing marriage to her. She immediately put me in touch with a showbiz lawyer named Robert Veit Sherwin who arranged such things. A friend of hers, a fellow fashion model from her pre-Hollywood days, "always took from him" when she wanted the Big Split.

I promised to get around to calling the lawyer, but my offstage professional life got suddenly busier. I was able to take television jobs that didn't interfere with my theatre gig, and I managed to get away from those nicey-nicey roles. I was cast on television shows as first a murderous psychotic alcoholic, then a cuckold who kills his wife's lover. To research the former I attended an AA meeting.

The only comedy part in a TV show came from Canada by way of Manhattan. It was from Frank Peppiatt and John Aylesworth.

This pair of writer-producers had moved away from Canada and for the moment had joined forces with Disney producer Bob Banner. The three of them wanted to make a pilot for a new one-hour variety series starring Dennis Weaver, who had gotten tired of limping through *Gunsmoke*. They wanted me in this new show for my Charlie Farquharson accent, but not the character himself. Instead I was to be Weaver's country cousin in a tight tweed suit with a bowtie, a cowlick, and freckles. I looked rather like a forty-year-old Alfalfa from *Our Gang*.

We taped the show one Sunday in the Ed Sullivan Theater on Broadway. That's where David Letterman now holds forth each night. It was intended to be a country version of the Perry Como Show. It never sold. Peppiatt and Aylesworth tried it again ten years later. They eventually called it *Hee Haw*.

83: HOLY ACRIMONY

I was being pressed fairly hard by Virginia and that divorce lawyer, who guaranteed that a fair share of my theatre income, a third, would go to my wife and children. From the other side I had a visit from Gloria herself, looking very nice in a new white suit. She came to my dressing room after a performance and we went out for a late supper. She told me that she was now living and working in Toronto for the CBC, answering audience mail. I had kept sending funny postcards to Martha and Mary, and Gloria said that they were much appreciated. Her parents had got her a car so she could go back and spend weekends with our daughters, and during the week she lived in a rooming house close to the CBC.

I admired her attempts to enter a world she had never expected to try before, but I realized she was here to reconcile our marriage. When she finally came to the point, I remembered Guthrie's advice about being true to myself, so I decided to be honest. Bluntly honest, it turns out. I said calmly, "I'm afraid you're not woman enough for me." That moment of cruelty haunts me still, fifty years later.

And that did it. She left the restaurant immediately, and I presume went back to Canada the following morning. She beat me to the punch in filing for divorce. She engaged the services of a lawyer. I put him in touch with Robert Veit Sherwin and the process of disintegration began. I realized I would have to provide a third of my income *ad infinitum* and told my agents to get busy scaring me up some extra-curricular work.

David Susskind hired me for his *Play of the Week* series to play yet another psychotic in a TV adaptation of the Broadway play *Climate of Eden* by Moss Hart.

Fortunately, Susskind hired me again almost immediately for another *Play of the Week*. This time it was for me a rerun of Sartre's *Huit Clos* (*No Exit*) which I had performed in Toronto with Lorne Greene and Honor Blackman, both onstage and in closed-circuit TV.

I don't remember much about the taping because by that time I was exhausted, between being a Jew full of a Dybbuk at night and a homicidal cuckold by day. Virginia became less a lover and more of a nurse and accompanied me everywhere. I finally moved into her place on the Upper West Side to save wear and tear on both of us.

I needed a night off. The solution? A Mexican divorce. My understudy, Michael Lipton, a genuine Jew, was ecstatic that the management allowed me to skip the Monday evening performance of *The Tenth Man*. Early, early Sunday morning, Virginia and I flew down to Texas and crossed the border Monday morning into Juarez.

Virginia would have a clearer memory of our trip. I remember little, including the trip back, getting on the plane, and throwing up a lot.

I was back in the play Tuesday night, while Virginia made plans for our wedding. I had been performing freebies on Sunday nights at a church in Brooklyn Heights. I gave readings from the Book of Job and other fun pieces, because the minister there was an old college chum, Bill Glenesk. He later achieved much more fame a few years later by being on the Johnny Carson show one night, where he officiated at the wedding of Tiny Tim and Miss Vicky. (That one didn't last, either.)

Joe Abeles, a kindly Broadway photographer, offered us his spiffy apartment for the ceremony. I got Bill Glenesk to perform his twee version of the ceremony, which made no reference to the Bible but was full of quotes from Shaw, Eliot, and Thornton Wilder's *The Skin of Our Teeth*.

I got Christopher Plummer to stand with me. At least during the ceremony. After the champagne he declined to stand but showed no inclination to leave and go back to his wife Tammy Grimes. I had introduced them when we were playing an out-of-town engagement in Westport, Connecticut.

As I got ready to go to the theatre, the only person actually leaving the wedding, Chris, sat there drinking champagne with the matron of honour. The matron herself was a blond *Vogue* model, Barbara Freking. I found out much later that she and Virginia had had a lesbian affair. I also found out just before the ceremony that Chris had just divorced Tammy Grimes. I felt responsible and suggested psychoanalysis.

Chris bristled. "You mean the thing that gets rid of all your neuroses?"

"That's the stuff!"

"Are you crazy? If I get rid of my kinks, what'll I do for talent!"

I was at the ceremony, but, due to my theatre job, I missed the reception. Duty calls. Only divorces rate understudies. One of the guests was a psychiatrist-advisor connected with *The Tenth Man*. As I left for the theatre he told me, rather full of champagne, I thought, that there was nothing between us newlyweds but sex, and it wouldn't last more than six or seven years.

There certainly wasn't any sex on our wedding night. I returned from the theatre to find Virginia dealing out the cards for us to play a game of canasta. Plummer was still there, up to his chin in Joe Abeles's bathtub, singing at the top of his voice to the nude matron of honour beside him, and wearing her bridal hat.

84: PRINCE HARMING

I spent fifteen months in that Broadway synagogue on Long Island, the longest theatrical run of my career. By that time I was a newly remarried man, and my bride was anxious to get away from another winter in New York. My California agent got me a plum job: Prince Charming to Shirley Temple's Little Mermaid in the NBC series of classic fairy tales that she herself hosted.

Before leaving for Los Angeles, we did a quick trip to Toronto the Sunday before Christmas to introduce my new missus to my parents. Also, my ex arranged for our two daughters to be brought down to Toronto for the weekend to hook up with their long-lost father.

Virginia had done some shopping for them: matching suitcases with their initials "M.A.H." and "M.M.H." In identical dresses, same colour as the luggage, they were dazzled and seemingly enchanted with the idea of their father being Shirley Temple's Prince Charming. I think I was a hero in the eyes of my children for the first time. My dear parents were probably witnessing the only second marriage in the history of our family. They were being very Canadian about it, quiet and respectful.

I don't even remember staying overnight. It was back to New York for my last two weeks in the synagogue, and then off to California on our honeymoon. To save money we would stay with her mother, who lived quite central to all our needs, as soon as we rented a car. Her mom was a manicurist who took the infrequent bus, even to meetings of the "Mothers of Hollywood Stars Club" in which she could boast about her daughter's film accomplishments without the slightest idea of what they had been.

First day in rehearsal at NBC Studios in Burbank was exciting. Most of the story of *The Little Mermaid* takes place underwater. Instead of swimming it meant flying in the air in one of Kirby's harnesses. I had such fun learning to fly that when lunch was called I stayed in that flying rig and swooped and looped to my heart's content.

Shirley decided that her Prince Charming should have curly hair. Last time that was tried on me was the publicity man at the Theater Guild, but in Hollywood I meekly submitted. I seem to have lost my bridle to the executive producer, Shirley Temple Black. She was really in charge, too, since she had previously been in charge of the American embassy in Ghana.

Speaking of love, there was very little of it on display between mother and daughter when I got back to our "honeymoon nook." Virginia and her mother seemed to be re-enacting scenes from *What Ever Happened to Baby Jane?* Evidently, Virginia had been used as a weapon between two divorced parents, and ended up living the life of an orphan in various convent boarding schools. Our honeymoon was really an opportunity for Virginia to hate her mother at close quarters.

All the wisdom she had acquired from years of analysis seemed to vanish. I pleaded with her to take it easy on the old soul, but she refused to let up. In the middle of one of these wrangles, I felt so desperate that while mother and daughter kept at it, I went into the kitchen, selected a sharp knife, and slashed my right arm (I'm left-handed).

That stopped the family fight all right. I went to Emergency and got my wound bound up.

The next day at rehearsal, my right arm was heavily bandaged. When anyone asked me about it, and to a man, and a woman, they did, I merely said, "Oh, tried to kill myself." Everybody laughed and we went on with the scene.

When I finally saw *The Little Mermaid* in my mother-in-law's now fairly peaceful living room, I saw a lot of the back of my head. The producer/star/ unofficial director and now film editor, Shirley, had left a lot of this actor's close-ups on the cutting-room floor. They included my best scene. Miss Moppet had had her way.

I was determined at this point *not* to stay in California. Virginia pleaded with me to extend our honeymoon in a warm climate. It never occurred to her to look for employment, as well. It upset her to think that I was homesick for Canada and a chance to be Charlie Farquharson again. I phoned my New York agent and told him I was available in the Far East.

He got back to me quicker than I expected with an offer from John Houseman to do another season of Shakespeare in Connecticut. I would rather have heard from Stratford-on-Tario, but I was intrigued. Orlando, the leading man in *As You Like It*, and Banquo in the Scottish play. A third production, *Troilus and Cressida*, was as yet uncast, because Houseman wasn't too familiar with the play. I was.

In the spring of 1961, I wanted out of a lot of different things, and one of them was California. I got back to Houseman personally and told him I wanted to play Thersites, this foul-mouthed character in *Troilus and Cressida*. He was surprised; he had thought of me as the romantic Troilus. But I thought the role of foul-tempered Thersites would give me the opportunity to introduce Charlie Farquharson to Shakespeare. And vice versa.

I also thought it was a chance to have a summer with my two daughters. Virginia accepted her fate. She preferred the prospect of living with my kin to an existence with hers.

85: BACK TO THE BARD

Instead of a rented car for the summer in Connecticut, I bought one for $50. It was a grey 1948 Mercury, and one of its many owners had given it a bright blue roof. Virginia dubbed the car "Natasha," after her Hollywood drama coach, Natasha Lytess, whose hair was grey with a blue rinse.

Rehearsals for *As You Like It* were very pleasant, because of my leading lady, Kim Hunter. She had been the original Stella in *A Streetcar Named Desire* and seemed thrilled to be doing the classics. Our director was Word Baker, an impish little munchkin who had become famous for bringing to the stage a little musical, *The Fantasticks*, which in time would become the longest-running vehicle in Broadway history. It opened in 1960 and finally closed forty-one years later.

He brought that same light-hearted spirit to Shakespeare, including modern dress. As the hero Orlando I wore blue jeans and a handsome denim jacket to match. In rehearsal, we soon found that adorable Kim Hunter couldn't begin to handle the poetry in the scene where she and

In 1962 at Stratford, Connecticut, Don in modern dress as Orlando in As You Like It.

Orlando toss couplets at each other. Baker's solution was to throw a ball into the scene. Orlando and Rosalind ended up playing a game of catch, hoping I suppose that the audience wouldn't notice what was being said. (I remember one performance when the ball bounced into the audience, and I ad libbed to whoever caught it: "I prithee sire, render to us the sphere of Vulcan!")

Rehearsals began for the Scottish play. Playing that role in our production was Pat Hingle, with a good ole boy Texas accent that he was unable to completely disguise.

In contrast, his Lady was the elegant, English-born Jessica Tandy. I had met Jessica before during our first season at our Stratford, because her husband Hume Cronyn was the son of one of London, Ontario's most distinguished families. He didn't appear with us onstage, although I greatly admired his film acting.

The mood of that grim Scottish play seemed to pervade our summer home when my family arrived just before the season opened. We had rented a cottage that would sleep four, but Gloria insisted that my mother come along to chaperone my daughters. Virginia was highly annoyed that she couldn't be trusted as a stepmom, but considering our California experience, I thought that having my mom, even with her bad legs, was more than a pleasant prospect. She even volunteered to sleep on the sofa, but I insisted on renting a bed, which we put in the girls' room.

The three arrived for a two-week stay, and I was shocked by what I saw. My mom had trouble walking, even though a few years previously I had arranged for an operation that tied those varicose veins. Martha, now ten, had put on what looked like forty pounds, while Mary, aged eight, avoided adult conversation by pretending to be a cat. All I could think was that I had caused all these drastic changes in my own flesh and blood.

But something good came out of all this. Instead of being resentful, the girls played up to Virginia as their fairy godmother-in-law. They told her that life in Gravenhurst with grandparents was okay, but they both wished they could live with their mother in Toronto. When Virginia told me this, I didn't hesitate to phone Gloria at her CBC desk in Toronto. By the time school started in the fall, Martha and Mary were sharing their mother's apartment in Toronto, to the probable dismay of her flatmates, who proceeded to move out.

The first two plays of the festival opened on alternate nights. *As You Like It*, game of ball and all, was first on deck, and its sunny atmosphere made it the hit of the season. The Scottish play got pretty vile reviews, except for Jessica Tandy. The production presented its usual atmosphere of ill luck, especially the lighting. Actors, especially the witches, poor bitches, would injure themselves trying to get on or offstage in all that murk. This led the cast to dub the butch female in charge of lighting the show "The Prince of Darkness."

It's always known as a bad-luck play, and toward the end of our season it really came to pass. One of the actors, a quiet fellow who seldom spoke, was due to replace one of the minor parts, Lord Lennox, because the actor who had been playing the role had to leave the season early. The quiet one had been waiting for this moment all summer, but he was told by some unfeeling stage manager not to bother; they were importing another, better actor to do the part.

What he did in reaction was commit suicide. Not in any ordinary manner, but the complete hari-kari ceremony, which involves slicing yourself with astonishing precision. He did this in his miserable little rented room while we were onstage. This happened during the last performance and was kept very hush-hush, but no one involved in that season can ever forget it.

Don with Kim Hunter in As You Like It *at Stratford, Connecticut, 1962.*

Before all that personal tragedy was the third production, *Troilus and Cressida*, the story of the Greeks invading Troy under command of King Menelaus to bring back his wife Helen.

The decision to costume the production in the blue-and-grey uniforms of the American Civil War led me to remind Houseman that the War between the States was a fight over slavery, not some blond bimbo. Nevertheless he went ahead with the Rhett and Scarlett *Troilus and Cressida*. They had already ordered the costumes.

I played Thersites, a deformed and scurrilous Grecian, the most foul-speaking character in all of the Bard's works. In this Civil War production he became the camp cook, in red underwear snapping my galluses, chawing terbacky (in my case licorice) and hitting a spitoon infrequently.

Houseman let me put all of Thersites's speeches together into one haranguing rant. I thought this was a good chance to introduce Charlie Farquharson. Tony Guthrie had told me that Charlie's accent and speech patterns were much closer to Elizabethan English than the current lingo spoken at Oxford and Cambridge.

The *New York Times*' Stanley Taubman approved of my performance but rapped me on the knuckles for picking my nose and leaving a deposit on a nearby prop tree. In retrospect, I apologize for a lapse in taste. But that speech, believe it or not, was met every night with what Charlie calls a *standing ovulation*.

With Shakespeare writing his material, it may have been the Parry Sound philosopher's finest hour.

86: EVERYBODY DOESN'T LOVE OPAL

That summer of 1962, lots of famous people seemed to wander backstage in Stratford, Connecticut: Charles Laughton, Tony Randall, Charlton Heston, Gore Vidal, and Joanne Woodward, all telling me how much they envied my lot as a classical actor. I was visited backstage by a man I had never met but admired tremendously as a comic performer, Cyril Ritchard. He is probably best known in America as Captain Hook to Mary Martin's Peter Pan. He came seeking my presence in a new work by the distinguished Broadway playwright John Patrick, who wrote one of my favourite plays, *The Hasty Heart*. At that time another Broadway success of his was in the process of being made into a film with Marlon Brando.

The play Patrick had just written was *Everybody Loves Opal*, which has now become a staple for aging actresses on the summer stock circuit. I read the script and thought it was terrible. It was about three swindlers who are trying to kill a harmless old bag lady for the insurance policy they had just sold her. My part, Brad, was the heavy of the piece, deluding poor Opal, a sweet, dotty old thing who lived in poverty and saved a little money by drying her old tea-bags on a clothesline. Eileen Heckart, a talented supporting actress who had anchored many a Broadway hit, was cast as Opal.

I didn't find the play funny, so I politely declined. But Ritchard just as politely persisted in persuading me. He even upped the weekly stipend. Finally, I realized that September was approaching and I had no other offers on the horizon. Also from Toronto came a large dentist's bill for my two daughters. I said yes to both, and the deal was sealed.

In the cast were *Guys and Dolls* veteran Stubby Kaye and a new actress with a delightfully smoky voice making her Broadway debut, Brenda Vaccaro. I kept wondering how I was going to douse an old lady with kerosene and at the same time make an audience laugh.

We opened in Wilmington, Delaware, on our way to the Longacre Theater in New York. Heckart as poverty-stricken Opal got a big laugh when she strung up all those used teabags on her clothesline. I got an even bigger laugh one night purely by accident. A tablecloth got caught up in my suspenders and, unknown to me, followed my movements crazily all around the stage. The audience howled as I pranced around the stage trying to free myself.

Cyril Ritchard and John Patrick wanted me to keep the business in, every night. To me it was a symbol of their out-of-town jitters with a new play that didn't quite work. But you can't repeat a lucky accident. Along with raves for my gymnastic artistry in the local paper came a dozen roses from Ritchard. On the strength of a single local rave review, both author and director took off and left us on the weekend before we were to open in New York, one in his Jag and the other in his Rolls.

We opened at the Longacre Theater, and to my surprise, the reviews in the press, on television, and on the wire services were not bad at all. Raves for Heckart, of course.

We lasted a month. I now faced the prospect of lining up for my first unemployment cheque. Supporting two households, plus two juvenile sets of teeth, was looking pretty formidable. But Christmas was a-coming, so I spent my last dime on a trip to Toronto loaded with presents for my kids. I decided not to risk Virginia's sharp tongue in the same locale as my parents. We stayed at a place close to Gloria and the girls' new home on Sherbourne Street. She had chosen this location because it was conveniently close to the CBC, where she had been promoted to editor of CBC's *Trans-Canada Matinee*.

The problem was how to make ends meet. Virginia got on the phone and got herself a Palmolive soap commercial. I did a couple of those prestigious low-paying TV shows on CBS like *Lamp unto My Feet* and *Camera Three* with the likes of other unemployed actors like Ed Asner and Larry Hagman. Lucky for me, the CBC came through with an offer to play the lead in a televised production of *The Lady's Not for Burning*.

The Inflammable Lady was to be Zoe Caldwell. Zoe was originally from Australia, full of the life of Down Under, and she later became a feisty Cleopatra to Chris Plummer's Mark Antony at our Stratford.

I had vivid memories of his own performance as Thomas Mendip while I scrubbed the floor in the background. I grew a beard and Virginia told me to dye my eyebrows to make myself more assertive. I think the thing that haunted me was that last fateful dinner in Greenwich Village with Gloria and the kids before they left for Canada. Before she slapped me, she shouted "You'll never be as good an actor as Chris Plummer!" In retrospect, she's right. But I still got a kick a few years later when Chris tried to imitate Charlie Farquharson playing Bardolph in *Henry IV, Part 1*, at Stratford, Ontario. Chris, you're a great, great actor, but don't plan on making a living as a farmer from Parry Sound.

As for myself, I swaggered behind my beard as much as I could, but I secretly doubted I would ever make the transition from juvenile to leading man. My rebel chieftain was a bit like Tony Randall playing John Wayne. Despite this, no sooner had I got back to New York than CBC called me again to play the one person who cared in *The Town That Didn't Care*.

I can't remember my careworn performance. I don't suppose you care, either. But I was about ready for a CARE package.

87: THAT BASTARD IS BACK

Good things started to happen to my career. *Variety* mentioned that *King Lear* was about to appear that summer in Central Park.

Producer Joe Papp had been successful in bringing Shakespeare to the park every summer for several years. He must have had a grant from the city, because admission was free, and the public flocked in. When I heard he was doing *King Lear*, I ignored my agents, who wouldn't be enthused about a salary of $175 a week. I phoned Joe myself and asked for an audition, because I figured it was time to let that Bastard loose again.

Papp sounded as if he had never heard of me when he said, "Okay, I'll put your name down on the list, but I'll have to have you read for the part."

Joe phoned me back a day later and said he had checked up on my Shakespeare credits, and I wouldn't have to audition. The Bastard was mine. I replied in my cockiest style, "That's too bad, Joe, because I was planning to come over there and knock you on your ass with my reading!"

This was still early spring, and I needed to get through till summer. Unemployment cheques were not the answer. Fortunately, Kim Hunter came through with an offer to co-star with her in Chicago in a production of *Write Me a Murder*, written by Frederic Knott, author of the successful play and film *Dial M for Murder*. He should have written longer on *Write Me a Murder*.

Nevertheless, it was an interesting interlude before I tackled the Bard again. Kim was gracious as always and great to work with. We had a ball onstage, without the necessity this time of throwing one back and forth.

The exciting thing about Shakespeare in Central Park was that the admission was absolutely free. Audiences would line up four or five hours in advance to get the best seats. I had been in that audience myself once before, to see George C. Scott play Shylock. It was quality stuff, and I looked forward to the prospect.

One of the things Papp pioneered in New York theatre was interracial casting. Many in our audience were "minorities." This time Joe was determined to have a black Lear. Frank Silvera, a handsome, silver-tongued leading man, was cast, and Roscoe Lee Browne, one of the finest speakers of verse I have ever heard, was the court jester.

The results were mixed, according to the press. The part of Lear remained just out of reach for the voice of Silvera, who showed his frustration nightly onstage, but Browne was a superbly witty fool.

I did amazingly well in the reviews. The *New York Times* said I was "a director's dream," London's *Times* said I was " a spirited Edmund," and *Variety* called me "a young Olivier." On the second night, Papp called out to me as he came backstage. "What do you want to play next, Harron?" I shouted back as I was leaving, "Harron's *Hamlet!*" He gave me a thumbs-up.

From these reviews I got my next job. It came from television's *Producers' Showcase*, with an offer to play the part of pretty-boy Christian de Neuvillette to my old pal Chris Plummer's Cyrano de Bergerac in a two-hour TV presentation for NBC.

Chris had just done the Big Nose part triumphantly at Stratford, Ontario. He later did it on Broadway in a musical version by Anthony Burgess and won a Tony, an amazing achievement for a classical actor. This time I was playing Christian in a shoulder-length, blond page-boy wig that made me look like early Ginger Rogers.

Our rehearsals were fraught with tension, not because of the play or the players, but because the Cuban Missile Crisis was happening at the same time, and there was the imminent danger of our world being blown up. However, Kennedy had his greatest triumph in forcing Khrushchev to turn tail and take his missiles home, so by the time we started taping, we were breathing a sigh of relief, along with the rest of the Western world.

Out of that TV show I got a job offer that had been a long time coming. Walter Kerr offered me the male lead in the London production of his wife Jean's long-running Broadway hit, *Mary, Mary*. I had auditioned for the New York production originally but was told I looked too young opposite Barbara Bel Geddes. Now I was cast opposite rising star comedian Maggie Smith, who I had seen on Broadway in *New Faces of 1956*. She was both funny and good-looking.

88: MAGGIE, MAGGIE!

In January 1963, I flew to London with Virginia to start rehearsals of *Mary, Mary*. My name would be over the title this time. I had also been co-starred in *Everybody Loves Opal*, but nobody noticed. We were to have the same director as the original New York production of *Mary, Mary*, Joseph Anthony.

But first I had to find a place to live. A "nice address" was what my English agent said. This happened when David Greene, a TV director I knew in Canada, had to leave his London townhouse to work in television in California. The rent was twenty-five guineas a week. My daughter Martha, who lives in England, says that that price would now be the hourly rate for such a "tony" residence.

But living in luxury in England has its limits. On our first night the heat went off at 10:00 p.m. and there was no way the North Thames Gas Board was answering the phone at that time. Virginia was no trouper in such circumstances, not used to bone-chilling damp. When she finally got the Gas Board on the blower, she was told by the authorities to stock up on sixpences. They had no advice for her on how to cope with the deafening roar of the lorries that thundered past our door at all hours of the night, providing Covent Garden with fresh veggies.

So the next evening we took refuge in London's finest asset, the theatre. We saw the comedy that Maggie Smith had just left, *The Private Ear, The Public Eye* by Peter Shaffer, and we roared at the campy and bitchy antics of Kenneth Williams. We were late getting to our seats and sat behind a tall man with a narrow head and a shorter woman wearing a mink coat that seemed to need Hollanderizing. When I whispered to Virginia that the man's head was obstructing my view of the stage, she replied, "Ask his wife to remove it. She can do it. She's the queen."

The next day rehearsals began and things seemed to go smoothly. Sharing co-star billing was an Australian actor, Ron Randell, playing the film idol Mary gets involved with. So it was a Brit, a Canadian, and an Aussie all playing Americans. Except that I noticed during the initial read-through that Maggie Smith made no attempt to sound Yankee in any way. I had seen her on Broadway doing a perfectly acceptable American accent. Instead of the Spencer Tracy–Kate Hepburn kind of sharp exchange that I had seen on Broadway, Maggie was playing the demure English rose, but with the razor-sharp wit provided by the dialogue that made fools of the American men in her life, including her husband Bob McKellaway, played by me as the chump of all time. I could only admire her strategy, because the British audience, prone to gentle anti-Americanism, would lap it up.

We opened in Brighton, at the Theatre Royal. This time Laurence Olivier, who lived in Brighton, popped in to watch Maggie, having hired her later in the season for his new National Theatre Company. I was told that he said about me that I had "good comedy timing." The *Brighton and Hove Herald* said "Donald Harron is a magnificent complex of bewildered emotions as Bob McKellaway."

That was the only good review I ever got. While Virginia happily prowled the antique shops in the Lanes, I enjoyed eating lots of fresh seafood, including mussels, which would later prove my undoing. Those mussels, I later found out, were caught in plague-ridden waters. Back in London, I was depressed beyond belief. By opening night I must have been impossible to live with, but Virginia knew better than to cross me.

Opening night itself, I was sick as dog, and most of my offstage moments were spent vomiting. It must have affected my performance drastically, because I remember wishing that I were dead. That opening night turned out to be the biggest disaster of my career. Naturally, my reviews were not good. One paper accused me of wildly overacting. I'm sure in my condition it was probably true.

Present in the audience that opening night was the one person who knew what was wrong. Woody Fisher, my ex-wife Gloria's kid brother, was on a honeymoon with his bride Beverly. He had graduated in medicine as a liver specialist, and that's exactly what was wrong with me. It took him about two seconds backstage to reach a diagnosis: infectious hepatitis.

I wailed in my misery, "How could I get a thing like that?"

Woody replied, "Three ways: anal sex, excessive drinking, or contaminated seafood." I told him about being mussel-bound in Brighton.

Naturally, I skipped the opening night party, but I told Virginia to go, while Doctor Woody drove me home and sent me straight to bed. Just as his father had done, he probably saved my life. Virginia left the party early and came home to tell me that nobody mentioned my onstage performance.

Next morning a Harley street specialist appeared, sent by the theatre producer to evaluate my health. The diagnosis was that I would be on my back for the next three months. This was financial disaster, because

I would not get paid for being in bed, as many famous concubines have done, and I couldn't afford to be unemployed for that long. Even in my liverish misery, I was determined to get back on my feet as soon as possible.

My understudy went on that night, and because of my condition, the cast was subjected to a series of large and probably painful injections which would not endear me to them in any way. The reviews were all bad for me, of course, but not that good for the play, either. However, Maggie Smith was the smash hit of the evening, and a long run was predicted on the strength of her performance. I did not appear onstage for the next six weeks. Another actor was flown over to replace me.

My father flew over to comfort me. He hadn't been back to Blighty since 1918, but because of my morbidity, he seemed to prefer to spend most of his time rooting around ironmonger (hardware) shops. The one thing he did do, which moved me even in my misery, was to offer to give me money, when I knew he couldn't possibly afford to. I wish that I could have been a better son on that dispiriting occasion.

Virginia did what she could to comfort, but the disease had really affected my liver and kept me in a sombre mood. I spent most of the time by myself, reading Kierkegaard and other melancholics. This resulted in temper tantrums. I remember throwing a Granny Smith apple at her as she fled out the door. This sour mood continued when I was up and about. We used to take separate sets of keys when we went out, in case we quarrelled in the great world outside and needed to take refuge from each other.

I got back to work in six weeks instead of three months, through sheer willpower and the need to get a weekly cheque. When I finally returned to the cast, it was to learn that Maggie much preferred performing with the replacement actor. The next few weeks were some of the worst memories of my life, constantly aware of my bad reviews and frosty relations with my co-star.

One night there was an unusual audience reaction. In the first act they roared with laughter on almost every line. After the intermission, we couldn't get a peep out of them. It wasn't till after the curtain call that the stage manager told us President Kennedy had been assassinated.

Next day Virginia and I went to the American embassy to pay our respects and ended up the evening after the show by having a fierce fight.

Later I found out that a lot of married couples had a similar reaction to that cataclysmic event.

The run of the play continued, with no communication between my dressing room and Miss Smith's. Memorable was a moment onstage when she addressed the English understudy for the other male lead, Ron Randell. The incident happened onstage in full view and full hearing of the audience, as Maggie withered this poor English actor by declaring "Why don't you get off!" I never spoke to her from that day on.

Maggie eventually left the cast to join Olivier in his National Theatre opening. Later she played Desdemona to his "Calypso Joe" Othello. Her replacement in *Mary, Mary* was Carole Shelley, who was an absolute delight to play with, and my London life brightened considerably. Incidentally, there was only a slight drop in the box office receipts after Maggie left.

The prospect of getting rid of two redheads in my life was cheering. My girls got news to me that their mother was thinking of getting remarried. That would certainly help my bank account. Her husband-to-be was Stephen Vizinczey, a writer of plays who also worked at the CBC after fleeing Hungary in the '56 revolution. He was six years younger than Gloria, and she later became the subject of his first novel, *In Praise of Older Women*. The fact that his "older woman" was also his editor contributed greatly to its success.

Because of that courtship, complicating the lives of my ex and her slightly younger suitor, I was able to bring my daughters over to England during the summer of 1963. That's where they first heard the music of the Beatles and eagerly bought their first two singles. They left these discs behind when they went back to Canada, and when the Beatles appeared on the Ed Sullivan show, there were frantic transatlantic calls to retrieve these treasures.

My mood and my attitude toward Virginia certainly improved when the daughters were around. We played games like "Who Am I" and "Essences" and even tried some improvisations. The one I remember was when Martha and Mary pretended to be swans on the Thames, the ones just across the road from us. The girls waddled about and honked, to our delight, but the true inspiration came when little Mary said to her big sister, "Somebody's coming! Quick, get into the water and look graceful."

When I was away at the theatre, the game-playing got more serious. Virginia eventually insisted on the Truth game, where the three of them had to reveal their true feelings. Once I arrived home and found all three of them in tears. When I was alone with Martha, I asked her what those tears were about. She said that she and her sister didn't want their mother to marry again. "He talks funny and I can't stand him."

Perhaps I was thinking of my own financial future when I said, "Okay, so suppose she doesn't marry him because of you. What happens when you're eighteen and ready to leave home? Your mother will be all alone. How will you feel then?" When the girls got back home they officiated at their mum's wedding ceremony in Rochester, New York, because our Mexican divorce wouldn't allow Gloria and Stephen to get married in Canada.

As I was leaving London, I got an offer from CBC Radio to do a daily recorded show (recorded at *my* convenience), which I could do in batches at the Toronto studios while visiting my daughters in their new home. My co-host would be Pat Patterson, a CBC stalwart, and the show would be called *Side by Side*. She would choose the music and I would choose the excerpts from talking records, poetry, plays, comic monologues, anything I wanted. The timing was perfect. All the shows would be recorded in one swell foop in the late spring. I could continue to watch my kids grow up, and maybe I could sneak in a TV monologue about Canadian politics from Charlie.

89: BACK IN CANADA

As soon as I got back to New York, I phoned Joe Papp about his 1964 season in Central Park. Both *Hamlet* and *Othello* were on the ticket. I reminded Joe of our previous conversation about me playing Hamlet before my fortieth birthday. Joe remembered but said he couldn't locate me because I was out of the country, so he cast an actor named Alfred Ryder.

"He's too old!" I snapped. Turned out that Ryder was over fifty and had to be replaced by his understudy before the opening performance. But this was well before that happened, and Papp offered me a role he thought was just as rewarding. "We're doing *Othello* with James Earl Jones, and I want you for Iago. You were wonderful as Edmund. Iago's the same kind of part."

I still can't believe my reply. "Don't call me. I'll call you."

I phoned my California agent, Sue Mengers, to see if anything was cooking on the coast. She gave the usual reply: "I'll get back to you." But the next day she did with the news that John Houseman was planning a summer production at UCLA with my old blacklisted friend and former Shylock, Morris Carnovsky, in the role he told me always dreamt of playing: King Lear. Two phone calls later and I was back to being that bastard again. I justified turning down Iago with the realization that the television industry had abandoned New York and fled all the way West.

Lear was a summer engagement. Before that was the CBC *Side by Side* assignment, which would keep me handily employed until then. It was when I checked into CBC in Toronto that I found out that *Side by Side* was to be a summer replacement for *Trans-Canada Matinee*. I would be working for my ex-wife.

Gloria was quick to inform me that nepotism hadn't gotten me the job. The choice had been strictly up to Pat Patterson. At the same time Gloria was doing so well in her job that she could financially support her new husband by persuading him to quit his job at that same CBC. When Virginia and I got to Toronto, Stephen Vizinczey was staying home in their Sherbourne Street apartment and writing his novel.

We had a pleasant five-week stay in Toronto with quite civilized relations between all sections of our double family. I also hooked up with Norm and Elaine Campbell and took Virginia for a meal at their home in Willowdale. Norm told me that he had a request from Johnny Wayne for the title song from our television musical *Anne of Green Gables*. They needed it to help celebrate the opening of the new Confederation Centre in Charlottetown.

The dedication of this new building was to be marked with a variety show featuring Canadian celebrity performers like Oscar Peterson, Glenn Gould, and Lorne Greene as master of ceremonies, plus the comedy team of Wayne and Shuster. But Johnny Wayne told Norman that there was nothing of the Island in the show and asked permission to do our little song with a local performer singing it. Norm agreed happily and so did I.

Virginia kept fidgeting in her seat at dinner and when I asked her what the problem was, she told me she was dying for a stiff drink. I told her to wait till we got back to the Waldorf and/or Astoria, because the Campbells were teetotalling Christian Scientists. It took Virginia three years to join what Charlie Farquharson would call Alkyholics Unanimous.

On other fronts, Virginia was a positive asset. She became a real pal to my daughters, especially the day when teenage Martha was home from school and got a phone call from the Metropolitan Police that they were holding her kid sister in jail! The cops wanted one of Mary Harron's parents to come down to the station right away.

First thing Martha did was phone Virginia, and together they appeared at the police station. My wife presented her ID, which said Harron, and asked to see her prisoner "daughter." Mary had been caught stealing an Agatha Christie paperback. Virginia, relishing the role of a distraught parent, assumed full responsibility for eleven-year-old Mary's dire plight. When Mary was released, the look on her face showed that she was quite ready to give up her life of crime. That included forging notes when she skipped school. She could have had a career as a master forger. I'm glad she eventually chose to be a film director instead.

On the way back home in the cab, Virginia gave Mary comfort rather than a lecture and swore Martha to secrecy about the incident. It was her finest hour. This forged a new bond and engendered a promise from both of us to bring both of them out to California for the summer. We would be able to provide them with a beach house in Malibu for the first two weeks. The girls couldn't wait to hit the beach.

King Lear was staged at Schoenberg Hall on the University of California campus. Carnovsky played the King rather like he did Shylock, but with more humanity. Most of the rest of the actors were from New York, lamenting the loss of television in the east and biding their time till they got an offer to go back to Broadway or Stratford-on-the-Housatonic. An exception was Lear's youngest daughter, Cordelia. This role was played by Katharine Ross, who elopes with Dustin Hoffman at the end of that film that includes the line "I have just one word for you ... plastics!"

We had packed houses, tumultuous applause, and rave reviews, which resulted in an extension of our run and a move in mid-July to a larger outdoor venue, the Pilgrimage Theater.

Transferring to the great outdoors from a small indoor theatre was an enormous technical task, complicated sometimes by the appearance of rattlesnakes from the surrounding hills. It also seems that our rehearsals went on till almost dawn and then resumed again early in the afternoon. Houseman's assistant, Gordon Davidson, who later took over the main downtown theatre in Los Angeles, was easy to work with and became a friend for life.

We opened to more rave reviews, and the *New York Times* critic flew all the way back to re-review us with another rave. The day after we reopened, I got an offer to guest-star in a three-part *Dr. Kildare*. One guest-star appearance a month would do us Harrons nicely. Nights belonged to the Bastard, but during most days I was a Scottish surgeon suddenly hospitalized, who ended up in a bed next to a nun played by Mercedes McCambridge. They let me keep my shaggy Shakespearean locks, assuming that just being a Scot made me pretty eccentric to start with.

90: THE PEN IS MIGHTIER?

September 19, 1964, I was too busy to celebrate my fortieth birthday. To get jobs in television, I cut my bastard locks to Steve McQueen–like proportions. The razor cutting was done for me by Jay Sebring, later to die a horrible death at the hands of Charles Manson, murderer to the stars, in that house of horror where Roman Polanski's pretty wife met a similar fate.

Speaking of houses, Virginia and I rented what looked to me like a Japanese ski lodge on top of Laurel Canyon. It was smaller and less prestigious than my previous "good address" on Summitridge Drive, but it had huge picture windows. No air conditioning, however, which led me sometimes to lead a life outside, provided there was no smog. Evenings were no problem, and it was a pleasure to invite some of our Canadian friends to dinner. Virginia was into her third dry martini when she turned to me and whispered, "When the hell are they going to serve dinner?" I tried to be as quiet when I replied, "Darling, you're the hostess."

I got a call to try out for the lead in a television series based on Jean Kerr's book, *Please Don't Eat the Daisies*. I guess the author had forgiven me for that opening night in London. I had never heard from either Kerr on the subject. The scriptwriter had kept the spirit of the original book, and we taped it in front of a live audience. Their constant laughter was music to my ears, but I realized I was only one of several actors trying out for the part. When the results came out, I was told I lost out because I have a "serious face."

Suddenly I got a call to go back to Canada and do a comedy special with Max Ferguson and my old high school typing buddy, Larry Mann. I don't remember much, but we had fun despite the fact there was no studio audience.

I took my Buster Keaton face back to L.A., where not only was I busy with *Burke's Law*, *Twelve O'Clock High*, and *The Man from U.N.C.L.E.*, but I started trying to write TV scripts on spec. Burl Ives was doing a series, *O.K. Crackerby*, in which he played an eccentric billionaire trying to control his spunky, unruly brood. He kept track of them by remote control, listening in on what they were up to at all times. My idea was that the kids were playing an innocent game of Monopoly, but billionaire Burl thinks their real estate exchanges are actual. So unknown to them, he starts buying up whole sections of Atlantic City, Park Place, Ventnor Avenue, various streets and estates for real. I got the idea from Ernie Kovacs when he told me that he used to play Monopoly with Dean Martin and Jack Lemmon, but using real money instead of that paper stuff.

My script idea was turned down by the powers-that-be because they felt it would be too much of a free advertisement for Parker Brothers games. The series itself folded a few weeks later, so I felt vindicated in my attempt to tilt at their windmill. I had an agent who was bemused at the idea of an actor turning out words on a page instead of merely memorizing somebody else's output.

Nevertheless, I went ahead and tried turning out a script for *The Dick van Dyke Show*. I had been to a taping of it in front of a live audience and was enthused by the fun the cast seem to have on set, even when retakes were required on the spot. So I wrote a story based on Rob's attempt to teach his wife a bit of American history. It was turned down, too, as being "terribly clever but a little too intellectual for our audience."

Speaking of which, the next day I got a call to do an episode of *Profiles in Courage*, the late John F. Kennedy's book about American history. Despite that, it was to be directed by an Englishman, Cyril Ritchard.

In the middle of all this I got a call from Mavor Moore. He had left CBC Television after its second season to take the helm of a new Toronto theatre, the St. Lawrence Centre for the Performing Arts. Having launched that, he was now the newly appointed artistic director of what was soon to become the Charlottetown Festival.

Mavor was calling from Charlottetown, where the Confederation Centre, the theatre-art gallery-library complex, had its gala opening the night before in the presence of Her Majesty, Queen Elizabeth II. The occasion was the meeting of the Fathers of Confederation, a fairly drunken group of men, next door at the legislative buildings exactly one hundred years before.

I remembered when Johnny Wayne had called Norm Campbell about this event months ago and Norm suggesting to me we let them have the title tune from our black-and-white TV musical. Evidently this was done, and a local Charlottetown girl, Maida Rogerson, was chosen to sing the song, amid all the high-powered celebrities. Wayne and Shuster had also written a special song for the occasion, "We All Sat Down in Charlottetown and Made Ourselves a Land."

Maida must have done a first-rate job, because Mavor told me that after the show the queen came backstage, and the first thing she did before greeting any of the lined-up celebrities, was to say to Mavor, "That's a rather pretty tune. Where's the rest of the show?"

"That's a Royal Command, buster!" said the artistic director of the new Charlottetown Festival. The reason Mavor was calling me was because Norm Campbell couldn't be reached. He was off in Denmark doing a movie for Disney about a ballet dancer. All I said was "Get the rights, buster!"

This was November. The festival was due to open the following June with a full season of shows, a Wayne and Shuster revue, an evening of Stephen Leacock comic sketches presented by John Drainie, and the touring production of the annual *Spring Thaw* review.

There would be a couple of weeks left at the end of the season to display a musical version of *Anne of Green Gables*. When Norm came back from Europe, he phoned me and said, "I don't think we should make a move in that direction until we get the rights!" This was December. Mavor didn't get the rights until the following April. Rehearsals were to begin in late June.

I decided not to wait. First thing I did was to go to Toronto and do more tapings of *Side by Side*, which had been renewed for a second season. The second task was to retrieve the original hardcover book that I had worked on for the television show. It had all my notes from ten years ago. Gloria told me it was still there in the bookcase.

I opened it and got the shock of my life. The middle of the inside of the book had been cut out in a three-inch square, and it was filled with cigarette butts. It struck me that my fourteen- and twelve year-old daughters had moved on. I wondered if they would still be interested in a freckled red-haired orphan.

By the way, there were no joints among the butts; none of what Charlie would identify as *That Mexycan laffin terbacker, wat they calls yer maruh-jewa-hyena.*

91: PHONING IT IN

Before I left Toronto, as 1964 became 1965, I had time to meet with Norm and Elaine. The original television version of our musical had been written with a lot of phone calls to Toronto when I was working in New York. Now it looked as if the same situation would exist for us between Toronto and Los Angeles. Sometimes Norman would have a tune first without any lyrics, and sometimes I would provide him with lyrics to set to music. We would get together when we could, but for both of us other work was beginning to pile up .

I sent Norman the lyrics for Anne's apology to Mrs. Lynde, in a format I had dreamed up all by myself. A first verse of fourteen lines, all ending in *ind* as in "Lynde." I sent a second verse of some ten lines all ending in *ary*. Then a third verse with the lines all ending in *ace*. Norman's reply to this was: "You are so ignorant about music that you create new forms!" He finally set it to a tune that sounds a lot like Puccini, and it turned out to be a comic favourite with audiences.

The convoluted rights to *Anne of Green Gables* were now held by the American conglomerate Farrar, Straus, and Giroux, instead of the original publisher, L.C. Page. There was no mention of British rights, or the Lucy Maud Montgomery Estate, which included her daughter Ruth, and Lucy's grandchildren, Kate and David. Mavor kept doggedly trying to get the dramatic rights, but they were not officially pinned down until Easter. The opening was now set for June.

I got a rash of TV jobs, including a three-part television film for Disney, *Willie and the Yank.* Willie is a Southern boy in the Civil War who captures a Northern general (that was me). Willie was played by Kurt Russell. One day the set was abuzz with the rumour that the "big mouse" was coming to visit. Lo and behold, there was Uncle Walt himself, all six foot four of him.

I also did back-to-back episodes of *Twelve O'Clock High*. Norm came to visit me during that first episode, and we would sit and have a confab about lyrics, until I was summoned to go back to the prison set, while I had a moment to think up another tune to which we could set lyrics.

He told me about the cast of our upcoming musical. Anne was going to be a little Texan, Jamie Ray, from Tommy Hunter's show, and the rest would drawn be from the cast of *Spring Thaw*. I was pleased about Peter Mews as Matthew, but not so enthusiastic about Barbara Hamilton as Marilla. When Norman asked why, I said that she was a superb comedian, but I didn't think she had the gravity to play a dour spinster, the most difficult role in our musical. Norman shrugged and said that the part was cast, and that was it.

I felt that with all my television activity I had really been letting the side down with my contributions to our musical orphan. This was to reckon without the amazingly multi-talented Mavor, who succeeded, even when the cast was already in rehearsal, in coming up with the lyrics to three of the best numbers in the show. First, Josie Pye's spreading the falsehoods of Anne's first day at school with "Didya Hear, Didya Hear!" then the new teacher's exciting exhortation to innovation in education, "Open the Windows," and finally the song both Matthew and Marilla sing about their inability to communicate, "I Can't Find the Words."

Mavor was the true godfather of the Canadian musical. His song "It's the Spring" in the first *Spring Thaw* was only the beginning of a succession of his songs and musicals, including *Candide, Johnny Belinda, A Christmas Carol, Sunshine Town*, and *Little Lord Fauntleroy*, culminating in the full-scale opera *Riel*. We could never have opened *Anne* without him.

The night our musical had its world premiere, I was not there. I was with David Jannsen in the Mojave Desert trying to avoid the scorpions under my feet. We were doing an episode of *The Fugitive*. I played a U.S. Army officer on a nuclear testing ground who finally relents and lets Richard Kimble go free. I wished that I had been in Charlottetown that night.

About four o'clock in the morning, I got an earlier-than-expected wake-up call. It was Norman shouting at the top of his voice. "We got away with it! Those Islanders accepted our version of their story!" My old nemesis Nathan Cohen was there, red as a beet from an afternoon spent lobster fishing. He fell asleep early in the first act!

Evidently, Nathan woke up for intermission and left his seat to go to the lobby. Norman thought he dozed off again in the second half. But my wily composer managed to siphon copies of *Anne*'s opening night reviews from the telegraph office, and they were all good, including Nathan's. Norm added, "Awake or not, Nathan's from Glace Bay. He won't dare say anything negative to upset Maritimers."

He also quoted something Nathan had said in print that night that has been used ever since by the festival: "Something wonderful is happening in Charlottetown."

92: LAND OF ANNE

The world premiere of *Anne of Green Gables* happened while my two daughters were visiting Virginia and me in Laurel Canyon. Despite their welcome presence, I felt obliged to make my first visit to Prince Edward Island to see for myself what we all had wrought.

It was toward the end of *Anne*'s brief run, and Mavor had announced that it would appear next season. The excitement was palpable when it was also announced that the musical accompaniment would be expanded from two pianos, a trumpet, and drums to include the entire Atlantic Symphony transplanted from Halifax.

Bubbling with enthusiasm and perspiring with relief after seeing the show, I made my way backstage. I headed directly for Barbara Hamilton's dressing room to tell her what a fool I was to ever doubt she was right for the part of Marilla. She interrupted my cooing about her wonderful performance to give me a hug and invite me back to her rented place that same night, along with the rest of the cast, crew, and musicians for a "ship-wreck" supper. This consisted of anything she could find in the fridge, which she would throw together in one pot and serve hot to the masses attending her hospitality. Barbara was not only superb at what she did onstage, she was one of the great hostesses of all time.

The Island weather was not at its best, and the next day, after a trip to Summerside to do some publicity, I came down with a summer cold.

This despite the fact that Island air isn't smog-ridden like the atmosphere in Los Angeles. As I snuffled my way to the airport, Mavor told me that the festival wanted another musical next year to play alongside *Anne*. He was the one who had presented my wartime play *Turvey* and wondered if I could "musicalize" it. I replied that with the team of Norman and Elaine Campbell, and himself at the helm, it could be possible.

Mavor also mentioned that they wanted a third show in the second season. He confided that he had been working on a Canadian setting for the classic Russian farce, Gogol's *The Government Inspector*. Mavor's title for the piece was *The Ottawa Man*, and it dealt with a crooked administration, mayor, and councillors in the Manitoba of a century ago. He asked me if I would consider playing the title role. I felt dizzy with the exhilaration of the idea.

Before I boarded the plane, I visited the little bookshop to find a piece of Canada to take back to California with me. The last time I had done this I had purchased Birney's novel *Turvey*. Now that book was going to become our second musical. In 1941 painter Emily Carr had won the Governor General's Award for her non-fiction book *Klee Wyck*. It told about her own life, how she was orphaned at an early age and ultimately triumphed with her paintings, despite the fact that everything seemed against her. She was eventually accepted by a fellow painter, Lawren Harris, and the other members of the Group of Seven. It would be another seven years before I would get a chance to help musicalize the tale of that other orphan on that other island.

But for the moment, as I boarded the plane for Los Angeles, I had never felt more Canadian.

93: HOME THOUGHTS AND A BROAD

I arrived home a changed man and was greeted by my little family, which had been through some changes, too. The bond between Virginia and my daughters, which had strengthened in Toronto, was starting to shred due to her incessant drinking. I was confronted by three sad females, not even buoyed by my exhilarating visit to Prince Edward Island.

When I talked about the possibility of coming back to Canada to live, that cheered up two-thirds of my family, but Virginia proceeded to lock herself into the bathroom and threatened to do away with herself. I reacted immediately. I tore outside and put my fist through the bathroom window, then cleared away the jagged pieces. This allowed my smaller daughter, Mary, to climb inside and open the bathroom door. A tearful Virginia emerged, cowed by the violence of my reaction. All she said was "It's all pain, isn't it. That's really what life is ... pain."

Maybe I shouldn't have indulged myself by going to Prince Edward Island, but in retrospect I had to be there. But without me, the visit of my two daughters turned out to be not what it should have been. When Virginia's mother was brought into the picture, neither she nor my daughters could seem to relate in any way. Virginia casually observed to her mother in the presence of my daughters, "Why is it that Canadian children are so much more boring than others?" I call this phenomenon the Stepmother Syndrome, and it didn't end with Virginia. It seems to engender a hostile relationship with my children. I should know about that syndrome — I've been through fifty years of it.

I took my daughters to the airport the next day, knowing that neither of them wanted to come back to California. Little did I know that by the time I could get back to Canada, both of them would be long gone. It was the success of Stephen's novel *In Praise of Older Women* that changed their lives. It took them away from me to Italy for a year, then grammar school in England.

One source of Virginia's real pain was that she had been to a fortune teller and was told to expect a divorce in our family within a year or two. That, and a complete lack of activity for her in Los Angeles, added up to depression. She had been involved, before my daughters came, with helping autistic children. The technique for dealing with them, according to Virginia, was to shout loudly at them to get their attention. From what I have learned since (one of our friends has an autistic son), the one thing you don't do is make a loud noise when you are trying to communicate.

What to do with a wife who doesn't know what to do with herself? I phoned her best friend in Malibu, and she came to the rescue with an invitation for Virginia to come by any time and shoot the breeze. At the same time, television work for me started pouring in.

Bob Goulet was so grateful to me for suggesting him for Lancelot in *Camelot* that he made me a guest star in his new series, *Blue Light*.

All I can remember is plunging to my death into a four-foot tank of water. Then came *Outer Limits*, *Voyage to the Bottom of the Sea*, and *Time Tunnel*. That's where I played Robin Hood, or rather the Earl of Huntingdon. But the athletic feats were all performed by a stunt double, a man in his late fifties who had performed the same tasks for Errol Flynn in the film.

In *One Step Beyond* I played a young English lord who fulfilled his family's curse by stepping off the parapet of his own castle. The director, John Newland, made the whole suicidal experience an enormous amount of fun. He was so enthusiastic about us working together that he asked me to suggest a play that he could direct, and I could play the leading role, to be put on at UCLA.

I suggested Albert Camus's *Caligula*, probably the most twisted psychopathic Roman emperor of them all. Such was my mood at that time, I suppose. It never happened, but as an alternative Newland told me about a television series to be filmed in Germany, *The Man Who Never Was*. I was to play identical twins on either side of the Berlin Wall. The reason the offer was definite was because the sponsor was a Shakespeare fan and insisted on me for the part, or rather parts.

In the middle of trying to figure how I could get a musical *Turvey* written came another offer from my old *Sleep of Prisoners* pal Leonard White. He was now the producer of a British TV series, *Armchair Theatre*, supervised by a Canadian, Sydney Newman. Leonard had hired another Canadian, Paul Almond, to direct a teleplay entitled *Neighbours*, with yet another Canadian, Toby Robins, as my wife, and starring ... Dick Gregory!

I was so excited to work with this iconoclastic black comic that I stopped figuring for the moment how the Campbells and I would turn out another musical. From my literary agent in Toronto, Matie Molinaro, came the news that another of her clients, Earle Birney, was not so enthused about the musical idea. He didn't think the gravity of the Second World War lent itself to songs and dances. I told her I would talk to him when I got back from England.

On the flight to London I went over my old playscript. Despite its three-act format, it seemed to fit naturally into the two-act pattern required by a musical. The first half would end with Private Turvey arriving overseas and tasting the delights of Piccadilly. I already had a thought for a musical number when he and a buddy meet up with the Piccadilly commandos (London prostitutes) and I already had thought up the first line: "We're having a couple of tarts for tea."

Being in 1960s London would only help to stimulate me further about wartime London, if I could find the time between rehearsals. The television play I was to do, *Neighbours*, was about a white couple renting out their London flat to a black couple. Dick Gregory was cast as a well-known jazz pianist.

Our first rehearsal felt like Old Home Week for me. Toby Robins and her husband Bill Freedman had been around the New Play Society since the early days. Producer Leonard White had been part of my life ever since his Cain beat up my Abel every night for Christopher Fry more than ten years before. Paul Almond, with his wonderfully energized look on life, had guided me through several TV plays, and I looked forward to being under his wing again.

The new elements were Dick Gregory and Ruby Dee. She was the wife of Ossie Williams, and together they formed an important part of the New York black theatre community. I had seen Dick perform his stand-up routine more than once. Not since Mort Sahl had a politically inclined comedian electrified me with his up-to-the minute content. I was a confirmed fan.

A problem cropped up in rehearsal. Dick couldn't remember a line of dialogue. My nights were spent, not being prompted by Virginia, who was more than capable of the task, but in both of us helping Dick learn his lines. He explained the reason for his difficulty: as a born rebel, young Gregory assumed that everything he was being taught in school was a tissue of lies. Especially in history class. Thus, as a child, he learned by forgetting, discarding everything except the few facts that struck him as true.

This same process occurred every morning in the limo out to the studio. In addition to his own thoughts, comedy material from America was sent to him daily by a master of the trade, Bob Orben. Dick would have me read the jokes aloud to him and would either accept or reject them. He kept maybe five out of the thirty or more sent to him. These he could weave into a half-hour monologue. But at the moment, the play was the thing.

The taping went surprisingly well, even though Dick was forced to contribute some of his inspired ad libbing, which didn't change the original intent of the content all that much. As we all hugged and congratulated one another, Dick announced that he was off to Wales that evening to meet up with the great philosopher, Bertrand Russell. Russell's secretary appeared and whisked him away for the meeting of the minds. I never found out what happened as a result, but Dick, after his time in England, became less of a comic and more of a serious spokesman for humanitarian and environmental issues.

94: BERLIN — BOTH SIDES NOW

For me it was on to Munich and the two-part pilot film for the TV series *The Man Who Never Was*. The news that what we had merely talked about in Los Angeles would now be done in Germany had come from director John Newland while I was taping *Neighbours* in London. The script had been revised, but it and I were still "a go" thanks to that Shakespeare-loving sponsor who had seen me in the Bard God-knows-where.

But the script changes had reduced me from a pair of identical twins on either side of the wall to a single agent impersonating a dead look-alike. It all took place in East and West Berlin. The reason we were filming in Munich was because it still had many bombed-out buildings, but no Berlin Wall. So filming would continue over New Year's in Berlin and Salzburg.

This was a big-budget operation, judging from the hotel suite they provided Virginia and me with in Munich. I just missed out on seeing a local production of Kleist's *The Broken Jug*.

If my present job continued, I was assured that the crew would amass enough European location footage that the remainder of the series could be made in Los Angeles. They would have lots of second unit stuff to use for the rest of the series.

This hardly solved my problem with the Charlottetown Festival. I couldn't expect Norm and Elaine Campbell to take root in L.A. while we tried to turn out another hit musical. In addition to that, Mavor Moore was expecting me to be on the spot, ready for rehearsal in his own play in Charlottetown in June. Virginia thought I was crazy to worry.

I decided to live in the present tense and relax about the future. First day on the set in Munich we filmed my initial confrontation with my dead double's family. The wife was played by that lovely English rose, Dana Wynter, and her brother was one of my own compatriots, Donald Sutherland. In those days the future big Canadian star specialized in bit parts, having just finished the non-speaking role of young Fortinbras to Chris Plummer's *Hamlet* for BBC-TV.

Next to film was my escape from East Berlin. But Newland felt that the Munich locale lacked credibility, and we should move to Berlin for more authenticity. We were booked into the Hotel Bristol-Kempinski in West Berlin, another luxury establishment.

Forget postwar drabness, West Berlin was lit up like Las Vegas. A bombed-out church on the Kurfurstendam twinkled with coloured lights like a Christmas tree. The cafés that littered both sides of it stayed open till three o'clock in the morning.

The first scene was my escape from East Berlin. My character had to climb the east side of the Berlin Wall, hang by his fingertips until the East German police (the Vopos) passed by, then pull myself up and over to the freedom of the West. I was introduced to the stuntman who was to do all this, except for the close-ups. He complained of a bad back and said he was unable to perform. I ended up doing all these gymnastics myself with the real Vopos watching me from a mere twenty-five feet away. They had their Sten guns with them. I assumed the weapons were at the ready, because not a flicker of a smile came from any of them.

None came from me, either, when I saw that my stuntman was still onboard the next day. I asked him if he was coming to Salzburg, where I was supposed to lie on a railway track and have a train pass over me. He assured me he would be there with balls on.

To relax that evening and to celebrate the entrance of the New Year, I suggested to Virginia that we take our passports and go through Checkpoint Charlie to see a performance of Bertolt Brecht's *Berliner Ensemble*. She showed no enthusiasm and instead suggested we go to a transvestite club in West Berlin. It had been a favourite of Hermann Göring's, even though it was forced underground by the Nazis. The present master/mistress of ceremonies was reputed to be an old flame of Göring's.

The next morning Virginia was badly hungover and didn't want to be included in the human race until much later in the day. I resolved to do what I hadn't done the night before. They kept your passport when you went through to East Berlin. I handed it to a large, unsmiling woman in uniform, and she didn't give it back. She told me it would be returned if I re-entered West Berlin at the same checkpoint the same day.

The streets of East Berlin were crowded with people, a lot of them from West Berlin, because this was the last day ever that they would be allowed to visit their relatives. The ban had been lifted just for the holidays, from Christmas to New Year's Day. People were very friendly, and some of them approached me for news of the other side. In my high school German I had to tell them I was a Canadian, a stranger on both sides of town.

I was directed to a bus that would take me to the Berliner Ensemble's theatre. It was now run by Brecht's widow, Helene Weigel, and she ran several of her late husband's plays in repertory. Fortunately for me, the play that night was *Schweik in the Second World War*, Brecht's dramatic "sequel" to Jaroslav Hašek's *The Good Soldier Schweik*, the classic Czech comic novel about the First World War.

The theatre didn't look at all as I expected. Instead of a Spartan, utilitarian building, I was faced with an intimate, handsomely decorated eighteenth-century little gem of a playhouse. The production surprised me, too. I had heard enough about Brecht's theory of "alienation": Don't try to charm the bloody bourgeois bastards, just dispassionately give them the facts.

What I saw that night surprised and uplifted me. There was a prologue to the actual play itself, and it was performed by enormous puppets in Nazi uniforms, spitting images of Hitler, Goebbels, Göring, and Himmler lumbering about the stage with voices provided by singers from the German State Opera, making a mockery of the style of Hitler's favourite composer, Richard Wagner.

That was just the appetizer. When the actors came on and went into a musical number, there was no orchestra. The actor concerned simply put a coin in a jukebox, and we heard a full musical accompaniment to one of Paul Dessau's songs. It was so clever and so economical. Trying it in North America would lead to serious trouble with the musicians' union.

The famous "alienation theory" didn't exist the night I was there in East Berlin. I saw a comic performance of great charm, about a deadly serious subject. It gave me great hope that I could make our own "war-is-hell" musical. Leaving the theatre, I was greeted by several members of the audience who recognized, from my fervent applause, that I was someone who appreciated what their national theatre was accomplishing.

They directed me to the bus that would take me back to Checkpoint Charlie. In the station itself I saw a most amazing sight. In front of one of the very last buses going back to West Berlin, family groups were saying goodbye to one another for God knows how long. This was New Year's Day, 1966, and that wall didn't come down until 1989.

I tried to guess who was leaving for West Berlin and who was staying behind. It was impossible to tell. The goodbyes were fervent as relatives took a last long look at one another. The last thing the driver did before heading back to West Berlin was to inspect the underside of his vehicle with a mirror on a long handle to make sure there were no escaping East Berliners. As I passed through Checkpoint Charlie, a smiling young man handed me back my precious passport and wished me a happy new year.

The next day we were off to Salzburg, Austria, that *Sound of Music* town. My mission there was simple. I would be photographed in close-up while my stuntman would lie under a train as it slowly rolled over him. Except that he never showed up. When I asked why, I was told, "He has chicken pox."

I replied with gritted teeth that I wasn't so sure about the pox part. Once again I would have to do my own stunt. The next day I decided to protect myself by buying a jockstrap, except that in Austria they are called suspensoriums. I was sent to a sports store to buy one. When I got there, all the clerks seemed to be sub-teenage girls, and I forgot the name of the garment. Instead, I asked for a "condom minimum."

This engendered a great deal of girlish snickering, but eventually I was shown what it was. The girl said, "Ve haff only liddles. You try?" I was so desperate I went in and came out almost immediately with my intent to make a purchase. The girl said, rather loudly I thought, "Oh, goot! Zuh liddle fits!" As I left, there was a good deal of tinkly laughter from the staff.

Next day I steeled myself for my ordeal. The train was already puffing in the station. My director, always positive, told me that all would go well if I lay still and didn't move. The difference between the bottom of the train and the tip of my nose was a close fit. I wondered about the distance between that train and my suspensorium. Virginia was nowhere in sight. I didn't blame her.

"Action!" shouted John Newland. I vaulted over the station barrier and rolled over under the train before it started its journey across me. I decided to close my eyes and avoid breathing. When I heard the train rumbling over me, I opened my eyes in spite of my careful plans. One quick look at the mass moving over me and I shut them again, very fast. I can't remember whether I prayed or not, but the scene was done in one take. The next word I heard was "Lunch!" I ate myself silly.

After finishing this pilot, I couldn't pass up the opportunity to see my daughters when we were only a country away. Before we took the train to Rome via Venice, Newland asked me to cross fingers with him for good luck, because we would soon know whether *The Man Who Never Was* would be picked up for the following season. This would happen after *Turvey* and *The Ottawa Man*, but I secretly hoped it wouldn't happen. I wasn't cut out for all these gymnastic heroics. My main function during this whole shoot had been making the crew laugh.

I longed for Charlie Farquharson to come back into my life.

95: HOME VIA ROME

I couldn't pass up the chance to see my daughters when we were only one country away. We took the train from Munich to Venice and then on to Rome. We arrived in Venice at sunset, the most beautiful I had ever seen, then on to Rome at an early hour of the morning.

Virginia had booked us into the Hotel d'Inghilterra because "that's where Tennessee Williams always stayed." I didn't wake up until ten the next morning and immediately phoned Velletri, where my brood was staying, almost forty miles outside Rome.

Stephen drove the girls into Rome in his brand-new Mercedes and that night we all had dinner in Rome. It was confirmed that Gloria and Stephen were moving to England, and the girls were ready to be enrolled in a good London grammar school.

I had been told that this was a possibility, and I was assured that I was given unlimited visiting rights. But the reality of the fact that my children would continue to be half a world away upset all my plans about returning to Canada. I had hoped to live in the same neighbourhood where they went to school.

Virginia was upset at what my daughters were wearing. She felt that Gloria had sent them to our elegant dinner in old, scruffy clothes. In her mind this was a definite ploy to get their father to shell out for some new Italian duds. She also suspected Gloria and Stephen of squandering my support payments. Instead of splurging on clothes, next day Virginia took the girls to a hairdresser near the Spanish Steps. They both emerged wearing the then-fashionable "beehive" look. It was fine for fifteen-year-old Martha but really ludicrous on her younger sister. I hugged little Mary extra hard as we said our goodbyes later that day. I hugged her sister, too, but I sensed that Martha couldn't wait to leave the provincial life outside Rome for the trendy excitement of 1960s London. Toronto was not in her plans.

As soon as we got back to Los Angeles, there was a message waiting from John Newland. *The Man Who Never Was* had been picked up for the fall. Virginia was ecstatic. I had mixed emotions. Next day came another message from Newland. The show was still going ahead, but there had been a sudden change of sponsor. The man who loved Shakespeare (and me) was out, and the new sponsor wanted Robert Lansing in the title role. Just like that, I was the Man Who Would Never Be.

Virginia was crushed. For once she didn't blame me for what happened and did her best to comfort me. I didn't feel crushed at all. I phoned Canada and found there was work waiting. More tapings of *Side by Side*, to be specific. This would allow me to deal with the author of *Turvey* and talk him into letting the Campbells and me make it into a musical.

Turvey had never been out of my thoughts all through my other adventures. I knew exactly what I wanted to do with the story of a Canadian sad-sack private in the Second World War.

Side by Side with the ever-bubbly Pat Patterson was fun to do again. Earle Birney was a different proposition. He wanted to stress the Hell of War, and he wanted the salty language to go along with it. In his original novel he had used euphemisms like "line up in alfa-friggin-betical order!"

Now he wanted the actual four-letter epithet. I knew this would drive the Christian Science Campbells up the wall, and I didn't think the foul language was necessary, either.

What changed Birney's mind was an actual meeting with Norm and Elaine one afternoon, and a piano recital with lots of ideas for the musical. He was particularly enthused about the number that Norm and I had been working on entitled "A Couple of Tarts for Tea."

The deal was signed the next day. Now all we had to do was to "cremate it," as Charlie Farquharson would say. Speaking of which, he came back into my life soon after I arrived in Toronto. It was in the CBC canteen where I met my old college chum, Eros, E. Ross Maclean from the pages of *The Varsity*.

Eros was now working for the CBC on its most popular public affairs show, *This Hour Has Seven Days*. Not since Andrew Allan's *Stage* series on radio had audiences felt compelled to tune in regularly to a Sunday night show. And this was not drama, but hard-core public affairs, delivered by professional journalists like Patrick Watson and Laurier LaPierre. To "leaven the loaf," as Eros put it, they had Bob Christie's daughter Dinah to sing original topical songs about current events. I hadn't seen Dinah since she was a kid backstage at Stratford telling actors in their dressing rooms when it was time to get back onstage.

Eros was worried that the ratings of the show had aroused a fit of jealousy from the news department. They felt the show was usurping their presence to present the news as facts. So Eros became concerned with upping the entertainment content of this public affairs show. He had remembered the original Farquharson monologue in *Spring Thaw* and seen a couple of my subsequent appearances in the old cap and sweater. He was now suggesting that a Farquharson monologue on some topical politics each week would alleviate the pressure from the news department.

I didn't hesitate for a second. Besides, I was having trouble pinning down Norman Campbell for lyric-writing sessions. Norm was not only one of CBC-TV's busiest producers, he was also on the executive of the union for television producers and directors. And they were talking strike! The only Campbell left at home to write lyrics with was Elaine. She succeeded in writing one of the best numbers in the show, a love song, "I'll Follow."

All of a sudden, Norm became involved with meeting after meeting. I suspect one of the issues might have been the rift between the news and public affairs departments, something in which I was about to become involved.

So, without further ado, Charlie Farquharson was thrown into the *Seven Days* mix. My first monologue was about Soviet Foreign Affairs Minister Andrei Gromyko paying a visit to the Vatican to have a talk with the pope, surely an unprecedented occasion.

Here's what I can remember of Charlie's comments on this unusual event.

Did yiz heer that serviette fella in charge of all yer forners affares, Andy Growmickey, had a oddience with yer Pope in his Vaticka-can? Yuh wud wonder how they cud git a oddience fer a rang-dang-doo like that? Becuz yew take that Gromickey feller, I bleeve he's nothin' but wun of them Commonists, and you take yer averidge Pope, he'd be morn likely a Roaming Cathlick!

I don't know if it was a direct result of that speech, but *This Hour Has Seven Days* lasted for only a few weeks more. The news department triumphed over public affairs, and Canadian viewers lost one of the most successful TV shows in years. The good news for me was that those CBC strike meetings had stopped because of it, and Norm Campbell and I were able to get together to work on the lyrics of *Turvey*.

96: ISLAND PAIR-A-DICE

In the late spring of 1966, I drove from Los Angeles to Charlottetown with a cat that yowled and a wife who didn't complain nearly as much. I've never mentioned this feline before, but he has a history of his own. When I started living in Virginia's apartment in 1960, he suddenly appeared at our door with a mouse in his mouth. He dropped it in front of us as a peace offering. I think it meant he wanted to have a home, and we were it.

Now it was six years later and Farley was still with us as he prowled and yowled in the back seat of my Volvo, most of the way to the Maritimes. It didn't help Virginia's frame of mind. She already knew I was thinking about coming home to Canada to stay. Her attitude was partly determined by that tarot card reader who told her, among other things, that I was about to embark on a decade of incredibly creative activity, and that activity could possibly include a divorce.

I've never put much stock in what's in the cards, but what's in the palm of one's hand is something else. I still remembered a reading I got from the wife of our family doctor when I was only five. She told me that I would make my living by my voice (she didn't mention that I can't sing two notes in the same key) and that I would spend a good portion of a long life (as revealed by my lifeline) under another flag. She also mentioned more than one marriage, without specifying how many.

In actual fact, despite Farley's serenades, Virginia and I got along better on that ten-day journey than we had before (or since). We spent one night in Las Vegas, where we saw Frank Sinatra and the Rat Pack. Virginia didn't care to renew acquaintance and we rolled on the next morning, eventually taking in the Grand Tetons and Yellowstone Park. Next was a glimpse of Mount Rushmore, and a three-hour wait behind a flock of sheep in Wyoming. Before I knew it we were on the ferry from New Brunswick to Prince Edward Island.

The thing that preoccupied me was the news that I was able to glean from my native land. It seems I was contemplating becoming a full-blown Canadian again at exactly the right time. Thanks to the original urging of Tommy Douglas, Ottawa had at last adopted national health care, a Canada Pension Plan (CPP), and a brand-new flag.

First thing I had to do when I hit Charlottetown was to find the Confederation Centre. I had forgotten from my first brief visit, and I knew the theatre staff could tell me where I would be staying for the rest of the summer. I asked at a gas station for directions and was rewarded with a brief lesson in a Prince Edward Island accent: "Turn roit at the loits."

I made a note of that significant vowel movement and found what I was looking for. The Confederation Centre building itself was located next to Province House, the place where our country's existence was first proposed.

At the centre I was given directions to the cottage I had rented for the summer. It was across the Northumberland Strait (there was a bridge) in a cottage community on the red sands shores called Keppoch. The cottage was of the kind I was used to in Ontario, as well as my grandparents' home in Dunbarton, Ontario. I settled in, happily reminiscing. Farley the cat climbed up into the rafters and didn't come down for days. Virginia had a somewhat similar muted reaction, because her idea of a cottage had been derived strictly from films starring Doris Day.

Next day I left cat and Virginia to their brooding and started rehearsals for Mavor Moore's *The Ottawa Man*. Mavor was directing his own piece and had assembled an impressive array of Toronto actors, including Eric House, Alfie Scopp, and Kate Reid.

Playing the daughter of Eric and Kate was a Charlottetown actress, Gracie Finley, who had distinguished herself in a local drama festival. She was still in her teens and had red hair and freckles. I asked if she could sing. She asked, "Why?" Obviously, she hadn't yet seen our musical. I told her she should take music lessons and get to play Anne of Green Gables, because she looked like an orphan. Gracie has reminded me of that remark ever since. Three years later she took over the part and has played it more often than any other actress.

I eventually heard from Gloria answering my request to have the girls stay with me in Canada. She turned me down flat, insisting that they would get a far better education in England. My reaction was to drive my Volvo too close to the bridge and put a big dent in the front fender. I replied in a blazing airmail that I might not be sending any support payments overseas. Gloria replied sooner than I expected that Stephen was interested in legally adopting both of my daughters. Things simmered down during the summer, and familial relations and legal obligations went back to what they had been. Part of the reason for this was the discovery by daughter Martha of four or five letters I had sent my girls, which Gloria had held back to punish me. Both girls told her that she was instead punishing them. The notion that they would let themselves be adopted by Stephen was out of the question.

So our family summer games ended in a tie.

97: ANOTHER OPENING, SAME SHOW

Anne was rehearsing at the same time as *The Ottawa Man* because the two productions were to open on successive nights, with *Turvey* to follow later in the season. One of the great thrills was to hear our score played at rehearsal by the entire Atlantic Symphony, and the masterful arrangements by John Fenwick, which are still in use today. I brought Virginia along that day and she had a whole new outlook on life on Prince Edward Island. This included a one-time fling with one of the local actors, which came from their sharing a mutual acquaintance in Hollywood. By this time in our cooling relationship, I merely made a note of it, determined to pay her back sometime with a fling of my own.

On opening night of the second season of the festival I was introduced by Jack MacAndrew, the director of public relations, to a Halifax singer who was a big star and selling more records than anyone else in Canada. I had never heard of her. Jack told her that I was a big star from Hollywood who had recently appeared in a film, *The Best of Everything*. She had never heard of me, either. This Catherine McKinnon girl had seen the film and was very enthusiastic about Johnny Mathis's recording of the title song, but she had no recollection of me being in the movie. So we started our relationship dead even. I wasn't surprised that she didn't remember me; we smiled socially at each other and went on our merry way.

The curtain went up on with the same cast as the year before, with one exception. In the part of Anne's villainous rival Josie Pye, last year's Gail LaPine had been replaced by a cute dancer named Diane Nyland. She was later to take over the entire festival for a while and as a director is still contributing mightily to Canadian musical theatre.

Nathan Cohen skipped the occasion because he had already reviewed *Anne* the first season. The thought that he would be there the next night for the opening of *The Ottawa Man* was something I banished from my mind.

There was a representative, Janet Roberts, from my New York agency, MCA, at the opening. She brought me news of Hollywood interest in our musical. She said this was because of its positive reception the previous season. The offer came from the Danny Kaye office. They were interested in the film rights. It was initiated, I am sure, by Norm Sedawie, former CBC music producer who now worked for Kaye. The offer stipulated that they hadn't seen the show but were interested in the libretto and the lyrics. However, they insisted that all the music be rewritten by someone more qualified, like André Previn.

I was furious at this slighting of our composer by a fellow Canadian and would have loved to let them know it. But instead Norm got on the phone and in his Christian Science manner turned down the whole ludicrous offer more politely.

After the opening night of *Anne*, Mavor Moore introduced me to Bob Johnston, now the producer of *Spring Thaw*. I had remembered him as an usher at the Museum Theatre in the early days of the New Play Society. He had just completed a successful run of the 1966 *Spring Thaw* and was planning next year's presentation, marking the 1967 centennial of Canada.

He had leased the rights from Mavor and wanted to know if I was interested in writing the centennial script. His idea was a Brit's-eye view of Canada by an English narrator travelling coast to coast. I disagreed completely with the concept. This was Canada's year in the spotlight. I would only consider a Canuck's-eye view, with the idea, in centennial year, of writing a hundred-year history of Canada in sketches and songs.

Selfishly, I figured it might be the best way for me to get reacquainted with my country after an absence of ten years. Bob agreed with my proposal. The cast would be chosen from some of the performers we had seen that night, like Peter Mews and Barbara Hamilton. Bob wanted me to perform, as well. I accepted his offer with glee, already plotting to find a place for Farquharson. It involved rehearsing in Toronto in December, followed by a cross-country tour that would end in the same city the following spring.

Dizzy with that new notion, I made my way backstage. There was a cabaret after the opening, organized by that same Jack MacAndrew, who eventually left the CBC that year and became the one-and-only in charge of public relations for the festival. He introduced the backstage audience to someone he referred to as "the Voice of an Angel."

It was the girl he had introduced me to before the show. She sang unaccompanied, and I don't remember what the song was, but she surely lived up to her title. The sounds were the best that I could remember ever coming from a human throat. Sitting with Jack, I asked if she'd be interested in appearing in the centennial version of *Spring Thaw*. His terse reply was that "she didn't need it." He told me she was already booked on her own coast-to-coast concert tour.

What Jack didn't know was something I learned from talking later with Catherine herself. She had been bitten by the musical theatre bug earlier that year when she guest-starred in the pantomime *Cinderella* at the Beaverbook Theatre in Fredericton. She told me she was so nervous on opening night that the character she played, Princess Crystal, ended up referring to herself as Crinsess Pristle.

Being the most popular singer in Canada in 1966 was something she had already accomplished. After seeing our musical, what she yearned for was sharing the stage with actors she had seen. I found that out the day after when I met Catherine and her younger sister Patrician Anne for breakfast.

I made Catherine the offer of a role in *Spring Thaw '67* and told her who had already signed up. The prospect of learning to do legitimate theatre under a mother hen like Barbara Hamilton was all that was needed. She said she would try to rearrange her schedule to fit in with our purposes. I found out later this involved cancelling the lucrative concert tour, which covered much of the same route we would be covering. Virginia thought she sang well, too. She seemed to accept the fact that Catherine McKinnon would become part of our existence.

98: ON TO "OTTAWA," THEN WE DO "WORLD WAR II"

The next night was *The Ottawa Man*, one of the rare occasions when the Charlottetown Festival did a non-musical play.

It was an out-and-out farce, making fun of post-Confederation bureaucracy, and it turned out to be a crowd-pleaser. Even my old nemesis Nathan Cohen approved, including my performance. I was the man of the title, a foppish upper-class English remittance ne'er-do-well travelling through nineteenth-century Canada with my manservant, despite the fact that I can't pay his wages because I'm flat broke. Suddenly, I'm mistaken for the new government commissioner that Ottawa is sending forth to examine the political doings in a Manitoba town.

The next night I had Norm Campbell stay backstage, and between my appearances onstage with Kate Reid and Eric House, the two of us, lyricist and composer, figured out that Kate would fit best into the scene in the pub as a boozy old crone with an unlimited thirst. Norm thought up the title first, "Buy a Drink for Old Mother." I went onstage, did a scene, and came back with the rest of the title: "And She'll Be a Mother to You." By the end of that night we had the song all written and ready for rehearsal the next day. We didn't care whether Kate could sing or not (she couldn't), but I was convinced that her talent and warmth would light up the stage (it did!).

The title role was played by Jack Duffy, a comic natural who had made his mark on American television among the cast of *The Perry Como Show*. One of the reasons he was hired was because he both looked and sounded like Sinatra. Returning to his native Canada, he became a *Spring Thaw* regular and brightened up the cast of *Anne* with his sleazy teacher who lusted after the prettiest girl in the class.

Norm and I were delighted with our luck to have him, and he and Elaine set about writing him a Sinatra-type love ballad. This actually succeeded in temporarily distracting the audience from the sad-sack character he played, while they all identified with the greatest crooner since Bing Crosby.

Alan Lund was chosen to direct *Turvey*. It was a case of natural selection. He and his wife Blanche as a dance team had been part of the successful "Navy Show" during the war. For *Turvey* Alan conceived a ballet based on a military assault course that trained commandos for battle. It was the most electrifying part of the evening. Lund also cast me as the army chaplain who lectures the boys overseas about the dangers of loose women. He quotes the Bible about an Old Testament courtesan named Rahab, and the soldiers are busy taking down her name in case they might get lucky. His sex advice to the troops was "Get a hold of yourselves, chaps!"

In the military hospital sequences near the end of the show, Barbara Hamilton was at her most hilarious as the overbearing, heartless Nurse Hart. She melts into a helpless mass of blubber in the final scene when asked to stand up at Turvey's wedding in the hospital ward.

Turvey was so popular with audiences that we revived it, with a few new additions, five years later. Someday I hope to get it done again, maybe during the hundredth anniversary of the First World War. It coincides with the fiftieth anniversary of *Anne of Green Gables*.

Hobe Morrison of *Variety* came to see both musicals. He sniffed at *Anne*, the hard-hearted son of a bitch, but he thought *Turvey* was the better prospect for Broadway, even though "the script needed a little work." Nathan Cohen seemed to agree with that assessment but thought that the whole idea was quite promising. So far, so good.

Hobe agreed with us that Jack Duffy was absolutely perfect in the role. Because of Hobe's enthusiastic review I received a letter from crooner Rudy Vallee asking to be considered for the cast of the next production. He was soon cast in the Broadway run of *How to Succeed in Business Without Really Trying* and made such a success of his role that I'm sure it took his mind off our little musical.

That 1966 season of the Charlottetown Festival was continually exciting, partly because Jack MacAndrew organized an impromptu cabaret every night after the show. I remember one night playing Matthew to Diane Nyland's Anne in a skit in which I repeated the well-known line from the show, "Anne of Green Gables ... never change."

And Diane replied with some disdain, "But, Matthew, *never* change? That's so unsanitary!"

Catherine McKinnon seemed to be around for most of that summer. She returned again and again from other professional engagements to sing in our cabaret for free. This was against a very different background offstage, in which three members of our cast were ending the summer by heading for divorce.

One of them, I found out *much* later, was me.

.

99: ONE FOR THE HISTORY BOOKS

Now I could turn my thoughts to my country's past century, the theme I had chosen for the centennial version of an annual review that I had been involved with on and off since 1948. I've always been a history buff and knew quite a lot of what went on in Canada between 1867 and 1955, but because of my twelve-year absence, I was a bit rusty on the years after that.

The show would be directed by Alan Lund and the score would be arranged and conducted by John Fenwick. The orchestra consisted of the same number of musicians that had played the first season of *Anne*, piano, trumpet, and drums. I didn't have to worry about the music or the lyrics because that was entrusted to the team of Marian Grudeff and Ray Jessel, who later created a fine musical about Sherlock Holmes, *Baker Street*, and for Charlottetown a musical version of Molière's *La Malade imaginaire*, entitled *Like Wow*.

I wanted a place for Charlie Farquharson in this centennial review but decided against saddling him with a narration throughout the entire show. Or anyone else in the cast, for that matter. The last thing I wanted for this show was to have it sound like a National Film Board documentary. An item in the *Charlottetown Guardian* caught my attention. Somebody named Pierre Trudeau had just been made minister of justice in Lester Pearson's cabinet. Zooming around Ottawa in a sports car wearing dark turtlenecks and leather jackets, he was fodder for Charlie.

Our minster of justiss looks more like a fidgitive frum justiss, with his turkleneck swetters, and his bare feet in his scandles, and sumtimes with his asscot around his neck. He drives wun of them sporty cars bilt so low to yer ground, fer to git her goin yuh has fer to leen back in yer srender posishun. That car look to me like wun of them forn eyetallyun jobs, yer Alfalfa Romeo.

But the item that really got my attention was about the minister of defence in the Liberal government, Paul Hellyer. He proposed, all by himself evidently, to have all three of our armed services give up their own colourful difference in dress and submit them to wearing the same uniform, what Charlie would come to label as *eunuchfication*.

So I set to work to write a fashion show for the Canadian military throughout the entire history of the country. Charlie could be the guiding farce behind all that, starting with *Jack Carter and Sam Plain, yer wolf and yer mount clam. Then onto yer Eye sick Brock and his Grenade-deers in that war wair we beet yer yank 18 to 12. Not to menshun that Ree-yell rebellyusness, and them Boar's Wores, not leevin' out Wirld War Eye and Eye Eye, and soon, here's me, Charlie Farquharson in this bran noo rig, gittin reddy fer Wirld Wore Eye-yi-yi!*

Hellyer's all-purpose uniform was in a colour that can only be described as Garbage Green. It was in force among our armed forces until Brian Mulroney stopped the nonsense some twenty years later in 1984.

For Charlie's unification uniform, our costumer Frances Dafoe made a dazzling uniform that started with a battle dress blouse in the usual olive drab, but attached to it was a wide sailor collar and below it wide bell-bottom trousers in the tartan of the RCAF. The cap contained the insignia of all three services.

Here's what I remember of the Eunuchfication monologue Charlie delivered across this country.

Hav yiz herd about this heer euchfication of our armed farces? Seems yer deportment of nashnul offensivness under ther minster Pall Hellyer has a mind to put all our navels, army, and airyplane fellas inta jist wun unyform. The hole bunch of them! All waring jist the wun unyform??? I don't think that sounds turbly sannytary!!!

Wun of then navel admirables is so upset about loosin his sailor sut with his belly bottom drores, that he has thretten fer to go down on his ship! In yer departmint of vetruns having affairs, sum of them deviationists thinks that this hole pogrom is gonna cost us taxed-pares bullions a dollers. Not mullion, bully, bullions! And fer what? Soze all our boyz in bloo'n grey and karky kin end up lookin' jist like them sibbilant serpents taggin' cars in frunta parkin meeters.

Why? Wellsir, the theery is if ther all drest the saim, our serviss-a-b ull men won't be razin hell with eech uther in pubs on sardy nites. Insted, they'll all be reddy fer to keep the piece.

But that's wat they bin doin' awreddy in places like yer Shiny-eye Dessert!! Yew noe wat?? I think Ottawa shud git the Hellyer outa there. Down with sich farced yewnitty. Divided we stand, yewnited we fall, and up yer kilt!! Not to fergit them belly bottom drores!!!

Virginia and I moved to Toronto in September, and I have very little idea of what she was up to, because I did nothing but stay indoors writing the show up to the moment we started rehearsing in early December. In the cast were several *Spring Thaw* stalwarts of past years. Peter Mews had been with all nineteen *Thaw*s, and Barbara Hamilton had been hugely successful in replacing the original star, Jane Mallett. Newcomers were Dinah Christie, comedy-lyrics star of *This Hour Has Seven Days*, and Catherine McKinnon.

Rehearsals seemed to go smoothly, and so did the first few performances in bilingual New Brunswick, in both Edmundston and Campbellton. The audiences were quite young, mainly high school students, mostly French-speaking but obviously fluently bilingual. The cast was amazed and heartened by their seeming knowledge of Canadian history, as they laughed at all our "histerical" jokes.

The show started with Catherine appearing as Canada's national bird, the mosquito. The first half ended with a basketball game conceived by Alan Lund. It re-created the Battle on the Plains of Abraham between the French (red team) and the English (blue team) both in shorts and singlets. But the outcome varied each night, depending on which performer from either team scored the winning basket.

The second half opened with Diane Nyland as a sexy Laura Secord wondering whether to give her Fanny to a Farmer. Barbara and Peter enacted Queen Victoria and Sir John A. deciding to let Canada have a birth. Then Charlie and the Eunuchfication fashion show. The show closed with "Sitting on Our Assets," a display of Canada's material riches. I remember myself as one of our arboreal forests, shouting "I've Got Shingles," and Barbara Hamilton as an oil pipeline, with a large append-age behind her. Perhaps a harbinger of what's to come with the current oil sands pipeline project.

After the bilingual kids, we were not to have such an understanding audience for a long, long time. From then on we faced mostly grown-up audiences who didn't seem to care that much about our efforts to amuse them.

Our next stop was our home-sweet-home Charlottetown, and disaster struck even before we opened. The business manager Bob Johnston had sent on ahead tried to commit suicide due to some private sorrow of his own. It happened the day before we arrived. The truck carrying our sets and costumes broke down on the road and was stuck for hours waiting for a ser-vice station to open. Consequently, the dress rehearsal in the Confederation Centre theatre went on until almost 3:00 a.m. The atmosphere was not helped by Virginia going around giving everyone personal notes on their previous two performances.

I don't know who was in the opening night audience, but they couldn't have been the same ones who cheered both *Anne* and *Turvey* the previ-ous summer. This January night they sat as if carved in stone. Toronto's *Evening Telegram* duly recorded the event, noting in its headline: THAW '67 SAVED BY THE PERFORMERS. The *Toronto Star* sent somebody named Peter Gzowski who praised pals of his like Dinah Christie, but zeroed in on me. "He has looked at Canada, and he has not been able to make it sound funny."

I realized that my work on this show was just beginning. The attitude of the cast changed with this abrupt turn in our fortunes. Part of the problem was the notes given to the cast by Virginia. Bob Johnston flew to Charlottetown and joined us for the bus trip to Fredericton. He took me aside and in a quiet moment told me that the entire cast was threatening to walk out if I didn't get that wife of mine off the bus. Evidently, she had been telling everyone how to do their job, at the same time complaining about everything Canadian. The last straw was the day she stole Barbara Hamilton's designated seat behind the bus driver and refused to move when Dame Barbara asked for it back.

The last straw for me was when she started to tell Lund how to direct the show. Virginia hadn't enjoyed roughing it on the road, and when I told her to take a hike, she was quite amenable to quitting the tour and sitting it out with her mom in California.

100: OHHHHHHHHH CANADA!

Virginia was gone, which left me with the main problem of this tour ... myself. I kept wondering if I hadn't really lost touch with my country after all those years away. I didn't blame the audience. After Fredericton our next stop was Sackville. We were delayed by a blinding blizzard. The audience in the theatre waited for six hours before we could get to them. I determined to keep on rewriting the show until I was worthy of that audience.

I felt just as much responsibility to my cast. The only positive in the ticket sales seemed to be Catherine's presence in the cast. She never complained about anything and bonded easily with the rest of the cast.

Everyone turned out to be real troupers as I restructured the script. I had the cast rehearsing one version of a skit during the day while they performed the old version at night. Just before Winnipeg I decided to change the opening Ice Age number, and instead of her usual mosquito, Catherine would sing the opening song as a horse. Diane Nyland forgot, too, and instead of whinnying like a horse she buzzed like an insect alongside the Voice of an Angel.

I decided to give the cast a rest and ad lib the changes myself. That happened when we played Timmins at forty below. We were booked into a movie house where the stage was too small to hold the nine-foot screen for our new magic lantern show. I decided to accept fate, dispense with the screen, and narrate the sketch myself. I guess the Northern Ontario audience identified with my Parry Sound accent, because I got more laughs than the real slides ever did. It loosened up the audience for the rest of the show. The audiences seemed to get warmer as we made our way west. By the time we got to Victoria, Audrey Johnston of *The Colonist* said it was "the best *Thaw* we've seen for years."

I was beginning to think I might have a hit on my hands, but on our way back east the reception cooled rapidly. The Trail newspaper called our show "a chilly mush of cold slush." By the time we hit Moose Jaw, real tragedy struck. The crew members, who had travelled the entire tour with us, were trying to turn yet another high school school gymnasium into a theatre. Our electrician, Lyle Ayton, was high up next to the ceiling rigging some lights when he fell with a horrifying thud. He was dead. I felt sick. I had sacrificed a man's life on this fool's errand. I didn't want to go on.

It went on against my will. Next stop, the Royal Alexandra in Toronto. We arrived back with Lyle's body for a family funeral. Mercifully, there was a week off before we had to do the show again. I dreaded the Toronto opening so much I decided to go to Montreal so I could prepare some material for a television special proposed to me by Frank Peppiatt about the Montreal World's Fair, Expo 67. Anything but thinking about what had happened in Moose Jaw. I felt the whole crackpot trip across the country had been a ghastly mistake with tragic circumstances.

Virginia flew back from California and went with me to Montreal. I didn't tell her at the time, but I had decided that the best thing to do would be to sneak back to California and make a living with the usual round of television shows. I was given a special permit to wander around the Expo site. It was a sea of mud with only a few weeks to go before opening day. The vast scope of the project impressed me enormously, and I wished I could change my feelings about retreating from my country in defeat.

I don't remember anything about the opening of *Spring Thaw '67* in Toronto, just the cameras flashing in my face at a lavish party thrown by Ed Mirvish after the performance. All I could think about were the hired assassins of the press who were about to attack me, and I slunk home and went to bed as early as I could.

It was four o'clock in the morning when I was jangled awake by a call from Dean Regan. He was at a pay phone and wanted to read to me the reviews. Herb Whittaker in the *Globe* said: "Harron's humour gives *Spring Thaw* its lilt." The *Evening Telegram*'s Ron Evans called it "Hysterical History" and suggested the show be taken to the Canadian pavilion at Expo "to show the world we're not the poor, pompous, opinionless clods they take us to be."

There was no review in the *Star*, not until the next day where Nathan Cohen did his usual axe job. "*Spring Thaw '67* has been conceived for an unsophisticated and undemanding public. Even on that basis, it does not do. By any other test, it is a grisly experience." But he was too late. The day before his review appeared the crowds were already lined up at the box office. It turned out to be the longest-running, most profitable edition of our national review in that theatre's glorious history. Six record-breaking weeks there were followed by a further two sold-out months in Ontario, ending at Expo 67 in Montreal. Don't ask me why.

Later that year, in the fall season, the first national tour of *Anne of Green Gables* was launched, including three weeks at Expo 67. When it hit Toronto in the late fall, Cohen ignored his origins and this time panned the show. The other Toronto critics agreed with the audience instead.

Bill Freedman came over from London to look at our show and liked what he saw. He brought with him Donald Albery, the owner of Wyndham's Theatre in London, and together they envisioned a separate London production of our musical in two years' time.

I decide to stick around Canada. Catherine didn't. We had formed an unspoken attachment on the tour, but as soon as Virginia came back to Toronto uninvited, Catherine made other plans. To make up for her financial loss after all those months, she did a tour of one-nighters that included stops in Central and South America. I finally caught up with her with a phone call to Surinam. I hoped that we would be able to work together again. That was the closest I came to declaring my feelings. The only commitment I could get was "We shall see." I knew that she wasn't interested in playing second fiddle to my current wife.

Virginia went back to California soon after that. After Christmas with the girls in London, I came back to Toronto determined to stay on in my own country. I began the year 1968 alone.

The 1967 tour of *Spring Thaw* had proved that Charlie Farquharson was alive and well. In fact, he started to eclipse my own acting career. One of the first jobs I got after *Thaw* ended was a film assignment from Revenue Canada. It wanted me to make a series of short films, five minutes each, explaining Canada's tax system to the general public. The tax people wanted to use Charlie's "simple-minded approach" for the task.

I was pretty dense on the subject of Canadian taxation myself, so before I wrote the scripts I decided I better go up to Ottawa and confer with some of the tax experts. They took me to lunch in their employee cafeteria that had prices so low no ordinary taxpayer would ever get near. I was hungry, so I did my darnedest to load up on all that free food. Even then the bill came to less than a dollar, and I had to pay it, just like the rest of these civil servants! Nothing was on the house with these government guys.

After lunch I talked them into letting me play seven different characters in addition to Farquharson: a Scots curler, a very senior citizen, a John Lennon–type hippie, an Arab sheik asking about oil depletion allowances, a female civil servant with a clipped British accent, a disc jockey on a Tax-a-Phone TV show, and a hospital patient swathed in bandages from head to toe. I had no agent in Canada at the time, so I agreed to writing and performing the seven scripts for a fee that they suggested — $1,500.

I had a good time doing the films, making the whole worrisome business of taxation easier to understand. I figured it was a nice way for me to round off the year celebrating our country's hundredth birthday.

But I waited around for months to get paid! When I finally got the cheque from Ottawa, well into 1968, it was followed a few days later by a reassessment of my 1967 taxes and a bill for ... I swear this is true ... $1,500.

No wonder Charlie calls it *yer deportment of infernal revenoors.*

101: ON MY OWN ... I THOUGHT

The year started off with an offer from Howard Cable, orchestra leader and all-round nice guy. When Jack Arthur retired after many years as the producer of the Canadian National Exhibition Grandstand show, starring such celebrities as Bob Hope, Roy Rogers, and Victor Borge, the task was handed to Howard to produce the next one. Because of the success of *Spring Thaw '67* in Toronto, he was inviting me to write the script and perform a Charlie monologue.

The title of the show was already chosen: *From Sea to Sea*, and the theme was the building of the first transcontinental railway. So my involvement with Canadian history would continue. It ends when the last spike of the CPR is driven in at Craigellachie, British Columbia, by Lord Strathcona.

The National Ballet was onboard, Howard himself would conduct a sizable orchestra, and Bob Christie was again called upon to play Sir John A. Macdonald. Fortunately, Gordon Lightfoot had just created his most impressive work, "Canadian Railroad Trilogy." Its rich lyrics and driving beat were what tempted me to accept the challenge and try something for which I wasn't really suited. But with the help of Pierre Berton's books on the subject and the help of Lightfoot, who offered to write a song about the Métis if I could get Catherine to sing it, I decided to sign on. But I was so worried about the football-field size of this big project that I consulted a teacup reader. She told me I was going to have one of the biggest successes of my career. I wondered later what she put in that tea.

This was eight months away. In the meantime Bob Christie and I decided to revive Jane Mallett Associates, mostly to provide a vehicle for Jane's talents. I chose what I considered the funniest book written in Canada in recent years. It was a satire on literary criticism written by a professor of chemistry at the University of Manitoba, Paul Hiebert, and he called his takeoff on bad poetry, *Sarah Binks, the Sweet Songstress of Saskatchewan*.

Nobody played the title role ... everybody talks about Sarah in retrospect at a special memorial service "to our dead local girl." Jane and I had been on the original radio adaptation by Tommy Tweed.

I asked Tommy to prepare a stage version, but he said he was too much of a radio man to change gears and suggested I do it myself. His adaptation was so well done that the transition to stage took minimal effort on my part.

I did it, and it was a labour of love. Bob played the Diefenbaker-like Prairie politician, Augustus Windheaver. I played the minister in charge of the service, Dean Pindle, DD. Jane Mallett played everything else, including Mrs. Pete Cattalo, who remembered her hired man Oley, as big ... in every way. There was also a Wagnerian soprano named Rosalind Drool and sung in full bel canto voice by Arlene Meadows.

We loved our audiences so much, we didn't want to part from them even at intermission! In all my years in the theatre, I don't think I've ever had so much fun in a play.

The reviews were a personal triumph for Jane Mallett. The only dissenting critical voice was ... guess who ... good old reliable Nathan. He didn't like the writings of Paul Hiebert in the first place, but he blamed most of what he saw onstage on Bob Christie and me as "the real malefactors of the mess. Like the coelacanth and the cockroach, a few vestigial forms of theatrical diversion turn up eons after they have outlived their purpose ... It is not to laugh, it is to weep."

At the same time *Spring Thaw '68* opened in St. John's, Newfoundland, to the usual round of "It's not as good as last year." Nathan wasn't there to assassinate it, but he might have been outdone by a new negative force, the jazz critic of the *Toronto Daily Star*, Patrick Scott. He went all the way to the outer reaches of the Atlantic provinces to declare that the new *Thaw* "had all the grace and charm of a giant squid." Despite this, producer Alan Gordon was already planning *Spring Thaw '69*. Brave chap. Glad it wasn't me.

At one matinee of *Sarah Binks* I heard a loud, familiar laugh. No mistaking it. Virginia Leith Harron had come back from California. She joined our audience at half-time, all affability, determined to make a crumbling marriage work. I had already arranged to bring my daughters to Toronto for their Easter holidays. Memories of their previous summer in California might spoil their visit. But Martha was very much the teenager, with an English boyfriend, and she left Canada after a week, because she was pining for him. Mary took refuge in Gravenhurst with her grandparents.

In the midst of all this, I got a call from California to do an episode of a television series about the FBI. Since no TV work was offered me in Canada, I took it. I took Virginia back with me but telling her it was too late for a reunion. I had fallen in love with Catherine McKinnon, and that was that.

I must say she became very reasonable about the whole situation, and after a consultation with my Robert Veit Sherwin, we parted ways. Virginia went to Mexico and settled for $10,000 cash and the proprietorship of my California car, the Volvo.

I found out much later that she became a teetotaller and a confirmed lesbian, now living happily with a wonderful female chiropractor in Santa Barbara. I have no contact with her, but both my daughters do. Martha never forgets her birthday and talks to her all the time on the phone from England, while Mary makes a point of visiting her in Palm Springs whenever she is in L.A. on business. So much for the Stepmother Syndrome!

Virginia and I parted ways at LAX, she temporarily to her mother's house and me to a motel room I was to share with Barry Morse. This was a much more amicable arrangement. Barry and I were playing FBI agents in a series of the same name. He was much more famous on series television as the man who pursued David Janssen every week on *The Fugitive*. But Barry Morse went back in English films to the early days of Alfred Hitchcock. He was full of the most wonderful stories about theatre, and he was one of the main reasons the Shaw Festival got off the ground.

First day on the set of *F.B.I.*, we both asked the director where the real agent was. He had always seemed to be there when we worked the series before, breathing down our necks to check on the authenticity of our every move. He would make sure our fedoras were on straight and not at a rakish angle and checked on how we entered a room with guns drawn. Our director sort of smiled and said, "Oh, he'll be along. Don't you worry."

It was not till mid-morning that he appeared, the same official who had checked on me the first time I did the series. Barry recognized him, too, but instead of that dark green suit and fedora to match, he appeared in front of us in white shirt and shorts and swinging a tennis racket. It seems that our man had gone Hollywood instead of vice versa.

Barry said the change in the G-man was just another example of LRP. Naturally, I asked what that was. He said his brother had been a London bobby, and he was asked if he never got tired of his occupation, pounding the same beat day after day. Barry's brother replied, "Not a chance, mate. Not when I get to watch Life's Rich Pageant flowing by!"

I gulped. Life's Rich Pageant was exactly what I was committed to create in a few months at the CNE Grandstand.

102: NATIONAL WET DREAM

Scripting a huge outdoor spectacle was a brand-new field for me, and I had a whole football field in which to do it. I had help. Howard Cable had arranged for David Yeddeau, one of the founders of the Royal Winnipeg Ballet, to act as choreographer. This involved not only the National Ballet, with dancers like Karen Kain just beginning their professional career, but a whole panoply of horses and carriages to convey distinguished politicians on and off the stage, plus work gangs with hammers and soldiers with muskets, and aboriginals with campfires. It's something Alan Lund would have tackled with glee, but I didn't have him on staff. Yeddeau was thorough, but painfully slow, with no real sense of the urgency of "getting on with it."

Catherine had a devoted fan in Gordon Lightfoot, and after I gave him a book about Louis Riel, he provided her with a folksong about the Métis, "Land with No Name."

And what was the theatrical climax of all this bustling activity? Charlie Farquharson wearing a huge sombrero so he could be seen by the people up there in the cheap seats. At least they were sitting high and dry. Outdoor pageants never seem to expect bad weather. It was entirely uncooperative for the entire rain-soaked two-week run! The heavens opened and it felt as if they never stopped.

One night Charlie did his CNR monologue in a driving cloudburst with electrical flashes that threatened to light up my entire future. Several actors refused to handle microphones. Since my name was prominently placed all over this show, I decided I had to brave the elements, mike in hand. As a comedian, I knew that there are more ways than one of dying in front of an audience.

Here is a sample of my waterlogged monologue for those sensible people who stayed home safe and dry that night.

Yiz minds how sum Canajuns seems to cum to their peeriods at yer end of a sentence with ay, eh? Like I better move to L.A., eh? Or I have to join yer Ay Ay, eh!

That's becuz that liddle word changes yer avridge sentnece inta a questyun! Ya mind our furst primed minster, Sir John Ay, eh? Well, him wuz of two minds about wether er not to git this hole cuntry raleroded.

Not till them Berdish Clumbyans tole him they wooden join his fathers of conflagellation, unless they got summit with steem rizing cumming round their mountings. If that wuz to happen then them westcoasters wud sine on as Canda's providence number sex.

So Sir John … Ay … yer father of us all, he set out fer to raze sum capitolists. Now, them Grits in yer common house oppsit-posishun they thunk yer John shooda riz the munny frum yer pubic sextors, instedda all that scratchin around his privates.

But wun quick way fer to became a malted millyumair in them daze wuz gittin a rail on. Bettern gold-brickin or counter-feetin.

And mosta them Canuck plutocraps had awreddy maid ther piles by railin in yer Ewe Ass. So becuz of ther ralerode ties with yer yank, wen old Mickdonald finely got hole of a tite wadda munny, it wuz frum them saim robber barns,insteadda yer publick trussed!

And he had two track teems workin frum eech coast, layin' fer eech uther, till they wuz sposed to meat rite smack in yer middle, hard by Moosejaw.

But wun sardy nite, wun teem all got sheetface drunk, and they cum out way blow Moosejaw … more like hard by Mooseknee.

The neether of them teems ever met. And nacherly, bein a guvmint projeck, they both kep on trackin and they eech end up at yer oppsit ends of our cuntry!

And that's how cum today us Canajuns haz bin raleroded twice, wunce by yer CP and agin by yer CN. And its sorta a chick-in-aig argymint to gess hoo got laid first.

One of the drenched citizens that night was Catherine's agent and manager, Paul Simmons. He watched as his client sang Lightfoot's song drenched to the skin. That was my Maritimer, out there every night, come hell or high water. Paul still maintains that *Sea to Sea* was a wonderful occasion. As soon as we finished, Catherine took off on a tour of Holiday Inns, again to repair her career, while her agent signed me up as a client.

The press the next day didn't agree at all with Simmons's evaluation. The *Toronto Star* blasted me in stereo. On one page was my old college chum from Vic, Ralph Hicklin, who had raved about our *Sarah Binks* six months before. "Give me anything but *Sea to Sea*, the new-type, dreary-type, indescribable-type spectacle that made its curtsey last night."

Thus ended one of the greatest disasters of my career. I wonder if that teacup reader who predicted my triumph is still in business.

103: MAN OF THE CLOTH

After that disastrous show, I decided to get out of Canada before they cancelled my citizenship papers. Since I hadn't seen my kids all summer, I phoned London to find that Martha was still there, but Mary was with Gloria and Stephen in St. Tropez. It was mid-September, and Martha had gotten over her attachment to whatever young man she had been temporarily linked with, so when I suggested I would pick her up in London and take her to the south of France, she was wildly enthusiastic.

Before I got on the plane, I got a call from CBC-TV's Bob Allen, who wanted me to play an inner-city United Church minister who was trying to encourage a group of disaffected urban youths in his congregation. I have always jumped at the chance to put my collar on backward, so I took the script with me.

I left the Vizinczeys' phone number in St. Tropez and was told that they needed my acceptance immediately, because taping started the week after next. Out of curiosity I asked, "So who turned it down?" Bob was absolutely straight with me and mentioned David McCallum, Keir Dullea, Robert Reed, and Aldo Ray. In other words, the CBC was hopeful to turn the script into a pilot for a series that could be easily sold in the United States.

Now they were reduced to hiring a lowly Canadian. With no other work in sight, I took a chance and accepted the offer. It was entitled *Reddick*, and I had the title role. Reading Monroe Scott's ninety-minute script on the plane, I was delighted with it. It had a completely contemporary feel about dealing with the new generation that was being called "hippies."

Martha met me at Heathrow, all excited about sunning on the Riviera. She was about due for a vacation, eighteen now and working as a volunteer visiting the poor, the old, the lonely, the sick, and tired. Martha told me that this had come as a terrible shock to her that people all around her in London lived in wretchedness and deprivation. But she admitted she was still bourgeois enough to look forward to getting away from it all.

The Vizinczey family was still living off the rewards of *In Praise of Older Women*, and a fellow Hungarian Canadian had already taken an option on it for a film. The extra money did something to mitigate both my daughters' cool treatment of their stepfather. The time spent on the beach with them was a very pleasant interlude for me. Stephen was already at work on his next novel, *An Innocent Millionaire*, and the leading character's father was an actor, based, he said, on me.

Back in Toronto I soon found myself in a rehearsal hall as the oldest among a passel of eager young actors. Some of them wanted to do improvisations based on the text. The director, Merv Rosenzweig, said that would be fine as long as they retained the original dialogue. Obviously, he shared a generation gap with me. We stuck to the script.

When we went on camera, the location was Bathurst Street United Church. It was soon to be called the Redlight Theatre, no longer God's house, and rented out to any organization putting on a play or shooting a television show. Now it's the home of the Randolph Academy, training young actors for live theatre, many of whom end up in Charlottetown in our *Anne* musical.

I was to preach from the same pulpit where my father had delivered the Sunday School anniversary sermon in 1926. In front of me was the font where I had been baptized.

According to the script, I was to be stabbed while delivering a sermon in this pulpit by one of the hippies I had been encouraging to express themselves. Catherine showed up at the church shoot for this after hearing that I was a single man again. On a lunch break we strolled hand in hand through Honest Ed Mirvish's Emporium a mere block away from the church. We looked like a married couple shopping for cheap bargains, and it was a pleasant experience.

When *Reddick* was shown to the television audience, the critical reception was so positive that a sequel was planned, and there was talk of a U.S. series. Fletcher Markle had returned to us from California and was determined to make this happen. The *Evening Telegram* critic said that my minister was so convincing, she was convinced I wasn't acting at all. I think that's supposed to be a compliment.

I ignored all rumours and vague promises and awaited the sequel. In the meantime, CBC sent me to the top of the world. There were 200

RCAF personnel at Alert, a Canadian Armed Forces base on Ellesmere Island. These guys were closer to the North Pole than anyone else on the planet, including those sneaky Russians. I was to be part of a CBC concert party, and they cast me as master of ceremonies. Because, as producer Ken Dalziel confessed to me, Gordie Tapp was booked somewhere else.

Charlie Farquharson was to be part of it, as long as he brought along his Eunuchfication uniform. Other members of the party were the current Miss Canada; black jazz singer Diane Brooks; magician Robert Downey, who brought along his birds (the ornithological kind); and Miss Canada 1968, a sweet French-Canadian girl named Marie-France Beaulieu.

We took off from Trenton in a Hercules cargo aircraft, which has very rudimentary seats on both sides of the plane. Our Herk didn't go directly to Alert. The route was through Greenland, where we stopped off overnight at the giant U.S. base in someplace with a Danish name.

We didn't give our little show there. The Yank troops didn't need us at all. Their recreation facilities would rival Las Vegas, the main feature being acres and acres of slot machines. Next morning we took off for Alert in a blinding snowstorm. At one point we were facing a headwind that seemed to be greater than the speed at which we were travelling. Clarinetist Lew Lewis took out a yarmulka and placed it solemnly on his head. Not much later the wind died down, and we were able to make some headway with our silent blessings on Saint Lou of the Clarinet.

Our arrival was in the middle of the day in pitch blackness. It was that time of year in the High Arctic, and the temperature when we finally stepped outside? Sixty degrees below you know what.

That'd be yer Fattenheat. I dunno wat it wood be in yer Selfishness, cuz Charlie is not yet familial with that metracal sistern of mezzuring everything in killyermeters and santapeeds.

Oney place further north than this Eltsmear ile blongs to Sandy Claws. Nun of yer innerwits wud be loony enuff to inhibit therselfs this neer to yer Norse Pole. That incloods carrybooze and polarized bares.

We were scheduled to do two shows that first day. This was so that all the personnel at Alert would get a chance to see us. The only other entertainment was a gymnasium where the inhabitants tried to wreck themselves playing floor hockey. Some of this, I was told quietly, was deliberate. The tour of duty up here on the extreme tip of Ellesmere Island was six months, and time was measured in Herks, which is the number of trips a Hercules would visit the base before any individual serviceman would be released to go south again. My informant told me, with anticipation in his voice, that he only had sixteen Herks to go!

The most intriguing mystery in our presentation, to both audience and us in the concert party itself, was the presentation of magician Robert Downey. He was a man of mystery to all of us, producing the birds from thin air, and returning them to the same element. The fact that he was a dignified, reserved alcoholic only added to our wonder. Apart from his magic act we never saw the birds in our travels.

Not only were both audiences the most appreciative any of us had ever played to, but after both shows we were treated to a fabulous buffet. We learned later that the goodies were made up from the troops' own rations, plus an amalgam of Christmas packages sent from home.

When Miss Canada learned this, she burst into tears and asked if there was anything she could do in return. The base commander, his face set straight as a die, asked her to donate and autograph a pair of her scantiest panties. I understand they are still on display on the trophy room wall, because Catherine saw them years later when she played the base. A pair of her briefs are also well hung there.

104: ALL MINE IN SIXTY-NINE

Soon after I got back from the land of frigidity, I phoned Catherine and asked her out to dinner. It was a trendy restaurant at the top of one of those Bay Street bank buildings, and the food wasn't really very good. On the way down in the elevator I proposed to her. She thinks it was because of the lousy meal, and perhaps she was right. I told her that we couldn't get married in Canada because of my two Mexican divorces. That meant a ceremony under another flag.

Coincidentally, I got a call from the Goodman Theatre in Chicago to do some Shakespeare. They had been connected with Stratford, Ontario, in some way since the beginning of that festival, and they wanted me to come and play Angelo in *Measure for Measure*. The reason I got the call, I think, was because my co-star, Clayton Corzatte, had been with me at

Stratford-on-the-Conn, and we got along well. Since a contract had been signed with Bill Freedman in London to open a new English production of *Anne of Green Gables*, I realized my only chance to get married would be under an American flag.

Before I donned tights again, I had to make a quick trip to England to check out Freedman's choice for our West End Anne. Norman Campbell was chained to the CBC, so he gave me his blessing on conferring my blessing on Freedman's choice. Her name was Polly James, and she was currently doing a panto in the far west of England. Any trip to England was okay with me, because it was a chance to see Martha and Mary. Coincidentally, Catherine was London-bound to do some television shows, so it would be a chance to break in a new stepmother.

I took a train down to see Polly in the panto and decided she passed my most rigid test ... she looked like an orphan. Catherine was involved in a couple of BBC Television shows, but she was able to spend New Year's Eve with Stephen and Gloria and of course my girls. Martha had a new boyfriend, an Algerian who spoke French and arrived wearing my ex-wife's former beaver coat. He was only five years older than Catherine and cooked ratatouille, and we all played an Italian version of monopoly with Venetian street names.

Just before midnight I took Catherine down to Trafalgar Square next to Canada House with two glasses and a split of champagne. As we toasted the New Year, I suggested we get married the following month in Chicago. Our relationship had survived a family dinner with my ex-wife, and I thought I should clinch the deal before she backed out.

Catherine said she'd have to check her schedule. I mentioned that the day after my Chicago Shakespeare gig finished, I would be on my way back to England to start rehearsals for *Anne*. She said that my closing night might interfere with her appearing on a bill with Henny Youngman in Saskatoon. And the night after that she was opening at the Royal York's Imperial Room. As it turned out, the Youngman date was earlier, so we had a window of one day in Chicago to get hitched. Henny would be playing a hotel in Chicago that very night, and Catherine thought he might make a nice best man. (Take my wife. Please!)

Measure for Measure was a pleasure, and I married Catherine during the afternoon before the evening performance. The ceremony was performed by a justice of the peace at the Ambassador East. My sister Mary was there with her husband Nick, and so was Catherine's sister Patrician Anne and their brother Rene. Henny Youngman turned up, too, with a case of Mogen David for a wedding present. Earlier that day, Catherine had phoned the hotel where Henny was performing that evening, and when he answered, he asked, "What are you doing for lunch?"

Catherine said, "Busy having a fit. It's my wedding dress. What are you doing *after* lunch? Would you like to see me get married?"

Henny was a bit late for the ceremony. He stopped to get himself paged, which was what he did in every hotel to attract attention. Unfortunately, this happened at the moment in the ceremony when the justice of the peace was saying, "If there be any just cause why this couple should not be joined in holy matrimony, let him speak now or forever hold your peace!"

"Mr. Youngman, paging Mr. Youngman!"

I had to dash back to the theatre for the evening performance of *Measure*. Catherine came later and remained backstage while I did unscrupulous, libidinous things onstage. She was still wearing her long white wedding dress. I was onstage when she was led past the row of dressing rooms. Co-star Haskell Gordon, who was flagrantly gay, stuck his head out of his cubbyhole as she walked by and said in the loudest possible voice, "I've had him and he's nothing!"

At the end of the performance, with the whole cast onstage, I brought Catherine out in her wedding finery. I told the audience I wanted to make an important announcement. "Ladies and gentlemen, I got married this afternoon." *Big* applause. I went on, "But the management of this theatre insisted that I come here this evening and attempt to rape this nice nun when I could have been much happier in my hotel suite with *this!*"

The audience cheered like a bunch of kids at a rock concert and rose to their feet in a standing ovation.

105: ANNE OF ENGLAND

Catherine was off to Toronto early to prepare for her Imperial Room debut at the Royal York. The honeymoon would have to come later. As a wedding gift, I wrote some topical Canadian material for her to deliver between songs. She protested that she was nothing but a singer and had no aptitude for comedy. After *Spring Thaw '67* I knew better. When I handed her the material, I said, "Try it, Crincess Pristle." Later I found out that she did try it and got good laughs. But I was told that when the audience roared its approval at her comic timing, she tried to shush their enthusiasm with "Oh, please, don't laugh." To a comedian, such a remark is grounds for mercy killing.

Later that morning, as I was about to leave Chicago for England, agent Paul Simmons phoned me and said Frank Peppiatt was desperate to talk to me before I disappeared overseas. The area code for Frank was that of Nashville, Tennessee. I knew that he and John Aylesworth had a successful series with Sonny and Cher in California, and I was puzzled about their connection with the capital of country music.

Frank sounded wildly enthusiastic about a new project he felt could rival the new hit series on NBC, *Rowan & Martin's Laugh-In*. Goldie Hawn's infectious laugh on that show had conquered America in the 1968–69 season. What Frank and John proposed was a country music series with added comedians doing a corny cracker version of twenty-second jokes, like *Laugh-In*. I was skeptical. I said, "Last time we did it, I remember it was a country-cracker version of *The Perry Como Show*."

Aylesworth got on the line. "It's not a pilot this time, Don. It's a whole summer series on CBS. Gordie Tapp is onboard, and we want you, too."

The working title was *Country Corn*, and they wanted Charlie Farquharson to be their news anchorman. I found out later that the reason they got the offer was because *The Smothers Brothers Show* was in trouble with the CBS management over their satirical attitude toward the war in Vietnam. Mike Dann, head of CBS programming, had called in Frank and John with their suggestions for a summer replacement for the rebellious brothers. That's why they suggested hick comedy and country music. CBS had been very, very successful in the cultural barnyard with comedy series like *The Beverly Hillbillies*, *Green Acres*, and *Petticoat Junction*, so they agreed to take a chance on two Canadians.

Completely flustered by this new development as I tried to make my plane for Heathrow, I told the boys, "I'm leaving for England right now, we're putting on *Anne of Green Gables* in London, and I can't be back until after the first of June."

Frank said, "Perfect. Just write us ten two-minute country-style local newscasts and bring them with you to Tennessee."

I think I said "Yes" to this wild notion and grabbed a cab to the Chicago airport. On the flight to London I tried to get into *Anne of Green Gables* mode, but the assignment of those hick newscasts kept intruding.

Turning my attention to the immediate present, I knew that *Anne* rewrites would be necessary for a British audience. I also knew that Norm Campbell would be pretty busy in London at the same time, because he was doing a television series with Liberace. He was already ensconced in a London flat with all six of his children.

I went to a rehearsal at the New Theatre in St. Martin's Lane, wartime home of the Old Vic Company. That's where Laurence Olivier made those blood-curdling screams as Oedipus the King and stammered to his death as Hotspur in *Henry IV, Part 1*. Next door to it was the Albery Theatre where *Anne* would actually be playing in three weeks' time, without the luxury of a pre-London run.

We weren't exactly heralded. Bill Freedman's idea was to sneak our show into the West End without any fanfare and hope to surprise the critics. On either side of our opening night we were flanked by competing musicals. The night before we opened, our competition was a musical adaptation of two Noël Coward one-act plays, one of them based on *Brief Encounter*. It starred Old Vic leading man John Neville.

The night after our opening, Betty Grable was coming in with *Belle Starr*, and on that very same night there was another premiere of a musical, an adaptation of H.G. Wells's novel *Ann Veronica*. Looming even larger on the near horizon was Broadway blockbuster *Mame*, with Angela Lansbury. No wonder our little show didn't attract much attention.

There was limited Canadian content. Bill Freedman and his wife Toby Robins were transplanted Torontonians. When I arrived, Toby was currently playing in a Restoration comedy with the Royal Shakespeare company at my old hangout, the Aldwych Theatre.

Alan Lund, who had directed in British theatre before, was fortunately retained as our director, and he brought along John Fenwick to supervise his excellent arrangements.

Bill had insisted on a local actress as Anne. I was hoping that Gracie Finley would be brought over, but since I had seen this actress's work,

I didn't disagree with Bill's choice. Barbara Hamilton was brought over as Marilla.

Peter Mews wasn't asked to bring his beloved Matthew to England. Instead Bill and Alan both wanted me to play the role. I told them that anyone who was married to Catherine McKinnon would be foolhardy to try to sing a note. I didn't add that I didn't want Matthew to end up sounding like Charlie Farquharson. Besides, I was saving him for Nashville.

Bill accepted and suggested we get an American actor who had just finished a successful one-man show in London portraying American newspaper columnist Art Buchwald. Hiram Sherman was already a West End favourite with the critics. As soon as I heard his name, I approved. We had worked together for two seasons at the American Stratford.

Two other Canadians came along from the Charlottetown company, Bob Ainslie and Susan Anderson. Susan would repeat her successful portrayal of Anne's best friend Diana. Alan chose Bob as Anne's heart-throb Gilbert Blythe. The rest of the cast were resident Brits, a couple of expatriate Americans, and an Australian who took on the part of new teacher Miss Stacy with great results.

Bill Freedman insisted on changes in song titles. Norman, Elaine, and I were told that *Mame* had a number entitled "Bosom Buddies," far too close in name to our duet "Bosom Friends." The lady teacher's number at the opening of the second half was "Open the Windows." It was seriously similar in title to *Mame*'s "Open a New Window." I suggested we use the last few words of our song as a new title but retain the song. So "Open the Windows" became "Learn Everything." But "Bosom Friends" had to be scrapped entirely.

This all happened while Norman was up to his neck in a television series with Walter Liberace. (You didn't know that was his first name?) When Norman was told about our "new song" crisis, it was Liberace who took action. He ordered a piano to be delivered to the Campbells' London apartment that very day. That night Norman, Elaine, and I gathered in front of Liberace's gift to deal with the crisis.

Norman solved it in less than ten minutes. He composed a song using the familiar phrase in the novel, "Kindred Spirits." Emboldened, he started composing a marching song for the school pageant near the end of the show, "Prince Edward Island, the Heart of the World." It's still in use today and is an audience favourite.

Both my daughters sat beside me in the theatre that opening night. Catherine had come from Canada for the occasion and sat on my other side. For some reason I wasn't enthused by what I saw. There was something ... oh ... non-Charlottetown about the whole thing. Maybe it was those sets, but I sat fairly silent at the party. Catherine couldn't understand my reticence but agreed to leave the cast party at the Ivy Restaurant early, and we went back to our suite at the Connaught Hotel. I promptly went straight to bed. Poor Catherine! What a transatlantic welcome she got from me after making such an effort to be there.

I awoke early, ordered breakfast for two, and found a copy of the *Times*. Only Catherine had the guts to open it to see if there was a review. The review was a rave. After breakfast, Bill phoned me to tell me that all the London papers agreed.

Our little musical turned out to be one of those classic showbiz sleepers. Six months later it was given the Plays and Players Award for Best Musical in the 1969–70 London season. Along with it came individual acting awards for Polly James, Barbara Hamilton, and Hiram Sherman, plus Best Single of the Year for "Wondrin'," the only ballad in our show.

Despite the rave reviews and those many awards, the show lasted only nine months in London. It was Bill Freedman's first and only theatre venture into the West End, so he was unable to commandeer the charabancs (buses) that bring in the out-of-town theatregoers. Otherwise we might have been there for years.

How can I explain my erring instincts about opening nights? Perhaps they are due to my nationality. Canadian critics came all the way over to London that month to bear out my pessimism. Urjo Kareda, representing the *Toronto Star*, gave us a good panning. Nathan Cohen showed up 200 performances later to give us his usual blast of hoarfrost to amend his 1965 rave review in Charlottetown. Is there something about the air on that island that affects city people? Because Urjo got married a year later and spent his honeymoon in Prince Edward Island, saw the show again, and this time gave it his enthusiastic blessing. Must have been a helluva honeymoon.

Speaking of which, Catherine and I finally had ours in Paris. I don't remember much about what we saw, except each other and a lot of Monet water lilies. All I know is we had a wonderful hotel suite, which I'm sure led to the creation, followed by the birth some months later, of our daughter Kelley.

We came back to London for the recording of the cast album, which was done at Abbey Road Studios. My suggestion for the album cover was to photograph four of the leading members of the cast trudging on that same pedestrian crossing on Abbey Road. I was vetoed. Aren't you glad I was?

I wrote the liner notes for the album on the way out to Heathrow. Catherine was flying back to Toronto to prepare for next month's appearance at the Calgary Stampede. I promised to join her in Calgary if I finished this new job in time. Before we both left for Heathrow, the word came that a Swedish production of *Anne* had been optioned. I never saw *Anne på Gronkülla*, but the theatre in Göteborg sent me a poster for the show to prove that it happened.

My destination from Heathrow was Nashville, the home of country music. About which I knew absolutely nothing! I was a fan of Stan Kenton, Rob McConnell's Boss Brass, and black blues singers like the Joes, Turner and Williams.

Little did I know it, but Charlie Farquharson was to have Nashville as a regular destination in his life for the next fifteen years.

PART IV

Tennessee Earning,
1969 to 1984

106: AMID THE ALIEN KORN

This was the project Frank Peppiatt had phoned me about in Chicago when he asked me to bring along ten newscasts. I cobbled them together between rewrites of *Anne* in London. I had the wit of England's best comedy writers to steal from, bright minds I used to work with back in the 1950s. These thefts from Norden and Muir usually involved outrageous, elaborate puns that I worked into Charlie's newscasts without any shame.

First thing I was told when I reported to Peppiatt and Aylesworth at the Nashville Holiday Inn was that their title of the proposed summer series had been changed to *Hee Haw*. The beginning of each show would be preceded by the mating call of a Missouri mule and a burst of banjo music. The show itself consisted of two headliners, country music stars, plus various musical guests differing each week. The rest of the show involved acres and acres of old jokes delivered in twenty-second bursts, one joke at a time, by all members of the cast, and appropriately enough from a cornfield.

Charlie in the first season of Hee Haw, *1969.*

The longest comic segment would be my own, a three-minute monologue delivered as a local news report by Charlie. The only member of the cast I knew was Gordie Tapp. He was an old hand at country music, having been a regular on CBC's *Holiday Ranch* with Cliff McKay.

We all gathered for our first get-together at Channel Five in a small studio, too small I thought for what they hoped to accomplish. The news studio next door seemed far more accommodating. Had I known it at the time, there were two stringers for that ten o'clock news show working to provide stories for the show, but neither of those two people got on air. Their names were Al Gore and Oprah Winfrey.

I didn't know any of the people in our studio, either. Catherine probably would have recognized most of them on sight, since she came from Don Messer and his fiddly-diddly gung-chang-chang kind of music. Gordie was enormous help. He introduced me to the queen of country comedy, Minnie Pearl. The public knew her as a goofy lady with the price tag still on her hat, but later I got to know her as Sarah Ophelia Colley, an elite member of Nashville society, and she also knew her Shakespeare, so we got along well.

The two headliners were Buck Owens and Roy Clark. I'd never heard of them. Gordie said they were the two most popular recording stars in country music.

I was then introduced to someone who had never been on television before. His name was Junior Samples, from rural Georgia, and he was there because of a fish that got away on him. His telling of it on local television must have been hilarious, because Peppiatt signed him up right away, even though neither he nor John quite knew what to do with him. He became one of the real celebrities on our show, with his inability to read a teleprompter.

There was a determined effort by Frank and John to provide eye candy on the show in the form of shapely ... well ... forms. Janine Riley and Gunilla Hutton, two blondes, had been imported from *Petticoat Junction*. For novelty in that department there was 400 pounds of fun in Lulu Roman, a comic stripper from Texas, who ended up not that many years later as a successful evangelist.

Archie Campbell was an experienced country comic who used a roving eye as a useful prop and ended up teaming with Gunilla Hutton in a feature called "Nurse Goodbody." Typecasting. He warned me, as a fellow comic, to be aware of the fact that there was a censor on our show, a leftover from *The Smothers Brothers Show*, where he must have been kept quite busy. But what was there to censor in our show?

One of the regular successful features was a barbershop scene in which Archie Campbell pretended to cut Roy Clark's hair. I wrote a gag for that scene that was meant to give the censor something to do. I stuck my head in the door of the barbershop and said "Bob Cox in here?"

Archie replied, "Naw. We jist do shaves 'n haarcuts."

The censor missed it and the item appeared on the show.

My own segment of the show had its own set. It was a small-town radio studio with a background consisting of egg cartons and a laying hen in a nest on either side of me. They would often cluck louder than my commentary, especially if they were about to lay an egg. On one occasion that summer I got so annoyed at being interrupted by their continual clucking that I turned to one of the offending chickens and said "Oh, buck, buck, buck ... *buck off* !"

The censor missed that one, too. I made one more attempt. I decided to write an item about cryonics ... which was all the rage that summer. It seems that baseball star Ted Williams decided, when the time came, to have his body put away in cold storage.

Sairy Lee poundcake is rite proud of her one-eighth Cherokee blud and has decide not to pass away rite away, but insted be inturd in a deep freezure at yer cryonicks institoot. Wair she hopes to stay until eether her diseeze goze out, or them Republickans gits back in.

Oney thing Sairy Lee worry's about is having them three ex-huzbins of hers stand in frunt of her display case and say "Thair she lays, jist as she wuz in life!"

My attempts at placating our censor with a joke about frigidity counted for nothing. He missed that one, too. I never did find out what happened to him after the end of our summer series.

Gordie Tapp contributed to the writing, and he says he got his country material from old issues of the *Family Herald* and *Weekly Star*. I combed the *Barrie Examiner* and the *Parry Sound North Star* for appropriate names for my newscasts, but I also combed my own past for eccentric names that had the ring of reality. Names of people I actually went to school with like Walter Bulleychuk, Dotty Rainesbottom, Harold Clockworthy, Ernie Gourlay, Gurney Bootland, Mavis Dongmans, Oley Finbogasson, Wick Smallman, Birdie Farrows, and Untzie John Sabino. Often I would mix the surname of one acquaintance with the Christian name of another to avoid litigation.

Here's a sample newscast from that first summer.

Charlie Farquharson here with yer KORN Hotflash News.

Yer Wimmen's Instytoot of Bent Falls had ther anal awards meetin' last nite, and wun of ther number becum housekeeper of yer yeer. It wuz giv to Daisy Cressy Defloyd Haskins Grosely Mulepeter on accounta she bin married and divorce five times, and evry time she dun it, she manage to keep the house.

Garnet Broadbent of Grinder's Mills darn neer jump to his conclusion last week wen he fell off of Moultrie Kelsall's barn during silo-fillin. With his confound frackture, Garnet don't expect to be back at work soon, as workmen's compensation has jist set in.

Here's a shockin story frum yer no-surprizes motel. Feg and Melva Sprunt dun ther honeymoon thair last weekend, but found out due to reno-vations that ther wernt no bed in their room. Yer mangemint tole them nuthin cud be dun about it till nex day and advize yer yung cupple to stand up fer their conjugular rites.

Vern Crabtree giv a tock to yung peeple at yer oro sex clinick. He was so embarsed about it he tole his muther insted that he had lechered them yung peeple on sailing. So she tole her frends that her boy Vern giv the tock all rite, but she dunno how, cuz he's only dun it the twice, and eech time his hat blew off!

Here's yer KORN News wether: our lokel frognosticater sez ther's a inter-mitten chants of pre-sippy-pie-tation. Hoo givs a dam as long as it don't rane!

This haz bin yer KORN News, brot to you by yer Grand Ole Opry brasseer ... stays up no matter how frantick the fiddlin' gits.

The results from the first show were immediate. It caught on like wildfire. One show registered a viewing audience of forty-five million! The thirteen shows were all repeated at the end of the summer, and a regular network year-round show was ordered by CBS network manager Mike Dann. The ratings may have been good, but there were critics who shook their heads. The *New York Times* was absolutely puzzled by the show's success. They should have quoted H.L. Mencken, who wrote years ago: "Nobody ever went broke underestimating the intelligence of the American people."

But the last word goes to the jazz critic from the *Toronto Star*, Patrick Scott, who wrote "If you watch this show, you don't deserve to own a television set."

107: SEX CHANGE OF PACE

Once I completed my KORN country news monologues, there was really nothing more for me to do on that first season, so I was able to join Catherine in Calgary for her starring stint at the Stampede Grandstand. While she regaled the western masses with her angelic voice, I was reduced to looking after her tiny Yorkshire terrier, Binky.

I realized that I was still a largely unknown quantity to the general public in my own country, and married to a Canadian star. There wasn't much I could do about it in Calgary, so I started to busy myself with a sex film I had promised to write for Bill Freedman. My interest wasn't in the boy-meets-girl kind of sex. It was in the much more kinky realm of gerontology — sexual relations between the generations. To be specific, a love affair between a very young man and a much, much older woman. I had seen evidence of this kinky state of affairs when I lived and worked in Hollywood. Now, since my libido was threatened and my testosterone was called to question by Columbia Pictures, I decided to assert myself in a sixteen-page film treatment.

My central character was a teenage farm boy who had a tyrannical father and a mother who died giving birth to him. The only person who ever truly loved him was his grandmother, who was now in her grave. In desperation he runs away from home to the big city of Toronto. He gets employment in a supermarket bagging groceries and rounding up shopping carts.

One day he helps an elderly woman who is having difficulty getting her groceries into a cart, and he ends up taking them home for her. The elderly woman represents for him the grandmother who gave him the only love he ever knew. But now he is of an age when love can be expressed in sexual terms. The woman can't understand his sexual attraction to her, but she comes to have feelings of genuine love for the boy, and they eventually "do the deed with two backs."

Unfortunately, the excitement of the act is too much for the elderly woman, and she dies as a result of the encounter. My film opens at that moment.

I sent the sixteen pages to Bill, and he showed them to Norman Jewison, who lived in England at the time. Norman showed my treatment to Hal Ashby, who was just finishing his script of *Harold and Maude*. This deals with a similar theme. Harold is a teenager, played by Bud Cort, who falls madly in love with an old crone, played by Ruth Gordon.

Hal told Norm that he thought my script was more believable than *Harold and Maude*, about a teenager who fell in love with an eighty-year-old woman. Hal's film became a kind of cult movie but also a financial hit. My script, *Once*, had to wait ten years to be produced by the CBC. It was directed by Gordon Pinsent and starred his wife Charmion King, and Jewison's daughter played his eventual teenage girlfriend. Toby Robins took the role of the social worker who cures the teenage boy of his delusion. I was delighted with all of them.

It got puzzled but highly respectful reviews from the television critics, and it eventually won an ACTRA Award for Leslie Toth, the actor who was making his television debut. I have never heard of him since.

108: ANYTHING TO DECLARE?

When Catherine and I got married, instead of providing her with a home, I moved into hers. It was a high-rise twenty-five floors above the street near Yonge Street and St. Clair Avenue in Toronto. I remember Catherine cooking our first meal there. It was an elaborate seafood dinner involving shrimp and sole, and in her opinion it was a disaster. It wasn't. I sat there and ate all that meal for two, while she took to her bed. She was very much a perfectionist.

After a few months of married bliss, I created the biggest gaffe of my life. This ideal arrangement of two lovebirds on an extended honeymoon was complicated by the arrival of my older daughter Martha, who had elected to give up the privilege of a free British university education to study instead in Toronto at my old alma mater, Victoria College. She arrived with no place to stay, and I decided that after a long absence from her father, she should stay with us.

All this was done without any consultation with Catherine. Entirely my fault. No wonder the Stepmother Syndrome swung into position as soon as this happened. Martha also brought along her French-Algerian boyfriend, whose British visa had expired. He wasn't allowed to stay with us, of course, but Martha was, at first, thanks to my selfishness.

My daughter also noticed that her rival-in-love for my affection was getting pregnant. When Martha mentioned this to me, I pooh-poohed the notion and said that due to Catherine's penchant for home cooking, we were both happy in love and putting on a little weight. The fact that all of Catherine's weight gain was in one place escaped my notice. Catherine herself must have given up waiting for me to notice and broke the news to me just as a big job appeared for her on the horizon.

As 1970 hove into view, I was again taken along as personal baggage for Catherine. This time it was to the island of Trinidad, where Catherine was hired by the Hilton Hotel chain to fill in for another singer who was pregnant and too close to term to perform. The fact that Catherine was also pregnant didn't seemed to deter anybody.

As extra baggage, I enjoyed myself thoroughly, anticipating the coming of Maas, the season of Carnival, and the joy of listening to local calypso singers and their topical tunes.

The third night of her engagement, January 9, Catherine insisted on going to bed early instead of socializing with her admirers. At four in the morning her water broke, and I phoned for the hotel doctor. It took a couple of hours, but eventually an enormously tall doctor appeared and took calm charge of the proceedings. Shortly after daylight, Catherine was moved from the hotel to the Rezvan Clinic to have her baby. I was dispatched downtown to buy diapers and various swaddling clothes.

Whatever sex the baby was, it was supposed to come out as a boy named Jason and arrive on March 17, St. Patrick's Day. Months before, Catherine and her girlfriends had gone through some sort of mumbo-jumbo ritual with a Ouija board, and that was the result. The fact that Kelley Harron, five pounds, five ounces, was a female preemie who arrived January 9, well before her time, cancelled the rest of the contract with the Hilton Hotel.

Flying home, we placed our precious cargo in a special basket and stuck it above us, where the carry-on luggage usually goes. Baby Kelley stayed there during the whole flight, oblivious to everything. When we arrived in Toronto, Customs asked if we had anything to declare!

The next task was to find a nanny. Martha was never considered, because she was too busy with lectures and boyfriend, and besides, the job required expertise. Catherine was doing some gigs with pianist Jimmy Dale, and he had a Jamaican nanny who looked after his little boys, so we lucked into hiring Gerry Leys, who became for me the linchpin that held our little family together.

As soon as Gerry was hired, Martha was asked to move out, even though Gerry would remain in her boarding house. I paid Martha an allowance to live by herself. She immediately moved in with her boyfriend, who was now getting a few gigs as a folksinger.

This arrangement turned sour when Martha got an offer through Victoria College to complete her B.A. at the University of Nice. With memories of our San Tropez holiday on the Riviera back in 1968, she eagerly signed on. Her boyfriend got drunk because of that, dragged her around by the hair, and ended up breaking her nose. I didn't see Martha again for three years, when she came back to Toronto and finally completed her B.A. at the same faculty as that Hick from Vic. My other daughter Mary took the easy route and went to Oxford, where she became editor of its magazine. When she graduated, she started a professional career in journalism, ending up as drama critic for *The Observer* and punk rock critic for *The Guardian*.

I had other things on my mind back in 1970. Like making a living. After two successful seasons, and winter, on CBS, *Hee Haw* was suddenly cancelled, despite our high ratings. The reason was pure snobbery. CBS head honcho Mike Dann, who had given us the original go-ahead, had been awarded a Phi Beta Kappa key from some learned cultural institution like Harvard. In keeping with his new status, he decided to clear out the barn and stable-ize his network.

He cancelled *The Beverly Hillbillies*, *Petticoat Junction*, and *Hee Haw* at once. This happened just after Catherine and I had purchased a lovely old three-storey house, including a garden for Kelley, in Toronto's Annex neighbourhood. Catherine made the down payment, but I needed to contribute my share of mortgage money.

Out of the blue came an offer from Stuart Griffiths in Ottawa to replace the host of *Anything You Can Do*, an afternoon game show. Stu had started CBC Television along with the ubiquitous Mavor Moore, and he was now working for CTV in the nation's capital. Without a thought about how I was going to manage to do the hosting job on a game show, I jumped at the chance to help Catherine pay for our new house and to play in that garden with our child.

109: OSAKA 70

The world's fair was held in Japan that year, and the Charlottetown Festival production of *Anne of Green Gables* was invited to participate. Before trundling off to Ottawa in the fall to my game show, I jumped at the chance to take Catherine to Japan in late spring.

As we set out, I knew that I wouldn't have much time to be a tourist. The sixth season of Charlottetown followed directly upon our return from Osaka, and the bill would consist of *Anne*, a new British musical import, *Jane*, based on *Jane Eyre*, and a revival of *Turvey*.

The flight to Tokyo was done in two jumps, Toronto to Vancouver, stay overnight, and on to Japan in the morning. Nowadays it's done in one jump, a flight of fourteen hours, which involves a lot of walking up and down the aisles of the plane and drinking lots of water. I prefer the old two-jump.

In Vancouver we were joined by some members of the RCMP Musical Ride. They were a jolly bunch, and as the plane took off again, the drinks flowed freely. Gracie Finley found three empty seats and was about to fall asleep when a Mountie appeared, sat in the aisle seat, grinned, and in a mild alcoholic stupor, promptly fell asleep in her lap. She couldn't budge him.

Why were we going to Japan with our Prince Edward Island show? Because the novel had been translated into Japanese shortly before Pearl Harbor. Despite the militarism of the moment, and being on the wrong side of their imperial war, it ended up in the Tokyo school system as *Akage no An* (*Red-Haired Anne*). The translation from English was done by Marura Oka. I met her grandaughter in Charlottetown in 2011, and she said the Japanese feel about Anne the way the Germans feel about Hamlet. That it's really part of their culture, and they're just lending it to us.

I personally think that *Akage no An*'s appeal is primarily to Japanese feminists. It's a strong statement about a little girl who doesn't take any crap from the boys, and instead bopped one on the head with her slate. One up for Women's Rib!

An is a boy's name in Japan, and the title sometimes causes confusion. The head of Toyota, in talking to Princess Takamado of the Imperial Royal Family, mentioned that he thought Anne would be a boy. The princess, who speaks flawless English, said sweetly, "So did the Cuthberts."

The plane landed at Tokyo's Narita Airport, many miles outside the city, but the whole area is one continuous city. Now Tokyo has more people within its limits than the entire population of Canada.

Before going on to Osaka, we were given a few days in Tokyo. I was anxious to see some Japanese theatre. I had seen kabuki in New York, but the kind of theatre that intrigued me was that shown in the movie *Sayonara* with Marlon Brando. As an American officer stationed in Japan, he falls in love with one of the stars of the all-girl Takashimaya Theatre. They were playing somewhere in Tokyo. Barbara Hamilton and Catherine were game to see them, too.

We set off together in a cab. Tokyo was the most confusing place I had ever been. There seemed to be no numbers on any of the buildings. But Barbara was undaunted and anxious to try using her newfound knowledge of Japanese. This consisted of two words: *wacky* meaning right, and *mickey* meaning left. She insisted on giving the poor taxi driver all these wacky-mickey instructions, but I think he knew the way, anyway, to the biggest girlie show in town.

The show itself was very glitzy, quite Las Vegas, except that the girls were covered up to the larynx. There were lots of pop tunes, some of which I recognized from Tin Pan Alley. There was no attempt at English subtitles, nor did there seem to be any need. But signs in English were a fairly common sight, even though most Japanese at that time spoke little English. Our hotel had what was labelled A TOOTH BRASH BENDING MACHINE.

The train to Osaka the next day was relatively uncrowded. Maybe the locals were unnerved by its incredible speed. Mount Fuji flashed by in a couple of seconds. By comparison, VIA Rail is the Toonerville trolley.

In Osaka the Charlottetown company was billed in a hotel close to the world's fairground itself. I was stuck in my room most of the time with *Private Turvey's War*, our new title. Catherine set off with the rest of the cast. She later reported that the crowds at the fair were full of tiny Japanese women elbowing their way through it all with a ferocity that would have made Gordie Howe very envious.

After our slightly drunken flight from Vancouver, the cast also made a point of seeing the film of the RCMP Musical Ride, which was done in the round, 360 degrees. They reported that the Mounties ended up looking like a firing squad trying to annihilate one another.

Our turn to perform came next, with the news that the crown princess would attend our opening. I decided to do what the Japanese audience was doing and rented a pair of earphones with the dialogue in their own language. Amid the flurry of Japanese, I recognized some strange pronunciations of once-familiar names. "Red-Haired An" was eventually adopted by "Massyou" and "Marirrer." Their nosy neighbour was "Missarynd," and An's potential boyfriend was "Gerbert Brize."

I didn't see the crown princess. There was no particular fuss about her arrival or departure. But if she was like the rest of that audience, she must have thoroughly enjoyed herself. Not that I was aware of this until the curtain came down to a thunderous ovation. The audience was eerily quiet until that time. The cast thought they were in a foreign flop. Not at all. Japanese productions of *Anne* started in 1976 with Shiki Productions and have continued at regular intervals until this day. The 2010 production in Tokyo and Nagoya continued all through the crisis produced by the earthquake, tsunami, and subsequent meltdown farther north at Fukushima.

The English version has toured Japan four times under the mantle of the Charlottetown Festival, sometimes with a full cast, including Norman's daughter Justine as Prissy Andrews and once, in a 1989 department store tour, with only four performers, Anne, Marilla, Matthew, and Diana. The same quartet did a tour in 1993 for the Japan Travel Bureau.

At Japan's most recent world's fair in 2005, director Duncan MacIntosh brought the current Anne, Jennifer Toulmin, to represent Canada's contribution. Kate Butler, Lucy Maud's granddaughter, came along and got to meet the granddaughters of the Japanese translator of *Anne*. Jennifer was chosen to represent Canada because she played a genuine Canadian heroine. During her visit, she signed over a thousand autographs for Japanese fans. Her face was on a baseball card, and by the time she arrived in Tokyo, there was already a nationwide contest to have a lobster dinner with Jennifer/Anne!

The centennial of the printing of the original novel was celebrated by Shiki in 2008 with a run in Tokyo from February to June followed by a tour of the rest of Japan. Norman and Elaine Campbell were special guests.

Back in 1970, I was still stuck in my room dreaming up the lyrics for the summer's revival of *Private Turvey's War*. I was busy with a number Earle Birney had suggested about the horrors of war. So I wrote lyrics featuring the black market in Belgium, which did deals with both sides of the conflict. It was entitled "War Is Hell, Private Turvey, War Is Hell, War Is Healthy for the Whole Economy!" Alan Lund also added a brilliant ballet in which his dancers in uniform are stifled by the government red tape that comes down from the ceiling.

I didn't perform in our musical this time, but Catherine did. When we took *Turvey* to the National Arts Centre in Ottawa at the end of the season, she took on the role of Turvey's girl, and eventual bride, Peggy. It was such a thrill to hear that voice singing the love ballad "I'll Follow."

Nathan Cohen's Ottawa review was out for the kill. He indicated that the early promise of the show five years before hadn't been fulfilled. As is typical in a politically charged atmosphere like Ottawa, there was a rumour about a bomb scare in the theatre. Cohen's answer to this was to state that "the bomb was on the stage."

There were cast changes in *Anne* that summer. Barbara Hamilton had relinquished the role to Mary Savidge, who played Marilla effectively with a slight Scottish accent. Susan Anderson, who had been Diana in both Charlottetown and London, announced that she was pregnant. Her place was taken by eighteen-year-old Glenda Landry, who had started with the festival as an usherette.

Gracie Finley offered to do the audition with her, and Glenda played Diana for the next twenty-two years!

110: WE FROTH 'EM IN GOTHAM

Gracie Finley and Glenda Landry (Anne and Diana) found themselves rooming together in New York. Shortly after the 1971 season closed in Charlottetown, our publicity director, Jack MacAndrew, got an invitation to bring our show to New York's City Center. A lot of concert versions of former Broadway musicals appear in this uptown location, without sets, on a bare stage.

This is off-Broadway by about ten blocks, but I have never felt that *Anne* is a Broadway show, despite urgent suggestions from many American tourists over the years who have enjoyed the show in Charlottetown. Having been in and at several Broadway openings, I feel the atmosphere is too brittle for the simple story of our orphan. London opening night audiences, in their ratty fur stoles, go to see a show; New York audiences, it seemed to me, go to see who else is in the audience, and most important of all, to be seen themselves.

The preparations weren't as thorough as they should have been, especially regarding the dancers. The floor of the stage was wood, not linoleum, and when Jeff Hyslop, as Gilbert, rehearsed his great slide during Act Two's shoe dance, he got a shard of wood in his thigh muscle. After that engagement, the festival company always carried its own special floor.

The television critics on opening night were brutal. They were on the phone to the networks with their reviews forty-five minutes after our curtain came down. "It's nuthin' but a kid show." "Not near as good as our own *Rebecca of Sunnybrook Farm*." We had to wait until the next morning to hear what the print critics had to say. They were far kinder. The *New York Times* was actually a mild rave.

After the brief New York run, both Gracie and Glenda were asked by the City Center management to stay on with the idea of mounting a new American production of our musical. They both said "No thanks!" and went back to the Island. It was different with the boys. Evidently, Gilberts were more prone to saying yes to the siren call of the Big City.

Three of our dancers ended up in the Broadway production of *A Chorus Line*: Jeff Hyslop, Claude Tessier, and Calvin McRae. Jeff went on to appear in the London production of *Kiss of the Spider Woman* and eventually the title role in an American tour of *The Phantom of the Opera*.

I reckon that no one alive has spent more time on the Charlottetown stage combined than Gracie and Glenda. Gracie played Anne for six years then married an Englishman and came back years later with two kids in tow. But she looked exactly the same as when she played Anne the first time! So she did it again!

Glenda can go Gracie more than one better. Two years ago, on our 2010 opening night, we had a special ceremony honouring her fortieth anniversary with the festival, eighteen years as Diana Barry and twenty-two as Mrs. Spencer, with the most provocative giggle you ever heard.

111: "I CAN DO BETTER!"

This chapter's title is the other half of "Anything You Can Do." It comes from the song that Ado Annie sings to Buffalo Bill in the musical *Annie Get Your Gun*. The television game show that I was now to host had the same title and was based upon the rivalry between men and women. This being a Canadian show, they competed for what sounded like pretty inexpensive prizes. The previous host of the show was leaving Ottawa for Montreal to host yet another game show, with a longer pedigree.

The essence of the show was undignified races, like contestants moving backward crab-wise, then squatting and entering the drop seat of a pair of long johns, extricating themselves from that, topped off with sitting rapidly on an inflated balloon in order to burst it. (In my graduating year from the University of Toronto, I remind you, I was awarded the Sanford Gold Medal in philosophy. I mention this only to gain your sympathy.)

The only game show I had ever watched before this was *Jeopardy*. To prepare myself for the fray, I started watching other game shows, not in the United States but on Quebec television. I wanted to see how an MC would do it in French. What I saw was a lot of devil-may-care Gallic gaiety. Maybe it's because French TV in Canada has no direct competition, either at home or in the United States. But instead of being complacent about it, the French performers throw themselves into the fray with wild abandon and enthusiasm, and it was often a joy to watch. I kept thinking about how lucky Quebec performers were and how overwhelming American television has become in the lives of the rest of us Canadians.

I decided that in my own way I wanted to be part of that insouciance. The job meant flying to Ottawa every two weeks, staying for three days and taping twelve shows, four a day in rapid succession. I had never done anything remotely like this ever before, but by watching the French guys at work, I assumed a devil-may-care attitude to counter my stage fright, and it seemed to work.

In the middle of my first season I received the startling news that *Hee Haw* had been picked up on the syndication circuit, which meant far more stations than CBS ever had. Everyone in the Nashville office had despaired when we were cancelled — except for our accountant, Sam Lovullo. He knew nothing about the entertainment business, but he certainly knew his balance sheets. So he set to work among the independent stations of America and sold our show into syndication … one station at a time.

At almost the same moment, the FCC (Federal Communications Commission), the government guys in charge of the content of the vast wasteland of television, decided that the hour between 7:00 and 8:00 p.m. should be designated as Family Hour, in which innocuous programming would replace the sex and violence most young children seemed to prefer.

With that ruling in mind, Sam had set out on his lonely trek to convince 400 stations to pick up a TV series featuring the stars of country music, not yet household words in any urban centre, with ugly old men telling even older jokes, but heavily endowed with robust, healthy young women. (Charlie Farquharson always referred to our *Hee Haw* honeys as *Fine upstanding holsteen lookin heffers frum yer Sillycone Valley*.)

This news of Nashville summer employment gave me even more of that Gallic devil-may-care attitude. The game show's relentless programming was beginning to wear on me, and I was starting to feel like a squirrel on a treadmill. I didn't need this show anymore, but try as I might, I never got fired. The more outrageously I behaved, the more the producers seemed to like it. I got them to let Charlie MC the show a couple of times, but he seemed relatively subdued compared to my usual Frenchified hyper manner. It lasted two whole seasons, and so did I.

A pleasant interlude was an offer to do a CBC show. The script was written by Norman Corwin, generally considered America's greatest writer of radio dramas. He passed away recently at 101, and I will always be grateful to him for writing for me one hell of a role in *The One Man*

Group. An added pleasure was the presence of the great man himself, who acted as narrator, playing himself.

My character was Charles E. Gumpert, prone to multiple reincarnations from the past. I looked up Peter Kenter's book *TV North*, and sure enough, on page 122 is *Norman Corwin Presents*, a series of teleplays. It was presented as a CBC anthology series, and besides me, other Canadian actors such as Paul Kligman, Barry Morse, Leslie Nielsen, William Shatner, and Gale Garnett, as well as leading American actors, starred in it. There's a sad note at the end: "The series bombed when syndicated in the United States but ran longer here." Ah, well, as the cannibal said, "I had me a nice bunch of parts."

When I went back to Nashville in early June, I found that we had moved from the CBS station to the brand-new Opryland facility, next door to the immortal Grand Ole Opry. I brought in my twelve newscasts, sprinkled with names that I had gleaned from Ontario rural newspapers and scrambled a bit to avoid litigation.

I recorded my newscast and was finished by lunchtime. I felt like an outsider in relation to the rest of the cast. There was nothing more for me to do, so I flew home late that afternoon the same day, feeling like a northern carpetbagger who had invaded the southland and escaped with a fortune. I had taped my contribution to half of our season, and wouldn't see any of my fellow Hee Hores until the next session in October.

I had to make arrangements with the game show to be excused for a couple of days. When I did go back to Nashville that fall, I had to wait until a square dance number was complete before I could go on camera with my KORN news. While waiting I listened to the music they were playing on their steel guitars and dobros. It was in an uptempo, new country style, not far from the soft rock popular with city kids. As I watched, my feet started to boogie a bit, using a step I had seen on the Detroit black music show *Soul Train.*

All of a sudden came the call from the control room to cut the music. Our producer called out, "Charlie, what in hell are you doin' with your feet?" I blushed and said it was something I had watched on another TV show. The director said, "Well, git out thar in front of the camera and keep on a-doin' it."

Now that I recall the incident, I think the moves I had been making were closer to a burlesque stripper than a black rocker. The result was no more northern carpetbagger. I was to be included in all the dance numbers, which meant that I would spend ten whole days in Nashville twice a year, June and October. I didn't know what the game show people would say about that, and frankly I didn't care.

112: AND THAT'S THE NEWS? GOOD NIGHT!

This was the title of a New Year's Eve television special that the CBC asked me to do along with Mike Magee, who had made quite a name for himself under another name, Fred C. Dobbs, as a regular old curmudgeon on Bruno Gerussi's national CBC Radio show. Fred C. Dobbs phoned Bruno every week from Grimsby, Ontario, where he seemed to get out of the wrong side of the bed.

Mike was in real life a nephew of E.P. Taylor, owner of Northern Dancer. As such, Mike became a horse-racing expert for the CBC, even though he seemed to be constantly losing money at the track. I found this out when Mike re-enacted my early-Chris-Plummer-syndrome all over again. When we worked together on the script (I did most of the work, because Mike didn't always turn up), he would constantly borrow money from me, and as promised, pay it back the following week. But sometimes the next day he would borrow it all back again.

For a relative of the ultra-rich who came from a privileged background and graduated from St. Andrew's College, Aurora, Mike had knocked around and been knocked around quite a bit, at one point becoming the night clerk in a seedy Vancouver hotel. From this experience he managed to dredge up about a dozen and a half eccentric characters, all different, and all performed brilliantly and hilariously.

Mike's only problem was that he didn't possess the energy to write material for this palette of variegated characters. I found that out when I ended up writing most of our script. But the CBC had decided that these two old farts, Dobbs and Farquharson, would be wonderful together on camera, so they assigned us a one-hour special to be broadcast the night before New Year's Eve, because they figured everybody stayed home in preparation for the next night's festivities.

Mike and I opened the show dressed as ourselves and as CBC news-casters, following which the camera would catch Charlie and Fred C. watching the show on a television set and making acid comments about themselves as those same news commentators.

The title came from the end of every CBC national news hour: "And that's the news, good night." I gathered some of my favourite Canadian comics, Peter Mews, Jack Duffy, and his cute and funny wife Marilyn Stewart, and we did our best to create a kind of mini–*Spring Thaw* in the middle of winter. Because it was the night before the night before New Year's, the ratings were high, and the CBC asked Mike and I to do it again the next year.

Between game show tapings the following week I thought about writing a book. Actually, the idea wasn't mine. It came from the husband of Catherine's best friend. She had married a sales representative of a book company. I told Al Mazeika, a Falstaffian Lithuanian with an infectious laugh and an enormous sense of fun, how much I had enjoyed a book by Max Ferguson that Al's company, McGraw-Hill, had just published.

Al suggested I write a Charlie book. This wasn't an idea I had ever entertained. I thought Charlie was best presented on television or radio, or maybe on a record so you could hear the flavour of his speech.

I told him I'd think about it. The more I did, the more I realized that what I wanted to write about was Canadian history, something I had tried to do in *Spring Thaw '67*. This time it would be just me on the printed page. I looked around the basement of my parents' home and found a copy of my old high school Canadian history textbook, written by Stewart Wallace. I remember sneaking into his lectures once or twice.

I had studied this text back in my first year of high school, 1936. On the first inset page was a photograph of our gracious king, Edward VIII, aka the soon-to-be abdicated Duke of Windsor, aka Mr. Wallis Simpson. In the middle of the book was another photograph, Sir John A. Macdonald, but the page had been folded by me so that it looked as if he was thumbing his nose at everyone. With these two jokes in hand, I felt better about starting this project.

Wallace's history started with the Vikings. I wanted to go back much further than that, like the Big Bang that had started us all off. I started work. Catherine said that while I typed my face would change entirely into that farmer from Parry Sound. Here is the beginning of what Charlie wrote.

Seems thair's two kinds of histry, yer oriole and yer anal. But I ain't got time fer to do this every yeer. I rite wen it's too wet to plow. Sept I don't reely rite, jist keep flappin' my gums wile the wife and former sweethart Valeda gits it all down soons it cums outa my mouth.

Histry is sumthin' yuh cant finish, so you mite jist as well git it started at yer beginnings. Ime tocking about our erth wen she wuz jist settin out ... oh, musta bin neons ago. Cuz yer erth, she's jist part of our universal ... that's yer hole rang-dang-doo all roll inta wun … incloods yer spiro's nebullous, alla them assteroids, yer Big Dippy, and the rest of them hevvenly constellapations.

So how did this hole rig git a shuv fer to git start up in yer furst place? Them sigh-entifficks don't seem to agree. Thair's sum as sez that our universal never got begun atall. They clame she's allus bin thair in her sollid stait, and thair she's gonna stay thru yer lite yeers and yer dark.

On yer uther hands, thair's sum of them assterollygists as sez the hole thing got start up with a ringtail snorter of a sponter-ainus de-cum-bustin. In uther wirds, things got off with a big bang. And yer intire perseedins has bin goin' downhills ever sints.

So thair you has yer two differnt theeses fer to play with. Yuh kin bleeve erth haz allways bin heer in yer sollied state, but the wife and me is kinda parshul to yer big bang.

The writing turned out to be a labour of love. When I sent a few advance chapters to the publisher, the reaction was encouraging. A computer buff in the editorial office did an estimate on possible sales and came up with an educated guess that indicated my book could sell as many as 18,000 copies. Since 5,000 was generally considered the definition of a Canadian bestseller, I was enormously encouraged.

I dedicated the book to a comedy mentor of mine, Tommy Tweed, who had written his own version of Canadian history, *Canada, Britain's Frozen Asset*, which was never published. Max Ferguson wrote the foreword, and in it he told Charlie that he would get no credit for writing the book. "I'm afraid it's a foreskin concussion that all the accolades for this tour de farce will go to a fella called Darn Herring."

Max's foreword was, in a sense, the first review of my book. The actual reviews were decidedly mixed. Some scholarly type in St. John's thought the misspellings were a disgrace; others complained about the plethora of puns. The exception was Irish expatriate Kildare Dobbs, who overwhelmed me with his column in the *Toronto Star* when he compared my constant punning and phonetic misspellings to his literary hero (and mine), James Joyce.

The 1972 *Histry of Canada* is long out of print, but that first edition seems to have sold 140,000 books at a cost of $5.95 per copy.

113: CHANGE THE ENDING!

While helping to open a new outdoor entertainment facility in Toronto, Ontario Place, I got a call from Paddy Chayefsky's office in New York. He had written a film script entitled *The Hospital* and wanted me to be a part of it. The role wasn't all that good, an executive assistant to the head of the hospital, and I would wear a tweed jacket and a frown throughout. Not much opportunity for comedy. But when I was told the director would be Arthur Hiller, I was enthused. Arthur and I had been involved with some radio broadcasts when we were both at the University of Toronto. He was just about the most engaging, pleasant fellow I had ever met.

So I signed the film contract and at the same time I got an offer from Norman Jewison. He had been successful leaving CBC Television and trying his luck in the United States. With specials featuring stars like Judy Garland and Frank Sinatra, he introduced the concept into television of the runway, a staple of any burlesque theatre. This allowed cameras to work freely among the stars onstage and not interfere with the audience. Now he was being wooed by Hollywood to do a feature film.

Norm asked me to do a screenplay based on Mordecai Richler's book *The Incomparable Atuk*. It was published twenty years before, and I would merely be the next in a legion of adapters who had tried to turn the comic novel into a film. It's about the adventures of an Inuit man who ends up in Toronto's cultural society of the 1950s, and it included a devastating takeoff on our mutual fiend, Nathan Cohen.

Mordecai himself had never tried adapting it to another medium. None of the other attempts had ever appeared on film, either. But Richler must have made a small fortune on the many unsuccessful adaptations of his novel. Norman was involved in this project with Czech director Miloš Forman, who later had great success with *Amadeus*, his film about the young Mozart. Now, evidently, he was willing to consider my approach to *Atuk*, because he considered the novel a devastating attack on American civilization.

This gave me a starting point. Richler's story takes place wholly among Toronto intellectuals. But I took a more international approach, starting with members of a New York advertising agency flying to one of those remote Arctic islands to do a photo shoot for a classy fur firm. But they find to their horror that there is no snow, even in the High Arctic, in the middle of summer. Disappointed, they make their way back to the plane. On the way they see some poor slob trying to spear a seal through a hole in the ice. This is Atuk.

In a flash of inspiration, they decide to take him back with them to New York. He will be the only authentic prop in their proposed fur shoot. Atuk smells too bad to be included in the passenger section of the plane, so he ends up in cargo. And when they land in New York, they put Atuk in a separate cab.

But they forget to fund the Eskimo, and the cab driver turfs him out of the car when Atuk attempts to pay his fare with a Canadian $2 bill. Atuk is dumped in Central Park and eventually ends up in their park zoo at three o'clock in the morning, happily cavorting with the seals.

When the zoo opens in the morning, Atuk is still there. But he is arrested for trespassing and ends up in a New York jail called The Tombs. Atuk's cell in The Tombs is shared with an enormous black man who resents his presence. But when he attacks Atuk, he gets a seal-knife in his gut for his pains. The wound is fatal.

When Atuk rejects the food shoved under the jail door, he proceeds to cut up the corpse of his fellow prisoner and eat his blubber. Can you imagine anything more politically incorrect? I told Norman and Forman that it was a metaphor for life in New York City ... dog eat dog.

Forman loved it, but Norman was very calm when he told me that the whole cannibalistic idea was just a little over the top. Undaunted, and with lots of time on my hands due to the smallness of my part in the Chayefsky film, I told Norman I could write him a sixteen-page treatment with a new idea.

This time it involved North America's upcoming water shortage. It started with a CEO demonstrating a flushing toilet to his investors and explaining that four gallons of water gets wasted with every flush. The only solution was to raise funds for a Canadian company to drain that country's water down into the States. But because of pesky regulations, the head of that company had to be a Canadian. That's where Atuk comes in as your token CEO. Most of the rest of my treatment script ended up in Las Vegas at the Hoover Dam. I never heard what Forman thought, but Norman let me know immediately. And to think that he and I are still friends! And he still lets me wear his dad's hat!

The next day I turned up at the hospital at 99th Street and First Avenue, where I would take film orders from another Canadian college chum, Arthur Hiller. This was the hospital where Chayefsky had researched his script .The hospital was located on the edge of Spanish Harlem and served as a kind of social centre for the Hispanic community.

I had no scenes with the leading actor, George C. Scott, but was told that he was going through his second divorce from the same wife, Colleen Dewhurst. His appearance certainly showed his stress. However, in the best tradition of method acting, he seemed to be "using it" as he portrayed a man on the edge trying to function in a hospital that was overcrowded and underfunded.

The script involved an expansion of the present hospital buildings, which necessitated tearing down several tenements across the street. Paddy wrote the ending of the film based on a book entitled *The Strawberry Statement*. This book was itself based on a strike at Columbia University that fizzled out due to a lack of interest. In Paddy's script this made the doctor more disillusioned by humanity than ever.

When we filmed the ending, it was an outside shoot involving the whole cast, including a strike scene with actors as pickets parading outside the hospital and carrying signs like SAVE OUR HOMES. The residents across the street thought the situation was for real, and they poured out of their tenement homes to join in the protest.

In the ensuing fracas a cameraman was injured, and two actors playing cops required emergency hospital treatment. Paddy was on the spot when it happened, and he wisely allowed real life take over from art. He let the locals change the ending of his script, which later won him an Academy Award.

114: CASTING SWIRLS BEFORE PINE

The title of this chapter is an outrageous pun based on the painting style of Emily Carr. It sounds like something Charlie Farquharson would say, but he was never aware of her existence. His art purview is limited.

The pun about casting swirls before pine appears in my script as a remark made by a local Vancouver critic at a showing of Emily's paintings in a scene I wrote in 1972 for the next Campbell-Harron musical.

I came back from New York to find that Fletcher Markle had television plans for me again. Encouraged by the success of *Anne of Green Gables*, he wondered if there was another Canadian theme I could provide as the basis for a television musical.

I had bought and enjoyed a second-hand copy of the Governor General's Award–winning book for 1941, Emily Carr's *Klee Wyck*. I had seen her paintings for many years, but not her words, which I found just as arresting, particularly her reaction when she saw the B.C. forest for the first time: "It is surging through my whole being, the wonder of it all, like a great river rushing on dark and turbulent, and irresistibly carrying me away on a wild swirl like a helpless little bundle of wreckage." I knew I had the title for a musical about Emily Carr.

I had been thinking about her life as a project for the stage in Charlottetown since 1967. It hasn't happened yet. But the television version did.

Norman Campbell popped in to give me news about our *Anne* musical's continued success. Since he was from British Columbia, I told him about my interest in Emily Carr, and he was equally intrigued. While in California I had worked on a possible screen treatment of *Klee Wyck*, which deals with her first involvement with the West Coast Native tribes, especially her fascination with their art of the totem pole, considered the finest expression of aboriginal culture anywhere in the world.

Klee Wyck means "Laughing One." The name was given to her by the Natives at a Christian mission visited by Emily and her older sister Lizzie at Ucluelet on Vancouver Island. The rest of her family might not have agreed with this benign title. To them their youngest child was a born troublemaker and rebel.

Nothing happened with my Carr project in Southern California because I had no clout with the movie industry. But I had hopes that someday I could present it as a possible Canadian film. At one point I showed the sixteen-page treatment to Tony Guthrie. He approved of its theme, although he was quick to remark that our Emily was pretty small potatoes in the world of painting. Time and monumental prices for her work has proven my favourite theatre director to be dead wrong.

Fletcher had no particular theme in mind for a ninety-minute television special, just something that could be the equivalent of our *Anne of Green Gables* success. Naturally, I contacted the Campbells. Only Elaine was home at the time, and she was wild with enthusiasm for my idea.

While in California I had come in contact with an Irish writer, Brian Moore, who had immigrated to Canada and written several successful novels. He now lived in L.A. We met more than once for lunch, and he suggested that if I wanted to complete my screenplay, I should apply to the Canada Council for a grant.

I did and was amazed when I received, fairly promptly for a government institution, an acceptance of my project and a cheque for $5,000. I envisioned various locales in the film, including San Francisco, London (England), Victoria, Vancouver, and various West Coast Native villages on both the mainland and the Queen Charlotte Islands.

This grant practically coincided with the offer from CBC. I cashed the check and flew out to Victoria, British Columbia, where I had tea with many dear old things who used to know Emily. Through their anecdotes, I got to admire this irascible, brutally honest woman with a wicked sense of humour.

At the same time I read all of Emily's works I could get my hands on. These included a book about her early years, *Growing Pains*; a further early-in-life memoir *A Little Town and a Little Girl*; a First World War memoir about her keeping a boarding house, *The House of All Sorts*; and her sketchbook *Pause*, which describes her frustrating time spent in an English sanitarium.

There was more than one memoir written by women who knew Emily personally, and they all contributed to the fascinating portrait. Although Emily lived until 1945, I wanted to end our musical treatment in 1927, with the complete revival of her career as a painter. This was the year, after such a long period of neglect and frustration, when she got a showing of her paintings in Ottawa and was finally accepted by her peers, championed particularly by Group of Seven member Lawren Harris.

I have no copy of my television script created from my teleplay almost ten years later! My stage version was performed for three consecutive summers in Victoria, starting in 1981, in the very museum that houses a collection of Emily Carr's paintings.

I finished the libretto for the television show between bouts of my game-show tapings in Ottawa. That's why the music and lyrics of *The Wonder of It All* were entirely the contribution of Norman and Elaine Campbell. The television version starred Catherine McKinnon as young Emily, and her physical resemblance to the original was uncanny. Carol Pearson gave Catherine a couple of shirtwaists that had belonged to Emily, which she wore on the show. Catherine was so nervous about my presence as author that she forbade me to be present at either rehearsals or tapings!

Catherine's love interest was played by Michael Burgess, making his television debut before taking on the onerous stage role of Jean Valjean in the musical *Les Miserables*. There were three Emilys, Big, Middle, and Small on television. Cynthia Dale was Small, Catherine Middle, and Irene Byatt played Big, the older, crustier version. The stage version that was done in Victoria during the 1980s had Margaret Martin as Emily Big. She headed an enthusiastic and industrious West Coast cast doubling, tripling, sometimes quadrupling their roles.

Lots of people came to see the show, but they were mostly from Seattle. A lot of Victorians seemed to treat Emily the way their elders used to. They ignored her. At first. The show lasted three seasons, and after the first one, the locals started coming in. Box office was always healthy, yet our musical closed with a deficit of $80,000. Our producer, Maureen Milgrim, said, "It's probably Canada's most underrated musical."

The title song was sung recently by Charlotte Moore at Elaine Campbell's memorial in the Glenn Gould Studio in Toronto. People who were there think it is the finest song the *Anne* team ever wrote. I agree, but I had nothing to do with it. Someday, I am sure, the whole stage musical will be done again.

115: SHH! IT'S THE NEWS!

I was back in Ottawa in the fall of 1972, finishing up the second season of that damn game show when I got the news that the series had been cancelled. Stu Griffiths might have been put off by my whoop of joy, but he immediately offered me something else much closer to my heart: a news satire show. With a fairly pleasant memory of two New Year's Eve specials with Mike Magee, I decided to take a chance.

Griffiths had been one the two chief creators of CBC Television. The other, Mavor Moore, told me that Stu was kind of a genius. I had found this out in an indirect way after working at his studio for the past two seasons. Stu spent most of his time in the basement of the CJOH building. Whenever anyone needed to find the president, all they had to do was go downstairs.

This meant that I would probably have free rein to do what I liked with this show. Stu said he didn't care about the content as long as Charlie Farquharson was onboard. This was 1972, and the series would start in the fall. In the late spring I agreed to do a half-hour pilot show complete with mock newscast, as long as Norman Campbell would be allowed to direct. Norm was one of the stalwart anchors of CBC Television, and CJOH was CTV. Chalk and cheese. If the pilot was accepted by Arthur Weinthal, CTV's head honcho, then there was bound to be concerned talks about a CBC director in charge. It was a chance I took.

I was also given a list of promising young comedy writers, most of whom lived in Toronto. The exceptions were two Ottawans, Ken Shaw, a gangly would-be stand-up comic, now perennial anchorman of the CTV six o'clock news in Toronto, and his comedy partner at that time, Barry Nesbitt.

I was to be executive producer, head writer, and casting director, and I realized I knew as much about all this as a hen knows about tap dancing. But it did give me a chance to choose people whose talents I knew and wanted to work with.

Accuse me of nepotism if you like, but I also took a chance on some-body who had never acted before, Catherine's younger sister, Patrician Anne. (Catherine explained to me the presence of an extra *n* at the end of her first her name. Evidently, when the girls' father was stationed at Shilo, Manitoba, the local priest was also the padre, and at her christening he was drunk.) The Patrician title suited her; she looked like a beautiful young princess.

Catherine and her baby sister did duets with the best blend of voices I have ever heard. One of the assets I recognized was that there were several good singers. Jack Duffy had a big band background, and Peter Mews had been part of a professional vocal trio. Since we needed a French token to represent Quebec, we found a Montreal lounge singer named Claudette, who was warbling nightly in the bar of Ottawa's Skyline Hotel while Catherine entertained in the main ballroom.

With so much vocal talent onboard, I thought I could solve a problem that affects news satire shows. One of the things that bothered me about *Saturday Night Live* was the difficulties they encountered ending a sketch. How do you do that if you can't find a good punchline? I decided that all of our sketches on the pilot would end with a song, preferably parody lyrics of some popular favourite tune.

There was another, more trenchant reason for hiring Patrician Anne, because she had been recently and quickly dropped from the *Singalong Jubilee* season when it was revealed she had Hodgkin's lymphoma. Some CBC Maritime executive made it known that he didn't want someone dying on one of their most popular shows.

We taped a thirty-minute news satire under the expert guidance of Norman Campbell. The one thing we lacked was a title. The inspiration came from Norman himself. He felt that people, anywhere, stop what whatever they're doing when the television news comes on.

He was in the CJOH green room when the news came on the TV set, and he heard somebody say "Shhhh! It's the news!" He thought we should begin every show with some kind of activity interrupted by someone shouting: "Shhhhhh! It's the news!" It became known among the cast when it became a series as simply "Shh It's!"

The basic idea of the show was very similar to *This Hour Has Twenty-Two Minutes*, with the cast playing many characters. But our show had a real newscaster to announce the various topics, Bill Luxton. He had the authentic newsroom voice, plus a delicious sense of humour. We also had the services of Rich Little's former comedy partner, Geoff Scott, who did wonderful vocal impersonations of political figures.

As Merle Macaroon, Geoff did an uncanny imitation of the voice of CBC anchor Earl Cameron, who was doing a nightly feature called "Viewpoint." Our version was called "Screwpoint," the point at which the Canadian public finally asks its government to ... you get the idea.

Barbara Hamilton was invaluable on the show, first of all as Charlie's wife and former sweetheart, Valeda Drain Farquharson. In between each sketch I decided that it required a comment from that rural couple, sitting up in bed in their nightshirts.

I remember only one line from all of the shows we did. It was when Evel Knievel tried to jump across the Snake River canyon on his motorcycle and ended up in the drink. Valeda's only comment to Charlie was *I hear that Eevil Connival muffed his dive.*

If Trish was nervous on the taping session of the pilot, she didn't show it. She did that first show playing a nun, a hooker, and a funny little old lady. She did all of them well and became a permanent member of the cast, despite difficulties she sometimes experienced when the cancer caused her to limp. But she never let it show on camera.

Claudette Farquhar became our separatist weather girl. She used a map where the province of Quebec towered over a shrunken version of the rest of Canada.

Claudette would, during this report, sometimes skip with a rope, and she was so physically endowed in the chest area that the whole exercise became eminently watchable. Another time she tap-danced as a little girl in a talent contest. Before she had a chance to finish, the poor girl was pelted with vegetables and loud boos from the cast as we ran through the closing credits. No wonder this shy performer stayed in her dressing room, only coming out when called to duty.

116: OHHHHHHHHHHH, DO IT AGAIN!

While I was awaiting the reception of our *Shh! It's the News* pilot, my publisher called me. They were delighted with the sales on Charlie's *Histry of Canada* and couldn't wait to do it again.

I must admit they had done a first-rate job of producing second and third printings. They followed this up at the beginning of 1973 with a *Histerical Calendar* featuring photographs of Charlie in various poses, with handwritten comments on certain past events on the various appropriate dates.

JANUARY: Photo of Charlie bundled up in Arctic furs and below the photo his comments on Arctic exploration: *She was Janyerry 11, 1914, up in yer Articks ware a iceman frum Manytoba, Veehellamure Stefannson, run a-ground (or a-floe, mebby) and got up to his perryscope in crushed ice. His ship's name was Karluk, and that's the same kind weer havin these days with our veehickle.*

About half the days of each month had handwritten notations about past events, like January 6, 1685: *La Sal gits within earshot of the mouth of Mrs. Ippy.* Or January 20, 1899: *Yer Dookybores immygrate outa Rooshya fer to cum heer and begin strip farming.*

This calendar sold well, but it didn't complete my obligation to my publisher. I owed them another book the next year, 1974. My literary agent, Matie Molinaro, asked me if I had a second book in mind. I told her that, as a sequel to Charlie's "virgin of our histry," I was thinking of committing the same kind of mayhem on my high-school geography text.

Wen I writ yer histry, I got it arse backerds. Jogfree is wat we started with, and histry is yer unholey mess we maid out of her.

Wonderful, said my agent. "But you don't want to give it to the same editor, right?" I had been very unhappy with my working relationship with the editor of my first book due to his high-handed treatment of the illustrations. "What if they stand by him?"

"Then I'll walk!"

She said that by contract I had to offer them something to publish.

The showdown came in the McGraw-Hill boardroom. I realized from the prevailing atmosphere that they would stand by the editor rather than me. When I was asked what I proposed to bring to them, I offered them the play *Adam's Fall.* I slapped my original copy down on the table.

Without looking at it, they turned me down. I expected this. I then proceeded to turn them down and walked out of that boardroom to six open mouths.

I was phoned later that same day by a McGraw-Hill employee, Bill Hushion, an affable fellow with a good sense of humour. Bill told me he was leaving the firm to go with another publisher, Gage, a branch of the Macmillan publishing empire.

In a matter of hours I had a contract for a second book, but I couldn't start on it right away, because the next day I got a call from Arthur Weinthal. His network was interested in producing *Shh! It's the News* on a weekly basis, but not out of their Toronto studio, CFTO. It would be done at CJOH Ottawa, because it needed the work after the cancellation of my game show. The director would *not* be Norman Campbell but somebody from their own Ottawa staff. Then came the real shocker. CTV would produce the show but wouldn't show it! Arthur said that the pilot show was very clever, but it would never register with any Toronto audience that lived above Bloor Street.

Before I could ask what the hell the point was of producing a television series without ever showing it, Arthur told me he had already sold the show to the brand-new television network, Global, which was beginning operations in the fall. The fledgling network had been taping TV shows like crazy to be ready for its September grand opening.

Most of those shows, it turned out, seemed to involve Catherine. I was aware that she was out of the house a lot. At one point, according to the fall schedule, she appeared in five Global shows in one day! She had her own interview program, plus a couple of weekly panel shows, and she had just been signed to co-host a nightly ninety-minute variety show! Eventually, they ended up doing three of those in one night!

I was ready, as Victorian ladies used to say, to loosen my tiny stays and take a deep breath. I realized that with this heavy schedule, Catherine couldn't be available for our own Global project. I was grateful that we still had her sister onboard, but Catherine was made of sterner stuff. She still made room for us in her hectic schedule, agreeing to appear in every other segment.

Our own schedule was formidable enough. With a mostly Toronto cast, we would fly to Ottawa on a Sunday, and each show would be taped all day Monday. Coming back from Ottawa Monday night, I would meet with the eager-beaver writers in my Toronto home early on Tuesday, and by Friday I would have edited and typed up a new half-hour script that would be copied Saturday in quintuplicate, brought by me to Ottawa Sunday night, for a read-through that evening with the cast.

Music rehearsals for the parodies would start early Monday with the ever-affable Champ Champagne and his tiny orchestra. He seemed to know every song ever written, a bonus when it came to the many parodies we provided him with every week.

My cast members were absolutely heroic in what they were called upon to do. For the actual taping of sketches all day Monday, we often had pages of script Scotch-taped to the various cameras and articles of furniture on the set. This was to help cast members with short memories, like myself.

The show would be edited in Ottawa on Tuesdays, then flown to Toronto on Wednesdays and shown to a Global lawyer for possible litigation on Thursdays, then finally exhibited to the public Friday nights at 10:00 p.m.

Thank the good Lord I had time to rest up before all this began! Except for the assignment of writing that second book: *Charlie Farquharson's Jogfree of Canda, the Whirld, and Uther Places.*

117: CHARLIE FARQUHARSON RETIRED BANKRUPT

Everybody took to calling me Charlie because of the success of the *Histry* book. This brought me the nod from Toronto's most popular radio station, CFRB. They wanted Charlie to write and perform a pair of three-minute editorials repeated twice every Saturday and Sunday.

As a hopeless newspaper junkie, this was a labour of love, to get paid for something I always did anyway, going through all three Toronto papers from cover to cover. All I had to do was choose two topics every week for Charlie's rural slant on things. I would take my two typewritten pieces to the station every Friday afternoon and sit in a tiny glass booth.

I worked a total of six minutes a week for CFRB, and it went on for fifty-two weeks a year. The earliest CFRB Charlie piece I could find comes from early 1973, which is pretty close to when I got started.

This is Charlie CFRB Farquharson talkin' at yiz on yer weak end.

And I think it's a darn shame to have that sexy-rotarian, the gradest race-harse since Mannerd-war, git retired out to be a stud wen he's oney sex years old.

Mine jew, thair ain't a man amung us wooden envy that kind uv a retired-mint pogrom ... Put out to pastyer with a buncha yung fillys, and gittin' pade fer doin it!! Unless of corse they do the hole sax thing by jist usin' yer artyfishul insinuation. But it duz seam a shame fer to bottle up a good draft horse.

Jist shows yuh how our world is goin' thru the changes, with two things becumming absolutely obsoleen ... Naimly yer big horse and yer small farmer.

Cuz on accounta them shoddy Arapeyuns with ther gas attacks on our pumps, weer gonna hav to find sum uther ways of gittin' round without our infernal combustin' injuns.

That may bring us back to yer horse, ware yer only polly-ution they giv out is sumthin yiz kin put on yer peeny bushes!

Cuz you take yer fowl air they got in yer sitty of Trawna, it's probly cause by them malty-nashnul big furms refusin' to take the lead outa thair plants.

What stopped all this after eleven years was the sale of station to its new owner, Dominion Broadcasting. The head of that company was the one who got me fired. I remember being at a party in Rosedale when he went by me while whirling some dowager in a fierce two-step. As he passed, he said to me, "You watch yourself!"

I laughed and said, "I always do!"

Next week I was told not to come to the station anymore with my pair of three-minute Charlies. The dancer who told me to watch myself because of Charlie's political views? Conrad Black.

118: SHHHHH! IT'S THE SH'ITS!

Back to 1973, and our first show of *Shh! It's the News*. The opening always included a reference to its title. In one instance three monks are pulling on bell ropes as they chant *Monasterium in quietus keepit*. (No talking!) But one of the monks keeps trying to speak to the other two, attempting to break his many years vow of silence. A television set comes down one of the bell ropes, and the other two shut up the loudmouth friar with "Shh! It's the News!"

First thing we taped each week was the Valeda-Charlie exchanges, both of them sitting up in bed in nightgowns, Barb in her curlers and me in my crappy old cap:

> CHARLIE: *Evrybuddy's gittin munny frum Ottawa sept us.*
> VALEDA: *We should apply to the guvmint fer saim sex bennyfits.*
> CHARLIE: *How cum?*

VALEDA: *Cuz we only hav sex on the thurd Friday of every munth.*
TOGETHER: *And it's always the same.*

After that I had to shave, leaving myself bare-faced to play other characters like Joey Smallwood, Robert Bourassa, Robert Stanfield, and John Turner.

We were on the air the first month that the new Global network was in operation, and dared to make fun of the experienced newsmen and correspondents they had hired to do the actual newscasts, able staff like Peter Newman, Peter Desbarats, and newcomers like Mike Anscombe. Our newscasters correspondingly had names like Peter Newsman, Peter Desperate, and Ike Back-comb.

A memorable moment from that first season was Jack Duffy's faultless impersonation of the vocal stylings of Frank Sinatra. The news item was based on Sinatra's hostile reception at a concert in Australia, after he appeared onstage and made several anti-Aussie remarks.

One of the reasons for the amazingly high ratings of our show was the fact that 1973 was the year that the American government, panicking over the Arab oil embargo, decided to go on daylight saving time in January instead of waiting until April. With our Friday night ten o'clock spot, the only opposition on TV at that hour was the local Buffalo TV news. Southern Ontarians turned to us instead. We used to joke on air about the fact that Global's name was a bit ludicrous, because it only "covered the globe" across Southwestern Ontario. Our on-air constant image was a winking red glow ball.

Nevertheless, the brand-new network tolerated our shenanigans because of the ratings, and the show was guaranteed a second season.

With this news, Barbara Hamilton, in Valeda's curlers, leaned over to me in our mutual bed on set and said, "Next year is International Woman's Year, Donnyboy. Whadda ya plan to do about it?"

"Barb, what do you expect me to do about it. Change sex?"

She said, "Yep. We've done the country mice, Charlie and Valeda, all season. Now it's time to include the town mice. I want to be a city stockbroker, with a walrus moustache just like my dad had. And you, Don Harron, can be my wife!"

I said I would take the summer to think about it. Looming ahead was the deadline for my second book.

The rest of the ratings for the first Global season weren't so good. Among the casualties were all of Catherine's shows, including the variety show *Everything Goes*. Evidently, everything went. Global had made a brave effort to become a truly Canadian network, and it had gone broke in doing so. Nowadays it's just another example of a Canadian distributor of American filler, except for their local and network news broadcasts, which are of a consistently high standard.

Catherine had managed to fit that show in with all her other assignments. During the last *Shh! It's* taping, she heard that *Everything Goes* had been cancelled.

As we made our way home, Catherine was understandably silent. She was still a formidable force in the recording business, and she still had her second Global season with our show, where she had proved herself an able comedian.

Next morning I woke up late, and the birthday girl was nowhere to be seen.

119: SEVERAL DEGREES OF SEPARATION

The day after the Harrons came home to Toronto would be Catherine's thirtieth birthday. *Thirty* seems to strike fear into the female soul like *forty* does to the male.

The week before I had arranged a surprise party with all our Toronto pals, as Catherine fussed over baby Kelley, two years old. In the morning I awoke to find Catherine gone. I figured the one place she could be was in our country house near Barrie. Eventually, that day, she turned up there, and she let me know there would be no birthday celebration. And furthermore, no marriage.

I realized that Catherine's career was paramount in her life. She was a big international star at eighteen. That's not easy to get over. When I first met her on Prince Edward Island in 1966, she was the centre of attention whenever we went out together. I was an unknown quantity, having been out of the country for more than ten years. Charlie Farquharson had been inactive for much of that time. In restaurants Catherine was surrounded by autograph seekers while I sat there ignored.

In a way, I could understand what she was going through. An article about me in *Maclean's* about 1954 was entitled "He Doesn't Want to Be a Star!" I have always felt that way.

Catherine seemed to feel that she was responsible for the failure of Global's variety show, when in fact she had been a distinct success. At our wrap party she was strangely silent, just as our shy French token, Claudette, had been throughout the series. Claudette came out of her dressing room only to work, and otherwise never uttered a peep. That last show there were two silent singers, Catherine and Claudette. They contrasted with the rest of the cast, who were loudly celebrating our renewal.

That birthday morning I phoned our nanny Gerry at her boarding house, told her to come over, and to bring all her things with her. She would be a live-in from now on. When Gerry died several years later, I realized the warm, firm centre of our family life had vanished.

Also that morning, I got on the phone several times to friends to cancel the surprise celebration. Meanwhile, the deadline for my book was fast approaching. A few days later I bundled Kelley and Gerry into the car and headed for the country house that we had christened Barrie Sound.

There was no sign of Catherine. I found out later she was back in Toronto, making arrangements to move into a handsome apartment in the centre of the city, but promising to visit our baby daughter frequently. A promise she kept.

Since Global had optioned a second season of *Shh! It's the News*, I asked Catherine to continue as part of the cast. It was an uneasy setup, but it seemed it might work out, because both of us, as registered workaholics, could be completely professional.

My editor at Gage, because it was an educational publisher, was an expert on the subject of geography, but he was also a Scot with a sense of humour. Like my history book, the companion geography started way back at the beginning, with:

Yer muther's erth having relayshins with yer soler sistern. Sum peeples think of erth as jist a ball, but that'd be mostly yer teenagers. After they gits older in to ther middle ages they starts to reelize she's flat at both ends.

I hate tuh tell yung peeples this, but our erth is not yer senter of things. Its jist a small dork objeck, spaced out amung a billyum uther hevvenly boddys.

These boddys is yer uther plants, Murky, Marse, Veenis, Poopter, Slattern, Napchewin, and that dog of a star, Plutoe. And nun of them boddys is too lifely, neether. On accounta we is all fix stars, jist sons of yer Son, havin' bin thrown offa its soler's plexus durin' a gas attack.

By daffynishun, yer Son is a big mass of hot gas wat shines by its own lite. (I got wun of those, too, naim of Orville Farquharson.)

Like it er not, yer Son is not yer big cheese neether. Its jist yer sentral heeting fer the rest of us, cuz its the hottest thing in our gal-ex-laxy.

If yiz catches a long, long peesa tale a-winding acrost sum hevvenly bodys wun nite, that'd be a cumit. They don't cum round too offen. Mine jew, weeve had yer Bill Hailey's cumit round the clock purty regler every millenema.

Yer cumit is jist a durty ice-cube, but burnin' with gas. It don't hang around too long, but fer a wun-nite stand, yuh can't beat her fer lite-in up yer part uv yer sky.

Yer meatier is smallern yer cumit, a sort of haff-assteroid wat broke off frum sum uther plan-it. Probly a chip offa yer old Murkry. (We had wunna those, but trade it in fur a shevvy.)

Us Farquharsons wunce had wun of them spaced-out objecks land in our falla feeld. Fer a time we maid a liddle munny chargin terrists, twenny-fie sents a hed, fer to git a look at her.

But Ottawar step in and sed we hadda pay tacks on our incum frum this heer Murky-meetier, on accounta our guvmint con-sider it imported iron, sints it cum frum a broad.

120: THE BOOK-EVERY-MONTH CLUB

That's a joke I used to make about the prodigious output of Pierre Berton. But I did write a book in a month, sitting out in the sun with my rusty tripewriter on a little balcony above our swimming pool.

It took me fourteen pages to mention Canada. I had to get through the various rocks of ages first, like *Cretin-ages, Messy Zoo-hick, Try-assid,* not to mention *Yer Plastiseen peeriods.*

In the middle of all this, I got a phone message from someone I couldn't dare refuse. No, not the Mafia. It was Whipper Billy Watson, WURLD champeen rassler, calling from Parry Sound. He wanted me to come up there on the weekend and do a telethon with him for Easter Seals.

My relationship with Parry Sound had its rough edges. In the first place I had never *really* been there! When I decided that it was the home of Charlie Farquharson, it was because the vowel in each of the two of those words that spelled out the town's name were absolutely perfect for Charlie's accent, a mixture of Lowland Scottish and Northern Irish.

Not too long after Charlie's beginnings, the local newspaper had printed an editorial to the effect that "Some struggling stock actor in Toronto claims to affect a Parry Sound accent. There is no such thing." On the strength of this notoriety, the promoter of the Parry Sound Winter Carnival invited me, or rather Charlie, to appear in it. Charlie was thrilled, but the job offer was vetoed by the town's mayor.

I phoned the number Whipper had left and got his Easter Seals assistant, Susan Brower. She told me that if I came, the Parry Sound Pipe Band would make me an honorary member. I told her to get in touch with the mayor. She called back within the hour. Either the town had a different mayor now or all was forgiven because of the success of my history book, of which Susan said, "Everybody in town got it for Christmas."

To hell with geography deadlines. Next day I was in Parry Sound and welcomed by the Whipper and Susan, who looked like a lady wrestler herself. But she had a heart of gold when it came to disabled children, and that weekend I committed myself to an involvement with Easter Seals that would continue for the next twenty-five years.

The moment of truth came during the telethon itself. I was dressed as Charlie when Whipper challenged me to an arm-wrestling contest. It was so ludicrous. Here was the heavyweight champion of the world! It made me answer with a hoot of derision. But Whipper said it was to raise money for the kids. When we went *mano a mano*, the son of a bitch took a dive and let me win!

Back to the grindstone, and the deadline. I did bring the book in on time. It appeared in bookstores early that fall, well before Christmas, and it was castigated by *Globe and Mail* reviewer Jack Batten.

Nevertheless, true culcher cannot be held down, and my fool book shot to the head of the Best Smeller list in its second week. It didn't stay there, however, but spent the rest of the season in a neck-and-neck battle with Peter Gzowski's book about *This Country in the Morning*. Gage didn't care which of us was on top. They suggested I wait another two years, and then, due to my appearances on *Hee Haw*, they would publish Charlie's version of *The Farmer's Almanac*, which could be sold in both Canada and the United States.

Little did I know at the time that a large percentage of the viewers of *Hee Haw* either couldn't read or had never been inside a bookstore.

121: MY DOUBLE DOUBLE LIFE!

Meanwhile, back in our base city on the Rideau, we were starting the second season of *Shh! It's the News*. Catherine and I were still living separate lives, but she was a regular weekly member of our cast.

My more immediate marriage was a fictitious one to Barbara Hamilton. During the first season of *Shh! It's*, Charlie Farquharson was her husband. In addition, this second season I was to become Barbara's wife. We decided to name the couple Charles (Barbara) and Valerie (me), and when it came to the proper surname, I thought the couple should be named after, if not the richest, certainly the oldest money section of Toronto, Rosedale. We could have called our upper-class couple Mr. and Mrs. Rockcliffe, or Westmount, or Shaughnessy, and it would have amounted to the same thing. Other than Charlie, Valerie Rosedale is the only other original creation of mine. Her voice pattern I got from a cousin of Jane Mallett's, and Valerie's laugh, which can only be rendered in print as YOFF, YOFF, KNOCK, KNOCK! I stole from a friend of one of my daughters.

Unfortunately, the costume department at CJOH was completely unaware of rich Rosedale bitches. They handed me a costume that I would describe as lower Kmart or maybe upper Goodwill. I wore it a couple of times but pleaded with them to let me wear something closer to Valerie's station in life.

Finally, someone got off their ass and brought me a second-hand tweed suit from an organization called WIMODAUSIS. It sounded like a social disease, but it was actually an upper-class charity run by the Wives, Mothers, Daughters, and Sisters of wealthy Ottawa families.

By the fan mail that season, Valerie was giving Charlie Farquharson a run for the money. Her first public appearance was in front of a sea of blue hair as the guest speaker on International Women's Day at the Canadian National Exhibition. The audience reaction was uproarious. I find that women have a better sense of humour about themselves than men.

Valerie's debut came about the same time as another more famous drag queen made her appearance, formidable Down Under Dame Edna Everage. Since we both adopted the same kind of harlequin glasses, people have assumed that one of us imitated the other. But that isn't true. We sprang spontaneously from our own different cultures. However, I yield to Edna's creator, Barry Humphries, as the greatest ad libber in the business.

I was cobbling together sketches and parodies for the following week's edition of *Shh! It's the News* when I got an urgent phone call from Trish, asking me to come over to her place immediately. Since it was only a couple of blocks away, I arrived on foot a few minutes later to find her house full of people I knew. They had gathered to celebrate my fiftieth birthday.

Valerie Rosedale, 1974.

I'd completely forgotten it was September 19, but Catherine hadn't. Remembering what happened on her own thirtieth birthday, she had used her sister's place to gather all our friends, including one named Vince Fournier — better known onstage as Alice Cooper. I had never met him and scarcely met him that night, so busy was I being affable to pals I hadn't seen in a long time.

I received a bunch of presents, mostly jokey ones, but the present I was hoping to receive I never got that night. It was to have Catherine come back home. My last glimpse of her that night as I left was her kissing one of our old friends.

122: CHARLIE TO THE IMAX

Our series finished its second season by becoming *Shh! It's the Snooze*. Our ratings were just as high as the previous season, but the other Global Canadian shows had dropped in popularity.

Almost immediately after our last show, my old friend from the Charlottetown Festival, Jack MacAndrew, was on the phone. He was now living in Toronto and in charge of variety for CBC-TV. He asked me about the possibility of continuing our satire series and wanted to know how much our show had cost. Like a fool, I told him. We had managed to do a network show three weeks out of four (we always repeated a week at the end of the month) for $5,000. I told him I expected a budget of at least twice that from the national government network, because my cast and writers had done it for two seasons for love rather than money.

He called me a month later and said the CBC would put the show on across Canada for the same paltry budget. I flushed with anger and turned him down. He accepted my decision without rancour and said he would look elsewhere.

He did and offered the same measly money to a bunch of young comics who were beginning to look to television after doing a successful stage revival of *Godspell*. They were now working at a downtown stage venue and calling themselves "The Second City," after a well-established Chicago satire group.

After its debut on Global, *SCTV* moved to CBC and NBC and finally Superchannel. The rest is historical. Toronto's *SCTV* stars are today all over the Hollywood map, while *Shh! It's the News* remains a distant memory.

Onward and upward with the arts. For me it was another twenty-six-show taping of *Hee Haw* and another book deadline for Charlie's version of *The Farmer's Almanac*, coupled with an offer to write and perform in an IMAX film!

I had been to Ontario Place a couple of years before to see this new screen process, which looked to me like 4-D, shown on the world's largest screen. Graeme Ferguson, the director who made the offer, was an independent operator with a very independent mind. He asked me to prepare a twenty-minute film script using this new medium and involving Charlie Farquharson. This in a screen process that usually featured three-dimensional views of the Grand Canyon, or ski runs down Mount Everest, that had audiences screaming because of their immediacy.

Graeme said the only limitation was that the film had to be made in Northern Ontario during the winter because the sponsor was the Ontario government. That gave me the title even before I wrote the script: *Snow Job*. The government wanted a story that kids would want to see, so I decided to make Charlie a minor character. The central one would be a female school bus driver, beloved by her youthful passengers because she didn't mind their antics or all the noise they made when she drove them to school.

One day the principal can't get his car shovelled out of his driveway in time to get to school, so he is forced to accept a lift on the school bus. He is so appalled by the behaviour of the kids and the noise they make that he fires the lady bus driver before they reach the school. As the kids pile out, unaware that their favourite driver has been cancelled, the principal suddenly gets a severe attack of stomach pains. He fears a burst appendix, and the bus driver, despite her being fired, attempts to get him in the bus to the local hospital. But the bus stalls in a snowbank, and she transfers the aching principal to a borrowed snowmobile.

Charlie gets involved when the snowmobile goes in and out of his barn while he is loading up his manure bucket. I wrote no dialogue for him, just a constant look of open-mouthed astonishment. As the snowmobile roars past him, Charlie slips on the ice below his feet, and the contents of the manure bucket empty on his tattered cap.

Instead of real manure, Graeme had the good sense to use endless packages of Shirriff's chocolate pudding, laced with a few dog biscuits and some wisps of actual straw for authenticity. We did the scene in one take, fortunately, but Charlie's hat smelled of chocolate for a couple of years afterward.

Before I got back to writing, other jobs kept popping up that summer. Jackie Rae had settled permanently back in Canada and was romantically embroiled with my sister-in-law, Trish. He suggested that Charlie should have a Christmas album. Catherine could sing some carols, and he would provide extra Christmas lyrics for her to sing. It all sounded wonderful, and I set to work, writing Charlie's version of Dickens's Scrooge, plus city and country monologues about the festive season, and ending up with his own version of "The Night Before Christmas."

I didn't know that some kind of feud had arisen between Catherine and Jackie over some European song he had given her to record. All I know is that the day we were to record the album, Catherine pulled out in a huff. I didn't know what to do, but Jackie did. He immediately put Trish in her place to sing songs like the "Cherry-Tree Carol," plus a number Jackie had written about the North Pole gnomes. We recorded the album with an audience, mostly kids, and I must say I enjoyed myself. And Trish, too.

Norman Campbell told me he had another ninety-minute slot open on CBC. I suggested we adapt a chapter of Stephen Leacock's *Arcadian Adventures of the Idle Rich*, a sequel to the much better known *Sunshine Sketches of a Little Town*. The follow-up novel is about rich city people, not small-town types, and the chapter I chose to adapt was "The Yahi-Bahi Society of Mrs. Rasselyer-Brown."

We taped it with a cast of seasoned farceurs, including Stratford's Helen Burns in the title role, Heath Lamberts and Paul Soles as a couple of fake Hindu mystics, and for the love interest an attractive young ingenue named Shelley Matthews, who was accompanied at all times by her fiercely protective fiancé, who later became premier of Ontario: David Peterson.

123: YER BI-SEXTENNIEL

In 1976, when I reported for duty in Nashville in October for the second session of *Hee Haw*, I had in my luggage thirteen news monologues and a freshly printed copy of my new book, *Charlie Farquharson's K-O-R-N Allmynack*. On the back cover were photos of *Hee Haw* stars, Roy Clark, Buck Owens, Minnie Pearl, Grampaw Jones, and Junior Samples.

Charlie in Nashville, 1976, signing copies of his record album Doesn't Anybody Here Know It's Christmas?

Our taping coincided with Fan Week in Nashville, and every country DJ in the United States was there. I had no trouble having a press conference with all these media folks, but they were less interested in the book itself, because you can't play a book over the airwaves. After the taping I was booked to start a national tour covering most of the States.

My tour started in Boston, of all places, the City of the Bean and the Cod, where *Hee Haw* had never played. Nobody knew who I was. I felt like a non-entity among celebrities like Cab Calloway, who had a biography to sell. It was a delight to hear him do "Minnie the Moocher" instead of the usual pitch for his book.

From Boston I went to another booksellers' convention in Chicago, but during the day I got so tired of being asked the same questions: Does Buck Owens really own the town of Bakersfield, California? Does Roy Clark have hair transplants? What's the price on Minnie Pearl's hat? Is Junior Samples really dumb? (Yeah, like a fox.) Is Nurse Goodbody's body really real? Are you really on the show? What part?

My reception was warmer closer to *Hee Haw* territory. One night I opened the show for Ray Charles in Columbia, South Carolina. The only thing I remember was getting instant applause when I shouted the slogan of the local college football team, the Gamecocks. Nobody laughed except me, inside, when I shouted "Go, Cocks, go!"

I next did a fundraiser in Knoxville for a burlesque theatre that hoped to become a repertory company, doing legit theatre for the students at the University of Tennessee. Knoxville is the area where Dolly Parton comes from. That year Knoxville was home to a world's fair, one of the smallest ever seen. The symbol was highly phallic, consisting simply of a cock and a ball, much enjoyed by my fellow *Hee Haw*er Archie Campbell, who was at the fair to sell his paintings at, I thought, exorbitant prices.

The telethon was sponsored by an academic group from the university. They were there that night, including the gentleman who had been chosen to head their theatre program, the distinguished British actor Sir Anthony Quayle. I had been part of a two-hour NBC *Producers' Showcase* when he played Robert Browning to Katharine Cornell's Elizabeth Barrett.

Evidently, Quayle seemed to vaguely remember me, and he approached me with a frown as I stood there in my Farquharson rags. He asked with an air of complete skepticism, "Are you the Donald Harron of Stratford, Ontario, as well as Connecticut?"

I allowed as how I was.

His frown got deeper. Looking me over, he said, "Good God, man, how have you come to this?"

I looked straight into his eyes and said with complete sincerity, "Just lucky, I guess."

The rest of the tour is now a complete blur, with the same relentless questions about country music thrown at me by someone who had never read the book. I was refused an appearance on *The Tonight Show* because I was told Johnny "didn't like puns."

The only interesting assignment was on Dinah Shore's daytime show. The guests that day included Oral Roberts, the TV evangelist. No one got a word in edgewise in the green room before the show as Oral held forth as if he was already on the tube. He had heard that I was a Shakespearean actor, and he was ready to give me his own interpretation of the Beard of Avon.

Instead I went on camera as the first guest, and Dinah described my book as a rather racy version of *The Farmer's Almanac*. She didn't really refer to any of the text and avoided mentioning the illustrations for Charlie's Horrorscopes, which included a drawing of Charlie having carnal knowledge of a sheep.

Instead she mentioned my involvement with Shakespeare and asked if I would favour her audience with a selection. I hesitated. The only speech I had retained over the years and performed three times onstage was the Bastard's soliloquy from *King Lear*.

I hesitated at first, then plunged ahead, wondering how Roberts would react when I shouted out the Elizabethan epithet "Fut!" He didn't move a face muscle. When Dinah interviewed him, he didn't make any reference to me or to the words of Shakespeare.

124: GOODBYE CHARLIE!

When I returned home after my dispirited U.S. book tour, I discovered that in my absence I had sold five times as many books in my own country without even being there as I had from being on the spot all over the United States. For the first time in my life I was sick to death of not shaving, of answering the same dumb questions, and having to be nothing more than Charlie Farquharson. The fact that Catherine wanted to come back and live with Kelley, Gerry, and me was the nicest homecoming present of all.

I found three interesting work offers awaiting me, none of which involved Charlie. First was an invitation from "old faithful" Norman Campbell to do a one-hour TV tribute to Sir Tyrone Guthrie, who at the age of seventy, newly knighted by the queen, had left us for the Great Festival in the Sky seven years before. He died on his mother's birthday. His wife Judith had been going through a bad patch, and as she watched, he threw away his heart medicine and died with a smile on his lips.

This belated tribute coincided with the twenty-fifth anniversary of the Stratford Festival. The year 2012 marked the sixtieth year, the Diamond Anniversary, of what Tony Guthrie started.

I suggested to Norman that the title of the documentary could be stolen from Oscar Wilde, with the letters *u* and *n* added, so that it became "The Unselfish Giant."

On camera I interviewed anyone connected with the early days of the Stratford adventure. The highlight was Douglas Campbell's description of Guthrie's funeral. Dougie had been present, and his warm, humorous recounting of the proceedings would have delighted our Tony.

The documentary opened with me riding my bike along the River Avon and up to the Stratford Festival Theatre, where I stopped, and said, "Twenty-five years ago, you wouldn't have known this place from a hole in the ground. Because that's exactly what it was. That hole became, as you probably know, the world-famous Stratford Shakespearean Festival. A lot of actors shared in the excitement of that first season, and we'd like to share it with you. We'd also like to pay tribute to the man who, more than anyone, was responsible for the success of that summer. His name was Tyrone Guthrie, and this theatre with its dynamic thrust stage is a memorial to his talent…."

This was followed by tributes from many of the stars and leading lights of the festival over the years such as Tom Patterson, Irene Worth, Bob Christie, Bill Shatner, and Tanya Moiseiwitsch.

When the documentary appeared in June 1977, Blaik Kirby of the *Globe and Mail* said it was the "the warmest, most affectionate documentary on record. I think you'll be moved by what amounts to a collective confession of love."

Mission accomplished.

125: LET'S SAVE CANADA ... FOR AN HOUR

The second Charlie-less offer in 1976 was from Paul Thompson, the founder of alternative theatre in Ontario. A zealot with flowing hair and a bushy beard, he looked like an Old Testament patriarch or John Brown, the body who started the Civil War. Paul was the creator of Theatre Passe Muraille, which put on "collectives" where actors researched and improvised dialogue.

He told me he had seen me as the minister in *Reddick*, the one who had started a youth group in his urban church. Paul suggested I play a real-life version of that same theme — actually, the man on whom the character Reddick was based, the Reverend Russell Horsburg, a United Church minister in Chatham, Ontario.

Horsburg had been hounded to his death by those who accused him of contributing to the delinquency of minors in his church youth group. Russell Horsburg was a charismatic saint to those involved with him in the youth work. The collectively researched and improvised play about him was to begin the following spring. I told Paul I would be onboard.

The third offer came from a totally unexpected source. It was from Quebec comedian Yvon Deschamps, a committed separatist. He had expressed interest in my Charlie character during an interview on television with Peter Gzowski, and this information was passed on to me.

Yvon, like me, had started out as an actor but developed a comic character that was so popular it swallowed up the rest of his career. He sold out La Salle Wilfrid-Pelletier in Montreal, the equivalent of Toronto's O'Keefe (now Sony) Centre.

When I talked to Deschamps, he had a zany idea for a satiric hour about national unity, or rather the lack of it. He and I would express ourselves on both sides of the question of separation, but in a comic way. Intrigued, I travelled to Trois-Rivières to see him perform in a two-character play. The character Yvon played was very much the sort of "little guy" made famous by Charlie Chaplin. After the play we broke bread and Yvon outlined his TV idea.

CBC Toronto would tape the show in the spring of 1977. The writing would take place in January and February. By that time Yvon had agreed to be in California doing something with Bob Dylan. I never did find out what they were up to. So Deschamps wanted me to come out to California for several weeks. Catherine and I had reconciled, and Yvon guaranteed me the CBC would pay for my stay, plus any members of my family I brought along. I was stunned. I couldn't imagine an Anglo nationalist like me having that kind of power with the Corporation. Maybe the CBC thought they could convert Deschamps to federalism with all that expense money. I told him I was in, and we shook hands on it.

Catherine and seven-year-old Kelley came with me to a motel on Malibu Beach in January. The years of separation had taken their toll on their relationship. Kelley really thought of Gerry as her mother-figure, and Catherine had a lot of catching up to do. We were thrilled to be away from winter and not to have to scrape the ice from our rented car's windows with a credit card.

Kelley and Catherine were off to Disneyland. Yvon and I got down to work. He told me Québécois didn't watch much Canadian English-language TV, but they seemed to know everything about American shows. So the first sketch we planned was a takeoff on the number one favourite American sitcom at that time, *All in the Family*.

Yvon played the role of the son-in-law, Meathead. In our version, he has an uncle who's a priest. (Montreal impressionist Jean-Guy Moreau doing a devastating René Lévesque.) We cast Al Waxman as Archie Bunker, and I got to play his wife Edith, singing their theme song, "Those Were the Days," in my high-pitched, off-key cackle.

Yvon scheduled a monologue for himself, entirely non-political. It was about *pa-père*, his grandfather. So I wrote a solo about the general plight of Canadian agriculture. As a part-time dairy farmer, Charlie had some sympathy for his counterparts in Quebec. Yvon meant the title of our show, *The Let's Save Canada Hour*, to be ironic.

But Yvon suddenly dropped his role of comedian and became devoutly in earnest as he presented the case for sovereignty (aka separation). He told our audience he was afraid that if Canada stayed together the French language that gave him his identity would totally disappear in the next twenty-five years. He kept repeating the phrase "I don't want to disappear."

This threw me completely, because I had planned to be light-hearted Charlie. It was too late to change my approach. Here is the gist of what I had to say.

We've had a separator in our cream shed fer twenny yeer, never giv us no trubble atall. That holyday ruckus they has down to Cuebec evry yeer, I bleeve it wuz call Sin John Papoose day, but it's now noan as yer Fate Nashon-ale.

But I think all Canajunjs is intrusted in our nashnul fate ... wether weer gonna be well-hung together, or git put to yer blocks as Sepritists.

Wat exackly do them Cuebeckers wants? I heer the thing most of 'em wants is a job. Jist like us Anglows, they wanna be gamefully emploid....

... this darn cuntry is alreddy seprit enuff. I think only thing wat keeps Canda together is the fack that evrybuddy in it hates Trontuh. That's the sorce of our reel nashnul unititty!

After we taped the show, we sat back and wondered about the reaction. To this day I can't tell you. It seemed to be ignored by most TV critics and resented by the mandarins in Ottawa.

By that time, I was involved in something else: Charlie's place in the world of commerce. The first commercial I did was for the Wintario Lottery, and the second one was for OFF, the bug spray, which allowed me to say several times in a loud voice, "BUG OFF!"

Then for a brief time Charlie became spokesman for the Bank of Montreal, when they introduced their first credit card. I attended a couple of board meetings, but I was pretty well ignored and they soon replaced me with Leslie Nielsen.

The fourth commercial took me back to California to do televised pitches for Del Monte. My pitch seemed to be based on the Canadian pronunciation of their product, Del Mont, eh? I feel it necessary to mention that these commercials were never particularly successful.

126: MAKING IT UP AS I WENT ALONG

Farquharson was temporarily off my calendar and I was into rehearsals with Theatre Passe Muraille for their next collective, *The Horsburg Scandal*. I had never before entered the world of theatrical improvisation. Of course, I had done a bit of ad libbing in Charlie monologues, but I had never improvised in serious drama. I took a weekly class in New York while I was in *Separate Tables*, with professional actors such as Farley Granger and Peter Falk, under the expert tutelage of the founder of the Neighbourhood Playhouse, Sanford Meisner. There I used to participate in highly improvised scenes. But I was always accused by Meisner of approaching improvisation too cerebrally. Sandy said I was being a writer, not an actor.

I found the same problem arising again in my attempts at making up dialogue in my role as the Reverend Russell Horsburg. Director Paul Thompson told me I was merely spouting warmed-over lecture notes from my favourite religious source, Northrop Frye. He was right. But Paul, who knew Horsburg when he was alive, said that he was never a United Church intellectual type. He was more of a YMCA-type summer camp director. So with my attempts at making it up as I went along, I was simply playing the wrong man.

I watched open-mouthed in rehearsal as truly experienced actors in the art of improv like Eric Peterson and David Fox effortlessly entered a world they only knew by implication. But nobody seemed to resent my fumbling attempts. In fact, they made me feel that I was their lunch ticket, the name value, as they managed to jolly me along and make me feel at home.

At home on Pinewood, things weren't so calm. My mother, sweet soul, had succumbed in her later years to what they called arteriosclerosis. Maybe now it would be labelled as Alzheimer's. The result was that she became unable to speak, but the warm light in her eyes and her smile never dimmed when I brought Kelley over for a visit.

My father told me it was time to take Mum to a rest home. The day we took her out of her own house, where she had been since a bride, her strength in resisting removal made me realize she knew what was coming. I was more worried about Dad coping by himself. He had always refused to wear his hearing aid, because he had won the Military Cross in the First

World War for his acute hearing, when he was in the trenches at Cambrai and overheard the Germans planning an attack.

Mum was in the nursing home only briefly and was transferred to a hospital. In retrospect, I regret taking her out of the home she had known since the early 1920s. The staff at the hospital all loved her sunny disposition, even though she was unable to speak. When Dad and I went for a second visit, it was a terrible shock to us to find that she had passed away just before we got there. Dead in her bed, my dad caressed and rocked her like a baby, as his tears flowed for his darling Dutzie.

Not only did I have to arrange for my mother's funeral, but also I had to find a retirement home for my father. I knew he could never stay in our family home without her. Preferably, I must find a place with vets from the First World War. With Mum gone, I knew Dad would go there voluntarily.

I phoned Paul Thompson and told him to get somebody else to play the reverend. I was concerned about the state of mind of my dad, my biggest fan, who had always encouraged me to take a chance on my chosen profession.

Paul went to extraordinary lengths to accommodate me, even to postponing the opening of the play for a week. It was at my dad's insistence that I go on with the play because he wanted to come and see it. I told him it meant I had to leave town, and I wouldn't see him for a month, because there was a four-week tour before we came to Toronto. Dad said he'd wait for that.

After Mum's funeral I went back into rehearsal, but I was filled with misgivings about my father's frail condition. He lasted only a few days in the vets' rest home and ended up in a Scarborough hospital close to where my sister Mary lived. She and her husband Nick were wonderfully attentive to him. They told me that Dad had been diagnosed with both diabetes and cancer.

When I visited him, I was told to bring no sweets of any kind. This was the man with the sweetest tooth I have ever known! Later, just before I left town on tour, I was told that his cancer was inoperable. I went to his hospital room and brought him lots of chocolates and ice cream.

We opened in the town of Blyth. The theatre there has since become successful as the most Canadian of all theatres in its offerings. Its mandate is to offer nothing but homemade fare. The audience was Charlie's kind of people, and at intermission my tea and butter tart were served to me by one of the theatre's volunteers from Wingham, considered by many as the best short story writer in the entire world: Alice Munro.

The Horsburg Scandal went on the next night to Listowel, in a train station that had been turned into a theatre. Everywhere we went we seemed to come in contact with people who had some personal knowledge of the subject of our play. Most of them defended his approach to youth and said he was totally innocent of the charge that he had sex with minors in his youth group. But the charge remained that he didn't discourage his teenage charges from having carnal relations. Some skeptics thought he might indeed be innocent of any physical involvement, but that he might have got his kicks from watching it. The tarnish some put on our hero was voyeurism.

Our next stop was the lovely little Victorian town of Petrolia, seemingly designed by Norman Rockwell. In 1882 it had been the oil capital of North America, and they never let you forget it, with names like Oil Street and Tank Street. The theatre was in the Town Hall, and still is, though it has since been replaced with a new one since the original burned down.

After a stirring reception in Petrolia, we prepared to invade Toronto. After the last performance in Petrolia, I got an urgent call from my sister, who told me Dad was fading fast. A furious three-hour drive to Toronto wasn't enough to get to him in time.

Another Harron funeral. Dad passed away five weeks after my mother. It's exactly the same interval between the deaths of my maternal grandfather and grandmother. It seems these long-married couples have a limited survival after the death of their loved one.

What did Theatre Passe Muraille do? They delayed the Toronto opening of the play so that I could have a week of mourning. I will always be grateful for that theatre's non-materialistic attitude and their respect for my family.

I don't remember much about the Toronto run, except that it seemed to be fairly successful. *Globe and Mail* critic John Fraser (now master of Massey College, following the tenure of Robertson Davies) referred to my character in the play as Horseburger. I'm not sure whether he was kidding. That part of my life seems to me as much a blur as Charlie's ill-fated American book tour. But I retain very warm memories of working with the gifted actors who persisted in their dedication while they hoped for bit parts in TV commercials and American films to finance the dedication to their real calling ... live theatre.

PART V

Good _Morningside_,
1977 to 1982

127: THREE HOURS A DAY

The next call I got was to do an interview on *Morningside*, a three-hour daily radio program that had replaced Peter Gzowski's *This Country in the Morning*. In just three years on the national radio network, Gzowski had replaced the railway as the real link that joins this country from coast to coast, and he sustained it magnificently. Now he was off to try the same thing on television. His former radio show was now called *Morningside* and had been taken over by hosts Harry Brown and Maxine Crook.

Harry was a Newfoundlander who had done everything in radio before moving to Toronto. He was a natural broadcaster, relaxed, charming, and wise. Maxine Crook was a perky, breezy type. When I did the interview with both of them, I found that they interrupted each other so much I often felt left out of the proceedings.

I had a much better time being interviewed by Gzowski on his new nightly television show *Ninety Minutes Live*. The program had become a kind of problem because the producer insisted on dressing Peter up in a suit and tie and styling his hair, instead of his usual rumpled informality. By the time I got on, it had already been satirized by the local Second City, referred to by the mock title *Ninety Minutes Dead*.

Peter wanted to interview not me — not Charlie — but my distaff side, Valerie Rosedale. So I dragged out of mothballs the grey wig, the harlequin glasses, the size-ten slingbacks, and the WIMODAUSIS tweed suit.

Peter was about the best interviewer I have ever been grilled by, and he was at his most charming that night. He arranged to have a little love seat where we could be together with a silver tea service in front of it. As I poured the tea with my legs properly crossed, Gzowski looked at my pantyhose, most of which was now visible, then turned to the live studio audience and said, "I hate to tell you this, people, but I'm actually getting turned on!"

Some months later I heard rumours that Peter was so despondent about the collapse of his TV dream that he would stay on in the studio long after the show, get morbidly drunk, and on one occasion tore up the store-bought clothes that had helped to destroy his image as Canada's down-homey nice guy. I thought if only he could be back in radio, everything would be all right. Instead he returned to where he had come from, to the print medium, wrote guest columns in newspapers and magazines, and went on to write several books. His return to radio would have to wait five years.

I was the one who got the call to do that three-hour morning radio show that he had created. The call came from the current producer of *Morningside*, Krista Meots.

We met at a little restaurant close to the CBC Radio building called The Edge. The lunch must have cost all of $3. Krista had worked her way through the CBC hierarchy until she was in charge of the largest chunk of their radio programming. For some reason she felt I was the right person to host her three-hour daily behemoth. Her light blue eyes sparkled with an earnestness and caring about this country's fate that put my own nationalistic fervour to shame. Television was becoming hopelessly cable-ized, and Canadian content was being sacrificed to sponsor greed. Only government radio was the national dream that could thread its way across our country every day from coast to coast to coast.

For fifteen hours a week I would get the chance to do something that even the prime minister couldn't: talk to the people of this country. But I felt that her confidence in me was unnerving. "I'm an actor, not a journalist. Let me come on the show occasionally as Charlie Farquharson."

She almost bristled. "I'm not interested in Charlie Farquharson, I'm interested in Don Harron! Think about it!" I reminded her that I had never interviewed anyone on the radio before, and in the brief interview she had referred to, I was the guest, not the host.

"Never mind," she said. "You'll get your first chance when you audition for us next week."

It happened. It was a hot, steamy August day and I was cooped up in a tiny room on the third floor of the old CBC building on Jarvis Street. I had done radio shows there many times, but always with a script. Talk about improvisation — the prospect before me made my experience with Theatre Passe Muraille seem minuscule.

I was given an hour to prepare myself for a one-hour version of *Morningside*. I would be interviewing several people, none of whom I would see beforehand, but one I would recognize as a well-known political figure.

Reams of research material were provided. I was left alone to peruse it all. I had a panic attack. I wanted out of that stuffy little room so badly that if I had been on the twelfth floor instead of the second, I honestly think I might have jumped to my demise.

But suddenly I wasn't alone. A bald man came into the room, smiled, and told me he was to be my secret interview. It was political legend Dalton Camp, who had volunteered to assist in an experiment that would never hit the air. He was so affable and full of wonderful small talk that I relaxed.

Morningside, 1977–82.

I remembered the old mantra I used to repeat to myself when I was auditioning for parts on Broadway: "I don't need this job, I don't need this job!" I also recalled that this national morning show for which I was now auditioning had been started eleven years before, not by a public affairs expert, journalist, or politician, but by a fellow actor, Bruno Gerussi.

The red light glowed, and I was on air (audition-wise). Suddenly, I was ad libbing about how strange I felt talking as myself, instead of Charlie. I picked up a copy of the *Toronto Star* and read aloud the headline on the front page. It stated that there had been a provincial election the previous day, and the Ontario Tories had suddenly been reduced to a minority. "And from Buckingham Palace, where John Diefenbaker is visiting Her Majesty the Queen, I'm sure that he is saying to Her: 'It's all the fault of that damn Dalton Camp.'"

Dalton roared with laughter, and we were off on the wings of talk. I can never thank him enough for his generous freebie.

The next item involved a couple of seniors from Ottawa who had their own TV show. They did all the work for me that day, because senior citizens never get a chance to have somebody listening to them.

There was also a young reporter on the line from somewhere in Northern Ontario with a hot story about being on the track of fissionable nuclear waste, dumped somewhere in the northern bush. There was a light interlude when I was expected to be a disc jockey, answering a listener's request of Bing Crosby's old theme song, "Where the Blue of the Night Meets the Gold of the Day."

I made the intro and relaxed, but suddenly the intercom from the control room told me they didn't have that record. This was a definite curveball they were throwing at me, and I was expected to talk my way out of it. Instead, I sang my way out of it, which took an enormous amount of gall, because I can't sing on key, but sometimes I can do passable impersonations. I remembered some of the words, even though I hadn't heard them in twenty years.

I remember a few sketchy details after that, then the hour was up. I was drenched in sweat. Dalton was cool and calm and congratulatory. Three days later I had to meet the top brass of the CBC for lunch, which included a bottle of champagne. I had won the nod by doing one-third of what would be required of me five days a week. I started to get the jitters again, but before I knew it, Krista Meots sent me on my way to Yellowknife to record a series of interviews that would be played during my first week of *Morningside*, which started on Labour Day.

128: THE VERDICT: FIVE YEARS

Let me tell you that I can recall very little of any of the radio interviews I conducted during those five years, 1977–1982. As soon as you finish one radio interview, you have to drive it forcefully out of your mind, so that it will be relatively clear for the next interview.

The show was on air right after the 8:00 a.m. news, because we broadcasted directly to the Maritimes. Then it was carried across the entire country in the various time zones. During my initial, pre-broadcast week in Yellowknife in September 1977, I remember talking to a Belgian priest, Father René Fumoleau. He had spent forty years among the Dogrib Indians, and his vision of hope for the Far North was breathtaking. I then visited the elders of the community of Rae-Edzo outside Yellowknife, who had decided that they would impose a temperance regime on their community. This was after they had succeeded in doing so and were all "dried out." I also remember a conversation with First Nations head George Erasmus.

I have broadcast on the spot from St. John's, Charlottetown, Halifax, Fredericton, Quebec City, Winnipeg, Regina, Edmonton, Calgary, Whitehorse, Victoria, and Vancouver. On the West Coast we found it expedient to record the show the night before, because I could talk sensibly to nobody at five o'clock in the morning.

The one attempt to go live at that ungodly hour was in Vancouver, and I ended up imitating the voice of my guest, Jack Webster, because he failed to show up on time for an early, early morning interview. The Vancouver producer suggested I go on to the next item, but I ignored this advice. Webster owned the B.C. airwaves with his own open-mike show, so I proceeded to introduce the Oatmeal Savage (as Allan Fotheringham has crowned him) as a proud new Canadian (he had been here for years and years) who spoke neither of Canada's official languages.

I loudly imitated his broad Scottish accent, and he (me) then castigated Don Harron for being a pompous pup. I replied by asking him how his non-smoking efforts were coming along. At that point the real Webster himself burst in from the control room, filling the studio with fits of his own laughter, as the interview continued as it should, with both parties shouting at each other.

Morningside followed thirteen minutes of national news, which often broadcasted a dirge of disasters. I was surrounded by a staff of a half-dozen experienced researchers who presented me daily with interview questions and sometimes suggested answers. One of these producers, Gary McKeehan, had played one of the hippie delinquents in my congregation when I played the Reverend Reddick. He and I agreed that the top of the show should have a sketch, a monologue, a mock interview with someone impersonating a political figure, anything topical that could cause a ripple of laughter on a grey morning.

Comedy soon became the key to start the show. The tears could come later. And they did come, believe me. There were a couple of occasions when, against my will, I bawled like a baby. The first was on Remembrance Day, when I read aloud some First World War letters from the trenches. Just thinking about my dad in all that hell was enough to trigger the waterworks. The second occasion was when the bilingual national anthem was booed at a Toronto Blue Jays game, and I recalled how proud my little seven-year-old daughter Kelley was in being able to sing "O Canada" in two languages.

I'm afraid I was entirely shameless in talking about my family, just like Kathy Lee Gifford did to Regis Philbin, I suppose. My wife and sister-in-law made surprise appearances on the show, rigged, behind my back, by the staff. When Kelley turned eight, she interviewed Richard Monette after he played the role of Dracula onstage.

Morningside is the hardest work I have ever done, and that includes field-pitching wheat in Saskatchewan. By the end of the day, I would be drop-dead tired. I don't know how Peter Gzowski managed it for three times as long as I did. He was in the studio every morning at 5:30.

Every Friday morning at 11:00 a.m. when I finished my week, I would get out of my chair, wave to Barbara Frum through the glass partition of the *As It Happens* booth next door, get myself to a CBC typewriter, and start pounding out my other responsibility, those two editorials for CFRB. I think I was the only guy who worked for a public and a private radio station at the same time. I was forbidden to mention Charlie on CBC, and of course private radio was Charlie's domain.

It was easy to pound out those two editorials for another station, because I had fifteen hours of research on the issues of the day, five days a week, to allow me to start typing Farquharson's point of view without hesitation. Here's a sample.

This heer's Charlie "nashnul secure-a-titty" Farquharson tellin yiz that our leeder of yer oppsit posishun, Long John Doofenbeeker wuz airin' hisself out hard by Vancoover this weak, wen them x-raited private-eye masheens found sum sizzers inside his brest pockit.

Fer Big John wen he flys, he's a clipper. Likes to keep noosepaperstuff frum yer daily scar or yer groping male. So he jist snips away like qwite yer cut-up.

But oh my gol, them R.C.S. of M.P.S. they air-lifted them sizzers frum him like they wuz dangeruss weppings, even tho' ther perfeckly blunt. Kinda like Deef wen he gits mad.

And he got mad this time, lemmy tell yiz. Didden Deef beef wen he wuz accuse by them mounty of bean a hi-jacker-offer hoo jist mite stick them nale-clippers in sum pile-its eers and shout: "Take this heer plain tuh Prints Albert!"

Valeda, the wife and farmer sweet-tart, she clames sheel never never take a chants fer to fly agin, becuz she allus carrys in her pirse a spair setta teeth. She sez if the gud lord had ment man fer to rize up and fly offa yer ground.he wud never hav give us Air Canda.

129: THE GOOD BOOK

When I signed on for *Morningside*, I was still tied up with *Hee Haw*. I did the CBC contract with an agent, my manager Paul Simmons. He shocked them by requesting I take all summer off. This was unheard of at the time. The rule was that CBC Radio hosts had a three-week vacation in August, and that was that. I had to be in Nashville at the end of June, and also for a couple of weeks in October.

To my astonishment the CBC agreed to this free-time arrangement. To take care of my October absences I suggested that the very first guest host in my absence be Peter Gzowski, who warned me that I would have to physically pry him away from that microphone on my return. By the time I got back for Halloween, Peter was flying to Edmonton to write a book about the Oiler hockey dynasty.

I had been taught the wonders of the Old Testament in lectures from Northrop Frye. When I started *Olde Charlie Farquharson's Testament* that day, I was determined to avoid making the text deliberately comical. I merely sought to express the words of the King James version the way Charlie would have said them in down-to-earth, wholly reverent terms.

I started where the Bible did:

> *In the big inning. Yer first book of Moeziz, called Jennysez.*
> 1. *At the start, there wasn't a thing. That'd be yer void.*
> 2. *Dark too. Absoloot kayoss. So God decided to do something about it.*
> 3. *He sed: let's hav sum light here. And there was, right off. But there still wern't nuthin to look at.*
> 4. *He kept yer dark too. Now he had two things going fer him, night and day.*
> 5. *He had the one foller the other so's he could keep track. That wuz all in one day's work.*

I numbered the verses according to the King James version, so that when I skipped verses, readers could still check my text with the original.

The book sold like wildfire. I remember several lineups of 200 people waiting to buy the hardcover edition. It got so I rarely had a chance for a proper lunch between book signings, and the process developed in me a hiatal hernia. This made me gulp great quantities of Gaviscon for dessert.

The most satisfaction for me was that it found favour with clergymen and chaplains and is now used as a teaching tool in some Sunday schools in Canada and the United States. It seems that Charlie had toured the States with the wrong book. *Olde Charlie Farquharson's Testament* didn't get scathing reviews from those whom Charlie would call *yer fuddled mentalists*. The *Globe and Mail*, tongue in cheek, compared it to the discovery of the Dead Sea Scrolls.

I didn't write another Charlie book for four years. Because of *Morningside* I didn't have time. Instead of writing a book, I read one, every day of my life for years, usually at night as I fell asleep, or at dinner when I would be so tired, I sometimes fell asleep face down into my pasta. I couldn't face an author across the mike from me without finishing what must have taken him or her many months, perhaps years, to write.

Morningside also brought me requests from every charity going. I did telethons, skate-a-thons, snowmobile races, blood donor drives, bonspiels, even fashion shows. But it wasn't Don Harron they requested. It was Charlie, and very occasionally, Valerie Rosedale. I was still officially connected with the Easter Seals and disabled children, but thanks to *Morningside*, I ended up shilling for contributions to prevent every disease known to man, or woman, or child. With the exception of leprosy.

I made this remark in 1982 when I accepted the North American Volunteer of the Year Award. The following week I got a letter of congratulations from Cardinal Léger in Montreal. Besides congratulating me, he was asking me to do a benefit for his leper colony in Africa.

130: TAKE THE FIFTH

A book that came out in 1980, *Farewell to the Seventies*, was a series of articles on that decade compiled by Anna Porter and Jack Batten's wife Margie.

I was astounded by a statistic in the book of which I was completely unaware. It stated that in 1972, 1974, 1976, and 1978, Charlie Farquharson books had outsold those of both Pierre Berton and Farley Mowat. I phoned Macmillan right away. Even though I still had to deal with the onerous duties of *Morningside*, I figured I could cobble together a book based on Charlie's CFRB twice-weekly editorials.

My fifth book would be entitled *Yer Last Decadent, 1972–1982*. The most important event for most Canadians in 1972 was the hockey victory in Moscow.

This wuz yer world serius of hockey agin them Serviette Roosians. We won this time with Polly Henderson's last minit goal, but if you look at the sadistics since '54 we have played them reds 410 time, and they hav beet us a lot morn we creemed them: 282 to 96 with 32 tie. But in '72 Polly Henders Sun finely beet them with 32 secunds to go. It wuz as Winsome Churchill wunce said: "our finesse tower."

The Olympics came to Montreal in 1976, and maybe they're still paying for it.

That liddle Frenchmare Jeens Dropout wuz deetermin' to put his town on yer map fer all posteerior ages.

Wen he wuz ast wair the munny wuz comin frum, he smile and sed: our Limpricks kin no more loose munny than a fella kin git preggerunt. Looks like he faled his rabbids test on that wun, by a billyun doller defickate! If yiz don't know wat a defickate is, look it up in yer Funken-wagon-all. It's sumthin' ya got witch is less than wat yiz had before, wen yiz had nuthin'.

The return to power of Pierre Trudeau came in 1980, and our first referendum on the separation issue.

Yer Grits wuz back in like Aerial Flinn! I hav spent most of my adultruss yeers under them Grits bean in charge of yer Commonhouse.

In Cuebec, Reamy Leveckyou finely ast yer big French questyun, "To wee or not to wee." Wen the eyes and nose all got counted up, terns out sepration wuz a big no-no.

Most Canajuns breethed a sy of releef and went back to sleep. That's wen Terdo started thinkin 'bout our consti-tutional, witch them Birdish had allways kep in the privy of ther cownsill.

So Terdo went all the ways over to Angland, to thair primed-mistress Marg Snatcher. To present his breefs to her.

Pee-air wanted that old privy paper pastry-ated over to us, so's that yer separendum we jist had, wooden becum yer never-endum.

After 1981 was the Year of the Disabled, 1982 can best be described as the Year of the Unable.

This wuz the yeer our guvmimnt finely admit it didden noe wair it wuz goin'. You take big Marg Lalond, our minster without yer energy to mind our resorces. His anser wuz yer nashnul elegy polissy ... th'ideer wuz to steel oil munny frum Elberta. Not all. Jist a lot.

This got yer west so riled up, no member uv Parlmint west of Thundermug Bay wood stand next to Lalond or Terdo at yer common house yoorinall. Becuz they figgerd if eether of them two seen yuh had a good thing runnin', they wuz morn likely libel to turn round and try fer to nashnalize it!

131: ANNE OF DISABLED

The most meaningful charity benefit in all my years of freebies was the one I did for the so-called disabled children of Easter Seals at Bloorview Children's Hospital.

The idea for this production of *Anne* came from Susan Brower, who had been married to a wrestler, Doug Brower. Sue was able to corral many professional wrestlers to charity events. She asked me to direct the production, but with nightmares of *Riel* still bouncing around in my memory, I declined. Our director, lucky for us, was a willing volunteer, Malcolm Black, who had directed thirty-three musicals on the professional stage. The Bloorview kids loved his constant enthusiasm as well as his teaching skills, and they returned his affection twenty-fold. Also, Fen Watkin, the Charlottetown conductor and piano player divine, gave us a lot of his off-season time to rehearse with the kids.

Don and Reggie Topping, the Easter Seals Timmy in 1980.

This production was for me the crowning effort in the twenty-four years I worked for Whipper Watson and Susan Brower through both Easter Seals and the Hugh Macmillan Centre. This production was to enable the disabled to show how really able they were.

We did the show twice, once at the Ford Centre Music Hall in North York, which has the finest acoustics I've encountered. The performance was a rousing success.

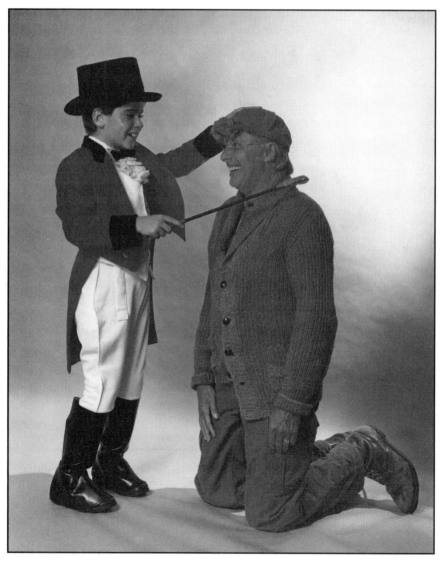

Charlie with Reggie Topping, the 1980 Easter Seals Timmy.

The second time was in the barn at Windreach Farms. These two showings will always be my favourite performances of our Canadian classic. My newest ally in work with the disabled was the owner of Windreach Farm, Sandy Mitchell. He was a millionaire born with cerebral palsy who gave his time and money to allow disabled kids to ride horses in a ring at the farm he built especially for the purpose.

This time our *Anne* was in front of mostly "underprivileged" young people, the beneficiaries of Sandy's special equestrian ring. The barn was an intimate venue that worked well for our Easter Seals cast. But this time we were without our Josie Pye, Michelle Kungle, so I was dragooned into playing the role. I must tell you that I was loudly booed from the audience by one young lady. I'm not sure whether it was my performance or the villainous character I played. I like to think the latter.

PART VI

Farquharson Rules,
1982 to 2012

132: BACK TO THE ISLAND

In May 1982, I performed my last broadcast of *Morningside*. It was my own decision. CBC management was prepared to sign me for another year, but I knew that five years was enough. I also knew that Peter Gzowski, after his television debacle, was waiting in the wings. His voice was so much better suited to the radio than my faint whisper.

Also I had an offer, along with Catherine, to appear in a two-person revue in Prince Edward Island at the Mackenzie Theatre. It was just across Grafton Street from the main venue where *Anne of Green Gables* was about to begin its nineteenth consecutive season.

"The Mac," as it was called, had formerly been a movie theatre. Now it was a kind of nightclub with a big sit-down bar and lots of tables arranged around a small stage that could hold up to half a dozen performers.

First, I had to trot off to Nashville for ten days to fulfill my fourteenth season there. At that time Frank Peppiatt and John Aylesworth, the original Canadian creators of *Hee Haw*, were thinking of selling the show to Bill Gaylord, the son of the man who had created WSM, the most successful country music radio station. He had also spawned the Grand Ole Opry, now a weekly television show. I hoped my Toronto friends wouldn't sell out, but six months later they did. I can't blame them. They were as whacked out physically as I was from *Morningside*.

Norman and Elaine Campbell had found a place on the Island in West Covehead. It looked from the road like Green Gables itself. They had us to dinner the first night, and it convinced Catherine and me that we should find a place on the island, too. There was nothing available in Charlottetown that summer, but we were told that a charming cottage was available some twenty-five minutes away in Stanley Bridge. I had passed through that village on my way to a radio interview in Summerside on my first visit to the Island, in 1965. I remember thinking at the time what an idyllic little village it seemed, and I had hoped to see it again.

The cottage was a Cape Cod–type residence that belonged to a surgeon resident in Summerside. Catherine wanted to buy the place the minute she saw it, but she waited till I expressed the same wish. That took about half an hour. We asked the proprietor of the local store if the cottage might be for sale. Ken McKay, who is also the unofficial mayor of Stanley Bridge, said he thought so.

After buying the cottage, Catherine and I set to work on our summer show. She already had a title for our two-person revue, which involved five characters, including Charlie Farquharson, Valeda Drain Farquharson, and Valerie Rosedale. Catherine's title: *My Many Husbands*.

Don as Donald Smith, Lord Strathcona, in the CBC Television series The National Dream, *1981.*

We did a takeoff on *My Fair Lady* in which Charlie teaches Catherine how to speak pure Parry Sound. Then Catherine reappeared with a monologue as Valeda Drain, and I followed with an appearance as Valerie Rosedale. I remember getting the biggest laugh of that evening for my "in drag" character.

Valerie said she was staying at the Rodd Inn, because of a long acquaintance with owner and proprietor Sally Rodd. In straying in her Rolls-Royce from the Rodd Inn, Valerie got hopelessly lost in rural Prince Edward Island and ended up asking directions from a young couple, obviously embroiled together in the back seat of their Volkswagen. Valerie is shocked by the young man's lengthy, profane response to her innocent request for directions. The line that got the big laugh was Valerie saying to the young man, "How far is your Rodd Inn?" It got just as big a laugh in Muskoka later that autumn when Valerie appeared at the Bigwin Inn, and even bigger in Fort Frances, Ontario, at the Old Log Inn.

We repeated our revue the following summer with new material and a new title, *Take Five*, because we were sponsored by the manufacturer of a multi-flavoured fruit drink with that name. The show was so well attended that in some cases we had to break the fire laws in order to seat overflow people in the balcony next to the man who operated the lights.

133: VALERIE'S TURN

Valerie had been such a hit that I seriously considered she should write my next book. I had already written some Valerie pieces for friend and editor Wayne Grigsby for his collection of satiric columns entitled *A Toronto Lampoon*. As a founding rock of the Granite Club, and an Apostle of Creed's, Valerie was happy to dissect her home bailiwick of Rosedale.

I first began my Rosedale experience as a schoolgirl at dear old Loathsome Hall, which extends itself in an archway over a road called Mount Pleasant. This construction keeps our pedestrian day-girls safe above the roaring traffic. Passing motorists look up at this structure and refer to it as "the bridge of thighs."

How do I happen to have the same surname as the place in which I live? I was christened Valerie Rose Farquharson, in the little Northern Ontario town of Nobel, distantly related, but not distant enough to that lout born further south in Parry Sound.

I was born to a mining man and an undermining woman, and when my mother sent me off to the local school I was regarded by the boys as the Nobel Prize! Which is why my mother sent me off to private school in Toronto. I am proud to be a Loathsome old girl, as opposed to other private institutions like Hav-a-gal college and BSS (far too much of that in Ottawa lately.)

I met my intended, Charles Dale of UCC, Upper Crust College, at a debutante cotillion at Queen's Park. I came out as the Tories were going in.

Meeting Charles, it was a case of like at first sight. We were eventually married in Timothy Eaton Memorial Church, which was erected to the ever-lasting glory of all Eatons, in loving memory of God.

I was very happy to change my name and get the Farquharson out of there. I became a Dale but insisted on keeping my middle name, Rose. So I signed the wedding resister Valerie Rose hyphen Dale. I must confess it took my husband until the third night of our honeymoon to talk me into giving up my hyphen.

Macmillan agreed to a Valerie book, and we decided that Valerie should do a takeoff on Peter Newman's successful Canadian equivalent to *Debrett's Peerage,* his *Guide to the Canadian Establishment.* We decide to call him Peter Parvenu, an Establishment groupie, and he hasn't spoken to me since. We used to talk about Stan Kenton recordings on *Morningside* interviews, because that's the only music Peter can relate to when he's writing his many, many books.

My lack of distaff experience prompted me to enlist the services of my daughter Martha to do the research. She ended up writing more than half the book, because after years of Farquharsonese, I experienced difficulty in expressing myself in proper English. Charlie came aboard to provide intros to the various chapters.

Valry Rosedale and me end up in Canda doo to our common incesters. Wen we start out we wuz all in yer saim boat.

Back home there wernt no lace curtings on her fokes shanty. Her peeple kep the pig in the house like everybuddy elts.

The book's title was *DeBunk's Illustrated Guide to the Canadian Establishment,* although it dealt solely with the Distaffe establishment, a Powder network of rich, successful businesswomen from coast to coast to coast. This included a billionairess who lived in a pleasure dome in the High Arctic.

Martha's research went back to the Chinese Imperial Court of Hwang Dong, way back B.C. to the days when they invented writing as well as gunpowder. The Chinese were writing poems on perfumed paper when we were still eating raw meat in caves. But distaff means spinoff, and Chinese women took up silkworms and spun a major export that started a female Powder Network which extends across time, and across the world. The main route from the Orient to Europe was called the Silk Road.

Valerie Rosedale riding backsaddle with her gillie, Charlie Farquharson.

In Canada it began with wampum. The purple and white beads were imported, no doubt from China, when the first Canadian immigrants made their way across the Bering Strait, thousands of years before Queen Isabella sent Chris on his craft. Evolved from the Chinese abacus, and strung on belts, wampum beads were the Native peoples' first written language, as well as the only solid currency North America has ever had.

Despite all this impressive research, Valerie's book was the first one of mine to end up on the remainder shelf after Christmas. Evidently, my reading public doted on Charlie and was indifferent to me in plain English.

Doing a book tour with Valerie was much more complicated than travels with Charlie. Selling those other books involved stuffing some rags into a bag, but Valerie required grooming, hair-dressing, and loads of makeup.

By the end of the tour, I was also hosting a talk show in Vancouver, which involved both live and pre-taped segments. When I interviewed Valerie, she was heckled from the back of the audience by Charlie Farquharson. Yet all three of them were me. All this technical razzmatazz we did before the age of computer graphics!

My favourite moment of the Valerie press tour came right after that particular show in Vancouver, when I was scheduled to be interviewed by the Oatmeal Savage, Jack Webster. I don't think he knew it would be someone other than me, and never for a moment did he recognize me. When Valerie appeared, he lost all objectivity and flirted outrageously, even hinting that I might like to join him in a post-Christmas retreat in the Hawaiian Islands.

I said, "For God's sake, Jack, it's me, Don Harron!"

He went beet scarlet, then roared with laughter, and we had a splendid, rollicking interview.

134: VANCOUVER COMMUTE

The Don Harron Show was a television talk fest that went coast to coast every weekday at 1:00 p.m. I wasn't the first to host that particular spot. I had been a guest on that same show with two previous hosts, Al Hamel and Alan Thicke.

How did I come to replace these two fellow Canadians? My audience figures on *Morningside* amounted to more than a million listeners, and this interested Arthur Weinthal of CTV. He called me the morning after I hosted the ACTRA Awards. I had done the show under the pain of a flu so rampant that I would lie down backstage between introductions, then get up woozily to talk to presenters like Barbara Frum, Kate Reid, and Pierre Trudeau, who referred to his reign in Ottawa as "Parliament Hill Street Blues."

Don, with Nellie, hosting the ACTRA Awards in 1983. Finally, a woman he can handle!

When Weinthal called me that next morning, I was barely able to speak, so he decided not to try to tape an audition but hired me directly on the spot! This surprised me because his CTV colleagues always referred to him as Doctor No. When I was feeling better, first thing that happened to me was being fitted for what seemed to be about a dozen and a half Pierre Cardin suits, jackets, shirts, and ties.

The main challenge of the job was the travel. I was expected to fly out to Vancouver every other week, tape a dozen one-hour shows in a bit more than half a week, and repeat this process every ten days. This would have been easier if I was able to land all the time in Vancouver. But to construct that airport, they had cleared all the trees, and this lack of vegetation created the conditions for a thick fog.

So half the time my plane had to land in Abbotsford, some three hours away, and I was forced to get on a bus. Which left me very little time before I was onstage with my first guests.

These guests, other than Canadians, mostly came from California. I was delighted to chat with travelling stand-up comedians like Jerry Seinfeld, Steven Wright, George Wallace, and Jay Leno. When Jay came on with his jutting chin, I asked him if he was here for the Brian Mulroney look-alike contest. The audience laughed so much that Jay asked me after the show for permission to use the line when he worked in Canada. Two years later I heard him say it while doing two-hour solo stand-up at Hamilton Place.

I also had the pleasure of interviewing one of my favourite humorists, George Gobel. He and singer k.d. lang sat next to each other, and I asked them if they went to the same barber, since both of them were sporting what we used to call brush cuts. There were brilliant Canadian comedians, too, like John Candy, who seemed able to impersonate anybody and was shy but proud about his attempts to lose weight at the Pritikin Institute.

Howie Mandel did his shtick on the show with a surgical glove. I had the nerve to ask him about his comedy beginnings at William Lyon Mackenzie Collegiate, when he threw a candy bar into the pool that looked like a floating turd. He then shocked his fellow students by gobbling it up with enthusiasm. It seemed as if he wanted revenge after that revealing interview. It came later that night at Punchlines, a Yuk-Yuk-like comedy club in Gastown, where Howie performed a guest spot. When he was heckled, he turned the mike over to his old friend Charlie Farquharson, with a Cheshire cat smile on his face.

Charlie in 1984.

I think I quoted from memory from my Jogfree book about where we were: This heer elder part of Wankoover is call Gasstown, and its divvied up tween yer hippyos and yer Gorjuss Straits. the rest of them animals is in Stanley's Park.

Back to the show itself. I was told by my staff that guests I had probably never heard of were the *real* celebrities on our show, guaranteed to boost the ratings. These were the stars of soap operas, and since I had never found time in my life to watch them at work, before or since, I depended on research to keep me informed, and often goofed terribly. I must say the soapsters were good-natured about my abysmal knowledge of their art.

Valerie Rosedale appeared to plug her book, as well as every other author that season, American, British, and even Canadian. Other memorable guests were Ella Fitzgerald, B.B. King, Paul Simon, Tony Bennett, Joan Rivers, Steve Bochco and the entire cast of *Hill Street Blues*, and Canadian stars such as Lorne Greene, Leslie Nielsen, Raymond Burr, and Michael J. Fox.

I did a topical monologue at the start of every show; many of them were written by Vancouver columnist Eric Nicol.

The Don Harron Show lasted two seasons, with about the same ratings as the two previous hosts. I didn't know it at the time, but there was a feud going on between CTV headquarters in Toronto and BCTV in Vancouver. I was caught in the middle. I wasn't sad to be dropped. I had accumulated enough frequent-flyer points. I was also flight-weary from being a transcontinental commuter often lost in a fog, both off-camera and on.

135: FUN RAISING

During my *Morningside* years, I was asked to perform again at the Stratford Festival. At the time it was impossible for me to take the time off from my radio assignment, so artistic director John Hirsch put me on the board of governors instead. When Hirsch passed away, another John, Neville, took over from Hirsch. I had admired him as an actor from my earliest days in London in the 1950s.

Catherine and I did a stage benefit to welcome Neville when he took over Halifax's Neptune Theatre. We lost this great actor to Alzheimer's a few years back, and he passed away quietly in Toronto in 2011. When he was at the helm in Stratford, he succeeded in putting the festival in the black, based on his own unerring decisions.

That's why I felt quite powerless at these bored meetings, pardon the pun. I felt that, like many boards of directors, we were there as window dressing for the decisions of the artistic director and his staff. My function was to act as a kind of court jester, making the others laugh between seconding motions.

But then I was put on a fundraising committee. At last I felt I could contribute. I thought we might raise a good bit of money for classical culture among the millionaires on Bay Street, if we could invite them to dinner and then have them sit back and watch other millionaires dressed up in Elizabethan costumes make happy fools of themselves.

We arranged the first of these at the Inn on the Park in Toronto, and the ticket price for dinner and show was $250. They sold without any effort, because my cast list included Conrad and Shirley Black, George Cohon, Julian Porter, Allan Slaight, Marlene Del Zotto, Ann Latham, and Patty Ann Burns. All non-enties in theatre annals but right up there on the Toronto Stock Exchange.

The evening was called *Much Ado About Something!* and the plot was very simple, based on Shakespeare's *Julius Caesar* with Conrad Black in the title role. The rest of the cast couldn't wait to stick their knives into him. But as in life, my script had the plot reversed, and while the blood flows for everyone else, Conrad is the only one who ends up in the black.

We rehearsed at the Black mansion on Toronto's Bridle Path. George Cohon would bring along goodies from his kitchen at McDonald's. One day he brought something new, Chicken McNuggets. I must confess I ate more than my share, in fact, most of them.

Conrad Black seemed to consider himself a bit of an expert on the Bard. When it comes to subjects like Napoleon and how many troops he had at Austerlitz, he certainly is. But he questioned a quote I gave one day from *Hamlet*. Not the words themselves, but the number of the scene in which they appeared.

Was it Act One, Scene One, as he claimed, or was it Act One, Scene Two, as I had quoted? Conrad stopped our rehearsal, went straight to his library and returned with a copy of *Hamlet*. He looked the quote up in front of me, his eyes widened in surprise, and he reluctantly said, "You're right." I must confess it was a lucky guess.

As a fundraiser, it was a big success, and the Stratford board wanted me to do another one as soon as possible. Ed Mirvish had made the Royal Alexandra Theatre available for free. I wanted to build the next fundraiser around Hal Jackman, who had proved to be an actor of professional calibre. He was a fellow graduate from Victoria College and had been active in Hart House productions. I wanted him to play Henry V in a takeoff on the then-current premier of Ontario, David Peterson.

I wrote the script that summer in Prince Edward Island and brought it back to Toronto on the day of the provincial election. As I sat and watched the election returns, my mouth dropped open and I tore up my script. David Peterson was out and Bob Rae of the New Democratic Party was in. Bob is another natural actor, so I decided to cast him as Hamlet. My next casting problem was where to fit Jackman, who had since become Ontario's lieutenant governor.

I called this fundraiser *The Shaming of the True* because the cast would be full of politicians. Hal came to me with a bee in his bonnet. He was trying to persuade the Ontario government to fund a new opera house. Instead of the heroic actor he was originally to portray, he wanted to appear as an ordinary citizen, begging the Ontario government for financial assistance. He asked me if he could borrow Charlie Farquharson's cap and sweater (by this time it had more holes than sweater).

So when Hal approached Bob (Hamlet) Rae sitting moodily on his throne, Hal, dressed in my Farquharson rags, got down on one knee and kissed the Socialist Rae's hand while he begged for alms for an opera house. This was the picture that got in all the papers.

Other members of the cast included Mike Harris, newly appointed leader of the Tory minority in the Queen's Park legislature. He seemed very grateful to be included when I cast him as Mark Antony. His lines were somewhat prescient of the future of what Charlie Farquharson later called *Mike Harse's uncommonly nonsensical resolutions*. Mike stood up proudly onstage at the Royal Alex as he proclaimed: "Friends, Ontarians, countrymen, don't lend me your arrears! I come not to tax, but to free you! "

Mel Lastman begged to be in the cast so he could get to wear an Elizabethan costume. But he also begged that he be given only one line, so we decked him out in orange tights and a purple bodice with puffed sleeves, and had him push a rack of cheap dresses from one side on the stage to the other, as he proclaimed his one and only line: "The Quality of Mirvish is not strained."

The third and final fundraiser I did for Stratford involved its own actors, past and present, as performers on the Royal Alex stage. For that reason I titled the show *Loitering Within Tent*. The main pageant itself was entitled *The Wars of Neuroses* and detailed a history of Canada from the Rebellion of 1837 to the most recent separation referendum of 1982.

Richard Monette was persuaded to come out of temporary acting retirement to play Pierre Trudeau, and Eric Donkin was superb as Her Majesty.

Chris Plummer topped all this off by appearing as master separatist Jacques Parizeau. He addressed something that was in the newspapers every day at that time, the Charlottetown Conference, where the Meech would inherit the earth.

136: BACK TO THE BOOKS

During the mid-1980s, Don Harron sort of disappeared from my work schedule. It was all Charlie Farquharson. I had signed up with a Vancouver talent agency, Speaker's Spotlight, and they kept Charlie pretty busy from coast to coast making custom-made speeches at luncheons and banquets for all kinds of commercial establishments.

I also started on another Charlie book, *Cum Buy the Farm*, which was published in 1987, a satirical look at the vanishing Canadian, our "small farmer." It had the same number of pages as my first book, *Histry of Canda*, and the cover had the same handwritten, homemade look.

No cow is too sacred for Charlie to flay as he casts his gimlet eye over the current political scene, whether it's Runny Ragin suffering from his Aides in yer Wide House, or Briney Bullrooney and his burrycraps up yer Ottawa. Along the way Marg Snatcher, Kernel Gidaffy, and Mikey Gorbachump are toppled by Charlie's irreverent wit. Finally, the only solution is for him to run for Pee Em on behalf of the FU party (Farmers Unite, of coarse).

Don in a dog collar again in Bill C. Davis's Mass Appeal, *Georgetown, Prince Edward Island, 1986.*

I was asked to help open a new cultural centre in North Bay, Ontario, where I would share the bill with Maureen Forrester and that superb a cappella group, The Nylons. When I got off the plane, I was suddenly seized by violent pains in my abdomen, so I stopped off on the way to the rehearsal and got some Pepto-Bismol in a drugstore. It didn't help. The pains got worse when I arrived at the new theatre and lay groaning in agony across the table in my dressing room.

I skipped the dress rehearsal. Somehow I dressed myself in my Charlie rags and made my painful way down to the stage in time to go on. There was a full house, and I got my first laugh after about twenty-five seconds. At that moment my pain disappeared and didn't come back until after I took my bows and left the stage. Immediately, I was again doubled up in agony, and to the stage manager I produced a strangled "Is there a doctor in the house?"

Before I could protest, I was bundled, Charlie rags and all, into somebody's private car and taken to St. Joseph's Hospital. There was no wait in emergency, thank God. I was put immediately into a bed in the ICU, mostly because the other wards were full. Somebody sedated me.

I woke the next morning remembering that I was supposed to be in Saskatoon the following day for a truckers' convention luncheon. I immediately phoned Catherine, told her where I was, and more importantly, where my Saskatoon Charlie speech was. Ever the trouper, Catherine grabbed Valeda's cloche hat and roll-top sweater and work boots and took off for Saskatchewan that night.

I spent the next ten days in that hospital bed while they tried to figure out what was wrong with me. The local paper, the *North Bay Nugget*, interviewed me, and the report went across Canada that I had collapsed onstage. The information kept getting more garbled the farther it went. A Winnipeg paper implied that I might have AIDS! I didn't know what I had, and neither did the hospital. The one bright spot in my existence was daily visits from *For Better or for Worse* cartoonist Lynn Johnston.

Heavily sedated, I tried to write some of my new book by hand, instead of on my trusty typewriter, which was absent. I also talked to Lynn about her doing some illustrations for a musical version of *Olde Charlie Farquharson's Testament*. To my amazement she agreed to do it, and when the time came a couple of years later, she was there for us. She probably gave up a fortune to do our project, but she said it thrilled her to be drawing Biblical characters wearing non-contemporary clothes.

After ten days the hospital gave up trying to figure what was wrong with me and sent me down to an internist at Mount Sinai, who was extremely thorough. I got X-rays, ultrasound, a barium enema (ugh!), and something called an ERCP, a tiny camera that goes down your throat and takes pictures as it peers at all your innards.

The results of all tests were negative, but the pain persisted, so they gave me some sedative pills. Back home, under duress, I tried to write more of the new book. My editor, Anne Holloway, called me up and told me not to bother. She said the stuff I was turning out was so full of bile that I had better wait until somebody found a cure for what ailed me.

That somebody was a woman in Penetanguishene named Isobel Fournier, an iridologist. That's a person who looks in your eyes and tells you what's wrong with you. Sounds ridiculous, but my granddaughter Zoe had been taken to Isobel by her mother (Martha) as a last desperate act after being told by a GP that her little girl had a virus.

My first-born Martha, always fascinated by herbology, heard about Isobel from friends who had consulted with her. Little Zoe was driven north post-haste. Isobel took one look in her eyes and told Martha that her daughter had no virus, but her insides were crawling with pinworms.

When I went there, Isobel took one look in my eye and told me I had gallstones. I told her that was impossible, and mentioned the camera at Mount Sinai that had explored all of my insides. Didn't impress her one bit. She gave me a diet to follow for a month, ending up with a douchebag full of boiling water and laced with garlic. This was to act as a self-administered enema to get those stones rolling out of me and into the toilet bowl.

Don as Hugh Hefner with Martin Short, 1986, in the episode "All's Well That Ends Strange" from the TV series Really Weird Tales.

From left: Catherine McKinnon, Charlie, Bill Carr, and Diane Leah in the musical Olde Charlie Farquharson's Testament, *1988.*

It worked. I wish I had collected those thirty to forty little boulders in that toilet bowl and mailed them to that internist at Mount Sinai. I still bow to orthodox medicine, mind you, but I also make a sweeping curtsy to homeopathy.

I resumed writing *Cum Buy the Farm*, which has the most variegated subject matter of any of my books: *aggrybizness, faminism, sy-ents friction, unpoplar meccanix, athaletticle supports, free traids, nukuler waists, relijun on yer nees, and up to yer arts in culcher.*

Stone-free now, I put that book to bed and turned to the musical version of *Olde Charlie's Testament*, co-written with Frank Peppiatt. The musical had been commissioned by Richard Ouzounian, director of Neptune Theatre in Halifax. He wanted it to appear onstage in the spring of 1988. We wrote the show, not around Charlie, but his son Orville. This part was played by Halifax comic Bill Carr, a former minister of the gospel, now well out of his pulpit and turned to stand-up comedy.

After Halifax came a tour of Nova Scotia, reminiscent of *Spring Thaw*, then we spent the whole summer doing it in a blue tent on Prince Edward Island. We were in the middle of a forest, next door to a motel that complained if our show ran past 10:00 p.m. The complaints stopped when the motel became host to a motorcycle gang that caroused till three in the morning.

In the fall of 1988 we did a month in Gananoque and another month at the Gryphon Theatre in Barrie. Then for another month at the Martha Cohen Theatre in Calgary. We finished the tour in British Columbia at a theatre in Richmond. Across the country we had received pleasant, sometimes puzzled reviews, but Richmond was where our show was severely criticized. It was by a *Vancouver Sun* food columnist, Lloyd Dykk, who was saddled with attending theatre, as well.

Years earlier he had panned our *Anne of Green Gables* when it appeared at the Queen Elizabeth Theatre. He now pronounced our current show as "the worst thing I have ever seen." The second night, during the curtain call, I made a speech to the audience: "I don't know Dykk, but I don't think he does, either. I intend to come back here next year to this same theatre with a brand-new show, to see if it comes up to the standards he mentions in his review."

Charlie in Olde Charlie Farquharson's Testament, *1988.*

137: WORKING FOR GOD, THEN MAMMON

After our tour, Bill Carr had moved from Halifax to Toronto with his brood and was now living in the house in which I was born.

First, Bill and I (I mean, Charlie, of course) did a film about trees and forest fires for what the Farquharson fellow called *yer Minstry of Nacheral Racehorses*. Then we did two short films for the United Church of Canada. One involved Charlie lying in a coffin for the entire film while Bill berated him for not making a will. Naturally, the film was entitled *Where There's a Will*.

Another film assignment was for the McLaughlin Planetarium, next door to the Royal Ontario Museum. We were contracted to film a show that would run in the planetarium daily from May to September. It was *Charlie Farquharson's Unyverse*, a look at the Milky Way and a tour of the solar system. Charlie was taken for a forty-minute ride through the cosmos, narrated by Bill Carr. This included all nine planets of our solar system, with stops at observatories in Chile and Hawaii, culminating finally in a chance for Charlie to ride a comet bareback. This was the planetarium's first use of video, with five newly installed projectors to give a 3- or even 4-D effect.

Oh my gol, jist lookit that Milky Way! Jist madge-in naiming a big rang-dang-doo like that after a choclit bar!! You take that hole constellapation ... Mars jist seams to be rustin' away, Joopiter is nuthin' but a big beechball, and Slattern with all them rings around it, jist looks like our bathtub! And I heer ther's jist billyums of Comit runnin' round, but not wun uv them fit to cleen the sink.

The research I had to do for this show got me really interested in the world of astronomy, and the unveiling of all these billions of new worlds. I felt emboldened enough to balance *Old Charlie Farquharson's Testament* with a book on science: *Charlie Farquharson's Unyverse*. The cover shows Charlie riding a comet and looking as if he's utterly spaced-out.

Charlie discusses the fastest unit of time, the nanosecond. (He says that it's the time it takes the car behind you to start honking his horn after the light turns green.) He also deals with quarks (*two pints*) *new-tree-nose* (*things peeples in Sudbury thinks of as deep, on a Sardy nite*) *yer Big Crunch* (*tuther end of yer Big Bang*), *and parrlell unyverses* (*uther opshuns*).

Canada reached its one-and-a-quarter centennial in 1992. I don't know what the technical term for that is. I know that in 2017 we'll be 150 years old, and that's called the sesquicentennial, and if the country is still around in 2067 that'll be our bicentennial. Charlie calls them both *yer sexycentenniel and yer bisextennial.*

Anyhoo, I decided that it was a good excuse to have another go at the history of Canada. I must add that my original publisher has been a good sport about the whole thing and sent me a letter declaring *Charlie Farquharson's Histry of Canada* now out of print, and granting me full ownership and all rights to my original manuscript.

So I began *Charlie Farquharson's Histry of Canda, Ree-Vised and More Expansive.* For illustrations I decided to use contemporary political cartoons. Most of them came from the pen of the great Duncan Macpherson, editorial cartoonist for the *Toronto Star* for many, many years.

The stuff in between covers the same events as before, but with different malapropisms and updates. Charlie's last chapter, "*Yer EpicLog*" is about the same phenomena that is still ruling the world ... globalization. A sample:

Now I ask yiz, wat's the gud of bean glow-bally competitiv, wen weer on our way to becumming jist the same as that thurd of yer wurld that's livin' blow yer slub-systems levels?

All them Yanks wants frum the resta our hole continence is cheep laber frum Maxyco and cheep nacheral reesorces frum us.

And all bizness peeples seams to be intrusted in is wat they call "yer bottoms line." That meens we hafta put our bottoms on the line wen it cums to deeling with big bizness.

138: CHARLIE'S A BROAD

Charlie Farquharson's Unyverse, published in 1992, was a science book and got me the best reviews of any of my previous twelve published efforts. Even the most negative review had a sense of humour about it, and was a kind of backhanded compliment: "*Charlie's Unyverse: A Brief History of Time*, as though it were written by a total imbecile. Amusing, and yes, informative."

But the book didn't sell very well. My kind of fan wasn't all that interested in science. The planetarium staff loved it and thought it should be placed on the high school curriculum, like the *Histry* and the *Jogfree*. Both of those books were on the recommended list for students, and I understand they're both still referred to in classrooms across the province. But *Charlie Farquharson's Unyverse* never got the nod.

Charlie's a Broad is a travel book, not a medical text on sex change, although the cover might give rise to some speculation on that subject. It shows Charlie on a street in Athens, with the Acropolis in the background, and our Parry Sound farmer is wearing the Greek national costume, the same one worn by those high-stepping guards that delight the tourists. But perched on top of his head is still Norman Jewison's father's old hat.

Figuring that most of my fans weren't teenagers but people my own age headed for the retirement of their by-now white heads, I decided to travel the world, with Catherine (Valeda) taking the photographs. Most of the tourists we encountered every summer on Prince Edward Island were seniors bringing along their grandkids for a first view of *Anne of Green Gables*. When we went on cruises, we found the same phenomenon. We took the Princess Lines Love Boat cruise from Singapore to Hong Kong in 1996, and we were the youngest couple onboard.

Don on the Queen of the Desert at the Pyramids, 1994.

I love cruises, because you can't be reached by phone and you can eat six times a day. On one Mediterranean cruise I gained six pounds in one week. To get material for the book, Catherine and I had to pay our own way around most of the world, hoping that book sales would cover it. But I had to find a reason for poverty-stricken Charlie and his Valeda to be able to travel to all those places. The answer: Lotto 649.

It wuz yer Blotto Sex Afore Nine wat dun it. Valeda, the wife and farmer swee-tart, had bin playin' them nummers games sints time in memorium. Not me. I figger tryna be a farmer nowadaze is enuff uv a gambol.

This pass Chrismuss the wife put wun of them blottery tickits in my well-hung-up-stockin, allongside a ornj and a bitta cole. It wuz the oney gift she cud think of fer the man hoo has everything. But munny.

Call it bug-inners luck, but this vergin click his furst go-round. Wen them balls hit on ther bottoms with my rite nummers, the wife pert neer had apple-plexy. Them liddle sfeers cum up with alla my nummers sep wun.

Catherine and I took the *Queen Elizabeth 2* from New York, thrilled with being onboard the Queen of the Seas. We waved as we passed Bedloe's Island and the Statue of Liberty.

Leenin over yer rales we cud see that big lady-statchel on Bedclose I-land, lookin' like a crotch between Annmurry and Marg Snatcher.

For Charlie landing on Irish soil was special.

We tuck a liddle fairy to git onshore. Ire-land look like a green pool table with smooth lumps. This is yer land of my ruts, ware us Farquharsons start out fer Canda wen our taters tern black.

All them tooryists gittin off with us, tocked about "gittin' Barney-stoned." Valeda snift, and sed she hadden cum all this way jist to git too famillyer with sum drug-taken dinashore offa the TV.

Valeda was anxious to get to Paris for some shopping, but first they had to get through England, not to mention all the sights of Towering London.

Us Farquharsons wuz of two minds. I wanted to go by yer Buckin' Hams Paliss to see yer Queens Calvary droppin ther horseballs on prade, but Valeda wuz determin to git to Ma-dam Two-sods. Gess hoo wun! She ast fer inflammation frum ther doreman and he wooden anser her, so she went away mad. Laider she found out he wuz jist maid of whacks!

Insted, we go to yer Ree-gint Park Zoo, watchin' a buncha chimp pansys havin' hy tee with eech uther.

The Farquharsons figured the best way to see all of Paris at once was to get to the top of the Eiffel Tower.

Valeda and me went all the waze up yer Eyefull Tower, ware thair's a restrunt, so we et pidgin pye wile thair fetherd rellativs sqwat and wotched us.

Having seen all of Paris at one meal, they headed for Holland and the sin city of Amsterdam, then through Switzerland to Venice and on to Rome.

We got thru Swishyland to Venus, witch is a kind of watertown, cant park yer car nowares. Now heddin' fer that interminal sitty, wair we seen thair roaming Colossal-semen. Thats wair us Christyuns use to be et up by yer Lion's club.

And now for the big jump, from Greece across the Mediterranean to Egypt.

Floo to Kyro, and hedded strait fer them peer-amids. Not to men-shun yer Sfinks, with its enema-mattick smile. Didden hav to wocka mile fer a camel! Valeeda now determin to join a peer-amid club back home.

We tuck anuther flite way down Abby Simpel way, fer to see them monsturd statutes of thair big fairos.

Then we tuck a boat backup yer niles. And it got us rite between yer tempels, in Ded Vally, hard by Luck Sore.

They both wanted to get back on their own "harth," so they took flight to London and booked a four-hour flight to New York on the Concorde.

They tole us this heer plain wood git us home even afore we got started. That's a exagregation, but not by much.

It's a funny lookin' burd, yer Conkerd, looks like kind of a long skinny siegull with a droopy nose, like it's peckin' fer durt.

Charlie still had a lot of curiosity about the rest of the world he hadn't seen yet.

We still got left haffa that Blotto Sex Afore Nine in mewchilly agreeabull funds. And with it, sumday Valeda and me plans to sircumsize yer uther haff of this old wirld.

It didn't work out that way. Catherine and I spent half of 1997 going to all those places in the Far East. The other half she was up to her eyeballs in opening a new restaurant on Prince Edward Island.

In the fall of that season, *Charlie's a Broad* came out in paperback. But the call never came from my publisher to do a sequel. I ended up pretty broke but happy that I had seen the world. But when it came to writing it up, you don't know the half of it. As Charlie says to Valeda when he stops his car all of a sudden, *Them's the brakes.*

139: ON THE ROAD. AGAIN!

Two game-changing things happened to Catherine and me in 1997. The first was the opening of the Confederation Bridge linking New Brunswick to Prince Edward Island.

Second, the opening of Catherine's own restaurant. That McKinnon girl always wanted to open one ever since I've known her. Even in Toronto she would bite into a hamburger and think that she could make one more palatable.

The news of a bridge to the mainland decided it. Next door to our place in Stanley Bridge was a private home, quite large, with a lot of land connected to it, enough for a parking lot. She cashed in some shares and bought it.

With only a copy of David Foot's book *Boom, Bust and Echo* and the hiring of a super-talented builder, Catherine also bought a little store that some people think was the one that Lucy Maud Montgomery had in mind when she wrote about Matthew Cuthbert going all the way to the village of Carmody to buy a dress with puffed sleeves for orphan Anne.

Catherine named the little tourist venue the Carmody Gift Emporium because that was the original name of the village of Stanley Bridge. She moved the shop just across the driveway from the restaurant.

During that initial season, we got the call to join a troop show that fall heading for the Middle East. Actually, we started in Cyprus and went on to El Gorah, a United Nations base in Egypt on the Red Sea, then on to Israel and the Golan Heights. Then over to Italy, where we would be flown to Yugoslavia to entertain Canadian troops in Croatia and Bosnia, probably during Christmas week.

There were eighteen people in our concert party in 1998, commanded by Bob Spencer, who had created a company called Bandworld, and this would be his twenty-second overseas trip for the Department of National Defence. We had a civilian technical crew of three, two Army chaperones, and nine entertainers. This included a country rock band, Coda the West, and three female singers. We were also supposed to have singer George

Fox onboard because Coda the West was his band, but he was too busy back in Alberta.

Instead we had an elderly comedian dressed in well-used but ill-fitting clothes: Charlie Farquharson.

Before we left, we did a preview in Toronto of the whole show in our own Limelight Theatre. Oh, have I never mentioned that? My business manager, Paul Simmons, talked Dave Broadfoot and I into taking over a Toronto dinner theatre. Not for long. We were too busy doing other things. Our best evening was when the Boss Brass turned up. Dave and I both did evenings of our own, but now it's a thriving murder mystery theatre under new management.

Next day we flew out of Toronto on KLM bound for Athens with a two-hour stopover in Amsterdam, then from Athens to Egypt.

We left for Egypt in a Herk, sitting in those basket-weave seats that make you feel as if you're lying in a hammock standing up! Our destination, El Gorah, is in the Sinai Desert, formerly an Israeli fighter base but ceded to Egypt by Henry Kissinger after the Camp David Accords.

The Sinai is divided into four strips from the Mediterranean to the Red Sea with checkpoints on the ground, each manned by U.N. soldiers who had thirty days on and thirty days off. They made the most wonderful audience, because among the military in this part of the world, boredom is a growth industry.

El Gorah is an outpost of the Multinational Force and Observers, assigned to monitor the Camp David Accord. They call themselves Pumpkins, because they wear orange berets instead of the U.N. blue helmets. There are only a few Canadians among the 2,000 troops.

We were there for two nights. While Catherine and the musicians rehearsed, I did a one-man Charlie show for the Canadians and the regimental dog, Patches. I wore my *Spring Thaw* unification uniform and did Canadian political jokes that would mean nothing the next night in front of *alla them forners.*

Do yiz mind that noo Federast leeder we now got in Canda? Pressed-tone Mannering? He's yer lockinjaw frum outa the west and haz riz up as a alturdnative to our present encumbrance, Blarney Bullroney.

I mind that Brine quite a bit. He's the wun with the moose jaw and a voice like a bumbled-bee in a jug.

But this new fella, Mannering, has got a voice like a cat cot in a car door!

I herd he had start up a moovemint call yer Refarm Party, and I wuz gonna vote fer him, but it's yer reform. That's a case of a differnt vowel movemint.

He arrove in Ottawa frum Elberter with a copy of yer ten command-mints and a hunnerd doller bill. So far he has broke neether.

Next night we did our full show in front of 1,100 CMFO troops. They went wild for the blend of country, rock, Maritime folk songs, and Christmas music.

Many recognized me as the news guy from *Hee Haw* and roared when Charlie confused El Gorah with the vice-president of the United States. They roared even more when I referred to their outfit, the CMOC, as "the Club Med for Officers."

140: THE OTHER SIDE

El Gorah is only eight miles from the Israeli border. Some of the kitchen staff drive to Israel every day for fresh water. The contrast between the two countries is stark. We drove through Egyptian territory with its new speed bumps and old land mines, often covered over with drifting sand.

On the way to the border with Israel, we were driven past bleak dwellings, none of them finished, nor likely to be, because the Egyptian government put a tax on completed residences. We saw new ones going up, and the excavation was being done with mere shovels. The Bedouin are now settled in one place as small farmers, so we never saw a camel. Goats and donkeys were tended by women as they gathered brush for firewood. We gave them the thumbs-up, until we were warned that this gesture is a sign for the need of water. And waving back is considered an insult.

The difference at the Israeli border was immediate. By contrast with Egypt's desert-like landscape, Israel is one huge greenhouse, open to the sky. We drove by but avoided the Gaza Strip and headed for almost the other end of this tiny country, past Tel Aviv and Nazareth, stopping at Tiberius on the Sea of Galilee.

Next morning we headed up to the Golan Heights by way of the River Jordan, where we stopped for souvenirs. There were samples for sale of

Jordan water, which has the same green colour as Palmolive detergent. At one point, on the way up Mount Hermon, we could see the borders of Jordan, Syria, and Lebanon.

Our Canadian welcome at the Golan Heights couldn't be warmer. The food in the mess was more modest than El Gorah but also more homey and familiar. We were to do three shows here, one each day, which necessitated going back to the hotel in Tiberius every night.

The first show, a disaster happened. The generator blew just as Catherine was singing "Farewell to Nova Scotia." It didn't faze her one bit. Without lights, or a mike, she finished the number a cappella, with some extra bel canto voice projection.

But the rest of the show was in danger of folding up. None of the instruments in the band were acoustic. When Catherine came offstage, she immediately went back on again to sing, a cappella again, some Christmas songs from her new CD. Then she introduced Charlie, and I came on and told every Farquharson joke I could remember. Our group was so hungry for Canadian entertainment, they didn't seem to care that I was shouting at them in the dark. The important thing is I was telling Canadians about themselves, and the laughter was reward enough.

The technical crew stayed behind and must have worked all night, because for the matinee the next day, all power was restored and the show went off smoothly. This time troops from other countries were involved as audience, with diplomatic and U.N. guests from Tel Aviv and Jerusalem.

The third show we gave that night was what the troops were supposed to get on the first night, and it was the best performance of the three. A lot of the same people came to see all three shows. It was explained to me that after waging peace on the Golan Heights, there's bugger all else to do.

Next day our bus took us to the Sheraton Tel Aviv. Here the weather is like Miami beach, and the traffic is like Toronto. We were given the day off plus an Israeli guide to take us on to Jerusalem and Bethlehem.

It was a few days before Christmas, and according to the guide in Bethlehem, there are usually long lineups to get in everywhere. For some reason we were able to walk into the Church of the Nativity right away.

With tourists from other nations, we stood in front of what was considered the location of the manger where Christ was born. We were all given lighted tapers.

Suddenly, in the silence, Catherine started to sing "O Holy Night." She was soon joined by others, of other nationalities, but all of them humming the carol in what seemed to me to be perfect harmony. The effect was sublime. When the song ended, everyone dispersed without a word. The squabbles in that same holy place during Christmas week in 2011 between the Armenian and the Greek Orthodox priesthoods are a sad commentary on tolerance in our present day.

Back in Jerusalem, we ate falafel, shopped for souvenirs, and then were taken to the Church of the Holy Sepulchre, where Christ is believed to have been taken down from the Cross. And then … I give you the exact words of our Israeli guide: "Then they schlepped Him over to the tomb."

The tomb was in another part of the church, and our guide showed us its probable location. She was by now more aware of our Christian sensibilities when she said: "And this is the place where He … uh … He probably awoke."

141: LOOKING FOR SOME ACTION

Next morning our bus took us to Ben Gurion Airport to fly to Ancona on the Adriatic coast of Italy, the base from which U.N. planes take off for relief missions to both Bosnia and Rwanda.

Our Bosnian itinerary was to fly to Split in Croatia on Christmas Eve, then travel on land to Visoko, the Canadian headquarters, on Christmas Day, there to do nine shows for the Canadian troops until the second of January.

There was a holdup. Fifty-five Canadian servicemen were being held hostage by the Serbs. The rumour was that Jimmy Carter was flying to Visoko to arrange a Christmas truce.

In Ancona, Sarajevo is only an hour by air, but the DND confirmed it was too dangerous for us to travel to either Croatia or Bosnia. Instead we were scheduled to fly back to Canada the next day, the day before Christmas Eve. That night, in our hotel in Senigallia we did an impromptu show in the lounge for the Canadian aircrews just back from Rwanda.

The next morning, as.we taxied for takeoff, some birds on the tarmac threatened to fly into the engines. The big Hercules screeched to a halt as the pilot aborted the takeoff, blowing out three tires. If no tires were available, we would be stuck there until Boxing Day. The tires had to come from Ottawa by way of Milan.

Next morning, Canadian Forces Base announced that Jimmy Carter had arranged a four-month ceasefire in Bosnia. Our bunch was thinking that we could have, and should have, been there. But we got word of another Christmas miracle. Ottawa had sent the tires from Trenton, and Milan was airlifting them on to us. We could take off for Canada as early as that afternoon!

Our takeoff was delayed for a wonderful reason. Another Hercules was to leave first, with a load of toys for the children of Sarajevo. The pilot wore a Santa Claus hat.

We got onboard the second Hercules. It was practically empty, except for us and a couple of uniformed personnel who were counting on getting home for Christmas Eve. Catherine broke out some champagne and we toasted our pilot, who appeared wearing a red plastic nose.

A Canadian Forces bus took us to Toronto. The Harrons arrived home just before midnight on Christmas Eve. I headed right for bed, but Catherine stayed up to stuff a turkey that she ordered from our butcher by long-distance phone from Italy just before we took off.

On our "twelve days pre-Christmas" tour we had set foot in six countries — seven, including our own.

142: THE YEAR OF OLD FARTS

In 1999, I was appointed by the federal government as Canada's representative to the United Nations Year of Older Persons. Even though I had been cultivating senility since the age of twenty-eight (when I first created Charlie Farquharson), I had never thought of myself as an old fart. My companion in this venture was Flora MacDonald, Canada's first female foreign minister. John Diefenbaker often referred to his cabinet colleague as "the finest woman to walk the streets of Kingston." She told me this herself with a wry smile.

Flora was named after the lover of Bonnie Prince Charlie, who escaped from Scotland to France in 1745. I remember visiting a seniors' home in Manitoba and being introduced to a woman who had just celebrated her hundredth birthday. She was anxiously awaiting that letter of congratulation from the queen. I said, "You have to meet Flora MacDonald. I'll get her. She's in the next room."

The centenarian's eyes opened wide as she said, "Fegs and havers! Is she still alive!"

The thing that depressed me about those geriatric rest homes was the awful silence. I was told that occasionally someone would come and play piano for the residents and they would have a singalong, but usually the place was a soundless vale of emptiness. I suggested that a sound system should be playing the big band music of the 1930s that these octogenarians would remember. I was told that this could be done. I trust it was.

Catherine was firmly set in place at our home in Stanley Bridge. Although her restaurant, Catherine McKinnon's Spot O'Tea, wasn't due to open its third year of operation until the tourist season began in June, she was already, in midwinter, planning a major extension to her solo enterprise.

We had appeared together in venues all over the island ever since our successful run at the "Mack" in Charlottetown. Now Catherine wanted to open her own summer theatre. There was room enough on the lot without intruding on the parking spaces. The contractor had a suggestion about seating for an audience. He knew of some church pews that would be ideal. The theatre itself was to be in the shape of a Nissen hut, one of those round

A hundred-year-old lady meets Flora MacDonald, 1999.

structures used for storage during the Second World War. A stage large enough for two performers and a pianist would be in front of those pews.

By the time I got back from the U.N. tour, the new theatre was up and ready for its first season, featuring the five-performer team of Catherine McKinnon, Valeda Drain, Don Harron, Valerie Rosedale, and Charlie Farquharson. Catherine even ordered a big sign to hang over the front of the building announcing that the star of *Hee Haw* was performing inside!

Speaking of vigorous athletics, my Year of the Old Fart ended in May 1999 with a six-mile walk in Calgary. Flora was fearfully fit, because she skates up and down the Rideau Canal in Ottawa. In summer she climbs mountains in places like Tibet. On this six-mile walk I was panting like a spavined horse as I dragged along after her.

The first summer season of Catherine's barn theatre was a big success. On opening night Norman and Elaine Campbell came for supper and stayed for the show. It was a good thing that I contributed by appearing in the barn that summer, because I felt less than useless when it came to the restaurant. Catherine worked so hard seven days a week, and she would come to our cottage straight from the restaurant to freshen up for our show in a state of near-exhaustion. I felt so guilty to be sunbathing as she arrived from her long day supervising the kitchen and singing "Happy Birthday" for celebrating guests at any of three meals.

Don and Flora MacDonald, 1999, the United Nations Year of Older Persons cross-Canada tour.

I tried to help running to the various local vendors who provided supplies for the restaurant. Otherwise, I didn't have much to complain about. The thirty-fifth season of *Anne* was going well in Charlottetown.

In 1997 there appeared a very personal book, *The Correspondence of Northrop Frye and Helen Kemp, 1932–1939*. It was published in two volumes by an American, Robert Denham, a Frye devotee. It was a delight to read about him gushing over a delightful witty woman I had actually met and enjoyed conversing at dinner with, even more than with that distinguished scholar, her husband!

The books were published by University of Toronto Press, and when I told them I wanted to do a stage presentation of the letters, they suggested I contact the editor. Bob Denham seemed to know who I was and was most congenial about me adapting the letters. I ended up presenting a reading of the letters onstage at Hart House Theatre as a three-night benefit for my alma mater, Victoria College. It was a non-profit exercise for me, but a labour of love.

The success of those staged readings set me thinking in the summer of 1999. Both the Fryes had passed on, but in perusing their letters, I was made aware of the fact that Helen had never bothered to read her husband's first great success, *Fearful Symmetry*, based on the life and work of William Blake. When I contacted his secretary at Victoria College, she confessed that she, too, had never read a line of it. It turns out that this masterpiece, unlike Frye's other books, was devoured by scholars, but was largely unread by his adoring general public.

That settled it for me. For the rest of the summer of 1999, I would start preparing a condensed version of *Fearful Symmetry* that everyone could enjoy. And occasionally take out the garbage for the restaurant.

143: SENCHRY TWENNY-WUN. YER OH OHS!

The above chapter title is how Charlie Farquharson describes the first ten years of our new century, as he deals with "yer furst decadence of yer Millenema."

As the new century dawned, I was still busy trying to cut a genius down to size. When I finished, I sent about half to Northrop Frye's number one fan in all the world, Gloria Vizinczey, naturally with some trepidation. She loved it. I finished and also sent it to Bob Denham. He expressed similar enthusiasm and sent it on to University of Toronto Press.

They turned it down. They said I was a non-academic source with no particular accreditation for the job at hand. They also suggested that it was a slightly frivolous project. The week they turned me down was the very same moment they brought forth from their publishing loins Madonna's book *Sex*. Go figure.

Catherine left early for Prince Edward Island to get her restaurant ready. I was offered a challenging part in the theatre at Petrolia. It was the role that George C. Scott was playing when he passed away suddenly, that of a quick-tempered blind English professor. He is confined to a hospital bed, to his intense frustration, and all the staff who have to look after him. It was a delightful role in a comic play with the most improbable title, *Wrong Turn at Lungfish*. It refers to the mistake aquatic animals made when they decided to leave the ocean to try to exist on land, leading, eventually, to the existence of human beings. I had a ball playing blind with my eyes wide open, pretending not to see.

Don with Lieutenant Governor Hilary Weston at the Order of Ontario ceremony, 2000.

During my run at Petrolia, I received an offer to appear in August in Toronto at Roy Thomson Hall in the "Royal Bank Seniors Jubilee." Since I was already booked in the Barn for the summer, I was to perform early in the week, when I would fly in from the Island. I turned up for the show and found a wonderfully warm atmosphere. There was a three-hour show starting at 2:00 p.m. and beginning at 11:00 a.m. music and dancing in the huge lobby until 12:30, when the audience would take their seats in the main auditorium.

Onstage was the great Salvation Army Band, playing old songs to the delight of the crowd. Thornhill Scottish Highland Dancers and the Scarborough Showstoppers were among many groups of dancers, most of whom were well over sixty and could still manage to kick themselves in the forehead.

I was one of a passel of comics. Backstage, I was waiting to go on as Charlie Farquharson when I noticed a performer who looked familiar. She was our separatist weather girl from *Shh! It's the News*. I hadn't seen her since then and that was twenty-six years before. Her name at the time was Claudette Farquhar (what a coincidence). She told me she had remarried an RCMP officer, Michael Gareau, but they were now divorced and she was living in Toronto. She was trying to restart her singing career, despite the fact that she hadn't warbled a note in twenty-five years!

No wonder she was nervous as she prepared to go onstage and sing in front of 2,500 people. Claudette was much relieved that she hadn't been booed off the stage, and we chatted as we waited for the finale. She told me she would love to do comedy as well as music and wondered if there was any old material from our *Shh! It's the News* series that she could borrow ... particularly parody songs.

I managed to get her some material before I took off for the Island. I was glad to be able to help someone who had been a part of my more inventive past. I remembered how shy she was and how she never dared to come out of her dressing room unless she was called upon to perform. Her bravery moved me and I was determined to help in any way I could.

Most people remember exactly where they were when the first of those two Manhattan skyscrapers was hit by that plane piloted by terrorists. I was in our bedroom at Stanley Bridge, cueing Catherine on her lines in a new musical.

The television set was silent, so we were totally unaware until we got a long-distance call from my daughter Kelley in Toronto. She told us to turn on the set and watch history being made. My first reaction was to cancel our performance in the barn that night. This was no time or place to wax satirical about politics.

I stayed in Prince Edward Island that summer until the opening night of the musical, *Menopositive*. Catherine had developed into a highly professional character actress, playing her part with an authentic-sounding Hungarian accent, and singing gloriously, of course. The reception was so successful that it became the only show in our barn in the summer of 2002.

144: FLAT ON MY O-HIPS

The second year of the new millennium was a very trying one for my health. First of all, I was diagnosed with prostate cancer, and the recommendation was that I undergo radiation therapy as soon as possible. This meant turning up at the hospital five days a week for eight weeks. The treatments themselves didn't bother me, but if I'd known what the result would be six months later, I might have questioned the project. They never told me that the enemy of an enlarged prostate is testosterone ... the thing that makes men manly! These radiation treatments were headed toward making me impotent! I found this out in 2003. They don't tell you this when you accept radiation. All the cancer doctors regard testosterone as the enemy of a cure. They wanted mine to dwindle to nothing, and with it went my chance of orgasm. I was outraged when I found out. But later, in a more reflective moment, I remembered something when I first read Plato's *The Republic* at university. On the first page there was an ancient Athenian named Critias. He expresses relief now that he has entered that bereft and benign non-orgasmic state of sexual impotence. I thought he was crazy at the time, but now I can bring myself to agree with him.

The exciting thing about 2002 was the invitation from the Shiki organization to come to Tokyo, all expenses paid. Catherine and I would be present at the opening performance of *Akage no An*. Shiki had been doing regular performances every other year or so since 1976, but this was the first time I was available.

The night before we were to fly to Tokyo I had a Farquharson gig at a golf club about eighty miles west of Toronto. I had some trouble getting there on time, because my right leg kept doing strange things. When I was called upon to perform at the banquet, I found I couldn't stand up without being very unsteady on my feet. The sponsors were very understanding, placed a chair in front of the microphone, and that night Charlie became a sit-down comic.

The journey back home wasn't as easy. Several times I had to stop on the road and raise my right leg up on the dashboard. When I finally got home, Catherine was fast asleep, so I crawled into bed, my leg throbbing. We had to get to the airport early that morning to go to Tokyo, but one look at my leg and Catherine headed the car, with me in it, toward Emergency. They put me directly into a hospital bed while Catherine phoned the Campbells to tell them the Harrons weren't coming to Tokyo. I felt so sorry for Catherine; this was her one chance to go back to Japan since 1970. They soon gave me a shot of penicillin and sent me home with instructions not to get out of bed.

Catherine was my nurse, administering penicillin on a regular basis. To reward her patience with such a grumpy patient, I booked a trip to Cuba the following spring. Meanwhile, plans were made for the summer of 2002. Catherine would play in her production of *Menopositive*, all summer in Prince Edward Island, which left me out of the barn schedule for that season. Instead, I got an offer to appear in the Royal Bank Seniors Jubilee.

Catherine and I got ready for Cuba. I was fine until the plane got above 40,000 feet, then my leg started acting up. I had to be helped off the plane into a wheelchair, and never once saw the beach the whole time I was there. Instead, I made regular visits to a Cuban clinic for shots of penicillin to cure the blood clots in my leg. Catherine did what she could to enjoy herself by herself on the beach, but the whole expedition was kind of a disaster.

Before she left for the Island we had a couple of engagements in Ontario. I remember one show at Blyth. As farm people they were particularly receptive to Charlie. I wondered if Catherine was miffed at my success, because after the show I drove home alone, while she got a ride with her piano player. When I questioned her about this, she simply said she merely wanted to gossip with a female friend rather than drive in silence with me.

It made for a slightly strained atmosphere when she took off for the Island to star in the all-female *Menopositive*. At Roy Thomson Hall I resumed contact with Claudette Gareau when we both appeared in another Seniors Jubilee. On the Island, *Anne* was finishing up its thirty-eighth season, and *Menopositive* was finishing its second season in the barn. I felt strangely distant from both. My thoughts were at Roy Thomson Hall.

145: THE BIG BREAK-UP, 2003

Things were getting pretty shaky on the marital front. At some point I became emotionally involved with Claudette Gareau. When Catherine discovered evidence of this, she put her foot down and said that relationship had to be over and done with. I agreed reluctantly and cut off all contact.

When Catherine was invited to present *Menopositive* at my old stomping ground, Petrolia, in the spring of 2003, I must confess that, in her absence, I resumed contact with Claudette in Toronto. One night I wasn't at our Annex home — I was in Claudette's apartment. Catherine phoned home, quite late, and was profoundly upset to find no one there. She told me angrily, "You don't know how to be in a marriage!" I agreed, and she suggested that since we were both booked in the same place all summer, that we use it as a testing ground for our marital bonds.

I must admit that I was entirely to blame for this disruption in our thirty-four-year marriage. I am not proud of my behaviour during the events of that fateful summer of 2003.

It was obvious to Catherine that things weren't working out. Instead of sharing a bedroom with her, I slept downstairs. One night I was startled out of a sound sleep by a glass of water thrown on me. It was Catherine, enraged, ordering me out of my own house. Nine years later she explained her action over a cup of tea in her kitchen by recalling something I had said to her about Claudette that enraged her. At the time I boasted that "We talked!" implying that Catherine and I lacked that kind of communication.

I hastily dressed and fled in the middle of the night, ending up at the Red Sands Motel about twenty miles away. That was to be my home for the rest of the summer.

Since I was only obligated to appear in the barn three nights a week, I decided to spend the rest of my time in Toronto. Not in our house, but in Claudette's apartment, where we planned a life together and purchased rings to bind us together. The second time I flew to Toronto I replaced my wedding ring with the new friendship ring. I was about to put my wedding ring away when it was seized from behind by a furious Catherine. I didn't know that she was on the same flight!

"Usual" wasn't the word I would use to describe the atmosphere in that dressing room for the last two weeks of our barn engagement. I was determined to fulfill my contract, and I must say that Catherine was completely professional in her appearances with me onstage, including the curtain calls.

Closing night was unbearably tense, but it never showed in either of us onstage. Professionals to the end, we took our bows hand in hand, then both signed autographs for members of the audience. Catherine suddenly announced that she was selling her restaurant and barn, and what the audience was witnessing was the final occasion in this building. I went backstage, didn't change from Charlie, just grabbed the rest of my costumes. The last look I had from Catherine was one of an unbearable sadness.

At the Red Sands, when I phoned Claudette, she said that she was flying to Moncton early that morning so that we could begin our life together as soon as possible. That was nine years ago, the year I turned eighty, and I must admit that I have never changed my mind about that fateful decision.

This has been the hardest chapter to write. I can now say that Catherine and I have resumed a relationship that allows us to share a cup of tea at her house in Toronto, which has been a great relief to our daughter Kelley.

146: SEE YOU IN COURT

I was now living in Claudette's apartment in East York. The first offer of a job in my new existence came from Ross Petty, to appear in his annual pantomime at the Elgin Theatre. Onward, ever onward. The pantomime that year was *Cinderella*, and I was to play her father. I never knew that Cinderella had a father, not one who was alive and on this earth at the same time. I knew that she had acquired one bitch of a stepmother, and two "sisty uglers." Ross wanted Charlie Farquharson to be in his show, so I was yoked to his own character; he played the bitchy stepmother in an unlikely marriage of inconvenience.

He also wanted me to play another role in this production, that of the king, the father to Prince Charming. I asked Ross how he wanted the king to be played. He replied he didn't really care. The king was a minor character as far as the major ones, Cinderella, the prince, and the wicked stepmother were concerned. So I decided to make the king so well-bred that he was actually unintelligible when he spoke, which was only during one scene during the show. But a fun scene it turned out to be.

Playing Charlie to a largely youthful audience was a new experience and a delightful one. The kids really seemed to dig Charlie's laugh, and I heard one or two attempts at reproducing it. So I decided, while I was onstage, to conduct a class in "How to Laugh Like Charlie." It wasn't long before I had a considerable portion of the audience barking like seals.

Meantime, offstage, arrangements were being made for Catherine and me to appear in court for a separation agreement. My manager, Paul Simmons, got me a lawyer, who had served well on behalf of one of his other clients. I turned out in the end to be a major disappointment for her, because when Catherine sold her restaurant and barn, I didn't feel I deserved any part of it.

Charlie shows his political allegiance.

I didn't see Catherine again until we met face to face in court that spring. She had just returned from a tour with Gordie Tapp that included stops in Florida and Palm Springs. I asked her if she did any comedy material on that tour. She broke into a smile and said she took along some parody lyrics from *Shh! It's the News*. She said that she got more laughs than my *Hee Haw* co-star.

The pleasantries ceased as soon as the lawyers arrived, and we got down to business. When it came to divvying up the real estate, I asked nothing from the sale of the restaurant and barn, and I used the proceeds from the Barrie house to pay off my line of credit. My lawyer was absolutely disgusted and stood morosely in the background while Catherine brought forth munchies from her kitchen and chilled champagne to close the deal. Outside the building, we shook hands and shared a brief embrace. Catherine retrieved her car from the parking garage, and I took the subway home to Claudette.

147: LIFE GOES ON EXCEPT FOR MY BEST FRIEND

Wayne Burnett of the Roy Thomson Hall Seniors Galas came to Claudette and me with the offer of a fall tour of Northwestern Ontario centres in a show to be called *Don Harron and Friends*.

Before this all happened, I got the shock of a lifetime. Elaine Campbell called to tell me that Norman was ill and not likely to recover. Claudette and I visited Norman and Elaine, not in a hospital but in some kind of Christian Science retreat. He didn't look all that different from the last time I saw him, but he must have been aware of what was going to happen. When I saw him, he had a copy of our second musical, *Private Turvey's War*, in his hands. All he said to me was "Get it on!" Then we talked about Prince Edward Island and another season of *Anne*, but I had the horrible feeling that I would never see my friend again. I never did.

I wasn't aware of any funeral, but there was a memorial service at the Inn on the Park a couple of months later. It was conducted by Robin Campbell, the eldest of their five children. At one point the lights in the ceiling started to flicker. Robin looked up and said, "It's Dad! He's criticizing the lighting for today's service!" The rest of the Campbell kids maintained the same lightness of spirit when they talked about their father.

I kept my promise to Norm Campbell about *Turvey* ... in a way. I arranged with playwright Jim Betts to get a one-night presentation of our second musical. It was at the Todmorden Mills Theatre, just off Pottery Road in Toronto.

There we assembled a top-flight cast of willing volunteers to pay homage to our beloved composer. In the cast was Norman and Elaine's second daughter, Justine Campbell, playing the part of Turvey's girlfriend. Turvey himself was played by Kyle Blair, a gifted young performer who was just finishing the season at Stratford. Turvey's more worldly companion, Mac, was played by Adam Brazier.

The music was provided by David Warrack, who also played the part of the Colonel at the Court Martial. I repeated my original role in the first production, the Chaplain, who gives a double entendre speech to the troops about chastity: "I expect you chaps on leave to avoid loose women, and get a hold of yourselves!"

After our presentation, I called Elaine Campbell to the stage. She told the audience that Charlottetown would be offering a scholarship in her late husband's name to a promising performer.

I haven't forgotten my best friend's last request. The golden anniversary of *Anne of Green Gables* will take place (I trust) in 2014. I am going to try to make that a Norman and Elaine Campbell year, with a production on the Charlottetown mainstage of our Emily Carr musical, *The Wonder of It All*. Also, to keep that last promise to my best friend, I would like to see in the MacKenzie Theatre a stripped-down presentation, with five men and five women, doubling and tripling their roles, of *Private Turvey's War*. Keep your fingers crossed.

148: IN THE GREAT NORTH COUNTRY

The time eventually came to think about that tour of Northern Ontario, which was still called *Don Harron and Friends*. The friends were all performers from the Roy Thomson Hall Royal Bank Jubilees, the most successful show for senior audiences in all of North America.

The most interesting addition to the cast for me was Claudette. She performed strictly as a singer, but her warmth and humour came through to the audience, and I could see her potential in the future as a comedic sidekick. She opened her set with a song that Noël Coward had written back in 1927, "It Doesn't Matter How Old You Are," and she made all the seniors in our audiences glad they came.

I was there as Charlie, of course, but I also did some talking as Don, with reminiscences about my career.

The month after we did the final Roy Thomson Hall show we flew to Thunder Bay. The very next day we played a high school in Geraldton, and the day after that, Atikokan, with warm receptions from both tour officials and the audiences.

For this tour I developed a skit in which I played a brand-new character, Hamish Moultrie Farquharson. He was a second cousin of Charlie's, straight from the village of Echelfechan, near Auchtermuchtie in dear old Scotland. In the sketch he proceeds to teach Claudette how to play golf, even though he was never a golfer himself, but a curler. "It's verra simple, curling. Ya bend down to get your rocks off, and somebody breaks wind in front of ye."

Mavor Moore gets an honorary degree in 2004. Don is just there to congratulate him!

The general Northern Ontario attitude was one of friendliness and a kind of gratitude for including them in our show plans. We played mostly in high schools, but also a couple of community auditoriums. Sioux Lookout was a big tourist centre for American fishermen, and in late September their private planes still filled the local marina.

At the end of the show I had to fly to Toronto for a one-night gig. My topic at the Royal York was the environment. Remember when that was in fashion? Here's part of what Charlie had to say on the subject.

Do yiz mind the time, neons ago, wen yer old muther's naycher turn down her thermalstats fer a cuppla senchrys, and with all that friggid-ity mange to extink a lotta indangerd speecies. Like yer dinashore.

That icy age left our erth pritty well uninhibited fer quite sum time, after having had the hots fer so menny yeers. And them hots is now back, big time.

Don with Claudette Gareau at his surprise eightieth birthday party at Windreach Farms, 2004.

Mine jew, thair's sum as thinks this glowball warm-in is nuthin' but a gud thing fer all us canajuns. Becuz we has spent menny a winter with nuthin to expeck but chilly- blains frum a sex-fut snowdrift. Warmin' up five degrease cud let our crops grow mebby all yeer round. But wut about the resta yer wirld. Is we cuntent to let them thurd-wurlders fry in ther own jooces? I hopes not!

I rejoined the tour for our final concert in Thunder Bay. Wayne Burnett had been with us all the way; out of the Roy Thomson Hall concerts he had formed an organization called COSAP, the Canadian Organization of Senior Artists and Performers. Wayne told me that COSAP had managed to get a Southern Ontario tour starting just after New Year's!

149: DOWN SOUTH (AS FAR AS WINDSOR)

There was no snow north of Thunder Bay for our fall tour, but that's because it was too early in the season. Our southern tour started off 2005, including St. Catharines, Sarnia, Chatham, Markham, Kitchener, North Bay, and Parry Sound.

The Chisholms
in Stratford B&B
Sunday,
February 13, 2005

Claudette and her greatest admirer, 2005.

In North Bay we played in the same Capitol Centre where I had held off the pain of gallstones until Charlie's last joke onstage. My rescuing angel from that time, Lynn Johnston, came back to the theatre to welcome us.

On to Charlie Farquharson country. The venue in Parry Sound was the newly christened Stockley Centre for the Performing Arts, which Charlie delighted in renaming *Yer Bobby Orrhouse of Ill-Fame*.

Charlie performs at the Canadian National Exhibition in Toronto, 2005.

All in all, from audience reception, Claudette and I were encouraged to consider a future touring Ontario with a revue-type show. After our one-night stand of *Turvey*, we joined forces with the musical director of that effort, David Warrack. David had plenty of his own material, original songs performed by him, which we included.

Our show was now called *Charlie Farquharson and Them Udders*. One of them "udders" was to be Valerie Rosedale. Claudette took on the task of revising and re-creating gentler, less harsh makeup for me than had been suggested by some makeup "expert" in the past. Here's a sample of what Valerie had to say.

I do wish the Canadian mint had more respect for our beloved monarch. I think that our new $2 coin is an absolute disgrace to the realm. It looks like a slug with a washer. It's being called a "double loonie." It has the queen in front with a bear behind.

The Americans seem to have more respect for royalty. I think it was entirely fitting that their composer, Mr. Gershwin, created an entire opera in Her Majesty's honour. It's called Corgis and Bess.

150: JIGGERY-POKERY AT THE PIGGERY

On our way down to Prince Edward Island in the summer of 2006, we stopped off in Quebec's Eastern Townships to see Claudette's sister Monique in Magog. Monique suggested we might like to see some English theatre while we were in the Eastern Townships. Close by in North Hatley there was a summer theatre, The Piggery. It had been a pig barn originally but was now a charming tourist trap for rabid summer theatregoers.

Before the show I was greeted by Hugh Macdonald, the manager of The Piggery. After the show, Hugh mentioned the fact that Dave Broadfoot had recently done a benefit for his theatre. I said, "This lady beside me and I do a revue, which we could do for you here." Hugh grabbed Monique by both hands until I told him that the performer I referred to was her sister Claudette. We agreed to come back the following summer and do two benefit performances for The Piggery.

The following summer, as promised, Claudette and I appeared at The Piggery. Hamish Moultrie Farquharson, Valerie Rosedale, and the inevitable Charlie were present. Claudette did a medley of French songs. Anecdotes from Don, then more songs, this time in English. Then we did a sketch in which Hamish teaches a French-Canadian woman how to play golf.

During the intermission, Claudette was instrumental in helping me transform into Valerie Rosedale.

I'm Mrs. Charles Rosedale. That's Missus, not Mizz. I think that Mizz always sounds like a wasp in heat. And I can assure you that I for one, have never been a wasp in heat. I loathe the term wasp: White Anti-Sexual Protestant.

I am feminine, but I'm NOT a feminist. I refuse to believe that women should be the equal of men, because I feel it would be a dreadful step down for all of our sex. I don't believe a woman's place is in the home, I believe a woman's place is in the country club. I would far rather be teed off on the back nine, than well-hung over a kitchen stove.

Thank you, Valerie. We ended the evening with a sketch where Charlie tries to order a meal in a Montreal restaurant, speaking entirely in his fractured French.

We have happy memories of the Piggery. Although we did the show for free, Hugh Macdonald allowed me to sell my books at the end. I've never had a better response than on those two nights. Considering the theatre had just over a hundred seats, more than $900 was collected by the volunteers.

As Charlie gave his otto-graft, he felt compelled to admit: *Them Cue-beckers shore deepreeshiates littercher.*

151: RUMPELFORSKIN

In June 2007, I did something a bit wacky. I decided to join Toronto's Fringe Festival with a play of the above title. I played the title role. It wasn't a large part — I didn't come in till more than halfway through. I think the impetus for me was to fill a gap from 1959, when I was in *The Tenth Man* and the only straight man to a bunch of elderly Jewish comedians. So I took a well-known fairy tale and wrenched it to fit my aspiration to play an old Jewish gentleman. I also wanted to do a gentle ribbing of several topical subjects: the Royal Family, Conrad Black, and the prospect of us soon filling our gas tanks with corn in the name of ethanol.

I solicited help from friends who were willing to work for practically nothing. Ticket price ten bucks to be divvied up equally between all of us. Ken MacDougall, who we had met and worked with at the Stirling Festival Theatre, offered to direct. His pals, Cyrus Lane and Joanne O'Sullivan, played the queen (it's the Fringe) and the miller's daughter who did the spin job.

Her father Horst, whose language I wrote as a takeoff on the polysyllabic verbiage of Conrad Black, was played by Patrick Masurkovitch, who had wowed us at Stage West in Norm Foster's *The Last Resort*. The clown prince was Christian Potenza, who was a client of my manager and therefore could easily be browbeaten into taking a rest from all those commercials he did. My witch, Gloria Valentine, had been with us before at Roy Thomson Hall, and we knew what she could do with an audience. My beloved Claudette doubled as producer and French maid, dusting till ready.

Coming back from the Island in September, Claudette and I were guests at the wedding of Cyrus and Joanne (Our "queen" and princess).

152: REMEMBER 2008?

It's memorable for me as the year marking the centennial of the publication of the novel *Anne of Green Gables*. It's memorable for the rest of the world, I am sure, as the year when the financial foundations of banking fell apart with a ferocity not seen since 1929.

It wasn't my idea to next write a book in English. Not after thirty-six years of success with Charlie Farquharson's broken Canadian efforts. Because of the hundred-year celebration of Lucy Maud's novel, Bill Hushion suggested I write about my forty-two years with the musical.

He introduced me to my possible publisher, Bill Bellefontaine, and we signed a contract. Soon after publication of *Anne of Green Gables, the Musical, 101 Things You Didn't Know*, he went bankrupt. I received all my royalties in the form of several boxes of my new book. I sold them personally, starting with the launch of the book at the Confederation Centre of the Arts in Charlottetown, just prior the opening performance, sometimes wearing Anne's trademark hat and braids. I rather liked doing this. Even when there were times when I hardly sold any, it gave me a chance to come in contact with the audiences visiting our show.

In case you never got a chance to read it, Chapter 100 is entitled "Anne of Saskatchewan." It all started with a request from the director of the Station Art Theatre in a place called Rosthern, one hour north of Saskatoon, to perform our complete musical with a cast of six actors. "Certainly not!" was my reply, followed by an additional comment: "Maybe seven?"

My book went to press before we had a chance to see this unusual venture, and when it opened in midsummer 2008, Claudette and I flew to Saskatoon to see it for ourselves. The theatre is located in the old railway station. A lot of the credit goes to the brilliant director Stephen Heatley. Claudette knew him, since she had taken his drama classes in Edmonton, and she also saw him play Matthew in a local presentation. The musical score was played by a solo piano, and it fulfilled the assignment completely. Altogether a triumph.

All of it was treated with a reverence that was lovely to watch. In a little place of 1,600 residents, they had sold out performances for a month. Mind you, the chairs were a little on the hard side, so Claudette and I offered to do a fundraiser for the theatre. We had brought the costumes from Prince Edward Island and Claudette's recorded music, and did a two-hour show. We raised $5,000, and a generous person matched that amount. They were able to get decent seating for the following season.

Norman and Elaine and I have seen so many variations of our musical, including a summer camp production where Matthew was all of fourteen years of age, a private school production that had a black Marilla, and a school production in Calgary that had over 200 people onstage for the picnic scene. When I asked why the Cecil B. DeMille–type crowd, the director said, "The rest of the kids in the school knew their parents were coming and wanted to be seen onstage in it."

153: THE STEPMOTHER SYNDROME

The one family relationship I have yet to solve is the daughter-stepmother relationship. For at least fifty years I have had to witness friction between my daughters and the new woman in my life.

The stepmother syndrome really flared up between my oldest daughter, Martha, and Catherine, wife number three. Martha got kicked out but got her revenge by ignoring Catherine the best way she could, though there is a mention of her in *A Parent Contradiction*, the biography of me that Martha published in 1988.

I suppose Marilla is technically speaking, not a stepmother to Anne Shirley, but their relationship took a long time to warm up, as opposed to the instant reaction of a Matthew. The Marilla-Anne situation was something that Lucy Maud had actually resolved by the end of the book, something that Norman and I never seemed to get around to.

Three years ago the Charlottetown Festival took *Anne* back to Toronto at the Elgin Theatre. It had been there several times before, including Barbara Hamilton's last performance as Marilla. The box office was kept busy throughout the run, despite the fact that the Toronto critics, all of whom had reviewed our show before, were decidedly cool this time.

I went back to the novel itself. At the end, in the last few pages, I found that our original author had provided our musical with what was missing. It's always been hard for a modern audience to believe at the end of the evening that Anne would give up a four-year scholarship to stay home with Marilla on the farm. But the reasons are all there in the novel. Because Marilla's constant headaches from eyestrain, she is in danger of going stone blind. At the same time, the dire financial situation of the Cuthberts is revealed. The local bank, in which they had invested all their savings, went under. Matthew knew about the danger in advance but was determined to be loyal to his old friend, the bank owner.

That's why Anne makes arrangements to lease the land at Green Gables to Diana Barry's father. She is also prepared to be a seeing-eye for Marilla while she stays home and studies the same subjects she would have taken at college. Stepmother syndrome solved.

It has arisen again between Claudette and Kelley, my youngest daughter. But Kelley says it should really be called the Don Harron Syndrome, because it's caused by me. Claudette agrees and says it is because I have always sided with my daughters.

But this time it may be resolved. Unknown to me, Claudette, after the loss of her sister at the end of November 2011, sent Kelley a Christmas card in the middle of December, hoping they could establish a friendlier relationship. Unfortunately, Kelley's neighbour in L.A. received it by mistake and only gave it to her several weeks later.

By that time, Claudette had given up ever hearing from her. But a heartfelt email arrived from Kelley the day the card was delivered. That simple gesture caused a flood of tears and much release of tension and stress. Maybe, between the two of them, they will solve the Don Harron Syndrome.

154: CITIZEN CANE

Charlie Farquharson has never been much of a success doing commercials. As Don Harron, I did have one successful commercial that ran for four years. It was for an insurance firm, Norwich Union, and I did the commercial while fussing about with food in the kitchen. Nobody seemed to be fooled by it, either, at least from the reactions of people who knew me.

But the commercial itself dealt with something universal ... death. The gist of the message was to encourage people to organize their own funeral and pay for it in advance. Which is why Doctor Death (me) was surprised to hear from somebody in Vancouver named Dorothy Sitek, asking me to be the spokesperson for an Anti-Stigma Campaign.

The stigma was against seniors who demonstrated their seniority by carrying a cane. Both Don and Charlie were asked to be part of a nationwide mobility program that involved television commercials, plus actual visits to seniors centres across this country. Charlie and Don were about to become the poster boys for senility.

Dorothy was a very pleasant lady. Together, with Charlie and me, we organized a series of cross-country presentations, ending up with a brace of TV commercials, derived from those experiences. Here's a sample:

> Hi there! I'm Don Harron, been in the business of making people laugh since I was ten years old, drawing cartoons with chalk on a big sheet of paper. Now, seventy-plus years later, as a senile delinquent, I make cartoons with my mouth. (CHARLIE LAUGH)

I'm still quite physically active, besides jumping to con-
clusions and pushing my luck. I can still touch my knees.
I'm getting used to lifting heavy weights, which, in my case,
is just the act of getting out of bed and standing up.

The one thing I'm afraid of is falling flat on my face.
I suppose, as a comedian, I should be used to that. I must
admit that falling down gets easier as I get older, it's the
getting up again that gets harder. That's what really gets
my back up, if you know what I mean. The Law of Gravity
must have been passed in Ontario years ago, but breaking
it by falling down doesn't have to mean the end of life as
we know it.

This was followed by a geriatrics expert, Dr. Janice Lessard, who showed
us all how to make sure we stayed ... steady as you go!

Then I talked about the habit that Flora MacDonald got me into at the
end of our United Nations Year of Older Persons — swimming.

155: "ANNE" IN JAPAN

I waited thirty-four years to get to see our musical in Tokyo. It was well
worth the wait.

Our Charlottetown Festival production had already toured Japan four
times, sometimes with the full company and sometimes with only four
performers. The latter were goodwill tours, like the one in 1989 for the
Keio department store chain. A quartet of actors did an hour-long version
of our musical, four times a day.

In 1991 the full festival company went on what is called the Non-no
tour. Not because they had a bad time, but because that was the name of
the company sponsor!

Our full Charlottetown production opened on Canada Day before a
glittering audience. It included members of Japan's Royal Family, various
embassy officials, including Ambassador Ken Taylor, and representatives
of the Canadian government. Dozens and dozens of bouquets were thrown
onto the stage at the end, followed by fourteen curtain calls. The next day

Ambassador Taylor held a reception for the company at the new Canadian embassy, with Crown Princess Nori as a special guest.

This was 1991, before the fifteen-year recession Japan experienced. Norman Campbell told me that when he and Elaine visited in 2002, a cup of coffee and toast in their first-rate hotel cost fifty bucks. There was another Charlottetown tour in 1993 for the Japan Travel Bureau. In all these visits from Prince Edward Island, there was no interference from Shiki Productions, which had been producing *Anne* in Japanese since 1976.

Kelley was instrumental in arranging our trip to Tokyo in 2010. Based in Los Angeles, she had kept in touch with "our man in Japan," Martyn Naylor. Together they persuaded Keito Asari, the founder and still head of Shiki productions, to fly us to Tokyo to see the current production, me from Toronto, herself from L.A.

The flight from Toronto is direct to Tokyo, and to me, fairly wearying. I don't know how long Kelley's flight was, but she was there already at Narita Airport to greet me, along with the girl in charge of publicity for Shiki.

First came a three-hour limo ride from the airport to our hotel in downtown Tokyo. Part of the reason it takes three hours is not the distance but the heavy traffic. I remembered from my previous visit in 1970 the lack of English signs. Now there seemed to be more English than Japanese, with many Starbucks here and there!

When we got to the hotel, the guide offered to take us on a tour of downtown. It was the middle of the afternoon, but Old Man Harron only wanted a tour upstairs to bed. Kelley took her up on it and they ended up at a Shinto shrine.

Later I did my share of sightseeing. What I noticed was the dominant presence of young people, all of them quite tall. We were informed back in Canada that Japan has the largest population of senior citizens. If it's true, then they must be resolute stay-at-homes.

Next day was the matinee of *Akage no An*. Martyn Naylor came along, mostly to see Kelley and myself, since he had seen the show more than once, usually in a much larger theatre. This time it was presented in a 600-seat theatre, about the same size auditorium as ours appears in most school productions in Canada. During the performance, Martyn was more intent on watching Kelley and me than what went on onstage. He had nothing to worry about — we both loved what we saw.

The first thing I noticed about the production was how much more youthful the adults were. The ladies from the church meeting at the top of the first act were in their thirties. In Charlottetown, they're in the fifties and sixties. This youthful quality existed throughout the show. Their schoolchildren were what they were supposed to be: little kids. In our festival there are a couple of young kids in our P.E.I. school. The rest of the class is populated by dancers in their twenties. Not that they don't serve our musical well, but it is essentially a story about the mingling of a child with a couple approaching old age. The Tokyo production bubbled with the excitement of being a kid.

Kelley did something about this. She contacted Charlottetown when she got back to L.A. and told them what a difference the presence of real children made to the spirit of the show. The festival paid attention! After forty-seven years, those in charge decided that a new director, a new choreographer, and a different set designer might revitalize an aging show.

In Tokyo I was invited to address the cast at the end of the show. In Japanese. My speech, written for me in Toronto by Toshiko Adilman, widow of *Toronto Star* entertainment columnist Sid Adilman, expressed my enthusiasm for the cast and my gratitude to the production company. I also chided the actor playing Matthew for giving up the role when he was still, at eighty, "just a kid." His grin was worth my making such a breach of international courtesy.

I was requested to repeat the same speech a couple of days later in the office of Keito Asari. He looked pleased and invited Kelley and me to return to Japan in 2013 to help him celebrate his sixtieth year of being in the theatre business. I have no doubt that a new production of *Akage no An* will be a part of Shiki's celebrations for him.

Productions have started to appear in some far-off places. We finally got a production in Australia and another in, of all places, Sri Lanka. The latest news of a production came from Iceland. Is it too much to expect that we might eventually see *Anne of Greenland Gables*?

156: END OF THE LINE

I retired in 2011 at eighty-seven, after seventy-seven years in the entertainment business. To mark the event I got involved in two ceremonies. The first was the seventy-fifth anniversary of my high school, Vaughan Road Collegiate, now called by the more auspicious title Vaughan Road Academy. This allowed me to make an Oscar-like speech thanking members of the Academy for inviting me.

I recalled a similar event fifteen years before, the golden anniversary of our seat of learning. On that occasion several of the girls I had dated in high school turned up, looking pretty damn good for their age. This time there were none of them in evidence. The most familiar faces were members of my old football team. They were familiar because twice a year we still get together for lunch and tell lies about our athletic prowess.

The second event was a *Hee Haw* reunion in May 2011 in Nashville. I hadn't been in the town in twenty-eight years. John Aylesworth was gone forever, and Frank Peppiatt couldn't attend due to poor health.

There were other empty seats in that gathering besides John Aylesworth: Junior Samples, Archie Campbell, Grandpa Jones, Minnie Pearl, the Hager twins, and Buck Owens.

The real star of *Hee Haw*, the reason the show happened in the first place, was Roy Clark, singer, instrumentalist, and master comedian. He was there in full form but in reduced circumstances. Not financial, he still had a healthy career, but he had just had a knee replacement operation and was taking it easy in a rocking chair.

In fact, there were rocking chairs all around in a huge semicircle as the various members of our cast, both musical and comedic, sat and reminisced about the show's twenty-five years. Gordie Tapp was the only other Canadian "snow-back" besides me. Dressed in overalls and that silly floppy hat he had also worn on Canadian TV shows like *Country Hoedown*, he did not look like a man about to celebrate his ninetieth birthday. He also weighed exactly the same as he had back in 1945.

The master of ceremonies was Bill Anderson, a major figure in the annals of country music. He introduced me as Charlie Farquharson and asked me to perform my last KORN newscast.

This event was arranged by Larry Black, who specializes in reunions of country music performers and makes a DVD out of the presentation. I received my copy of the DVD and am grateful for the gift of excellent memories. The show still appears with some regularity on Sunday nights in North Carolina, and this has given me the most awesome fan I could ever wish for.

Her name is Wendy Jernigan. She used to watch the show with her grandmother when she was a young girl, and she tracked me down on Facebook.

Wendy and I have been corresponding ever since, largely through the Internet skills of Claudette. The exchanges have been voluminous. But Charlie is the basis of her adoration, and recently she sent along a Charlie Farquharson doll.

Claudette drove me to North Carolina in the spring of 2012 after our stay in Hollis, New Hampshire, where Toby Tarnow, our very first Anne, directed a revival of our musical that she first did six years ago.

After those visits, it was back to Prince Edward Island and a busy schedule walking our neighbour's Golden Lab. That was about it.

• • •

These days I go online to read the newspapers, but I won't go near Facebook, or YouTube, or anybody's blogs, or Tweets, or Twitters.

That's a world in which I have no place. I'm just too old to be online all the time. That also includes stand-up comedy, competing with much younger talents who spout the F-word every ten seconds. Another reason, besides my short-term memory problem, is my balance. Physical, not mental. Sometime, going to the john in the middle of the night, I perform involuntary gymnastics en route, caused I think by the lack of blood flowing to my cranium on such short notice. Speaking of short, as in term, my memory has not improved in that department. Every day I forget the names of friends I see almost every day!

There's nothing wrong with my long-term memory. I am constantly made aware of how similar this part of our twenty-first century is to the events that marked my career beginnings as a ten-year-old in 1935. There was the same emphasis on the lack of jobs, jobs, jobs. In power in Ottawa was a Conservative government led by Prime Minister R.B. Bennett. He may have been a Sunday school teacher at one time, but he turned out to be a grim taskmaster. He resolutely ignored the problems of the unemployed, and they found it necessary to march from Regina to Ottawa to state their case. Out of it came a third political party, the Co-operative Commonwealth Federation, and a Baptist minister who found it necessary to leave his pulpit and preach the Christian point of view in politics.

The most shocking aspect of our contemporary political life is the federal government's ignoring of our climate crisis. I worry for the future, not of me but for my grandkids. The same familiar echoes exist down below the border, with the business of business drowning out the cries of the have-not 99 percent trying to occupy their share of the ground dominated by the 1 percent who have and continue to hold. Barack Obama, the bringer of Hope in 2008, has turned out to be no Franklin Delano Roosevelt. He has tried to do the impossible, to be a conciliator and make peace with those in Congress and the Senate who oppose his plans.

Another unwelcome aspect of my old-age forgetfulness is walking around with my fly open. Entering this no-fly-zone is not deliberate, I can assure you. I am partly assured by the fact that a lot of famous people have walked around with their flies open. For example, Winston Churchill. When he was about to address the student body of Westminster College in Fulton, Missouri, in 1946, making a speech that announced the beginning of the Cold War, he sat on a dais in front of that body with his fly open.

Sitting beside him was the British ambassador, who leaned over and said, "Sir Winston, your flies are open."

But Churchill's reply should be celebrated along with his wartime speeches. Winston simply said, looking down at his open fly, "Fear not. A dead bird never leaves the nest."

Readers who look at the front jacket of this book might be a bit shocked to see Charlie Farquharson in dire need of a haircut, not to mention a new set of duds. But most shocking of all seems to be the a gap in the middle of his upper front teeth. Charlie just bit down too hard on some of Valeda's home cooking and is content to live with the gap in his appearance. Considering the current financial crisis, it must be obvious that our "vanishing Canadian" can't afford such fripperies as a visit to the barber or a dentist. Universal health care is not all that universal in Canada; it doesn't include looking down in the mouth for free.

Valeda sez her best way fer to git rid of rinkles is take off her brass-ears and let yer law of gravelty do its work. Next, she plans on going on a diet to stop that calorie stampede. She sez she is thick and tired of it. Valeda thinks haff the peeples in this cuntry is overwate. Witch is a big round figger, but that's exackly wat the wife wuz tryna avoid. Seems to me that haff the wirld is starvin wile the tuther haff goze on a diet.

Valeda went on a diet last yeer. Only thing she lost wuz her sents of yumor. The wife tern out to be a poor loser. So now she expecks me to loose wate by waring that thermos undy-ware, wat allows yuh to stew in yer own juices.

Helth Canda and yer Departmentof Welth and Hellfire thinks we shud all do more fizzical jerks. Wants evrybuddy runnin round in ther undy-wares, jogglin' til our breth cums in short pants.

Our neer naber, Oscar Rumble, is 72 and duz wat he calls yer sweetish yogurt. Puts his laigs round his neck like a regler extortionist, then stands on his hed fer ten minits to let yer blud rush past his browse. Finshes off with a icy cold shower and a brisk rub-me-down with a stiff brush til he feels rosy all over. Only thing worries Valeda bout this is his wife's name is Letitia.

Gittin' retired is even worse than gittin tired all the time. All I gots garnteed is that 65-pluss handout frum yer Federast Guvmint. No malted-nashnul corpulation is gonna penshun me off. No extry-hospitabull or dentical plans haff-pade by emploirs. Farmers is yer leest pertecked of all yer seenyer sittizens-to-be. We wirked 7 daze a week, 14-hour shifts without over-times pay without no costa-keepin-up-livin' clozzes, no sick-leeves, or workmen's constipation.

I noe a feller hoodid retire. Used to be a implement sailsman sellin trackters, til wun day he got a deer john letter frum yer John Deer peeple. He wuz giv mandible-a-tory retiredmint, witch jist meens "git offa the pot!" I ast him wat its like been retard. He sed yuh gits up in the mornin' with nuthin' to do, and yuh goes to bed 18-hour lader with only haff of it dun!!

But wat's a farmer got fer to retire on? We is the leest perteckted of all yer seenry-sittizens-to-be, incloodin' them baby bloomers. Accorn to yer Ottawa sadisticks, thair is lessen 250 thou farmers left in the hole of our cuntry. Most of us is wat them sibilant serpents calls marge-in-all. Witch meens we ain't werth fussin' about wen it cums to bean gross about our nashnul producks. We is seen as bottom-rung suppliars, and i think our bottoms is by now pritty well wrung-out.

Yer cost-of-keepin'-up livin' indecks is still givin' us the finger. That bludget Flaherty brung down, I kinda wisht he'd brought it up agin. (My old muther used to say Flaherty will git yuh nowares!)

Guvmint don't seam to do nuthin' fer the pore peeple of this cuntry, both yer old and her indignent. That bludget wuz sposed to simulate yer conomy ... it giv them fine-anshul typhoons lots of munny, sposed to creemate jobs fer the rest of us. But it never wirks out that way. Them capittle-ists takes the guvint tax brakes and puts the differrnts inthair pocket, giving the workmen jist thair in-differents. Wellfare fer the poor, and free enter-er-prize fer the ritch. And then they tellus weer livin' beyond our meens. It's the pot callin' the stummick preggerunt!

All us have-nuts gots garnteed in our fewchers after we leeves our pastyers is that handout frum yer Common House fer them as is over-sexty. Over-sexty what? Rite now, I think it's five, but they keep nudgin' us retired-ease closer to three scores and ten.

Minejew, I understand the guvmint will giv yiz yer Canda penchant erly, if yer willin' to be marked down cheeper and cleered out sooner. It's wat they calls "premachoor congratulations." But i skipt yer haff-price bargin and helledout fer yer full amount. That's why ther ain't gonna be no freedom '85 fer me. I'm still a sun uv toil cuvvered in a tun of soil, workin' seven daze a weak, sumtimes 14 hour a day, and no pay fur overtimes.

You non-farmers is 95 pree-sent of Canda's copulation. That meens most of yiz is free frum the drudgery of raisin yer own fud. To sitty peeples fud is sumthin yuh gits in a can offa shelf in yer soopymarkit. Farms is treeted like anya uther bizmess today. If they don't perduce, they gits shet down like a wore-out goldmine. Big bizness is allwaze lookin' out fer them as kin git the goods to them cheeper. That's why they luvs to deel with maneline Chiner.

Farmers haz bin awair fer quite sum time that we is on the list of yer indanger speechies. The price we git fer wat we raze is gittin' lowern a preg-gerunt dacks-hound. Hardly enny of us is gittin' by without bean sudsiddyized by Ottawar. So sitty peeples considers us a drane on ther pubelick purse.

Gon is the time wen Canda wuz consider yer world's bredbaskit. Weer bean outclass in this deportmint by both Chiner and Injure, ware even our best sitty jobs has bean out-sore-assed !

Bout yer only way us Farquharsons will ever git ta be in the munny is if Valeda wins yer Blotto Sex Afore Nine. Evry week she dips inta her aig munny and plays them numbers games. Nex thing ya noe, she'll be wantin' to go south.

I meen hard by Orillyuh, wair they has wun of them caseenys with all thair slut masheens. Our pervinshul guvmint wud be happyer than hell fer to hav Valeda cum and pull them leevers. Cuz yer queens porkers is the bunch as runs them! And that way, they gits thair well-fare paiments back the same day!

Oh, dear. Let's hope that Valeda's numbers come up before Charlie's. As for me, this is my last book. When I was taking this weighty tome to my editor, I was making some last-minute corrections with my pen. I was in a taxi on the way to my publisher, and I asked the driver to go a little slower over the speed bumps.

"Why?" he asked.

"Because I'm trying to write a book."

"What the hell do you wanna do that for? You can buy one, easy."

He's right.

YER END

Index

Page numbers in italics refer to images and their captions.